THE INDIAN VILLAGE COMMUNITY

THE INDIAN VILLAGE COMMUNITY

EXAMINED WITH REFERENCE TO THE PHYSICAL, ETHNOGRAPHIC, AND HISTORICAL CONDITIONS OF THE PROVINCES; CHIEFLY ON THE BASIS OF THE REVENUE-SETTLEMENT RECORDS AND DISTRICT MANUALS

BY

B. H. BADEN-POWELL, M.A. C.I.E.

GYAN

Published by

GYAN

Gyan Publishing House
5, Ansari Road
Daryaganj, New Delhi-110002
Phone: 011-47034999, 9811692060
E-mail: books@gyanbooks.com

Distribution Network
gyanbooks.com
India, USA, Canada, UK, Australia, France

ISBN : 978-81-212-6004-6 (PB)
First Published, 1896

2nd Impression 2021

Printed at: Gyan Press, Delhi.

The
Indian Village Community
Author: B. H. Baden-Powell

THE

INDIAN VILLAGE COMMUNITY

EXAMINED WITH REFERENCE TO THE
PHYSICAL, ETHNOGRAPHIC, AND HISTORICAL CONDITIONS OF
THE PROVINCES; CHIEFLY ON THE BASIS OF THE
REVENUE-SETTLEMENT RECORDS AND
DISTRICT MANUALS

BY

B. H. BADEN-POWELL, M.A., C.I.E.

1896

PREFACE

No apology will be needed for the publication of a book devoted to an account of the 'Village Communities' as found in the several provinces of India. In this department, at any rate, there is a distinctly vacant place. But an apology is very much needed for the imperfect manner in which the attempt to supply the want has now been made. That there are mistakes of detail I cannot but fear; that there are other defects will be only too evident. But the errors will at least be such as admit of ready correction by superior knowledge.

There is another matter for apology. The accounts of the Indian village which have hitherto appeared are either brief and generalised, or they represent an ideal rather than an actual form of the institution. There has been no means of testing such accounts; and it is small wonder that a particular theory of the Indian village has become accepted—and, indeed, sometimes taken for granted—by the ablest authors when discussing the rules of Hindu law, or tracing the history of institutions. It is impossible for any later writer wishing to give a faithful account of village-tenures to avoid pointing out the errors which an abstract and unified conception of '*the* village' can hardly fail to produce. But, to borrow a phrase of Professor Ashley's, 'the piety of the disciple takes a controversial form' solely with regard to this theory of Indian villages; and he intends neither to undervalue the works alluded to nor to show any want of respect for their authors.

Finally, I cannot but anticipate that one class of readers may be inclined to reproach me with not having more explicitly pronounced a judgment, if it is only a provisional one, on the facts set out. But, in truth, the present state of the question seems to me to be such that a contribution to the materials for a decision will be more useful than any deductions which I could formulate.

Whatever conclusions have hitherto been drawn from the phenomena of the Indian village have proceeded, almost unavoidably, from a slender basis of fact; they have been drawn, too, in disregard of a number of circumstances, the importance of which in forming a just opinion will be obvious as soon as those circumstances are explained. I confess, therefore, to have felt more concerned about marshalling the facts of the case and setting forth the conditions under which those facts are found, than with elaborating arguments and conclusions. Nevertheless, the book will, I venture to think, bring out with tolerable distinctness the view that the 'joint-village' of India is not the universal or the most ancient form; and that the common-holding of land (where it is not the result of some special voluntary association) is traceable only among the superior tenures of the Hindu-Aryans and the later tribes who settled in Northern or Upper India. Or, if I may state the matter somewhat more particularly, that the so-called joint-village followed, and did not precede, the village of separate holdings; and that in those cases where it represents a section of a tribal or clan territory, it derives a rather delusive appearance of being held 'in common' from certain features of clan life and union; while in the very numerous cases in which it is a small estate connected with an individual founder, the joint-ownership depends solely [1] on the existence of the 'joint-family'—

[1] That is, allowing (as above) for certain cases where a group of colonists or others has been formed by voluntary association and has cultivated on a joint-stock principle—a matter which has obviously nothing to do with 'archaic' custom.

i.e. on the law or custom of the joint-inheritance of a number of co-heirs in succession to an original founder or acquirer. How and when the joint-inheritance and the joint-family came to be invented may be a difficult question; but if the idea of the joint-family is not primitive, nor found among all tribes or races, and is rather the special creation of the developed 'Hindu' law and custom as such, and if it is only found among other tribes after more or less contact with Hindu-Aryans, then the joint-village cannot be demonstrably a primitive, still less a once universal, form of land-holding.

B. H. BADEN-POWELL.

OXFORD: *September* 1896.

CONTENTS

CHAPTER I

CHAPTER II

CHAPTER III

CHAPTER IV

CHAPTER V

CHAPTER VI

CHAPTER VII

CHAPTER VIII

CHAPTER IX

CHAPTER X

MAP

Errata

Page 136, line 24 ; *for* Ahŏm *read* Ahōm
„ 153, line 25 ; *for* The Ho adds Mundā *read* The Ho and Munda
„ 177, note (*bis*) ; *for* Kanāra *read* Kānara
„ 187, note 1 ; for *Khsatriyā* read *Kshatriyā*
„ 210 (note), 219, 283 ; *for* Dakhān *read* Dakhan
„ 279, line 28 ; *for* mājra *read* majrā
„ 287, 311, &c.; the more correct name of the clan seems to be *Çandel* not *Çāndel.*

LIST OF BOOKS REFERRED TO

The following list includes such books or periodicals as are quoted by abbreviated titles, or need explanation as to the particular edition or reprint made use of.

'S. R.' = 'Settlement Report' of the several districts. The date of publication or the author's name is added where there have been several such reports.

'D. M.' = the 'District Manuals' for the several districts of the Madras Presidency, and which contain the information found in the other provinces in the 'S. R.' or in 'Gazetteers.'

'Agricultural Statistics' (Returns of Land-tenures, &c.). Those referred to are called 'Returns of the Agricultural Statistics of British India,' published from time to time by the Revenue and Agricultural Department of the Government of India (Calcutta: Superintendent of Government Printing). The table showing 'Varieties of Tenure, &c.' is 'Form I–E 3.'

'Ayīn-i-Akbari' (translation), vol. i. by H. Blochmann; vols. ii. and iii. by Colonel Jarrett (Bengal Asiatic Society: Calcutta, 1873–1894). This is the celebrated work of Abu-l-Fazl, giving an account of the administration of the Mughal Empire in the reign of Akbar.

'Archæological Survey of India Reports.' Serial volumes from 1862 (the earlier ones are by Sir A. Cunningham). This series is distinct from that of the Archæological Survey of *Southern* India. (Quoted as 'Rep. Arch. Surv.')

Baden-Powell, 'The Land Systems of British India.' 3 vols. (Clarendon Press, 1892.) (Quoted as 'L. S. B. I.')

'Bengal: a Statistical Account of.' (Ed. Sir W. W. Hunter.) 20 vols. (London: Trübner, 1872.)

'Berār Gazetteer.' (Ed. A. C. Lyall.) 1 vol. (Bombay: Education Society's Press, 1870.)

'Bombay, Gazetteer of.' (Ed. James Campbell.) 25 vols. (Bombay Government Central Press, 1880.) Some of the volumes are not yet out. (Quoted as 'Bombay Gazetteer.')

Caldwell (Rev. R., D.D.). 'A Comparative Grammar of the Dravidian Languages' (Introduction and Text). 2nd ed. (Trübner: London, 1875.) (Quoted as Caldwell, 'Introduction.')

Campbell (afterwards Sir G.). The Essay on 'The Tenure of Land in India' alluded to is found in 'Systems of Land Tenure in various Countries: a Series of Essays published under the Sanction of the Cobden Club.' 2nd ed. (London: Macmillan, 1870.)

'Central Provinces Gazetteer.' (Introduction and text.) 1 vol. (Ed. C. Grant), 2nd ed. (Bombay: Education Society's Press, 1870.)

Cunningham (Sir. A.), 'The Ancient Geography of India' (1. The Buddhist Period), vol. i. (only this volume published). (London: Trübner, 1871.) (Quoted as Cunningham, 'Anc. Geog.')

Elliot (Sir H. M.), 'The Races of the North-West Provinces of India, &c.' Ed. John Beames. (London: Trübner, 1879.) 2 vols. (Quoted as 'Elliot's Gloss.')

Elphinstone (The Hon. Mountstuart), 'History of India.' 6th ed. (E. B. Cowell). (John Murray, 1874.) (Quoted as Elphinstone, 'Hist.')

'Fifth Report of the Select Committee on the Affairs of India, 1812.' Vol. I. Bengal, Vol. II. Madras. Madras Reprint of 1883. (Quoted as 'Fifth Report.')

Forrest (G. W.), 'Selections from the Minutes and other Official Writings of the Hon. Mountstuart Elphinstone.' (London: Bentley, 1884.) (Quoted as Forrest, 'Elphinstone Minutes.')

'Gazetteer.' See under Bombay, Panjāb, North-West Provinces, &c., &c.

Grant-Duff, 'A History of the Mahrattas.' Bombay Reprint of 1873. 2 vols.

Hunter (Sir W. W.), 'Bengal MSS. Records, &c.' 4 vols. (W. H. Allen, 1892.) (Quoted as Hunter, 'Bengal Records.')

Hunter (Sir W. W.), 'Orissa.' (Smith and Elder, 1872.) 2 vols. (Quoted as 'Orissa.')

Ibbetson (D. C. J.), 'Outlines of Panjāb Ethnography; being Extracts from the Panjāb Census Report of 1881, treating of Religion, Language, and Caste.' (Calcutta: Superintendent of Government Printing, 1883.) 4to. (Quoted as Ibbetson's 'Panjāb Ethnography.')

India: Census Report of 1891. My reference is to the Parliamentary Blue Book, which is a summary with tables, by J. A. Baines, Census Commissioner, 1893. There is a fuller report published by the Superintendent Government Printing, Calcutta, for all India, and the series of Provincial Reports published by the local Governments.

India: 'Imperial Gazetteer of.' (Ed. Sir W. W. Hunter.) 14 vols. (London: Trübner.)

India. 'Statement exhibiting the Moral and Material Progress.' (Parliamentary Blue Book. Two parts, with Maps and Tables.) These are published decennially. My reference is to that of 1883, written by J. S. Cotton, B.C.S.

Lassen (Prof. Christian), 'Indische Alterthumskunde. 2nd ed. 4 vols. (Leipzig, 1867.) (Quoted as Lassen.)

Laveleye (Emile de), 'De la Propriété et de ses formes primitives.' (Paris: Baillière, 1874.)

McCrindle (J. W.), 'Ancient India as described by Megasthenes and Arrian.' (London: Trübner; Calcutta and Bombay: Thacker, 1877.)

McCrindle (J. W.), 'Ancient India as described by Ptolemy' (1885).

Madras: 'Manual of the Administration of the Madras Presidency.' (Government Press. 3 vols. folio.) Vol. I. is paged separately for each division—History, Ethnology, &c. (Quoted as 'Macleane's Manual.')

Maine (Sir H. S.), 'The Early History of Institutions.' (John Murray, 1875.)

Maine (Sir H. S.), 'Village Communities in the East and West.' 3rd ed. (John Murray, 1876.)

Malcolm (Sir J.), 'A Memoir of Central India, &c.' 2 vols. Reprint of 3rd ed. (Calcutta and Bombay: Thacker & Co.) (Quoted as Malcolm, 'Cent. Ind.')

'Manu, The Laws of' (translated by Georg Bühler), being Vol. XXV. of the 'Sacred Books of the East.' (London: Trubner.) (Quoted as 'Laws of Manu.')

Mayne (J. D.), 'A Treatise on Hindu Law and Usage.' 4th ed. 1888. (London: Stevens & Haynes.)

Muir, J., 'Ancient Sanskrit Texts, &c.' 4 vols. (Quoted as Muir, 'A. S. T.')

'N.-W. Provinces Gazetteer.' 14 vols. (Allahabad: North-West Provinces and Oudh Government Press.)

Oppert (Gustav), 'The Original Inhabitants of India.' (Constable, Westminster, 1893.) (Quoted as G. Oppert.)

'Oudh Gazetteer.' 3 vols. (Lucknow, 1877.)

'Panjāb Gazetteers,' in separate district volumes of various dates. (Government Central Press, Lahore.)

'Papers on Mirasī Right selected, &c.' (Madras: Pharaoh & Co., 1862.) (Quoted as 'Mirasī Papers.')

'Rājputāna Gazetteer.' 3 vols. (Calcutta: Superintendent of Government Printing, 1879.)

'Royal Asiatic Society Journal.' (Quoted as 'J. R. A. S.')

'Society of Arts Journal.' (Quoted as 'J. Soc. Arts.')

Tod (Lieut.-Colonel James), 'Annals and Antiquities of Rajast'han, &c.' Third reprint. 2 vols. (Madras: Higginbotham, 1880.) (Quoted as Tod.)

Wilson (Prof. H. H.), 'A Glossary of Judicial and Revenue Terms.' (W. H. Allen, 1855). (Quoted as Wilson, 'Glossary.')

Zimmer (Heinrich), 'Altindisches Leben: Die Cultur der Vedischen Arien.' (Berlin, 1879.) (Quoted as Zimmer.)

NOTE ON THE SPELLING OF ORIENTAL WORDS

Technical terms in the Indian languages are printed in italic letters and transliterated, as far as possible, on the system used by the Royal Asiatic Society.

The reader not acquainted with any Indian dialect will have no difficulty in pronouncing the words if he gives the *continental* sound to the vowels; or comparing them with *English* words :—

a—ā, as the *u* in '*cut*'—the *a* in '*father*.' The sound of English *a* in 'flat' is unknown to any Indian language.

i—ī, as 'pit'—'peat.'

u—ū, as 'pull'—'pool.'

o—always full, as in 'depôt.'

e—always as the 'ay' in 'hay'; 'ai' as the 'i' in 'fire'; 'au' as the 'ou' in 'bough': 'y' is always a consonant.

Of the consonants, it is hardly necessary to say anything for the English reader, except to notice that the 'g' is always hard; and that the 'j' is employed with its usual (English) sound. The inverted comma or apostrophe indicates the Arabic *'ain*; and the two forms of the Arabic *kāf* are distinguished, as 'k' and 'q' (in the latter case without the conventional 'u' added). The kh and gh (underlined) indicate the gutturals; ñ in a final syllable indicates the nasal pronunciation. 'Th,' it may conveniently be added, is never sibilant (either as in 'thin' or 'this') in any *Indian* dialect;[1] it is 't' with an added aspirate. I may call attention to the ç, which=ch, and saves the awkwardness of writing Hindī forms when the letter is both aspirated and reduplicated, as often is the case. In familiar words printed in ordinary type, I have retained the 'ch,' as there it seems more natural.

I have used a modified spelling for the common words *raiyat* (*ra'īyat*), *Tāluqdār* (*Ta'alluqdār*), and *mauza* (*mauẓa'*). Indeed, when these words are written in any dialect that does not use the Persi-Arabic alphabet, they are actually so spelt (very nearly).

When necessary to indicate the language or dialect, an initial has been added in brackets: S=Sanskrit, H=Hindī, M=Marāthī, A=Arabic, P=Persian, Tam=Tamil, Tel=Telugu, Karn=Kanarese, or the Karnatā language.

[1] It may be in Burmese; and, though it is frequent and varied in classical Arabic, it is not so sounded in Indian use.

THE

INDIAN VILLAGE COMMUNITY

CHAPTER I

THE INDIAN VILLAGE AND ITS FORMS IN GENERAL

SECTION I.—THE COMMONLY RECEIVED VIEW OF VILLAGE-TENURES

IT may safely be assumed that the term 'Indian Village Community' will not sound strange or unintelligible to English readers. As to the meaning which the term conveys, it is not so easy to feel confident. Our standard histories of India usually present us with a picture (more or less detailed) of what 'the Indian village,' as an institution, is; and some of the passages in which these accounts are contained have, not undeservedly, become almost classical. We also, at the present day, instinctively connect the idea of 'village community' with that of a survival of ancient forms of common ownership of land, a survival which the intense conservatism of Eastern countries has made possible. There is no one book, as far as I am aware, that, dealing chiefly or solely with village-tenures, contains the collected evidence regarding the details of their history and their varied forms; it is not surprising, therefore, that such knowledge of the subject as has become current is of a highly generalised and often theoretical character.

It may be useful to recount briefly what is usually held regarding Indian villages, and see how far we can accept familiar ideas as a groundwork for a more detailed examination of the subject. It is understood, to begin with, that the country dis-

B

tricts are almost everywhere divided up into groups of holdings which, for want of a better name, are called 'villages' or 'townships.' Here and there, and sometimes throughout whole provinces, it is remembered, the ownership of 'villages' has been absorbed by the growth of a wider landlord interest, as, *e.g.*, in Bengal, and Oudh, and part of Madras. In these cases the superior tenure has overshadowed the villages, and they have become mere groups of tenants, or have always been so, being located by the landlord himself. Otherwise, the villages are independent, and represent, in fact, the primary form of land-ownership in general, and as such, constitute the chief agricultural feature of numerous 'districts.'[1] If for a moment I may illustrate the general state of things with reference to familiar English institutions, without unduly implying any connection between the institutions themselves, I might say that in some cases villages have been swallowed up in great 'manors,' under the lords of them; and in this case the village-organisation has often decayed. In other cases the villages have escaped being so absorbed, either because no 'lord' has arisen over them, or because such lords as once possessed them have disappeared, being destroyed by war or stress of times; or, more curiously still, because such villages have become little 'manors' of themselves; the lordship that has grown up has either been conterminous with the village, or has broken up into a number of fragments which are 'villages.' In all the latter cases we have 'villages' as the independent elements of the agricultural system, with no 'lord' over them except the state or the ruler.

So far,[2] the general idea is quite in correspondence with the reality of things. But when it is further inquired what is understood to be the nature of the 'village-community' or 'township,' it will probably be most frequently answered that the village, though existing in some variety of form, approximates in general to a single type, of which the important

[1] The 'District' (sometimes called Collectorate) is the administrative unit into which each province is divided. In some respects it answers to the 'county' in England. See my *Short Account of the Land Revenue &c. of British India* (Clarendon Press, 1894, p. 22).

[2] And allowing for cases where, owing to physical conditions, village-groups are not formed at all.

feature is that there is some kind of 'holding in common' of the village area, either still surviving at the present day, or which existed in former times. The village is further supposed to consist of the group of connected families which probably once acknowledged blood-relationship, but now, having lost the recollection of it, is only held together *by the land* occupied in common. For this reason the term 'village community' as applied to India has been generally taken to imply not only a local group of landholders, but something of a communistic type as regards the property in land. Some writers also have made use of such terms as 'rural communes' or 'village corporations'—terms which we may allow to pass, though they can only be used by way of a rather loose analogy.

At this point the popular theory becomes, I fear, open to several objections. The most serious is that it generalises in a way which is not warrantable; it ignores the fact that, even taking the widest possible view of the subject, two types of village must be recognised—one that has, and one that has not, any appearance of joint or common ownership. In the latter type, which for convenience we call the *raiyatwārī*, there is no evidence that the holdings were ever otherwise than separate and independent. But even in the 'joint' type, it is almost equally important not to confuse the whole of the villages together, but to recognise the very different principles or bases of union which exist: the joint-village on a *tribal* basis is very different from that which depends on succession of joint heirs to an *individual* founder, and that, again, is different from the group formed by families on no tribal and no aristocratic basis, or on voluntary association. The whole argument of this book is not so much to throw doubt on the general idea of early communal ownership, as to insist on the specific facts of Indian village history, and to the *qualified sense* in which such collective ownership as is deemed predicable can be asserted. It is especially necessary to point out that in all cases the collective ownership has nothing to do with any social community of goods; it is a question of some bond of union among conquering and superior tribes, or among a family proud of its descent from some aristocratic founder.

Even so preliminary and general a criticism of the usually

received theory of Indian villages may be open to the objection that it also calls in question to some extent the general conclusions which have the authority of the late Sir H. S. Maine. May I say once for all, that in respect and admiration for the author of the *Early History of Institutions*, and of the *Village Communities*, I yield to no one? But it seems to me that the author himself would have been the very last to hold that no modification of his theory was ever possible. The results arrived at in these well-known works are professedly only probable conclusions from such evidence as the writer had before him at the time, and which he certainly did not regard as complete. It can hardly be doubted that the information available when Sir H. S. Maine wrote was very far from being what it has since become. None of the reports on the Panjāb frontier tribal-villages were written—or at least were available in print; and the greater part of the best Settlement Reports of the North-West Provinces, Oudh and the Panjāb, are dated in years subsequent to the publication of *Village Communities*. Further, the Settlement Reports of the Central Provinces, the District Manuals of Southern India, and the Survey Reports and Gazetteers of the Bombay districts, were many of them not written, and the others were hardly known beyond the confines of those presidencies. In this fact I find the explanation of the total omission in Sir H. S. Maine's pages of any specific mention of the *raiyatwārī* form of village, and the little notice he takes of the tribal or clan constitution of Indian races in general, and of the frontier tribal villages in the Panjāb.[1]

If, however, it has become necessary to modify our conception of collective-ownership as applied to Indian villages, and to recast some other conclusions, this modification will in no respect suggest any diminution of the value and authority of the works alluded to. They will still continue to be our lasting possessions not only as models of lucid exposition, but as per-

[1] This is the more remarkable because Sect. III. in the *Early Institutions* deals with the clan and kinship; but the author evidently had seen nothing directly to connect the clan and the village in Upper India; he turns away to suppose the village-group to belong to a stage when kinship is largely forgotten and when the land (always supposed to be held in common) is the chief bond of union.

manent guides to scientific method in the collection and use of materials. Indeed, it is not too much to say that we owe to Sir H. S. Maine's invaluable pioneer work the very possibility of further advance; since his work has constantly suggested the lines of inquiry which our later detailed reports have pursued.

But some readers may further be disposed to regard the Indian case as necessarily concluded by a general verdict on the European evidence as to archaic common ownership of land. It would be quite beyond my scope to discuss the wide question of early 'collective ownership' as a universal phenomenon of ancient times; but more than one of the hitherto received proofs or instances has of late years been rendered at least questionable owing to the re-examination of texts and documents; and some cases of apparent common-holding supposed to be ancient have turned out to be comparatively modern, or to be explainable on other principles. I would not, however, venture to approach the subject, except for the one reason that if it is really the fact that in all the countries of the West ownership of land 'in common' was a recognised feature in a certain (archaic) stage of social progress, then, no doubt, it might afford an *a priori* reason, inclining us to believe that the Indian evidence must support a similar conclusion in the East. But I submit that under the circumstances of doubt that exist as to the European phenomena, the Indian case may with advantage be dealt with on its own merits, and without any predisposition one way or the other.

At any rate, I think that we have every right to insist that the distinct existence of a type of Indian village in which 'ownership in common' cannot be proved to be a feature either of the past or present should be duly acknowledged; and that it is hardly possible to appeal to '*the* Indian village community' as evidence in any general question of archaic land-custom or of economic science, if we first obtain a single type by leaving out of view the wide area of country which furnishes divergent forms or features. And further, when the details of the history of the Northern Indian villages are so much better known, it becomes imperative to give due weight to the fundamental differences of structure and origin which exist among the 'joint' villages themselves; for these differences must largely affect the sense in which we predicate 'holding in common' or 'collective ownership' of any or all of them.

In the first place, then, in deprecating the absence of all acknowledgment of two broad types of village in India, I think that I do not misrepresent the opinions actually expressed by Sir H. S. Maine when I conclude that distinctive evidence regarding one type of village was not before him—that type which I have called the *raiyatwāri* village, in which the separate holders (or *raiyat*), whatever spirit of union they may have possessed, never represented co-sharers in a unit estate nor acknowledged any form of common ownership.[1]

The following passages appear to me to be conclusive on the subject. 'Over the greater part of the country,' writes Sir H. Maine,[2] 'the village community has not been absorbed in any larger collection or lost in a territorial area of wider extent. For fiscal and legal purposes *it is the proprietary unit of large and populous provinces*' (the italics here and elsewhere are mine). This may indeed be understood to allow that other provinces may exhibit some differences; but there is no hint that any such differences may involve a distinction in principle, as they really do. And in another passage in which the author emphasises his desire to recognise considerable variety, it is still evident that it is only variety within the general lines of common holding; it does not extend to distinguishing or accounting for the *raiyatwāri* principle. 'In the account of the Indian cultivating group which follows,' he says, 'you will understand that I confine myself to fundamental points, and, further, that I am attempting to describe *a typical form to which the village communities appear to me on the evidence I have seen to approximate*, rather than a model to which all existing groups called by the name can be exactly fitted.'[3] This unity of general type indeed necessarily follows from the way in which collective ownership is assumed to be universal as a primary stage. And the general type is accordingly presented of a group of persons not only connected (really or by a fiction) by common descent, but who

[1] The word *raiyat*, sometimes written phonetically *ryot*, is (correctly) the Arabic *ra'īyat*, and means 'subject,' 'protected,' &c.; hence any landholder subject to the Crown or to a landlord.

[2] *Vill. Comm.* pp. 12, 13. [3] *Ibid.* p. 107.

also own the land in common or collectively. This typical community is distinguished by the absence, originally, of any one headman superior to the rest, the co-sharers being represented by a council of heads of families or houses. Recognising also that there often are inferiors and dependents (tenants) included in the village group, the author considers that these also formed part of the 'brotherhood.'[1] The brotherhood, in fact, forms a kind of 'hierarchy,' the degrees of which are determined by the order in which the various sets of cultivating families have amalgamated with the community.[2]

In another place the author, speaking of ideas of ownership in land as prevalent in India generally, remarks that ownership was understood, 'but joint ownership by bodies of men was the rule, several ownership by individuals the exception.'[3] And in an interesting passage in the *Early History of Institutions*, the village group in general is traced to some form of expansion of the single family, in which the sense of common descent is gradually lost, and 'the assemblage of cultivators is held together solely by the land which they till in common.' In India, even where division of the culturable holdings has introduced separate ownership, and the waste only is held in common, *the Indian village community is a body of men held together by the land that they occupy*.[4]

Now, such a general typical description cannot be applied at all to one class, and that by far the largest, of Indian villages. The form of village of which it is to a great extent a true representation is confined to India north of the Vindhyan Hill series —*i.e.* to the Panjāb, the North-West Provinces, and Oudh, probably in former times including the northern part of Bengal known as Bihār. A few villages of the same kind are found in Upper Western India (Gujarāt), and there are wide-spread

[1] *Vill. Comm.* pp. 123, 175, and compare p. 179, where some interesting remarks are made on the position of the grain-dealer in the village.

[2] *Ibid.* pp. 176, 177. This is something quite different from there being merely different grades of social rank in the village, such as landlord, tenant, farm-labourer, low-caste menial, &c.; it is something within a general 'brotherhood.'

[3] *Ibid.* p. 222.

[4] *Early History of Institutions*, pp. 77-82. (The italics in all these passages are mine.)

traces of formerly existing shared (or landlord) village estates in the Dakhan and in certain parts of South India. But, broadly speaking, this form of village was never universal: it always implies, as I have said already, the growth of some individual overlordship or some settlement of conquering clans or expansion of families with their own notions of equal right and superiority to inferior races: it never extended generally over the greater part of Eastern, Central, Western and Southern India.

A better idea will be formed about the relative importance of the areas in which the *joint* and the *raiyatwāri* villages respectively are the prevalent kinds, if we set down the Provinces, with their area and population.

—	Provinces	Area in square miles	Mean density of population per square mile
Joint villages prevalent	The Panjāb	110,667	188
	N.-W. Provinces	83,286	411
	Oudh	24,217	522
	Total . .	. 218,170	
Separate ownership or *raiyatwāri* villages prevalent; traces of joint-villages once in existence locally, and from special causes	Bengal	151,543	471
	Bombay and Sindh	77,275 / 47,789	207 / 117
	Madras	141,189	256
	Ajmer [1]	2,711	200
	Coorg	1,583	109
	Central Provinces	86,501	125
	Berār	17,718	163
	Assam	49,004	112
	Total . .	. 575,313	

As to the second point—the real nature of the collective ownership that is observable in the northern Indian joint-village

[1] In Ajmer and in the Central Provinces the revenue system has produced artificially a new proprietary title to the villages; but it is undoubtedly the fact that, in both, the villages were naturally *raiyatwāri*. I have alluded to the probability of joint-villages once existing in the Bihār districts forming a part of Bengal. On the other hand, the sequel will show that in Oudh and the old Hindu kingdoms of the North-west the *raiyatwāri* form of village was originally prevalent among the lower castes and aborigines when the Hindu Rājās held the dominion; so the one case at least balances the other. If I added the Native States of Rājputāna, Central India, and the Nizām's Territory, the *raiyatwāri* area would preponderate still more.

—my observations must be reserved to a later stage. Before any remarks on the subject would be intelligible it will be necessary to consider a number of other matters. It will be desirable, therefore, at once to present the reader with a sketch which aims at placing before him the two forms of village in contrast. It is easy to describe the *raiyatwāri* village, because in the nature of things its form is one: more difficult is it to sketch the other type, because its forms are several—that is to say, putting aside minor modifications in details of internal constitution, there are some fundamental distinctions which co-exist with a certain outward appearance of uniformity.

Without further prelude, however, the attempt to present each type of village in its proper character must be made.

Section II.—The Two Forms of Village-tenure

A. *The Raiyatwāri Village*

In this form of village, so widely prevalent, the group of holdings in no sense forms a 'proprietary unit;' and the term 'community' is properly applied to the group of landholders only so long as it is employed to indicate the connection which a group of cultivators must have when located in one place, bound by certain customs, with certain interests in common, and possessing within the circle of their village the means of local government, and of satisfying the wants of life without much reference to neighbouring villages.

It is quite possible that when the first Dravidian and other tribesmen formed villages on this pattern, there was some general idea of tribal union, and that every member of the clan was entitled to receive an allotment sufficient for his wants; but there is no trace of any common holding of the land occupied; the several portions of the village are allotted or taken up severally, and are enjoyed quite independently from the first. I make this allusion to the clan or tribe, because in the countries marked by the prevalence of villages of this type we are almost always able to note evidences of a tribal stage of society which will be described in due course. There were clan-divisions of territory, containing a number of villages, each under its own headman or chief, who was a natural and essential part of the institution. This alone places this form of village in contrast with the other form, in which, as Sir H. S. Maine has prominently remarked, the 'headman' is not originally a feature of the constitution. It may be concluded with reference to any possible numbers of the earliest agricultural tribes, as well as to the immense area of the country, that the villages were at first scattered over the jungle-clad plains at considerable distances apart, but within certain general boundaries of clan-territory. Each village group contained a number of household or family holdings, the holdings being larger or smaller as the means and the requirements of each suggested. In the oldest customs we shall find special allotments of land reserved in each village for the chief, for the worship of the deity, and so forth; but there is no community of interest in the cultivated lots.

The cultivated area is naturally surrounded by waste and woodland, which may extend for some distance before the 'sphere' of another village is reached. We have no evidence, as far as I can discover, of any formal tribal or other procedure for allotting the several *village* areas within the territory occupied by the tribe or clan. The area available for tillage was very large in proportion to existing tribal numbers; and the naturally connected groups of families could settle where they pleased within the general area recognised as belonging to their clan. As the headman or chief of each village was always an important personage, it was doubtless by his influence that the site for clearing and settlement was selected; and several neighbouring headmen in consultation could prevent any clashing of interests, even if such occurred, which is not likely.[1] Under the influence of established custom—that potent factor in Indian affairs—we find in later times that the headman regulated subsequent extensions of the cultivation and disposed of disputes about the occupation of fresh lands. When a Rājā was (perhaps in still later days) established, it was always understood that there was no appropriation of waste land without permission, though in practice such appropriation was often tacitly allowed, and indeed

[1] I am alluding, of course, to the earliest agricultural villages founded by the original settlers, who could hardly have found any human enemies, but must have found the available area enormously in excess of any possible requirements.

freely encouraged; for the early State authorities were only too glad to see more land cultivated, because the King's revenue share of the produce, which was from very early times his chief resource, was thereby increased.

Thus, the waste adjoining the village was not the 'common property' of the village, any more than it is at the present day. And consequently in early times the boundaries between village and village were rarely, if ever, defined. It was only if one village was at enmity with the next that some definition of 'spheres' would be made. There is reason to believe that only the *clan* territories were more definitely demarcated, and that encroachments on these would have led to resistance. I have been told of cases among the Assam clans, where one group would turn out in war array to prevent a neighbouring group trespassing on their grounds. This is in the hill country, where each group-area consists of a large tract of 'jungle' and only a certain part of it is taken in hand at a time, by reason of the practice of shifting cultivation.[1]

It is only reasonable to suppose that from the earliest times of tribal settlement the several tribal or clan areas were jealously guarded. But a general sense of right of some kind over a given neighbourhood is quite consistent with very vague ideas of actual ownership; and there is not the smallest reason to believe that in any early non-Aryan village the adjacent waste was ever regarded as a definite property available for partition at the option of the resident group of cultivators; nor was it supposed that each man had a right to an area of waste proportioned to his arable holding, or any other share such as is always recognised in case of the waste belonging to joint or landlord villages. All traces of early custom show the villages just in the same condition in this respect as *raiyatwārī* villages of to-day. It should be remembered that the waste was always used for grazing, and that hay-fields and hay-cutting are still generally unknown;[2] hence there would be no need for dividing

[1] This is described at p. 53, *post*.

[2] In the hills between Simla and the plains, where there is no forest but a large expanse of hill-side which does produce hay, there is an exceptional custom of marking out the area into 'doles' or strips (*ghāsnī*), which are allotted among the landholders; and the area is only used for

grass lands into 'doles' for hay, as in the English village of former days. Hence, too, there would be no opportunity for a sense of ownership to develop. It is doubtless this absence of definite claim to anything beyond the appropriated and cleared holding that made it so easy for the first rulers to assume their (very ancient) right to the waste. But wherever a village was made over by a Rāja, who of course professed to assign the State-rights only, to some courtier or other grantee, the latter immediately seized on the adjacent *waste* as one of the most useful parts of his grant, and cultivated it, as far as the necessary area for grazing, &c., permitted, for his own profit.

So little was the waste adjacent to the old *raiyatwāri* villages deemed a 'property,' and so rarely was it demarcated, that in the Revenue-settlement arrangements of the Mughal Emperors, or possibly at a still earlier time, it was sometimes necessary to define the limit of waste attached for grazing or other uses to a village; and this process was effected by the primitive expedient of sending the village watchman to stand on the edge of the cultivated fields and shout. The waste reserved to the village use was then held to extend as far as his voice could be heard.[1]

common grazing when the hay is cut. These lands are not the property of the hamlets, and pay dues to the Rājā. I do not know of any instance in the plains where artificial cultivation of grass is resorted to. No doubt there are places where the natural grass, which springs up chiefly during the rainy season, is subject to a certain customary protection before grazing or grass-cutting is allowed. But, speaking generally, hay-culture is unknown.

[1] It is curious to note that the origin of the familiar Indian measure of length, the *kos* (2 *kos* = 3 miles), is in this rough method of estimating distance. The word *kos* (*kroça*) meant the distance to which a voice would reach (*J. R. As. Soc.* April 1894, p. 238; and for an illustration see the paper on the Burmese version of the *Sāma Jātaka* in the same number, p. 222). The indefinite length was gradually converted into a fixed measure by substituting a given number of *danda*, or poles, of four cubits each. In the *Ayīn-i-Akbari* (Jarrett's Trans. ii. 414) there is an elaborate account of the imperial *kroh* or *kos*. In Hunter's *Bengal Records*, i. 87, there is an interesting notice of the subject; but the learned author is perhaps only speaking generally when he calls the waste within earshot the *joint property* of the resident husbandmen (in Bengal). It was only when a village was made over to a grantee that the waste was

So much regarding the *waste* area. As to the *residence* of the landholders, a central village site is usually established within the group of arable lands. But circumstances may cause outlying hamlets to exist also. In this village-site the headman (called *pātel* in Central India, but there are many other local titles) had a residence larger and better built than the others. In the Central Provinces the headman's residence is often spoken of as the *garhī*, or fort; and in former days, at any rate, it was large enough to afford accommodation for the whole of his family and its dependents. Instances have occurred where the headman made his house a veritable fort of refuge, and defended his village against marauders or the attacks of enemies.[1]

It is sometimes stated that the headman was at first the nominee of the ruler, and that the office *became* hereditary.[2] This is certainly not the case; the hereditary headman is a distinctly original feature, and is traceable to old tribal times. But it was inevitable when the plan of taking a revenue by means of a share of the produce was introduced, and some kind of public administration was organised, that the ruler should enlist the efforts of the headman on the side of the State and recognise his office and give him some additional privileges. As a matter of fact, I believe it will be found that the first action of the Rājā, when that stage of society was reached, was not so much to deal with the existing headman and his old tribal authority, as to introduce a sort of second headman (*māhato* of the Dravidian villages), who rather overshadowed the original chief, because he was necessarily literate and could keep accounts. In time it was found that both were useful, and both were officially recog-

claimed as distinct property under the grant. For an ordinary *raiyatwāri* village of old times, as at the present day in Bengal, the waste was only *used* by the villagers; it could not be broken up, still less partitioned or alienated, without leave of the authorities, or later of the landlord.

[1] See *L. S. B. I.* ii. 464 (note), where there is a reference to the Chānda S. R.

[2] See, for instance, Elphinstone, *Hist.* (6th ed., Cowell), p. 69. It will often be noticed in villages of Dravidian origin that the 'headman' is regarded as too dignified for executive duty; he gives orders and decisions, but has a deputy (*çaughala*), also hereditary, who attends to practical business (Grant-Duff, i. 28 and note).

nised. However this may be, the second officer was the prototype of our modern village *paṭwārī*;[1] his office, like everything in India, became hereditary; it is still allowed to be so to some extent and on condition of the efficiency of the heir. On him the cultivators rely for a knowledge of the official entries in the Records, and the survey details of their holdings; he it is who makes out the receipts for their payments, and is the general adviser. All village accounts and village statistical returns are made out by him. He also is the village notary for matters requiring written documents such as bonds and land-transfers. The antiquity of this office is only second to that of the headman.

The headman was always, at least nominally, the superior, for he had, and still has, small magisterial powers and various duties of police and protection. The office was remunerated by an important holding of land—often the best in the village—which, in some cases, the ruler allowed him to hold free of revenue. Besides this there were various much-cherished privileges and precedence rights. The aggregate of these rights and privileges (*mānpān*), together with the official land, constitute what was afterwards called the *waṭan* (dialectically *vatan*). As the whole was hereditary, it could be partitioned; and in some cases of necessity was even sold or mortgaged.[2] Otherwise, so strictly hereditary and held by the *family* was the *pātelgī* (headmanship), that in former days the male heirs of the last *pātel* sometimes held the office jointly; and as, of course, its actual duties and responsibilities could only be performed or discharged

[1] This officer is commonly called *paṭwārī* in Bengal and Upper India; in Madras he is *karnam*, and has other local titles; in Bombay, *kulkarnī*; or, if stipendiary and not hereditary (in certain parts), *talātī*.

[2] There is every reason to believe that the village chief's *ex-officio* land was always hereditary; but of course these special features of family ownership followed from the general adoption of Hindu social and religious ideas. In *J. R. A. S.* iii. 350, Colonel Sykes has given a translation of a long award relating to a dispute about partition, which incidentally shows what a number of rights and privileges there were to be divided. The headman's precedence was laid down in detail: *e.g.*, he had a right to throw the first cake into the *Holī* festival fire; the right to have the pipes played first at his house at the *Dasahra* festival; and to have his cow's horns first gilded at another festival, and so on. He also had certain dues of grain (so many *ser* in each *maund*), called *gūgrī*; certain dues in oil, hemp, pots, shoes, cloth from the weaver, &c.

by one at a time, they adopted a sort of rotation. The hereditary land was a much-cherished family possession. Similar holdings were enjoyed by the accountant and, on a smaller scale, by the artisans and menials of the village, to be described presently. But it is worth while mentioning that the Arabic name used for this special holding (*waṭan*) superseded any older indigenous name, as this institution was wisely preserved by the earlier Muhammadan kings of the Dakhan; and the revenue- and land-terms employed by them became locally current.[1] The Marāthās, on the other hand, used to impose a heavy *joḍī*, or rent-charge, which must have destroyed the value of such holdings; and in some districts their harsh arrangements for revenue collection caused the wholesale disappearance of the old *pātels*, and with them of course the *waṭan*. Indeed, in the central districts, land held on this tenure is *now* almost exclusively found in certain districts in the Central Provinces and Berār.[2] It is well known in the Southern Presidency, where, however, the term *waṭan* does not seem to be in use.

[1] *Waṭan* means 'home'—that which is the hereditary and intimately valued property of the family, as opposed to any land they might hold by purchase or on managing lease or other slighter tenure. When such a holding and privilege was attached to any hereditary official or member of the family he was said to be *waṭandār* = holder of a *waṭan*. The very fact of this distinctive possession shows that the headman was never owner of the whole village. The strong attachment and loyal adhesion to the *Pātel* in Central India is vividly portrayed by Malcolm (*Memoir of Central India*, i. 12, and ii. 60). Great Marāthā chiefs valued the title of *Pātel*. If deserted villages had to be re-established, strenuous efforts were made to discover some descendant of the original headman (Malcolm, i. 18, note).

[2] We shall see in the sequel that the plan of setting apart a special holding in virtue of office for the headman and other village officers can be traced back to early Dravidian times. In the Laws of Manu we find the King directed to let the headman of the village, as well as the officer of larger revenue divisions, have a certain portion of his land free of revenue charges. The *waṭan*, it will be remembered, was not a State grant of land, but an old customary hereditary holding in virtue of office; the only connection of the State with it was the privilege of remission of the revenue dues. It may be well to add that, in some reports, the terms *waṭan*, *waṭandār*, are used as synonyms for hereditary land and its holder in general; but this is not strictly correct. Owing, however, to the sale, &c., of *waṭan* lands, it is possible that plots may be claimed as

Besides these two principal officers, who usually in large villages had deputies or assistants, there were others, such as the village watchman, and the guardian of boundaries, and the messengers. In irrigated villages there would be also an official to regulate the distribution of water.

But something else was wanted besides officers to make provision for the self-contained life of the 'community.' A village group established perhaps in the forest at some distance from any other village, to say nothing of larger towns, would need some purely local means of providing for the simple wants of daily life. And therefore villages of this, and, naturally, of the joint type also, have always solved the difficulty by attracting to themselves a body of resident craftsmen and menials, who are not paid by the job, but are employed by the village on a fixed remuneration, sometimes of a bit of rent-free (and perhaps revenue-free) land, sometimes by small payments at harvest, as well as by customary allowances of so many sheaves of corn, millet, &c., or certain measures of grain,[1] and perquisites in

on this tenure, though there is no existing connection with any headship or other office.

As may be expected in a Dravidian country like Madras, the *ex-officio* holdings of the headman, and also of the *karnam*, or village accountant, and sometimes of other members of the village staff, are well known throughout the villages of the Presidency. As to the special holding of the headman in Madras, see *Mirāsi Papers* (1862), p. 396, and many other places. We find the village watch enjoying this remuneration (*grāma-kāvel*), and a similar privilege to certain district police. The *vattiyan*, or sweeper, has his hereditary land, and so has the *panjāngan*, or village astrologer, who fixes the propitious dates for ploughing, sowing, and reaping (pp. 180, 405).

[1] This custom of paying the artisans and menials by allowances of grain (taken out before the division of the crop between the King's officers and the cultivator) is very ancient. It is found in every province, either accompanied by a small grant of land or as the sole allowance. So various are the modes of payment that I can only select one or two characteristic examples, which in this instance I take from the joint-village provinces. Details will be found for Madras in Macleane's *Administration Manual*, i. (Ethnol.), 102 (note), 154; *Mirāsi Papers*, pp. 180 ff, 405, &c. For Bombay, any district *Gazetteer* may be consulted: *e.g.* Ahmadābād (iv. 47), or Ratnagiri (x. 139), Broach (ii. 385), &c. The usual features occur of small land '*vatans*,' or allow-

kind. Each is also given a house-site in the village, or in some cases, as in Madras, in a group outside it, forming a sort of suburb.

The list of artisans varies in different parts, though of course some, being indispensable, are found in all cases, such as the blacksmith, potter, shoemaker or cobbler, carpenter, washerman, sweeper, and a barber, who also is surgeon, and is the proper person to carry messages connected with negotiations for betrothals. In some villages there is a dancing-girl; in others an

ances in cash or grain or both. (See also Berār *Gazetteer*, p. 205 ff. It may be necessary to explain that the villagers supply the materials for the work to be done, but do not pay for the labour; a stranger getting a job done would pay for both.

As a case in point I may instance the Gujrāt district of the Panjāb (*Gazetteer*, Gujrāt, 2nd ed. p. 97). The village servants are paid by grain-fees, with allowances of so many bundles of the crop before threshing, as there described: and the 'bundle' (*bharī*) of wheat or barley means the bundle tied by a string of *three straws length*. The blacksmith affords a good example, as his work requires a supply of iron and also charcoal. He never provides the iron for the tools he makes (reaping-hook, spade, ploughshare, &c.), but he does provide the charcoal for the forge, unless, indeed, an unusual quantity will be required—as in making a great pan for sugar-boiling. And in general, it is noted, the blacksmith is allowed as a perquisite, the roots and branches of any tree cut by a village proprietor. As a sample of the custom of grain payments in the North-West Provinces, I may quote from Mr. Hooper's Basti *S.R.* (1891), § 64. In a village called Dhebaruā, the following persons take shares of grain (called *jeora*) amounting to four *panseri* (measures of two *sers* or four pounds avoirdupois each) for each 'plough' of cultivated land in the village: the barber, washerman, carpenter, blacksmith, and cowherd. These also receive a further allowance (called *kalyānī*) when the 'business of the threshing-floor is over.' Another series of smaller shares are allowed to the *Pandit* or astrologer who determines the propitious seasons for sowing, &c.; to the *kahār*, who attends on visitors, such as the *dāroghā* of police, the revenue officer (*chaprāsī*), and the 'exorcist' (*sokhā*) who secures the village from evil spirits, and sets up the little posts called *Jāk* and *Jāknī* outside the village. This person, by the way, is often of the aboriginal tribes, *because these are supposed to have the power of exorcising the spirits of their old country*. The three last-named only get half a *jeora* and no extra *kalyānī*. Besides these regular allowances, certain other deductions are made from the grain heap before it is divided between the tenant and landlord; for example, five *anjuri* (double-handfuls) go for charity to Brahmans and *faqīrs*. The ploughman's wife is allowed to take up as much as she can hold 'for luck.'

astrologer to announce the propitious seasons for agricultural operations; in one account of the primitive villages in south-west Bengal I find mention of a 'witch-finder.' And in Berār (in the Amrāoti district) some of the villages pay a *gārpagāri*, whose duty it is to *avert hail* by his incantations.[1]

This residence in a more or less isolated group, with the common use of the adjoining waste or grazing ground, submission to the village headman, and common employment of a local staff of artisans and menials, were the chief circumstances which formed the bond of union in a *raiyatwāri* village. Probably at their first foundation the village families were more closely connected by clan ties than they are now; and there may have been some further feeling of 'community' on this ground. The nature of the revenue-system which early Governments adopted in dealing with these villages must have greatly influenced their solidarity. When the old custom of the State grain-share was quietly followed out, the headman managed the whole, and every holder in the village knew what he had to contribute. But in after times, when this system, with its natural complications caused by deductions and allowances on this account and on that, and by the calculation of average yields, proved too troublesome, the practice arose of fixing lump sums in cash, for which various speculators contracted, and thus elements of oppression were introduced. The government of the village by its own headman was interfered with; lands were sold and mortgaged to the bankers and others who advanced, or were security for, the revenue; and in general the old order was upset, lands abandoned, and the original holders ejected. The result of Marāthā mal-administration especially must have been to disturb greatly the old holdings, and, in fact, in the long course of years, to make the village population a very mixed one.[2] I am unable to trace

[1] Berār *Gazetteer*, p. 206. In *L. S. B. I.* i. 150, I have given some further lists of village craftsmen and servants. In the Marāthā villages, the complete number was supposed to be twelve, hence the term *bāra-balūte* for the body of village artisans and menials. *Balūta* (M.) is the grain-fee or allowance = *merāi* of the south.

[2] It is one of the things much to be desired as regards village statistics that we should have some means of knowing how far the western and southern villages under the *raiyatwāri* system still consist of land-

at any former period, anything resembling a community of property between the different holdings, or anything in early Dravidian custom that may have led to it. The individual holding now passes, on the death of the holder, to the descendants jointly, under the Hindu law; and they subdivide it, as far as circumstances permit. If the family is too large and more land cannot be had, the sons come to terms, and some sell their shares and seek new homes or other means of livelihood. There is, of course, no joint responsibility of the separate families for the Government revenue.[1] The headman alone is, or was, responsible for such village expenditure as entertaining guests, celebrating a festival, and the like. In former days he, and the officers of the superior revenue charges above him, used to levy a tax, or cess, called *ṣādir-wārid*,[2] to meet such expenses.

It only needs to be added, in conclusion, that the *present raiyatwār* holder of land has, legally speaking, a somewhat peculiar position, which is the result not of his original rights, nor of the intrinsic nature of his tenure, but of subsequent historical developments, especially in connection with the later claim of the rulers to be superior owners of all land. This point, however, will be more easily explained at a later stage; and as the modern legal nature of the tenure in a *raiyatwāri* village holding does not affect either the character of the village form or its principle of constitution, there is no occasion to pursue the question at present.

holders of the same clan or caste; it *may* be that there is more of this than *prima facie* we should be disposed to expect.

[1] The head of each family is alone responsible for the revenue of the holding; the revenue system also has its rules for allowing partition among the heirs on the death of a landholder, and for the separate shares being erected into separate 'numbers' on the revenue register, provided they do not go below a minimum of size.

[2] This means literally 'going out and coming in'—referring to the arrival and departure of guests. The levy seems to have been the occasion of many abuses. See Elphinstone's *Minute* (G. W. Forrest's Reprint, p. 280). 'The expenses of the *patel* on public affairs . . . are defrayed by a tax on the village. . . . This tax . . . is a great source of profit to the *pātels* and *kulkarnis*.'

B. *The Joint-Village*

If we now turn to the joint-village of Upper India, we have no longer a simple form to deal with. Without any previous knowledge of details, it will be obvious that, there being a *joint-tenure* of the village, that which is joint may be in time wholly or partly divided or partitioned: this alone will produce some variety of condition. And when estates are *joint* the principle of union need not be the same throughout. The former incident produces only minor varieties, including such as arise when the strict scale of shares gets forgotten or altered. The latter, in fact, produces important classes, in which the *principle of sharing* is different. Some indications of such a difference are given by those writers who speak of the 'aristocratic' and 'democratic' constitution of villages. This distinction is not a convenient one; but it is quite true that some villages are so far 'aristocratic' that they hold in *fractional* shares which indicate a family property held in descent from a dignified (possibly once princely) ancestor; others are 'democratic' in the sense that the groups of families have a real common descent, but have adopted a more equal mode of sharing, or that they are voluntary associations of settlers. Neither term, however, serves to indicate the important class of villages whose joint constitution is due to some form of *tribal* union and to surviving *tribal* or clan custom. I mention this fact, and only mention it, at this stage, because there is some obviously consequent danger of error in any generalised account of the joint-village, even when it has been acknowledged as a separate type. There are, however, certain features which all forms of joint-village possess in common, and these may be usefully described.

In all cases the entire area of the village forms something like a unit estate.[1] The adjoining waste is here an integral part

[1] The village is not always, strictly speaking, itself the unit estate. It may happen that a connected group of co-sharers have come to be owners of an estate comprising several geographical villages, and that the different branches of the family have not divided the whole so as to make the separated shares consist each of one or more entire villages. Each branch may have taken its share partly in one place, partly in another. Hence the real unit, for revenue purposes at any rate, is the

of the property, and is at the absolute disposal of the owners as much as any other land. Consequent on this universal and ancient fact of unity, the waste is included by the Survey in the boundaries of the village, as well as the arable; and when the waste comes to be partitioned, it will be so on a definite principle, usually, but not always, having relation to the existing shares in the arable area.[1]

It is also in consequence of these essential features that the modern Land-Revenue Administration is able to treat the village as one estate, liable for one lump sum of revenue which is distributed over the holdings or among the co-sharers according to their own principle of constitution: the whole body is jointly responsible, until what is technically known as 'perfect' partition severs the bond.[2] It is quite possible, and in former days was usual, to partition the holdings for several enjoyment without dissolving the common responsibility.

The body of owners who thus, whether their lands are partitioned or not, still hold together and have a certain joint interest in the village, arises in various ways, which will appear

maḥāl, or group of lands held under one and the same title; and registers are prepared to show the list of lands brought together for this purpose on paper, but actually lying, some here and some there, possibly, through half a dozen *mauza* on the map. Still, there are a very large number of cases in which a single village is also a *maḥāl*, or estate. In the Panjāb it is quite usual.

[1] In provinces like the Panjāb and the Central Provinces, where the area of waste was very great, and it would have been impossible to suppose it all really appropriated to one or other village, a special rule was laid down at the Land Revenue Settlement for allowing a liberal portion to each village; the surplus was reserved to Government on the general principle that waste not occupied belongs to the State. Such surplus areas (called *rakh* in the Panjāb) are utilised for grazing reserves, for forest purposes, and for colonisation when a scheme for irrigation can be carried out. In the North-West Provinces, except in some special districts, the whole of the waste was included in the village boundaries; and the Revenue Law contains some special provisions about the area in case it is so large as to be beyond the requirements of the village.

[2] 'Imperfect' partition merely defines the severalty holdings, leaving the body still jointly liable for the revenue. 'Perfect' partition goes further, and in fact constitutes so many new and distinct estates. The law may differ in different provinces as to the freedom with which this 'perfect' partition can now be applied for.

presently. I wish first to repeat once more that in all cases they are either a ruling, conquering, and often non-agriculturist caste, who have taken the superior or landlord position *over an earlier existing village group of cultivators*, usually of aboriginal or some mixed or humbler descent; or else *they have founded their own village in the virgin waste*, either by their own exertions, if agriculturists by nature, or by aid of tenants and dependents. But in either case, the village owner, or body of village owners, has the same sort of superior title. It depends on the locality which origin is the more common. The North-West Provinces official is extremely familiar with Rājput and other village owners, whose lordship was established over existing villages by various means, and not unfrequently has resulted from the prior existence of a territorial chiefship, which being afterwards partitioned among the family has left a number of individuals or families in possession of single villages. To the Panjāb official such a proceeding is less familiar; the joint-villages in the plain districts are much more frequently the direct foundations of individuals and clan-groups and colonist associates, who were agriculturists by nature and themselves cultivated the land; but they have the same ideas of united and superior ownership.

It is not at all necessary that the joint-village should be actually held undivided. In some cases it is so held; and the reason for it is plain; but in the majority of cases there is a complete separation of the individual or household holdings, and this may have been so from the moment of first settlement. Very often the arable is divided, and the waste not, either because it is more conveniently kept as a common grazing ground,[1] or because it is not yet wanted for the extension of cultivation.

As to the extent of land included in the 'village,' in many cases the estate is of what I may call a normal or average size, varying from a few hundred to a thousand or two thousand acres; it represents the limit to which the original grant extended, and to which the body of descendants have succeeded by in-

[1] As I have elsewhere remarked, *grazing* is usual, unless, from the absence of grazing land, stall-feeding has to be adopted, with such grazing on fallow fields as is possible. Hay-growing is not practised in the plains; hence divided meadow-land is not known.

heritance, or the limit of the settlement of the particular group who own it, or it is the result of a distribution of a larger area among certain branches of a family. But we shall meet with some cases where a great area (of many thousand acres) has been occupied by a whole clan and divided by them into certain main divisions for each of the minor clan groups; and it is only gradually and ultimately that separate 'villages' have emerged. There are also cases in which an extensive area was originally acquired by one family which has in the course of time multiplied into a clan, and so covered the whole, also without the intervention of any proper 'village' grouping at all. Here, again, time usually produces a fission into 'villages;' but there are instances of great areas still held directly in numerous individual equal shares, and to these it is difficult to apply the term village. Taking, however, the average-sized village, there is little in external appearance to distinguish the *joint* from the *raiyatwāri* form.[1] There is, of course, the group of residences—sometimes a central compact group, but often several scattered hamlets.[2] Close to the village is a tank or pond, hollowed out by the process of digging the clay to make the sun-dried bricks of which the cottages are built; there is a dry dusty space around the group of houses where the cattle stand and where the weavers stretch and prepare their webs. There is also the village tree or grove, and the meeting-place of the villagers, sometimes with a raised platform of masonry to sit on. And the village will have its mosque or temple, and its cemetery, if Muhammadan. The conditions which attract a group of permanent menials and artisans to serve the village are the same as in the *raiyatwāri* village.[3]

But with the village officers there is a difference. The *patwāri*—whose native title we inadequately attempt to translate as

[1] Except that in Bombay and Madras, the revenue system being different and adapted to the *raiyatwāri* village, there is *now* a method of demarcating field or holding boundaries which is peculiar and strikes the eye of anyone familiar with the system, telling him that he has come into a *raiyatwāri* district. Perhaps also the *raiyatwāri* village has oftener the central residence of the headman as a prominent feature.

[2] In the next chapter will be found some account of the village buildings and the circumstances which produce compact residence-sites or the contrary.

[3] See p. 16.

'accountant' or 'village registrar'—is, of course, to be found. Receipts have to be given, village accounts kept, and statistics prepared, as much in joint-villages as elsewhere. But, as Sir H. S. Maine has pointed out, there is no real 'headman.'[1] The management of the affairs of the joint body is properly by a committee of heads of houses, or *panchayat*. But some one must represent them at the Collector's office and be their spokesman, and also be responsible for the duties which the State may require of the village owners. Hence, at any rate, in modern times, a headman, whose hybrid title (*lambardār* = holder of a 'number')[2] indicates his recent origin, is appointed; and his office is allowed to be in some degree elective, while it also tends to become hereditary if the next heir is qualified. As most villages are divided into certain main sections or *pattī* (of this hereafter), there will be a *lambardār* for each section. In the Panjāb, where the *pattī* are often numerous, it has been found necessary to have a further single representative of the several section-headmen; such a person is called the *'alā-lambardār*, or chief headman. These officials, as I may call them, have now certain duties under the Criminal Procedure Law with regard to reporting and aiding in the discovery of crime, and in surveillance of bad characters; they have also certain responsibilities connected with realising the revenue; otherwise they have only such authority as their public duty and their family dignity and personal character give them: they have nothing of the formal supremacy and precedence of the genuine old *pātel* of the *raiyatwāri* village. Nor have they any holding of land in virtue of office. The *panchayat*, at the present day, has indeed lost much of its ancient power; partly owing to the partition of lands, partly owing to the facility of reference to the district law courts. In most cases it is hardly

[1] *Ante*, p. 7.

[2] The name dates from the first quarter of this century; the 'number' refers to the Collector's list of village landholders with a serial number attached to each name, showing who is directly responsible for bringing in the revenues of each section of the village. The Mughal system of revenue management, which was in most cases essentially *raiyatwāri*, unless a landlord or some definite superior was dealt with, recognised the principal man in the village (or more than one), without, however, defining any official functions, as the *muqaddam* = the first or forward man.

in existence at all; but it will still assemble in connection with some social or caste dispute. I confess, however, that I do not know what is meant by the *panchayat* controlling the course of cultivation, except in the comparatively rare case of some peculiarly situated colonist villages, where the associated members preferred to determine at the beginning of each year what lands each could and would cultivate.[1] For by far the greater number of villages the cultivating holdings are either partitioned (and in one large class of villages have *always been so from the first*) or are held year after year in severalty by tacit consent, and nothing of the kind is required. Perhaps the most frequently surviving occasion of the *panchayat's* action is in connection with the adjustment of accounts which, in some villages, still takes place annually or after each harvest. Then the proportion in which the revenue-dues are to fall on the different holdings may need to be adjusted; and in any case the headmen (*lambardārs*) have to recover their expenditure under the head of *malba—i.e.* common expenses of the village, such as entertaining strangers, repairing the *paṭwārī's* office, expenditure on the village mosque or temple, charities, religious offerings, and the like. The co-sharers may object to some items as not properly common expenditure.

One other feature deserves to be remarked on, as it may occur in any kind of joint-village. In the many cases in which the co-sharing proprietary body are of non-agricultural caste, or of such a caste as regards farm-work, or at least handling the plough, as degrading, or where they have established their landlord position over the heads of an earlier cultivating body, the larger part of the land will necessarily be held by tenants.[2] The co-sharers will only have taken into their own direct possession the several home-farms (*sīr*) which each enjoys. Some of these tenants, no doubt, will be in a privileged position in virtue

[1] And there are also certain villages *situated on the banks* of a variable river, where a portion of the land liable to unforeseen changes from river action is never permanently allotted, but managed from year to year for the joint benefit.

[2] This is quite common in the North-West Provinces. In the Panjāb, on the other hand, the village-owners are most frequently also the cultivators. That is why we so seldom meet with any reference to *sīr* lands in the Panjāb.

of their possibly expropriietary character or other circumstance as defined by the Tenant Law; in other words, some may be 'occupancy-tenants,' others, 'tenants-at-will.' In some cases, especially in the Panjāb, there are tenants who not only are allowed to have occupancy rights, but they pay nothing beyond the Government revenue on their land; they owe this position most frequently to their having consented in former days to come and help the village body in cultivating enough land to meet the heavy assessment of some rapacious Sikh Governor. But I am not aware that in any case tenants form part of the 'brotherhood,' or that they can be represented as occupying a grade in any sort of hierarchy formed by the 'brotherhood.'[1] The proprietors alone have a voice in the management. Tenants, even when they are of so privileged a class as to pay no rent beyond the Government dues, usually pay a nominal fee—perhaps a load of manure annually—for their house-site; they often cannot sell the cottage; and it is a question of local custom whether, on leaving the village from any cause, any tenant or artisan can sell the house-timbers. No doubt good tenants will be under the protection of the co-sharers; but they have no voice in the village council, no concern with profits or losses, nor any share in the waste, beyond a probable right by custom of grazing their cattle there. Still less are the artisans and menials part of the 'brotherhood' in any degree whatever: they are always of different (usually lower) caste. Indeed, the idea that, *e.g.*, a body of proud Rājput co-sharers would acknowledge their cultivating tenants, and *a fortiori* the potter, the carpenter, or the *çamār*,[2] as part of their brotherhood, only in a lower degree, is something quite grotesque.

[1] *Ante*, p. 7. It is quite possible that a person may have been in past days formally admitted as a co-sharer (*khātādār*), and in time gets supposed to be of the 'founder's kin;' but that is quite a different matter from coming as a tenant, however independent and however valued.

[2] The low-caste cobbler, who has as a perquisite the skins of cattle dying in the village. So far from the brotherhood including anything beyond the actual co-sharers, absconding members who have returned and got readmitted to the village and yet have been unable to pay up the arrears on account of which they formerly threw up their holding will very often not be allowed to resume their full position, but be admitted as a sort of tenant without voice in the management or share in the profits.

The co-sharing body, especially if they are of one clan, or are the joint successors to one man who founded or acquired the village landlordship, are often desirous of excluding strangers, as well as securing to themselves the chance of augmenting their own holdings. This desire gives rise to a custom of pre-emption, which is not inconsistent with the fact that, in former days, the pressure of a heavy revenue-assessment compelled them to take in special tenants, or even grant shares in the village to outsiders. Nor, of course, does the feeling prevent the custom (in some localities) of admitting the family Brahman to a share. In general, the intending vendor, whether of his whole share or of any field or plot, must offer it at a fair value to one of the existing co-sharers (usually in order of blood relationship to himself), and then to the members of the same subdivision, before selling to any outsider.[1]

So much may be said regarding the features of joint-villages in general: but it is impossible to form a just idea of such villages as they actually exist in the different districts, without understanding the principles on which the body of proprietors who own the whole village are united together, and on which the real or apparent collective ownership depends. The matter cannot be fully stated or illustrated, because some other matters have first to be considered. But I have already indicated, as a ground for caution in attempting a general description, that, apart from all those minor varieties which are the result of what I may call 'wear and tear'—the alteration of the strict shares, and the more or less complete partition of joint-lands—there are several clearly-marked principles of joint-constitution. The application of one or the other is at once indicated by the *mode of sharing* the village. It is hardly necessary to add that the

There are various customs regarding this readmission of absentees; for, especially in former days, sharers often found themselves unable to pay the revenue and live on the holding; they would go away until better times, and seek, perhaps twenty years later, to return.

[1] The custom varies locally. It is only effective if the other co-sharers are able to buy, or are willing to redeem the mortgages which are sure to have been made before the sale is proposed as a final measure. It may be doubted whether the custom has done much to prevent the lands of the less successful passing into the hands of money-lenders or capitalists.

difference of constitution implies a corresponding difference in the mode of origin or foundation.

The first principle of formation depends on there being a *considerable clan*, of which the village is part; indeed, in these cases, the 'village' is often, as I have said, a very secondary consideration, and the co-sharing extends over the whole of a clan-area, or over some primary divisions of it much larger than ordinary villages.

The second principle is always connected with the normal *village* area, and is observed in that large class of cases where the village body is a group of descendants from an *individual* founder.

A third principle, which involves a variety of forms of sharing, may be also spoken of; and it applies to all cases where the *clan* or tribal principle does not appear, and where also the special features of the sharing in descent from a single aristocratic founder are not observed.

The two salient cases of *clan*-settlement, and of *individual* or *joint-family* settlement, may be a little further explained, something in this way:

I. A whole clan has conquered or occupied a suitable district. Under the guidance of its patriarch and chiefs, the land is apportioned in the first instance in large tracts for its several main sections, or minor clans; these effect among themselves the final allotment to households and groups of households, which ultimately form villages. More commonly, however, the appearance of a *clan*-settlement is due to the fact that a single enterprising family, having no pretensions to nobility or territorial rule, had originally located itself on a wide area—which good fortune preserved to it intact; on this the existing clan-group has gradually grown up till it has filled the whole. At first there was perhaps only a father and four sons; but now, not only do the descendants occupy the whole territory, but they may have split up into villages all of the same clan. In these cases, some rule of equal division, such as we shall hereafter describe as the BHAIĀCHĀRĀ method, nearly always occurs. It is quite a distinct and characteristic method.[1]

[1] The term *bhaiāchārā* itself has unfortunately become misused in our offices, and has got applied to other forms also; but this is a detail which I cannot here enter into.

II. In the other principal form, the estate originated with one man (or possibly two or three brothers), to whom the village was granted, or who simply usurped the superior position, or who gained a footing as farmer of the revenue or as purchaser in later days at an auction sale for arrears of revenue, or otherwise established himself in the management. New villages, too, have been constantly founded by individual enterprise, with or without the grant of a Rājā or local potentate.

Very frequently, too, under this head come the cases, occurring more especially in the North-West Provinces, where the village bodies are descendants of former chiefs or of Rājās, or of scions of princely houses or adventurous chiefs who once had a regular (or irregular) territorial rule; but the rulership has long passed away, and remnants of the family, represented by two score or more of descendants, have clung to a village here, and two or three villages there, and have then become peasant *landlords* where they once were *rulers*. In all this class of cases, the principle of sharing is, or originally was, not one of 'democratic' equality of right in the area obtained, but one depending on *the place in the table of descent from the founder or acquirer*, the different heirs each taking the 'legal' share that belongs to him by the law or custom of inheritance. This is what is called the PATTIDĀRĪ principle of sharing.[1] Properly speaking, each takes his share in the land or in the proceeds, if the land is undivided, and pays the corresponding fraction of the revenue and other burdens.[2] If the waste has remained undivided and is afterwards partitioned, the owners will share it in exactly the same fractions as have determined their holdings in the arable. This is the admitted theory; but naturally it often happens that in the course of years the strict shares have been forgotten or changed, and members not really of the founder's kin—perhaps members of the wives' families or other 'helpers in time of need'—may

[1] See diagram at p. 31, note.

[2] In estates of this kind the joint heirs may hold undivided for a long period. But the profits and burdens will be shared on the same principle (*pattidārī*). From a *tenure* point of view there is not the slightest distinction between the joint-landlord and the severalty-landlord village, as long as the ancestral share principle is followed in sharing the profits in one case or the fields in the other.

have been admitted to shares. Shares may also have been sold to outsiders under stress of necessity. Accordingly, where *all* remembrance of the correct fractional shares is lost, and each now holds simply on the basis of his *de facto* possession, and pays the share of the revenue and charges according to an acreage-rate agreed on for the number of acres actually held, the village is officially put into another class—it ceases to be *pattidārī*, or 'ancestrally shared.' It also is often the case that a part of such a village has been divided and part not; *and* the divided part is held in modified shares, or on mere *de facto* possession, and the rest still on the strict shares. All these are what I have called minor varieties, which must not detain us at this stage of our inquiry. This *principle* (*pattidārī*, or ancestral sharing according to the law of joint inheritance) is simply the result of the joint succession of all the heirs together. It is in villages of *this* class that it can truly be said that the village is the group which is held together *by the land* which it occupies 'in common' —*i.e.* as joint-heirs or co-sharers. It is also in villages of this class, as distinguished from those first mentioned, that we hear of a person being a '4 *āna*' sharer—*i.e.* owning one-fourth of the estate, or being a '2 *āna* 3 *pāi* 15 *kaurī*' sharer.[1] These terms could not properly be used of the other estates where the shares are so many equal lots, or are expressed in terms indicating the peculiar method on which the clan or family has arranged the valuation of its land for the purpose of equitably distributing the revenue and other charges; nor where the holdings are merely so many acres, or so many 'plough' lands, not being *shares of the unit estate area on any principle whatever*.

When a *pattīdārī* village is divided—and this may have

[1] In these cases the whole estate is treated as 'one rupee;' occasionally the whole is 'one *bīghā*' (land measure); but as the usual divisions of the currency or the square measure would not suffice to meet the numerous small fractions of a much multiplied body of co-sharers, various artificial sub-divisions have been invented. If the strict ancestral principle is maintained, the fraction indicates also the share of revenue payable; and to say that a man owns a '4 *āna* share' in the village is synonymous with saying that he pays '4 *ānas*' of the revenue; it indicates not only that he owns one-fourth of the village, but is consequently responsible for one-fourth of the assessment.

occurred many years or generations ago—as soon as the existing co-sharers were numerous enough to require it, it is found that there are major and minor divisions. Sometimes there will be a primary division into *ṭarf*, either because one whole section became Moslems and the rest remained Hindus, or because two different parties originally founded the estate together, or both got hold of it together, by conquest. But more ordinarily the first main divisions are called *pattī*, and these often represent the original shares of the sons of the founder and, naturally, are considerable in extent and limited in number.[1] Of course it is only in a very few cases of late foundation that the present representatives of the *pattī* have any personal memory of their head. Inside the *pattī* are the next grade of divisions called *thok*, and then the *ṭūlā*, (or *ṭolā*). Under one or other of such final or 'primary' divisions are grouped the many subordinate later families; but their divisions receive no new designation. So much may be ventured in this preliminary statement, as to say that in all probability the general prevalence of the three primary, or larger, divisions in descending grade is essentially connected with the close-kindred of the first founders—representing the shares of the founder's son (*pattī*), grandson (*thok*), great-grandson (*ṭūlā*).[2] In all families, and in clans as well,

[1] Or in a diagram:

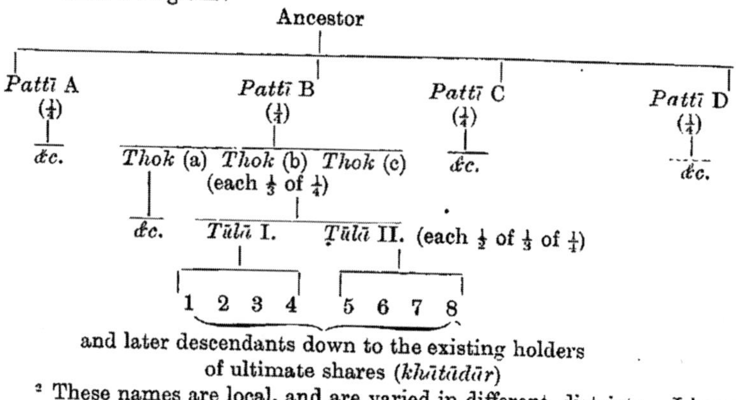

and later descendants down to the existing holders of ultimate shares (*khātādār*)

[2] These names are local, and are varied in different districts. I have met with the following series:

Ṭarf, thok, naglā
Patti, thok, ṭūlā
Patti, thok, behrī.

this series forms the natural basis of the grouping of the after-coming kindred. When occurring in villages, it marks the *completion of the first group* of close-kindred; and as the descendants from each branch multiply, they retain their own close-kindred connection subordinate to one or other of the 'primary' groups. It may often be observed that long after the primary partition has been carried out, some of the subordinate groups remain 'joint' among themselves. The different sections of the estate may also have different customs of sharing: one may have lost knowledge of the proper shares, and adhered to *de facto* holdings and so on.

Exactly the same primary divisions may be observed in clan or tribal settlements, and in those areas held on the *bhaiāchārā* principle, where a commencement was made with a single family which (in the first instance) could only divide on this principle. But here the areas for each branch were calculated, not as equal fourths, or other *fractions*, of the unit area, but in some other way. And when there is the clan feeling in operation, it may happen that, subsequent to these primary divisions, no further attention is paid to precise shares, but all get, as far as possible, equal lots, according to the number and requirements of each family—as long as the area available admits of such a plan. In rarer cases we shall find an entire clan (*e.g.* on the Panjāb frontier) following the ancestral fractions throughout—in fact, carrying the *pattidārī* principle through the whole body; whereas in most cases it is only found in the limited group of descendants of a single founder in a village. Within either of these two great classes of joint-village—these groups illustrating each a different principle of formation—there may be several minor varieties, as I have already indicated.

III. Where the village is not tribal, and also not *pattidārī*, there may be several modes of sharing the land, the detail of which had better be reserved until a later stage; but one of them may perhaps be mentioned here—namely, when the village is formed by a voluntarily associated body of colonists, who agree to be 'joint' as regards their liability to the ruler, or for the general purposes of aid and defence, and who may also hold the land on various plans. One is a kind of joint-stock cultivation, in certain known shares, each sharer taking for the year only, a certain area of land to cultivate; or the produce of the whole might be divided according to the shares. Another method of association will be described, in which the holdings were made out from the first and were distributed by lot. I will only add that villages originally *raiyatwāri*, and which did not happen to have fallen under any superior family, may in modern times become 'joint-villages' by the action of the Land-Revenue system; and so joint-villages may be artificially created.

This general sketch will suffice to call attention to the real distinctions that may exist under the general denomination of 'joint-village.' It is right, also, to remember that these different kinds, with their minor varieties, in the Upper Indian Provinces, have long acquired an additional appearance of uniformity by reason of the application to them all of a system of revenue management which, varying much in detail, is essentially the same in all the provinces, and by reason of the uniformity of the nomenclature applied in the official records and returns.

But before closing this chapter of preliminary statements, it will be well to explain how it comes about that the primary distinction insisted on between the two diverse types of village —the *raiyatwāri* and the joint-village—has not hitherto been more fully recognised, or, if recognised, has not been allowed due prominence.

In the first place, most of the extant accounts or notices of villages in histories and memoirs are based upon the earlier published Minutes of various administrators which obtained celebrity, and have thus got copied from book to book. Now, in the first instance, these original documents were written solely from the administrative point of view, and to justify or recommend a certain practical course of present action; and it is often forgotten that our earlier Indian worthies were great masters of administration, but this did not necessarily imply that they had a special knowledge of historical details or an aptitude for land-tenure investigations. They had not either the means or the time to examine village-tenures from the point of view of the student of ancient institutions or of the historical economist. Moreover, each was usually closely connected with some one part of India, and his remarks properly apply to that part only. Locomotion was not then as easy as it is now, and public officers had not either the opportunity or the need to pass frequently from one province to another. Elphinstone, for example, was able to give us a good picture of the *raiyatwārī* village of the Dakhan, but he was not familiar with the details of the northern village; on the other hand, Holt Mackenzie (and after him Thomason) knew well the village of the North-West Provinces, but evidently had not studied those of the South or of Central India. Indeed, in Holt Mackenzie's time, the Central Provinces were not yet annexed, and the Dakhan was only beginning to be settled provisionally.

Various later writers, especially those not practically acquainted with land-tenures, have endeavoured to combine together the different accounts of village-tenure which they found on record; and, seeing that each of the existing authorities spoke of one kind of village—that which was characteristic of the province under his care or observation—they naturally supposed that there was one kind only, and that they might regard the different features described, as all belonging to varieties of one species. Thus in the elaborate treatise on the *Law Relating to the Land Tenures of Lower Bengal*, forming the Tagore Lectures for 1874–5,[1] the author, living in Bengal Proper, where the village system (originally *raiyatwārī*) had fallen into decay under the influence of the Zamīndār landlords, and having no direct experience of villages, collected with exemplary diligence all sorts of materials, and combined them into one picture of 'the village'; with the result of presenting in his pages a form of 'community' which does not, and never did, exist.

But some still later writers, having perceived that the *raiyatwārī* village, as now existing, is obviously different from the joint-village, have attempted to argue that it is a form

[1] Calcutta, 1876: Thacker and Spink. Another example, one easier to refer to, is in Elphinstone's *History of India* (Cowell's 6th ed.) At p. 69–70 is an excellent account of the *raiyatwārī* village which the author knew directly, and at p. 71 he has added a general account of the northern joint-village, which, though unfortunately wrong in some minor points, yet clearly explains the essential features of the co-sharing landlord class. But the editor's notes in Appendix V., especially those marked E, F, and G*a*, are likely to mislead, chiefly through mixing up totally distinct matters.

which has resulted from a natural 'evolution' of common ownership into severalty; and they set forth the stages of this process in a manner which, plausible as it at first appears, does violence to many unquestionable facts. They have also found a cause for the supposed change, in the wars and intestine commotions and tyrannical oppressions which they assume to have broken up the 'communities,' and converted the villages into miscellaneous groups of now independent landholders, only loosely held together by the circumstance of local aggregation and by the authority of the headman.[1] At this early stage of our inquiry it would be inconvenient to go into details about the progress of ideas of ownership or the fallacy of the evolution argument, but it may be stated that, if such a view were correct, and that all villages began by being held absolutely in common, and gradually became more and more divided, till at last modern individual ownership was perfected, the *raiyatwārī* villages must all be much later in date than the joint; whereas the evidence is all the other way,[2] and some relics of very early Dravidian villages, *e.g.*, show no sign of any common holding; moreover, the *raiyatwārī* village gives no indication of being a decayed or altered form of anything: the position of the headman and the land-allotments held by the village chiefs—both of them foreign to the joint-village—are ancient and original features. It is perfectly true that there are in the South, and in Bombay, traces of what were apparently once jointly-held villages which have decayed; but an examination of these cases, which we shall afterwards make, will show that they were local and special tenures due to exceptional causes; and that in the Dakhan ancient local lordships had probably been established which passed away, and, the shares of the overlord-families having lost their owners, the villages reverted to what was in fact their original *raiyatwārī* constitution. But when it is attempted to be argued that the Marāthā and Mughal wars, and the oppressive

[1] Both these views will be found in Mr. J. D. Mayne's valuable and compact treatise on *Hindu Law and Usage*, which, when I left India, had reached a fourth edition. See p. 219 of this edition.

[2] We shall see hereafter, for instance, that the *raiyatwārī* was the form known to the author of the *Laws of Manu*, and that it existed in the ancient kingdoms of Oudh under the Rājās, and in Rājputāna.

government of the former, caused the wholesale conversion of the villages in the West and South, it may well be asked how it was that similar wars, and the repeated invasions that occurred, did not change them wholesale in the North? For it is notoriously the fact that the North was just as much the scene of wars, invasions, and turmoils, as Central and Southern India—indeed, as regards Madras, more so; for the Southern Presidency was never really subdued by the Muhammadan conquest, any more than it was reached by the original Aryan invasion; and, though there were local invasions and cruel oppressions, there were still parts where no great changes could have occurred. Yet *raiyatwāri* villages are there universal in all the districts alike.[1] The joint-village community, we have often been told, is peculiarly strong, and able to withstand the shock of armies and the fall of empires; how was it, then, that it survived all over the country north of the Vindhyas, and generally succumbed in the east, west, centre, and south?

I do not, of course, doubt that it is quite possible for a shared-village to fall into poverty and ultimately to present a series of repeatedly alienated and now miscellaneously owned fields, the cultivators of which have lost all sense of union; but such a possibility does not account for the wholesale change, over wide areas, of the strongest form of village into another form; nor does it explain how the supposed decayed form comes to be uniformly endowed with special marks and features which we are able to trace back to very early times.

On the other hand, it will be observed, it would be quite easy for *raiyatwāri* villages to be changed into joint-villages, as doubtless they were in many northern districts, by the simple fact of conquest and the consequent establishment of overlord-families who formed a new *stratum* of superior co-sharing owners, and so constituted *the* village community, the older cultivators

[1] And where joint-villages appear they are exceptional and are assigned to special causes and origins. In any case it is remarkable, on the view I am combating, that the 'Jaghire territory' (Chingleput district) of Madras happens to be a district more cruelly ravaged and desolated under special attacks, than almost any other part of the Presidency; yet this is the *very part* of Madras where the (exceptional) joint or *mirāsi* villages were *best* preserved in evidence!

sinking into the position of tenants. This may happen, and certainly has happened, not only in individual cases, but over whole districts at once, as actual examples in the sequel will show.

We must now proceed to that detailed consideration of village tenures which will justify what has here been asserted in a preliminary way; and I will only add to this already lengthy prefatory note that, in order to understand the real history of villages, we ought to take into account all the factors of the case. We must first note the physical and geographical conditions of India, both as regards the bearing they have on the natural inclination of *all* tribes and races who have found a home in India to form village groups; and as regards the bearing they had on the spread of the Aryan and other Northern tribes, who had so much to do with shaping Indian ideas and customs of land-holding.

We must, then, gather together what evidence we have regarding the early non-Aryan races of India and their land customs; and also proceed to notice the effects of Aryan influence on these, the real establishers of agricultural land-holding in India.

Having thus disposed of the geographical, climatic, and ethnic antecedents to the formation of village groups, we shall be in a position to appreciate various local illustrations of the actual growth and condition of villages in different parts of India, as these appear from the really authentic sources—the Settlement Reports of districts, and other similar manuals written expressly on the subject and on the spot. These will make it plain how villages arise out of *tribal* conditions of society, as well as out of *individual effort*. Finally, we shall be in a position to consider what 'collective ownership' or 'holding in common' really means when applied to the class of village which we call 'joint,' and how ideas of ownership in land seem really to have grown up in India.

CHAPTER II

THE GEOGRAPHICAL AND PHYSICAL FEATURES OF INDIA AS AFFECTING THE MOVEMENT OF AGRICULTURAL TRIBES AND THEIR FORMS OF LAND-HOLDING

It would not be fair to criticise too closely the meaning of phrases frequently met with in books on India which seem to indicate a belief that the villages are chiefly, if not solely, traceable to 'Hindu' (Aryan) influences, or which assign to the Aryan element an almost absolute predominance in the population of India. But it will be allowable to point out that the non-Aryan races have of late years been more carefully studied, and their importance as affecting the origin of many existing castes and tribes is now generally recognised. And certainly the result of such further study has been to establish the fact that the non-Aryan races had a good deal to do with building up the existing village land-customs. Hence it is that whatever concerns the movements and the permanent location of these races, and whatever has in after times influenced the movements of Aryan and other invaders, has its interest and importance in our inquiry. And there are certain geographical features of India, more especially connected with its mountain ranges, which have had an obvious effect on the movements of at least some of the tribes—facilitating those movements in one direction, and restraining, if not altogether stopping, them in another. In the third chapter I have endeavoured to give a brief sketch of the population—past and present—of the Indian provinces, as far as it is connected with agricultural life, because the names of the different tribes and people must occur again and again in the course of our narrative, and it is desirable that something should be said in explanation of those, in some cases unfamiliar, names. This second chapter is, in fact, the natural if not necessary preliminary to the third.

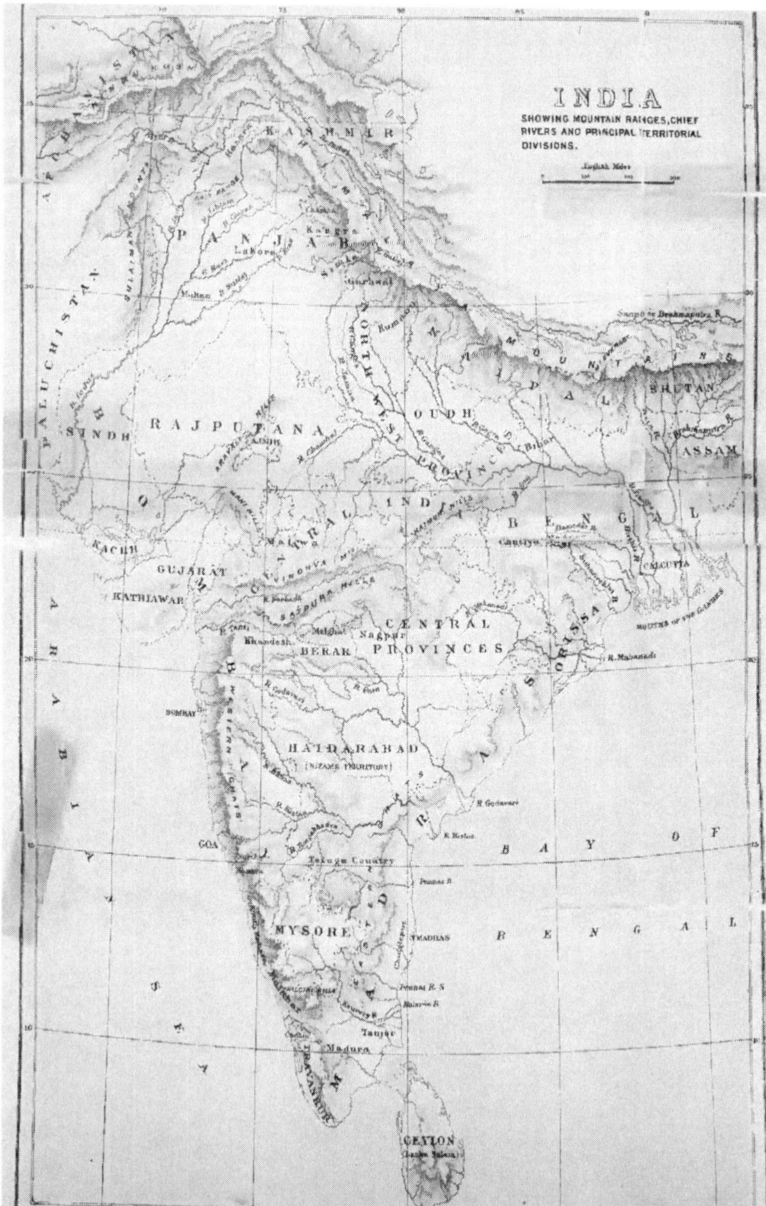
INDIA
SHOWING MOUNTAIN RANGES, CHIEF RIVERS AND PRINCIPAL TERRITORIAL DIVISIONS.
English Miles
KASHMIR
PANJAB
AFGHANISTAN
BALUCHISTAN
SINDH
RAJPUTANA
NORTH WEST PROVINCES
OUDH
BHUTAN
ASSAM
CENTRAL INDIA
BENGAL
CALCUTTA
KACHH
GUJARAT
KATHIAWAR
CENTRAL PROVINCES
BERAR
ORISSA
BOMBAY
HAIDARABAD
(NIZAMS TERRITORY)
GOA
MYSORE
MADRAS
BAY OF BENGAL
ARABIAN SEA
CEYLON
Tanjor
Madura
Telugu Country
Nagpur
Khandesh
Kangra
Lahore
Multan
Malwa
Longitude East from Greenwich
Longmans Green & Co. London, New York & Bombay.

There is also another matter which comes under the head of physical features and their influence. It is impossible to doubt that while social customs, and often purely natural liens of kinship, have been the main factors in determining to what extent sections of tribes and clans, as well as closer degrees of kindred, continue to keep up their connection or effect a certain fission and separation into groups, the 'village,' regarded as an aggregate of land-holdings, was suggested, not to say necessitated, by the physical features of country and climate; indeed, this is sometimes shown by the absence of villages and the substitution of isolated homesteads or small hamlets in certain localities. Lastly, the opportunity of a general chapter on the physical factors of our problem may be taken, to explain certain forms of agriculture or modes of cultivation which indicate the stages by which permanent land-holding may be gradually introduced.

SECTION I.—GEOGRAPHICAL FEATURES

(1) *The Northern and Western Hill Ranges*

If we look at a map of India,[1] it will be obvious that all invasions of tribes by land must have been from either the north-east or north-west end of the Himalayan chain. Any considerable migrations across the central ranges are as little probable as they are without any traditional or historical suggestion. If we look first to the north-east corner as a convenient starting-point, it will be observed that there is nothing to prevent tribes from the north-east coming to the Brahmaputra Valley, to the central and southern hills of Assam, and to Eastern Bengal generally. How much farther such tribes would advance into Central Bengal would depend on whether they were met by other people whose presence sufficed to check their progress. As a matter of fact, the tribes from this quarter, which belong to a distinctive group, did not affect the population far into Bengal Proper, as we shall afterwards see. But many of them found a congenial home in the outer slopes and valleys of the

[1] Throughout this section it is necessary to assume that the reader will have a fairly good map of India before him, showing the chief rivers, mountains, and provinces. It is impossible that the remarks made can be intelligible without such an aid.

Himalayan Mountains; and it is curious to observe that these outer districts of the hill country, as well as the *tarāi* or malarious jungle country below it, became peopled, albeit scantily, by early Mongoloid races. The descendants of these early settlers, some unchanged in race and much degraded, others improved by more or less admixture with other tribes, are found in considerable numbers throughout the whole of the outer ranges almost up to the river Indus itself.

But beyond the possibility of Mongoloid tribes entering India from the upper north-east end, there is little at present to call our further attention to this quarter. The chief interest lies in the geographical features of the north-west Himalayan frontier, of the Indus Valley, and of those of the broad but low ranges of mountains which divide Upper India from the Dakhan. The whole question of the facilities which existed for the advance of the Aryan invasion is connected with the north-west Himalayan passes and those more westerly routes through the hills beyond the Indus Valley. The Vindhyan Hills, on the other hand, afford an explanation as to why limits were set, as they were, to any Aryan advance *en masse* to the south, and why Southern India remained isolated and only accessible to later Aryan influence in a totally different manner. The Vindhyan Ranges, too, are interesting by reason of the curious sort of 'refuge-ground,' if I may use the phrase, which they afforded to some of the earliest tribes which occupied Indian soil, and whose institutions can still be clearly traced in the plateau country formed by the eastern terminal ramifications of the mountains.

But first as regards the northern and western passes into India. If we glance along the great line of Himalayan Mountains as far as a point about due north of where Peshāwar is marked on the map,[1] we shall notice that while one chief line of northern barrier mountains goes on more or less directly to the west, and bears the local names of the 'Hindū-Kūsh' and 'Safed-koh,' another series, roughly parallel to it, forms a southern or outer Himalaya, including the Pīr Pinjāl, which bounds Kashmīr, and further east the Dhaulādhār, &c. At the western

[1] In the Parliamentary *Statement of the Moral and Material Progress of India*, 1883, will be found an excellent map of the *mountain systems* of India, and another of the *rivers*.

end this southern range branches off and turns southward, forming a western frontier for India and skirting the Panjāb and Sindh. Of this western hill-barrier there are two main lines or ranges; the outer one, next the river Indus, is lower in general elevation and terminates sooner; the inner one, or Sulāimān Range, continues, though with diminishing height and under other names, almost as far south as the delta of the Indus.

Both the northern mountain ranges (at the north-west corner) and the western (Sulāimān) barrier are traversed by several *passes*. And these passes, speaking generally, are in a double series: first crossing the highest, or farther rampart, and then crossing a second or plainward line of mountain crests before reaching the level country of the Panjāb or Sindh respectively.

Naturally, clans with their leaders, or conquering princes with their armies, coming from the more northern or north-western regions, would enter the Himalayan group of hills by the north-west passes about Kābul. It is also quite possible for hardy northern races to have remained a long time among the valleys and slopes of the mountainous region about the Upper Indus and its affluents, lying, roughly speaking, between the northern high-line of the Himalaya (represented by the Hindū-Kūsh and its continuation east and west) and the *outer* line of the same group. Once across the northern main ramparts, it would be possible to extend a settlement into the intramontane valley of Kashmīr and the neighbouring valleys of Chamba, &c., as far east as Kāngra. Whether or not the tribes made such a settlement in the Hill Country, it would still be necessary to cross the remaining ranges in order to emerge on to the plains in the vicinity of Peshāwar, or of the Jihlam River, as did Alexander.

In the case of tribes coming from the north-west and following this general route *towards the plain country*, it would be possible either (1) to go south along the Indus Valley, which presents an open country, all the way to the sea; or (2) to spread over the outer hills and also the level plains of the Panjāb. Once having reached those plains, the tribes and their followers could advance eastward with no other difficulty than that of crossing various rivers, to the Ganges plain or valley, and to the rich tracts of Oudh and Bihār. Ultimately Bengal Proper and the Ganges mouths could be reached without any serious physical obstacle. Supposing, again, that other tribes chose the Indus Valley route, or perhaps entered India lower down—*i.e.* more towards due west—these would naturally occupy Sindh or would proceed to the Southern Panjāb. If it was in their mind to go still further south, their line of progress would be by Kaçch to Western India, as we shall presently see.

(2) *The Vindhyan Barrier*

Across the middle of India, just where the continent begins to taper to its triangular form, and south of the Chambal, the Jamnā and the Ganges rivers, there is a broad but rather low series of hill ranges, which forms, as a whole, a continuous barrier almost from west to east. At either extreme end the barrier can be rounded; but the whole central portion has, as a matter of fact, for many centuries afforded a practical line of demarcation between 'Northern India' (the basins of the Indus and the Ganges), and the Dakhan and Southern India. This barrier does not strike the eye so much till its entire features are taken in. There are, in fact, a whole series of variously named ranges, which it may be permitted to generalise under the collective name of 'Vindhya.'

If we consider the main lines of greatest elevation, we shall here also observe two general 'ramparts.' The great valley of the Narbadā (or Narmadā) river forms a convenient line to guide the eye.[1] Along the north of this, there is one continuous and comparatively high line of hills—the Vindhya proper—which continues far eastward in the Kaimūr Hills. At the western extremity—at some considerable distance from the coast—this range turns somewhat suddenly northward, forming the line of the Mahī and Arāvāli Hills; it thus encloses a partly barren, partly fertile, table land of which the rich plateau of

[1] These features are especially obvious in the outline map of the hill systems in the *Statistical Atlas*, 1885, prepared by the Government of India for the India and Colonial Exhibition, and sold by Messrs. Eyre & Spottiswoode; and better still by the beautiful map of the Hill Ranges printed with the Parliamentary (periodical) Statements on *The Moral and Material Progress of India*.

Mālwā is the most noticeable feature. But it leaves the whole country west of Mālwā to Kaçch, Kāthīāwār and the coast, open to the north; the desert country being the only obstacle.

On the south side of the Narbadā, comes the second 'rampart,' marked by the great range of Sātpurā Hills, the Maikal, Mahādeo, Melghāt, and other ranges. This southern line unites, at its western extremity, with the line of 'Ghāt' or Sahiyādri Mountains that extends southward along the western shores of India at a limited but somewhat variable distance from the sea coast. Below the junction is an opening into the Taptī Valley which would give access to Berār, and thence without difficulty to the plain of Nāgpur, in the region of the modern 'Central Provinces.'

But on passing the second or southern high line of the Vindhyan group, the country does not subside to a dead level, as Northern India does when the last of the Himalayan outworks are passed. For this reason the Vindhyan group, as a whole, does not stand out sharply and separately on the relief map; the whole of the country inland of the Ghāts and south of the Vindhyas forms the somewhat elevated but varied table-land of the 'Dakhan.'[1] This table-land is brought up on the east as well as on the west side, by a range of hills along the sea-coast. The range called Sahiyādri or Western 'Ghāt,' already mentioned, is higher and more continuous and in general much nearer to the sea-coast than the so-called 'Coromandel' Ghāt skirting irregularly the eastern side of the Madras Presidency.

The general result of such a conformation is, that the whole of Upper Western India is also open to an advance of tribes from the Indus Valley or by the lower passages of the Western Sulāimān frontier. The route is across the open desert of Kaçch and on to Gujarāt.[2] Once in this position, it would be a matter of no great difficulty either to turn eastward and domi-

[1] The dialectic form of 'Dakshinā,' or 'southern' country, variously written in books as the 'Dekhan,' 'Deccan,' &c.

[2] In early times there was, in all probability, a different conformation of the country, and the river Indus had its mouth in the Bay of Cambay. But this does not affect the use of the route spoken of. (See an interesting paper on Gujarāt by Mr. A. Rogers in *Asiatic Quarterly Review* for April 1896, p. 380.

nate the Narbadā Valley, or, by the Taptī, to reach Berār, the Gondwāna country, and the western plains of the Central Provinces. South and east, however, of the Nāgpur Plain the country again becomes hilly and inhospitable, so the further advance will not be likely.

On the other hand, tribes reaching India by the north-west passes, emerging on the Panjāb and proceeding in an easterly direction towards the Jamnā and Ganges Rivers, would find, as I have already explained, the Panjāb and the Ganges Plain as far as Assam open.[1] But should such settlers have tried to extend southwards in anything like large bodies, across the wide series of Vindhyan Hills, they would be checked by interminable forests and hills. It is not until later times (apparently about the eighth century) when the country south-west of the Chambal River, Bundelkhand, &c., had been occupied from the Ganges Plain, that the Mālwa Plateau was reached, and thence northern chiefs led their armies through the Mahī Hills into Gujarāt and through the Vindhyan passes to the Central Provinces.

Thus, while the Vindhyan barrier generally restrained the Aryan advance to the south, it did not affect the western extremity of the continent; and in Upper Western India we have consequently to take account of a double series of Aryan movements. First, in remote times, Aryan tribes came without hindrance from the Indus Valley; next came Turanian or Scythic tribes; and then, in much later times, Hindu Rājputs from Mālwā or Bundelkhand and Rājputāna.

All *later* movements were facilitated by certain passes in the Vindhyan lines themselves. There are two principal openings through the higher 'rampart.' One, at the eastern end gives access to the *upper* Narbadā Valley (Jabalpur and Mandlā). The other, at the western end, not only gives access to the *lower* Narbadā Valley owing to openings, by Mhau and Indor, in the northern range, but also, by an isolated and somewhat wide opening in the southern Sātpurā range, to the Dakhan itself. This latter opening is commanded by a fine scarped and table-

[1] Indeed, when once Bengal was occupied and the mouths of the Ganges were reached, adventurous parties could, and did, go by sea to Arakan, Java, and Ceylon (Lankā).

topped hill, called Asīrgarh,[1] crowned with a once extensive fort. It is not surprising that this place has again and again been the object of attack by northern armies seeking to reach the Dakhan from Delhi and Āgra. It was taken by storm, on the last occasion, in the Marāthā war (1819). The Mughal Emperors in their endeavours to conquer the southern kingdoms by an advance from Ajmer and Āgra had always to take account of this pass.

The passage at the eastern end is that now made use of by the railway from Allāhābād to Jabalpur.[2] Indeed, the existence of the railway and other modern roads rather blinds the tourist of to-day to the real character of the Vindhyan hill country as it must have been in old times. 'Not many years ago,' writes Mr. (Sir C.) Grant, 'the passes which would now scarcely excite notice but for the boldness of their scenery were looked forward to days beforehand with dread by cartmen, and most of the carriage of the country was effected by pack-bullocks. The valleys were sufficiently smooth and easy in fair weather, but a few hours' rain would convert the track through them into a trough of deep black compost, in which every step was a labour to the most lightly laden animal.[3]

It may be worth while, in conclusion, to notice how the actual condition of the 'Central Provinces' (immediately beyond

[1] See *Imperial Gazetteer* (2nd ed.), i. 338. A good view of the fort is obtained by travellers on the Great Indian Peninsular Railway from Bombay to Allāhābād.

[2] I venture to think that Lassen (i. 112, 2nd ed.) attaches too high importance to this east-end route when he calls it the 'Hauptverbindungsstrasse' ('chief line of communication) between Hindustān and the Dakhan.' It never served to do more, in early times, than enable an Aryan, or more probably semi-Aryan, royal family to establish a local lordship in the Upper Narbadā Valley (Jabalpur and Garhā-Mandlā). It seems also to have led only *into* the valley, and not given access further south; at any rate, the Haihaya kings whose dominion was early established in this region only extended their sway to the districts of Chattīsgarh (Raipur and Bilāspur) in the immediate vicinity. All history shows that, apart from the access to Western India by the Indus Valley route, it was the passes at the *western* end that can be correctly described by Lassen's phrase as giving access from Hindustān (*i.e.* Upper India).

[3] *Central Provinces Gazetteer*, Introduction, p. xx.

the Vindhyan 'barrier') shows the effects of the geographical features I have sketched. The northern or Narbadā Valley districts contain most of the Aryan or northern element, as might be expected; not only because they are nearest the north, but because the valley was from the earliest times more or less open to approach by the western (Indus Valley) route. Here it was that one of the most ancient of the Aryan or quasi-Aryan (Rājput) rulership was established in the well-known dynasty of the Haihaya, whose first capital was at Maheswar.[1] After the progress of the Hindu Aryan tribes in Rājputāna and Bundelkhand and Mālwā, no doubt there would be more and more intercourse with the Narbadā districts and Gujarāt. But in reality it is known that the chief influx of Hindī-speaking people from the north of India only occurred within the last three centuries (since the reign of Akbar).[2] And the establishment of Hindus with their Brahman priests has resulted in the gradual absorption of many of the earlier races. But 'below the Ghāt' the country is more Dravidian, including a Marāthā element from the west, and a Telugu and Uriya one from the east and south.[3]

Another point deserves mention in connection with these Vindhyan ranges. Not only have the western and central hills served as safe retreats for the relics of tribes like the

[1] Maheswar is now in the Indor State. Cf. *Central Provinces Gazetteer*, Introduction, p. cxxvi. 'It [the Narbadā country] was ruled by chiefs called as usual Rājput, but these seem to have been days in which Rājputs had not been thoroughly assimilated with the Hindu caste system' [which, I may add, was hardly then in existence]; 'and it is quite conceivable that they may have reigned as a semi-foreign tribe directly over the aborigines without the intervention of any class of Hindus.'

[2] *Central Provinces Gazetteer*, Introduction, p. xv. The gradual absorption of the population within the ranks of Hinduism was, as we shall afterwards see, begun very early by Brahman hermits. Hills and woods which completely stayed the waves of tribal emigration or the advance of large armies proved no obstacle to wandering hermits and those who sought the merits of ascetic life in the forest.

[3] As a matter of fact (*Census of India*, Parliamentary Blue Book, 1891, p. 156), the Hindī-speaking population is now 60 per cent.; the original Dravidian-Gond element still a little over 9 per cent., while the Marāthā element from the west represents 19·6 per cent., and the Uriya from the east, 6·35 per cent.

Kolī, the Bhīl, the Māriā, and Kurkū, who have not been assimilated with the general 'Hindu' population, but the eastern extremity (South-western Bengal and Orissa) has its special features. Here there is an extensive plateau-land in the province of Chutiyā-Nāgpur (corrupted into Chota-Nāgpur) and the adjoining 'Hill States.' In this we find the refuge-ground of interesting races. For the country is at once fertile within and inaccessible from without.[1] Accordingly we find examples of the so-called Kolarian tribal land-customs, as preserved by the *Santāl*, *Ho*, *Mūndā*, &c., as well as the *Urāoñ* and other admittedly Dravidian tribes. It was mainly owing to the local features of this region that these tribes were able to establish a permanent home, and to find land to cultivate, while they retained their own peculiar customs, safe from external attack. Hill ranges have often served as the refuge for ancient tribes; but they afforded no facilities for the permanent location of agricultural villages. On the contrary, they often directly invited a nomadic life and subsistence by the chase; and where cultivation was adopted as a necessity, it was carried on by a method of temporary clearing to be described presently. Tribes placed in these situations have ended by remaining, or perhaps becoming, quite nomadic and uncivilised, or else by descending into the plains, and more or less completely losing their individuality in the mass of low-caste Hindu agriculturists or farm-labourers. The districts of Chutiyā-Nāgpur, on the other hand, though shut in by the hills, contain so much culturable land, that tribes finding a secure home within their precincts were able to establish permanent cultivation, and so to develop their natural tendencies towards this form or that of village organisation. Thus we can observe in the plateau lands, relics of early agricultural customs which we should seek in vain in the forest-clad hills of the other Vindhyan ranges, and these, under the circumstances, we may believe to be really

[1] 'The central table-land on which the tribes rallied is admirably adapted for defence. The approaches to it are from the north, north-west, east and south, and are exceedingly precipitous, the paths winding up defiles which a handful of resolute men could hold against hosts of invaders.' (Dalton's *Ethnography of Bengal*, Calcutta, 1872, pp. 150–235). See also an interesting article on 'Chota-Nāgpur: its People and Resources' in the *Asiatic Quarterly Review* for April 1887.

ancient, since there was no external influence (at least till quite recent times) to destroy them.

It is not, of course, claimed that geographical features explain everything; hill ranges which have proved barriers to the Aryan advance may not have always been equally impervious to other tribes coming, perhaps, from other quarters and moving very gradually, in small sections and under wholly different conditions. But the features above described had a very clear connection with the facts of the Aryan advance, the occupation of the Indus Valley, the early Aryan connection with Upper Western India by that route, and the subjugation of the Ganges Valley or Plain, as well as with the fact that no extensive Aryan movement south of the Vindhyas took place.

We cannot, however, derive any definite information from such features when we try to account for the first origin of the ancient Dravidian races; and how it is that we find people with more or less distinctively Dravidian elements in their language at once north and south of the Vindhyas, on the border of Bilūchistān, and throughout the Madras territory.[1]

Section II.—Physical and Climatic Features bearing on the Forms of Agricultural Settlement

(1) *General Remarks*

The great diversity in abundance of rainfall and general moisture which now exists must at all times have been experienced in different parts of India, and the striking differences in soil, climate, and vegetation which follow from these differences will naturally have had a great deal to do with the permanent location of groups of settlers and their customs of land-holding.

[1] The question whence the Dravidian races came is so purely a matter of speculation that it would be altogether foreign to my purpose to touch on the subject. It may only be suggested that if they ever came from the west, following the indication afforded by Dravidian elements in Bilūchistān, they would naturally have taken the Indus Valley route and gone first to Western India and Southern India, where they would have multiplied and remained comparatively pure and unmixed; while those of the races who gradually extended to Upper India, would be largely influenced by the stream of Kolarian and Tibeto-Burman races from the north-east, to say nothing of other possible northern tribes.

Such climatic variations are accompanied by differences in the crops which it is possible to raise, and in the sort of treatment necessary to the proper utilisation of the soil. Different tribes may also prefer different climates; and if they happen to have markedly diverse customs we may find peculiar tenures in one place which do not occur in another. It has been observed in the Panjāb that the location of Muhammadan village-communities usually follows the river lowlands, where cultivation is less troublesome, and a crop more secure, though the climate is less healthy. The Jats and hardier agricultural races, on the other hand, follow the higher lands, where the soil is good but the labour of raising a full crop is more considerable; the climate, however, is drier and much healthier. The customs of these villages are not, in fact, markedly different, Yet, if there had chanced to be some striking contrast, we should have had the spectacle of customs changing with the contour lines of the map. I cannot help thinking that it is the peculiarity of Indian climatic conditions that has prevented the early agricultural tribes from following certain methods of co-aration and other customs which seem to be always found among the early Celtic and Teutonic tribes of Europe.

In Wales, for example, in a moist and cool climate, the ground is covered with short grass suitable at all times more or less for tribal grazing—and this we know to have been the principal resource; the tribes were more pastoral and predatory than agricultural. What land they actually wanted for the yield of bread-corn, they could easily reclaim every year by simply ploughing it up. Every tribesman had cattle which he brought to the work; strips representing a day's ploughing—or some similar area—were arranged; and the harvest was divided with reference to the number of strips which fell to each tribesman's share. The harvest over, the short grass and herbage would again take possession of the fields, and if the tribe moved its home, or required new ploughlands, nothing would be easier than to settle on a new site for the purpose.

Anything of the kind would be impossible under any of the ordinary climatic conditions of Indian provinces. Hence we never hear of tribal co-aration. Small holdings may be worked by people each of whom has only one bullock, so that they must combine forces. And in some places local customs will be found of gathering together a number of ploughs to treat a large area, and giving a feast to all the helpers.[1] But that is not co-aration such as we see in ancient Europe. We have also instances of jointly-worked village-colonies, where no permanent allotment of the fields was made, apparently for a long period: the village heads determined each year what land each co sharer should take in hand; but that again is not co-aration.

The fact is that no system of the kind would in most cases work. In all the numerous places where dense forest has to be contended with, the fields, once laboriously cleared, must be *kept* clear, or the work would be undone in a few weeks or months;[2]

[1] *E.g.* the *atari* custom in the Akola district of Berār (*Gazetteer*, p. 65).

[2] It may be not quite useless to explain to English readers that the work of clearing land and keeping it safe from the encroachment of the jungle is in many parts of India a task quite beyond the experiences of European agriculture. The following passage, relating to the clearing of jungle country in the remotest parts of the Central Provinces (*Gazetteer*, Introduction, p. xxi), gives a graphic sketch of the ancient difficulties of 'first clearing.' Of course the nature of the difficulty varies from district to district; in one place the contention is only with a hard soil, for which irrigation has to be laboriously provided; in another, it is with rank deeply-rooted grass of the *Saccharum* and other species, which springs again if a vestige of root be left, and soon chokes the ground with great tufts of leaves and tall flower-stalks twelve feet high; in another, it is deep-rooted jungle of *Prosopis* and other dry species. Wherever there is 'semi-tropical' forest and undergrowth, as in the country described, the labour, as well as the risk of fever, is great. The writer of the extract which follows speaks of the life of a settler, even in modern times, being 'a constant battle against tigers and malaria.' 'At present,' he says, 'it is almost incredible how quickly the ground which the hand of man has patiently gained, inch by inch, is swallowed up again by the jungle, when the pressure of regular occupation is for a moment intermitted. Sir W. Sleeman, writing in 1826, records how a few days' ill-judged zeal on the part of a mere underling threw a flourishing tract of country out of cultivation for years. . . . There had been a bad season, and yet the collection of the revenue had been pressed on, in one of the wilder subdivisions of the Narsinghpur district, without allowance or consideration, by an over-zealous collector. The hill cultivators . . . deserted in a body; when better times came it was found impossible to repopulate the deserted villages, for they had been so grown over by jungle in a year or two, that the very village-sites needed clearing, and

and this not only invites the separate demarcation of fields and develops the sense of a strong claim to what has been so laboriously won, but it almost naturally produces a union of families in villages ; for people cling together when they not only need the help of one another in the fields, but when they are liable to be harassed by wild animals, and subject to much sickness—at least till a large open space has been cleared and good drinking-water obtained—and where the demons of the woods and the spirits of the solitudes have to be propitiated, beings who excite in the minds of the primitive tribes an amount of superstitious dread which it is hard for us moderns to realise.

In other places the village lands require irrigation of various kinds ; this is obviously opposed to easily shifted cultivation ; it also requires fixed fields and a determination of shares in the water. We shall afterwards notice that among the earliest allusions to agriculture in the Vedas we find the water-course mentioned, and also the field measured with a reed and separated by a balk or lince from the neighbouring fields.

In the dry plains of the Panjāb and the Ganges Doāb, early cultivation was probably confined to the immediate vicinity of the rivers, where the soil was moist, and where wells, if used at all for watering the land, would have been, as they are now, mere pits in the soft soil. It must have been some time before the people learnt to cut canals inland from the rivers, or to sink deeper wells, and raise the water by some mechanical device. Here, then, we see no opportunities for co-aration and the indeterminate occupation, by whole clans, of large areas of land.

In the Hill Country and intra-montane valleys of the North Country, again, the nature of the soil would require the permanent terracing of the hillsides, the establishment of small irrigation works along the hillside—or else the permanent utilisation of all such level alluvial deposits as naturally become the sites of rice-fields. Or, again, just below the hills, we find cultivation often carried on solely by aid of occasionally flowing, or permanently

tigers had so readily occupied the new coverts thus made for them that even travellers shunned the country.' This state of things would be reproduced even more easily in well-watered and tropical parts of the country, in East Bengal, Burma, &c.

flowing, streams, which are made, by very easy and primitive devices, to water the land. There is little opportunity for changing the fields, which, moreover, are usually terraced or embanked with some labour. But the most serious and general obstacle to easily moved agricultural settlement in the plains is the labour of clearing the soil already alluded to. Nothing suggests the open-field system of shifting settlements and the co-aration of the whole.

To be sure, the extensive use of fallows is an early resource of primitive agriculture; and in the drier climates land is easily exhausted; but here it will generally be found that each holding is large enough to include an area that is fallow while a small portion of it is under cultivation; they do not shift the entire village or the entire tribal group of cultivated holdings from one location to another. Temporary cultivation is practised on alluvial lands, which are unstable, and on certain soils where either there is only occasionally sufficient moisture or some local peculiarity. And this generally occurs where the herbaceous vegetation dries up after the rains and can be removed by burning.

There is, however, one general method of temporary cultivation which is still extensively practised in the remote districts and among the less advanced tribes. It is confined, however, to the forest-clad hill country in parts of the Eastern, Central, and Southern Provinces of India. It will be worth while to devote some attention to it, for it is connected with the customs of locating tribes and the allotment of territory; and while, on the one hand, it seems to render the idea of fixed ownership of land more or less impossible, on the other hand it initiates various customs of united labour, of responsibility for keeping fire away from the clearings, and of the establishment of small family groups, as well as larger clan-settlements, in their defined boundaries. Ultimately we see how it gradually becomes modified into a permanent right in the soil.

(2) *Shifting or Temporary Hill-cultivation*

The essential element is the existence of hills with a convenient slope and a sufficiently dense covering of vegetation to yield an amount of ash which will suitably manure the ground.

It involves also the distribution of certain beats or areas which can be taken up in rotation; and this gives the first idea of right over a considerable territory only a limited portion of which is under treatment at any one time.[1] The first point is, as I have said, to select out of the wooded area the slopes that have a suitably thick clothing of vegetation and are sufficiently gentle. This latter is important, since if the slopes are too steep, the 'monsoon' rain, descending on the surface bared of its tree-shelter, would erode the soil and wash away the seed.

On the selected area, the working members of the families, armed with their heavy knives (of the type of the Burmese *dā*), cut down all the smaller vegetation, bamboos, grass, and small trees, which are then gathered in heaps to dry in the sun; in some cases the larger trees are not cut, but ringed or 'girdled' and left to die standing. At the end of the hot season, and just before the summer rainy-season begins, the dry material is set on fire; and when all is reduced to ashes, these are raked over the soft forest *humus* soil, and seed (millet, hill-rice, and sometimes cotton), being mixed with the ashes, is dibbled into the ground with a hoe. As soon as the rain falls the seed germinates, and the family labour after that consists in repeated weeding and in guarding against the attacks of wild animals.[2]

[1] This form of cultivation is known by various names. It is *jūm* in Bengal, *kumri* (or *kumarī*) in South India, *yā* or (in the Hills) *taung-yā* in Burma; in the Central Provinces and neighbourhood it is *daiñyā* or *dahyā*, the enclosed cleared fields being called *bemar*. It was known in the outer ranges of the Himalaya, within the last century or still more recently, under various local names, *çīl*, *korālī*, &c. It was by no means unknown in Europe. In Styria it is still practised under the name of 'Brandwirthschaft.' The French 'sartage' is, however, not the same thing: that is a method of lightly burning over the soil to manure and improve it; it answers more to the *rāb* cultivation of Western India, where the permanently cultivated rice fields are lightly covered with leaves, bamboos, small branches, &c., and burnt, partly for the sake of the ash manure, but still more, I am told, for the benefit to the surface-soil by the slight calcining action of the fire. There is an account of the *kumri* cultivation on the West Coast, in *Bombay Gazetteer*, xv. (part ii.), 188, 189, and *South Kānara D. M.* i. 209.

[2] Which latter is sometimes a very formidable business. For example, in the *Central Provinces Gazetteer*, an account of the cultivation as practised by the Baigā tribe is given. There they seem to rely

When the crop is reaped, the soil may be considered sufficiently fertile for another year's cultivation; but it is soon exhausted, and then a move has to be made to a greater or less distance according to locality. It depends on the extent of suitable slopes with sufficiently dense vegetation, and the relative numbers of the tribes, whether the same place is returned to after many years (20–40), or after the *minimum* number (5–7), in which a sufficient growth will cover the land and afford material for the next burning. In scantily populated ranges, no care is taken; and the fire applied to each cleared area is allowed to spread over the adjoining forest, many square miles being annually burned. But where the area is more restricted, the 'villages' have a well-understood system whereby the fire from the prepared blocks must be prevented, by cleared lines, &c., from spreading to neighbouring blocks; and a system of fines and compensations would be enforced in case of neglect.

To a great extent the allotment of these tribal areas is regulated by Nature. There may or may not have been a conflict of interests and fighting before a peaceable location is effected; but the natural barriers of river, ridge, and valley appear usually to be followed as intimating the limits of clan-territory and its sub-divisions.

It is extremely interesting to be able to trace the stages by

on burning the large wood as well as the smaller stuff; sufficient being cut 'to cover pretty closely the whole of the area. . . . In May and June, just before the setting in of the rains, the wood and the brushwood in which it has fallen is set fire to; and almost before the fire is out the Baigās may be seen raking up the ashes and spreading them over the surface of their field. This is done with a bundle of thorns or long bamboos, until there is a superstratum of about an inch of ashes spread over the ground.' The grain sown consists of millets and *Kodo* (*Paspalum sp.*) and a poor hill rice. 'When sown, the field is fenced round very roughly and strongly; small trees are felled so as to fall one on to the other; the interstices are filled in with bamboos, and the boughs are carefully interlaced so that the smallest kind of deer cannot effect an entrance.' Where bison or buffaloes are feared, which would burst through an ordinary fence, they bury a line of broad-bladed spears (*dāñsā*) at about the spot where the animals would land if they jumped the fence. Watching an opportunity, they frighten the wild cattle, inducing them to rush the fence, when some of them are sure to be wounded and perhaps one or two killed; and the herd never visit the field again.

which this nomad cultivation begins to change into permanent allotment of holdings and to the fixation of villages. Such a process has been observed in parts of Burma, where the Karen population has come to press on the land and is unable or unwilling to move elsewhere. The rich soil at the bottom of the valleys first becomes permanently cultivated, and the slopes above, still cultivated by burning the vegetation, are nevertheless divided out, and worked in a strict rotation, under severe penalties and well-enforced responsibility in the case of fire being allowed to spread to the areas not yet ready for cultivation.

Sir D. Brandis has given an interesting account of the Karen tribes in the hills between the Sittang and Salween Rivers [1] who had attained this stage of progress. 'These Karens,' he says, 'have two classes of cultivation: along the valleys and ravines are extensive gardens of betel-palms, with oranges and other fruit trees carefully irrigated and admirably kept. These gardens are strictly private property; they are bought and sold, and on the death of the proprietor are divided in equal shares among his children.' He then describes how on the drier slopes above, *taungyā* cutting is practised; but the limited area available and the necessity for carefully fostering the vegetable growth [2] which yields the ashes necessary for sowing the hill-rice renders special arrangements necessary. And he continues: 'The whole of the *taungyā* grounds of one village are divided into a number of plots, each plot being owned by one of the proprietors of the village. Well-to-do people own from twenty to thirty plots situated in different parts of the village area.' The boundaries of each village are most distinctly defined, and jealously guarded against encroachment. The boundaries of the plots also are defined. 'These plots are sold and bought . . . and when a proprietor dies his *taungyā* grounds, with his gardens, are divided in equal shares

[1] Quoted at length in my *Land Systems of British India*, iii. 506 ff. Sir D. Brandis was familiar with these tribes as Conservator of Forests, and again visited them twenty years later, when he was Inspector-General of Forests to the Government of India.

[2] The vegetation that springs up after a season of shifting cultivation is interesting botanically, and is very different from the original forest. In the Karen Hills, the vegetation for burning is chiefly a tall reed-grass (*Arundo sp.*) interspersed with old gnarled trees, which are pollarded so that the leaves and branches may be burned on the ground.

among his children.' . . . 'I have here spoken of the people as the proprietors of their *taungyā* grounds. They claim, however, only a kind of imperfect proprietary right. They hold their plots as against each other, but they recognise that the State has a superior right in the land.' So far Sir D. Brandis: for my own part, I may suggest that this may be a relic of the feeling that, as waste land belongs to the State, as of old it belonged to the tribe indefinitely, so land which is yet, so to speak, in a stage between waste and cultivation, has not yet completely become private property. It will be observed, however, that the plots are rented, bought, and sold; this implies that the State right is after all of a limited kind; or more probably, perhaps, that the native mind does not regard the concurrent existence of two kinds of right as at all antagonistic.

In some places we may observe the change which has led tribes, without deserting the hill country, to take to the terraced cultivation which is so commonly observed in hill districts; in the Himalaya, for example.[1] There is usually some level ground at the bottom of the valleys, and perhaps some alluvial level area formed by the gradual accretion of mud and detritus from the mountain torrents; and this is suitable for rice-land. With this valuable area of permanent cultivation, the desire grows to remain in the same vicinity; and so, gradually, the best spots on the slopes above are selected and terraced or banked up with the stones picked out of the fields; if rice can be grown here, it is soon found possible to conduct the water of a hill rivulet to the spot by means of a contour channel along the hillside. These are sometimes contrived with considerable skill.

I do not know whether it should be considered a relic of the old forest-burning method of cultivation, or whether it is merely due to a prejudiced clinging to an early method of manuring, that it is still a feature of the West Coast holdings, in Coorg, Kānara, &c. (and I have noticed the same thing in Chutiyā-Nāgpur on the east side), that every cultivated farm holding has allotted to it a certain portion of grass and jungle

[1] I have been shown places in the Simla Hills and elsewhere where the peculiar vegetation of the slopes indicates that they had once been treated by the process of shifting cultivation perhaps no more than fifty or sixty years ago.

land, not only to supply grazing for cattle, but more especially to yield branches and stuff to burn on the rice fields. This is irrespective of any general grazing area or forest that is available in common.

(3) *Instances where Village Groups are not found*

The first case to be noticed is that of the British Himalayan districts. It is not difficult to understand that where there is only a limited area of flat land in a narrow valley, and occasional patches of good soil with not too steep a slope on the hillside, single homesteads, or very small groups of two or three families together, must take the place of the villages of the plains. The consequences of this from a tenure point of view are, perhaps, not immediately perceptible; but in reality there can hardly be any doubt that the peculiar natural dispositions of culturable soil and waste have had a great effect: (1) on the arrangements made when Rājput conquering chiefs assumed local dominion, and (2) on the modern system under our own Land-Revenue Settlements. But still more interesting (3) are some ancient customs still traceable, which largely depended on the physical conditions, but may also be due to peculiarity of racial custom.

It happened that the Kāngrā district became British territory (now under the Panjāb Government) in 1846. The Kumāon and Garhwāl districts, farther east, also came under the North-West Provinces administration in 1815. And we have good information about both, especially in the interesting reports on Kāngra, with its outlying dependencies, by Mr. Barnes, and later by Mr. (now Sir James B.) Lyall. It will be necessary to premise [1] that both these districts were probably inhabited from early times by people who belonged to the North-Eastern or Tibeto-Burman stock. races now much altered and blended with Hindus (Aryans), who came later. It must have been a comparatively easy task for a chief of superior race and with a small hardy troop of followers to establish a local rulership in these hills; for the isolated holdings were too scattered to combine for defence, and the petty independent chiefs had no cohesion. We find the Rājput Rājās claiming all the land as conquerors. But

[1] Further detail will be given in Chapter IV., dealing with Land Customs.

they did not interfere much with these existing holdings, nor as a rule tax them exorbitantly for rent. The waste and the forest became the Rājā's; and, in Kāngrā at any rate, he enforced the claim strictly. The State officers soon arranged the scattered farms and hamlets into circles for rent-collecting and other Government purposes.[1] These circles afterwards were treated as 'villages' when the districts came under the British Revenue Settlement.

In the Kāngrā Hills, separate homesteads are found (*lārh, lārhi, bāsā*), or where it is possible small villages or hamlets are built together and called *grāoñ*. As all the waste and forest belonged to the Rājā, the cultivators only claimed to have the customary use of the hillside and grass-land for grazing their cattle. But sometimes the waste and the cultivated fields were so intermingled that the whole group together seemed to constitute some different form of 'village' tenure. This, however, is not really the case, as Sir J. Lyall points out.[2] I have alluded to this detail, not that there is any necessity for explaining it, but because the remarks on the subject made in the Report were the occasion of introducing a vivid picture of the agricultural settlements in the hills, as they occur under the different conditions which the gentler slopes and occasional open valleys afford. This I cannot do better than quote:—

A glance at the outward aspect of these *mauza*[3] [writes Sir J. Lyall] will, I think, make it clear that this degree of difference of tenure in the waste has mainly arisen from physical causes. Take first a *mauza* in the irrigated villages. The low and tolerably level parts of the area, which can be conveniently flooded from the water-channels, form the *hār* or open expanse of rice-fields. This land is too valuable and too swampy to be lived upon; the houses of the landholders are seen closely scattered along the comparatively high and dry ridges or rising ground. Each family has a garden, orchard, or small field or two round the house or houses in which it lives (*lārhi-bāsī*); the rest of its holding is made up of fields scattered

[1] Locally called in Kāngrā *kothi, hākimi, magdaī*, &c., and by other names elsewhere.

[2] *Kāngrā S. R.* (1874), § 17, pp. 14 ff.

[3] *Mauza* is the Revenue-office term for a village as defined in a map; the term was doubtless purposely used in the Report because of the artificial nature of the groups adopted for Settlement purposes.

here and there in the *hār*. Near the houses are long strips of grass like village greens, on which the cattle graze in common. Now, in a village of this kind it is evident that the idea of boundary in the waste between family and family has not the chance of arising. . . . Next take a *mauza* in a country where there is no irrigation, but where the features of the landscape are bold—that is, where open arable slopes and plains alternate with steep unculturable hills. Here the houses of the landholders will be seen scattered over the surface of the arable land, the fields of each family lying with few exceptions compactly round the houses of the family. . . . The general grazing grounds are the hill sides which surround the arable land. Here, again, there has been no opportunity for the growth of a feeling of boundary between family and family in the waste as a whole. Thirdly, take a *mauza* in an unirrigated country . . . composed of a mass of low steep hills intersected by hundreds of narrow valleys or ravines. . . . There is little culturable land, and what there is is scattered here and there along the tops of the ridges and edges of the ravines. Culturable and unculturable lands are everywhere intermixed in about the same proportion. . . . Each group of houses is surrounded by waste sprinkled with fields. Each family, as it has grown from its ancestor the first settler, has brought under the plough all the culturable land within its reach, but has still within the orbits of its fields much waste—enough, or nearly enough for the requirements in the way of grazing.[1]

Here naturally nothing would tempt anyone else to make use of the included waste, and equally naturally in time it would become regarded as belonging to the group within whose 'orbit' it lies, though not actually its 'property.'

These little groups of separate farms were all held from the Rājā as superior landlord; they had, as I have already said, to be further organised in circles for rent-collecting purposes; but the effect this produced on the soil interests cannot be classed under the head we are now considering. Similarly, the application of a particular Revenue system in modern days, and the

[1] The length of the extract that would be necessary prevents my adding some interesting remarks (p. 16) on the smallness of the hamlets in narrow and malarious 'irrigated' rice valleys. 'Not only in Kāngrā but in Gurdāspur and in other districts,' says the writer, 'I have noticed an extraordinary difference in the growth of families in irrigated and unirrigated estates. In one case the pedigree table expands hardly at all; in the other it soon shows a list of descendants almost constituting a clan.'

formation of 'estates,' which go to swell the total of villages in the official returns, is a purely artificial arrangement.

It would be impossible to pass by the Valley of KASHMIR, for which a Revenue Settlement has recently been made, and under which it is hoped an altogether new era of prosperity has dawned for the long-suffering population. Mr. Walter Lawrence, who made this Settlement, has given us a charming account of the valley.[1] In the more completely mountain country of Kashmir, in such localities as the Kishngangā Valley, and the hills on the confines of Hazārā, as well as about Kishtwār, Badrāwār, and on the borders of Chamba, all of which I myself have visited, the villages are formed of little groups of chalets wherever the site is sheltered and there is water and sufficient space for the houses. The cultivation is on terraced fields forming separate holdings grouped together as far as circumstances permit, just as in Kulu or Chamba. In the 'Valley' itself, where there is more space, larger villages seem to be formed; and in one case Mr. Lawrence speaks of a village with a normal population of 165 families, and the usual village menials and artisans appear; indeed, the Mughal rulers seem to have introduced a village system. But I cannot find any trace of a community holding an area of land in common, even where the extent of country would permit such a thing. No allusion occurs in Mr. Lawrence's account to any tenures. I presume that it was impossible to trace any early forms of land allot-

[1] *The Valley of Kashmir*, by Walter Lawrence. London: Henry Frowde, 1895. These hills and valleys seem to have been early inhabited by Aryan clans who at that time could not have developed caste and other later Hindu institutions. It seems also the Nāgā or serpent-worshipping races were there also. It is remarkable that the Kashmir dialect more nearly resembles Sindhī (Lawrence, p. 454) than other Prakrit derivations. And Sindh must have been originally occupied by Aryans in the same stage of progress as those of Kashmir. Afterwards Buddhism prevailed, and we have a long list of Hindu kings, who had, evidently, much communication with India, and became 'regular' Hindus as time went on. In the seventeenth century the Mughals conquered the valley; and after them Pathāns and Sikhs exercised, in turn, a cruel rule. All rights have been set at naught for generations past, until now when, thanks to the enlightenment of the Council of Regency, a proper Settlement has been made. The theory, I presume, still is that the State is the owner of the soil; but the peasantry will at least have a secure hereditary possessory title.

ment, and that for generations past the Rājās' ownership, and the official oppression to which the people were accustomed, must have left at best only a certain hereditary occupancy as the ostensible tenure. Speaking of the villages in the Valley, Mr. Lawrence remarks that each house has some space around it: 'instead of the ineffable dreary and unvillage-like look of the Indian hamlet, we have in Kashmir the picturesque homesteads dotted about here and there. All have their little gardens and courtyards.' In this courtyard is the wooden granary, like a sentry-box; and here, too, the women sit to husk rice and separate the maize from the cobs. 'Most villages,' adds Mr. Lawrence, 'have a delightful brook, on which is a quaint-looking bathing-house, where the villager leisurely performs his ablutions. One of the prettiest objects in the village is the graveyard shaded by the *Celtis australis* trees, and bright with iris—purple, white, and yellow—which the people plant over their departed relations.' [1]

The hill districts of KUMĀON and GARHWĀL lie more towards the centre of the outer Himalayan Range; they show very much the same features as have been noticed in Kāngrā.[2] The 'villages' of the plains are replaced by 'detached hamlets scattered along the sides and bases of the mountains wherever facilities for cultivation are afforded.'[3] I do not find any special form of land allotment noticed; but the assumption of the soil ownership by

[1] Quoted from a paper in *Journal of the Society of Arts*, xliv. 492.

[2] Reports on Kumāon and Garhwāl, by Traill and Batten, collected in the Agra reprint (1851). There is also a 'Statistical Account of Kumāon' in the *Gazetteer*, and much information for those who care to dig it out of the bulky Report by Sir H. Ramsay on the Kumāon Revised Settlement of 1873. Unfortunately, at the early date when the first Reports were written, it was not yet the fashion to inquire into the ancient customs in detail. The Reports are also much spoiled by a feature which might seriously mislead an unwary reader. The Board of Revenue had prescribed by Circular Order a general mode of recording and describing village-tenures under the usual terms *Zamīndāri*, *Pattīdārī*, and *bhaiāchārā*, about which we shall hear in the sequel, and which only suited the villages of the plains. Accordingly, both Messrs. Traill and Batten thought it necessary to attempt to use these official terms, and sometimes have to apologise for the hill-tenures, that really they *will* not, as doubtless they ought, fit into the frames provided by the Board of Revenue!

[3] *Sketch of Kumāon* in the Collected Reports, p. 11.

the conquering Rājās led to the separate homesteads and small hamlets being regarded as 'Crown' tenancies; and, just as in other States, the rent collections were managed by forming 'circles' of hamlets under officers locally known as *Kamīn* and *Thokdār* or *Siyāna*. These agents, again, selected a headman (*padhān*) in each hamlet or group of hamlets to collect the rents of the individual farmers. Thus a more or less artificial appearance of 'villages' arose. And in Kumāon, apparently much more generally than in Kāngrā, the Rājā made grants or assignments of his superior right in the land; and the resulting title was called *thāt* (or *kot* if the grant was for the support of the relatives of a soldier slain in battle). All sorts of persons, astrologers, Brahmans, courtiers, dependents, and even the royal cooks, got such grants. At first they were 'freehold,' since the royal revenue due on them was either remitted or was taken by the grantee for the service on account of which the grant was made. In course of time the revenue remission was rescinded, but the 'proprietary' title remained. The grantee 'proprietor' was entitled to take into his personal possession, and use, one-third of the land. Here, again, was another source of artificial villages. For when the heirs of the grantees succeeded jointly, some semblance of a joint-village estate arose, and, under the North-West Provinces Revenue system, the estates were treated as *mauza*, or villages, and shown as such in the statistical returns. Notwithstanding these grants, however, a large proportion of the hamlets in Kumāon, and especially in Garhwāl,[1] remained as independent groups of cultivators, and are only aggregated for administrative purposes.

In another widely different part of India—along the WEST COAST—we have another instance of the absence of villages. This country comprises the districts of North Kānara, South Kānara, and Malabār. It may be described generally as consisting of a strip of uneven but fertile land between the sea and the Western Ghāt mountains. Many spurs run down from the hills beyond, and the level country is constantly intersected by rivers and estuaries, and by ravines which widen towards the coast and are filled with rice cultivation; while

[1] *S. R. Garhwāl*, in the Collected Reports, p. 129.

the whole country is studded with orchards and luxuriant palm-groves.[1]

In NORTH KĀNARA, as the country approaches the districts of Belgaum and Dhārwār, and above the Western Ghāt or Sahiyādri Hills, something like villages are formed, and there are some appearances of a staff of village officers and menials. In Kānara generally, the house of a cultivating family stands, separately, in the neighbourhood of the fields held by them. The single holding is North Kānara is called *sthal.* The aggregates of these holdings formed for official and administrative purposes throughout Kānara appear to have been variously arranged at different periods, and especially by the Mysore Sultans or other sovereigns who introduced the Perso-Arabic revenue terms. A small group of two or three holdings (having, I suppose, some connection among themselves) is called *majare*, which is a local form of the Arabic *mazrā*, (H.) *majrā*. The more natural aggregate is called *grāma*, which also is a group of a few holdings. I think I am right in supposing that the *grāma* was the original subdivision of the *nādu*, of which we shall hear much in the sequel. Where there happens to be a somewhat larger aggregate of residences it is called *mauje*, which is the (A.) *mauza*. Whether this is regarded as distinct from the *grāma* I am not informed. For administrative purposes several (5 or 6) *grāma* are again aggregated into a *māganē*.[2]

The houses are mostly built of laterite, which is a material locally abundant, soft when first cut, but hardening on exposure to the weather. Or else laterite pillars are built, and the walls are of mud. A large proportion of the ordinary peasant houses are thatched; but that is not from poverty, but from the ancient custom which confined the use of tiles to temples and the houses of the Brahmans and the ruling classes.

[1] North Kānara is under the Bombay Government, and is described in the *Bombay Gazetteer*, xv. 411–15. South Kānara is in Madras; there is a pleasing account of the country in the *South Kānara D. M.* i. 8.

[2] *Bombay Gazetteer*, xv. 412. The old Mysore Government made use of a larger aggregate, called *hobali*. I understand that this is now disused. Cf. *South Kānara D. M.* ii. 6. I presume that the figures at p. 8 refer to the population in a *māganē*.

The system of land-holding here, which depends on the past history of the country, has no reference to village aggregates whatever; and we shall hereafter see that the *warg*, or superior holding, often consists of several plots which are not necessarily in the same *māganē* even.

In MALABĀR the general facts are similar. Here, among the upper classes of landholders, the single house is often a handsome structure standing in the midst of a square enclosed orchard, approached by a castellated gateway, and solidly built. It contains several connected families, for the joint-family idea is strong among them.[1] Here also we have the grouping of a number of holdings into *grāma*, *taṛa*, &c., and these again, for administrative purposes, into *amisham* (*amshom* of the books).[2]

More will appear on this subject when we speak of the landholding customs; and we shall then see how far the state of things depends on Dravidian custom, modified by caste and the Hindu law; but it is clear that the isolation of the holdings is in the first instance caused by the physical features of the country—the broken ground, the frequent ravines and valleys, at the bottom of which the rice lands lie. It is interesting to observe that in the fourteenth century Ibn-Batūta noticed these features: he says that the whole coast-line afforded one long journey under trees, and that the people had all of them separate houses in the midst of their land.[3]

One more example of the absence of village aggregates, and that entirely due to physical circumstances, may be taken from the SOUTH PANJĀB—a country presenting about as complete a

[1] *I.e.* among Nāyar and Brahman families. Logan, *Malabar D. M.* i. 89, 131, 133, 153. The feeling for separate households is shown by the numerous words in Malayālam for houses of different kinds; the cottage, the ordinary house, the mansion, the menial's hut, the Rājā's palace, the chief's house, &c., are all distinguished.

[2] The aggregate known as *deṣam* is of a different character; it was an early aggregation made solely for military purposes, each group having to provide so many soldiers.

[3] Quoted *D. M. Malabār*, i. 86, where there is also a pleasing account of the arrangements of a higher caste dwelling in the midst of its orchard and surrounded with a high bank of earth and an interlaced hedge. It is too long to quote, and would be spoiled by condensation.

contrast to that last described as can well be imagined. In the districts below Multān, and part of Dera G͟hāzī K͟hān, the country is so rainless that anything like permanent cultivation is only possible either along the banks of a river, or by aid of small canal cuts taken off from the river, or by the aid of wells. which again can only be sunk up to a certain distance inland—*i.e.* away from the river. The 'well' (*i.e.* the area protected, or at least partly watered, by the well) becomes the unit of property throughout the tract that lies next beyond the river-moistened belt. Thus, in the Multān district, Mr. Roe writes:[1] 'In the tracts near the rivers, the lands generally belong to Jat tribes, and here we find regular village communities. . . . Away from the rivers the villages are generally merely a collection of 'wells' which have been sunk in the neighbourhood of a canal, or in more favourable spots in the high land. In these there never has been any community of interest; in very many cases there is not even a common village-site: each settler has obtained his grant direct from the State, sunk his well, and erected his homestead upon it. Under our Settlements, the waste land between these wells has been recorded, as a matter of course, *shāmilāt-dih* (common of the village); but originally the well-owners had no claim to it whatever.'

(4) *Physical Features which invite Village Formation*

Having described some of the physical causes which tend to *prevent* the formation of villages, there remain to be noticed, on the other hand, those features of Indian climate and physical condition which would have directly encouraged the aggregation of groups of cultivators, even if tribal ties or a strong sense of family life had not already predisposed them to settle together. These causes have, in fact, operated universally, and are sufficiently obvious when stated; they are calculated, however, to invite aggregation of some kind, but do not go further in producing any particular form of that aggregation. Wherever they have operated, 'villages' are a feature on the map, irrespective of the internal structure of the groups, whether as aggregates of independent households or as co-sharing bodies.

[1] *S. R. Multān* (1883), chap. ii. § 69. It is just the same in parts of Dera G͟hāzi K͟hān, Fryer's *S. R.* 1874, § 216.

I need hardly repeat what has been said about the difficulty of first clearing the jungle-clad, black-soiled districts of many of the central and southern parts of India, or in the dense forests of the eastern districts. No single family could settle alone. A fair-sized clearing must be made as soon as possible, for the sake of health; and the need of co-operation for defence against wild animals injurious to crops and even to human life, for carrying out the cottage-building, tank-digging, forest-clearing, and other initial works, is obvious.

Even in dry open districts the help of a number of hands would be needed before cultivation could be fairly started.

In very dry countries, where cultivation is impossible unless a well or canal-cut can be provided, circumstances may, as we have seen, tend to the establishment of separate farms or land-holdings with reference to the well or other irrigation source; there may also be conditions which admit of cultivating groups, but at the same time limit their size. In the Bannu and other frontier districts of the Panjāb, where there are low hills furrowed by many torrent beds which for the most part have water only during the short rainy season, there are well-established customs of sharing the water, by means of a system of channels and temporary dams, whereby the water is led on to certain groups of terraced fields. The customary rules provide that each dam must be removed after a certain number of hours; or that it can only be raised to a certain height, so that when the flood reaches that level the surplus water may pass on to the fields of another right-holder. The point here is, that the size of the village may be largely determined by the number of fields which the available water-supply will reach. In the same way, wherever there are but limited 'tanks' for irrigation (*e.g.* Ājmer and Central India), the size of the cultivating group must naturally regulate itself accordingly.[1]

[1] The word 'tank' is said to be of Marāthī or Gujarāti origin. Wilson's *Glossary* gives *tānkeṅ* (M.) and *tānkh* (Gu.); it has no reference to our English word of the same form. The irrigation-tank is sometimes a depression in the soil, or the head of a valley dammed up artificially, and so situated as to collect the rain running off the high land all round. Some 'tanks' are vast sheets of water never completely dry.

Defence against enemies is another obvious reason for aggregation. In unsettled times, cultivation is hardly possible except within reach of some chief's fortress [1] or other place of refuge; and in those provinces where the open level country has allowed of 'village' settlements, the families keep together for mutual help. Each group has to be prepared to defend itself against sudden attack. Accordingly, in many parts of India the village dwelling-place has been built with mud walls and stout gates, within which the cattle may be secured and the cultivators find refuge against a foray.[2] In later times, too, oppressive revenue officers had often to be resisted.

This allusion to the dwelling site of the village reminds me that, though the aggregation of houses in the centre of the holdings is a very common feature, it is by no means universal. This difference often depends on physical conditions; but in former times it must have depended also on the state of the country as regards peace: homesteads or small hamlets scattered about the village area would have to be abandoned (and were so frequently) during the wars and invasions that so constantly occurred. It is mentioned in one of the Lahore Settlement Reports that the villagers used to come and ask the Government Settlement Superintendent for permission to have their homestead outside the regular village site, as if this were an exceptional measure which formerly would have been dangerous.[3]

This may be a convenient opportunity to pass in review the several provinces, as regards the form of village residences, whether they are compact groups of houses (either walled and

[1] We shall meet with an example of this in the hilly table-land of the Dakhan districts.

[2] Grant Duff mentions that Sivāji, the founder of the Marāthā rule, fearing to encourage 'the village and district authorities to resist his government as they frequently did that of Bījapur,' . . . '*destroyed all village walls*, and allowed no fortification in his territory that was not occupied by his own troops.'—*History of the Mahrattas*, i. 197.

[3] Possibly, however, the application was made because the petitioner expected to be allowed a sufficient area for his house, to be made free of revenue: this he could have got in the *ābādī* or central site, the area of which is, in the Panjāb, always unassessed, but he might not be able to secure a remission on part of his fields.

gated or open), or whether small groups of houses (hamlets) are the prevalent form.

In the MADRAS Manuals I have not found any general account of the subject, although it is evident that, putting aside the special conditions of the west coast districts, the plain country in general appears to present similar characteristics. So much I gather, that the flat-roofed houses characteristic of the Dakhan are not in use, but that mud-built cottages thatched with palmyra palm (*Borassus sp.*) are common. It seems also to be a general feature, and one apparently derived from the original Dravidian village customs, that each house had its 'croft,' or garden and yard, and that the menials of the village were aggregated in a sort of suburb (*çeṛī*) just outside the village.[1] Madras villages in general (I gather from various scattered indications) are compact groups, and, as usual in Dravidian countries, the whole social organisation is complete—the hereditary headman with his *ex-officio* hereditary holding of land, the village accountant, and the regular staff of village artisans and menials paid by grain fees as we have already noticed.[2]

As to BOMBAY, I have not yet seen a general account of the Dakhan,[3] but from scattered notices in the district reports, I gather that the villages are generally compact, and that flat-roofed houses are common, the poorest sort of huts being thatched. The general use of sun-dried bricks or of mud walls compacted together, or of burnt brick with mud cement, not only in this part of the country but in India generally, is not only to be ascribed to its cheapness. There is no doubt that thick mud walls are much cooler than brick. The circumstances of life in the Dakhan districts seem to make compact villages necessary. It would appear that at one time families of superior race had established their lordship over the villages, and they probably held control from the *gaḍh*, or forts, built on the eminences with which the irregular table-

[1] *Macleane's Manual*, i. 100; *Godāvari D. M.* p. 87.

[2] *Ante*, pp. 16, 17.

[3] Vol. i. of the *Gazetteer*, which may be expected to contain a general sketch of the physical features, population, and social conditions of the Dakhan districts, has not yet appeared.

land abounds; as such 'barons' would have constant feuds among themselves, compact villages would be a necessity for self-protection.[1]

In the richer districts of Gujarāt—a province which has often and not unjustly been described as the Garden of India—the villages seem well to do, and furnish an excellent specimen of what village-building can attain to. The account deserves to be quoted:[2]

> The whole population . . . (a practice which doubtless dates from old times of insecurity) live together in the village itself, which is generally situated near the centre of the area. There are sometimes hamlets subsidiary to large villages. . . . The village, containing from 100 or less to 2,000 or 3,000 inhabitants, is always built beside a tank or large embanked pond shaded by noble trees, among which is the temple of the local god. On one side of the tank, and in front of the village, is an open space where the cattle assemble to be watered morning and evening; and here is usually a deep-chambered well with a long flight of stone steps leading to the water. . . . Here also at nightfall, on earthen seats round the stem of an aged tree, the village elders assemble to smoke the *ḥuqqa* and talk over their simple topics. The village itself is occasionally surrounded by an earthen wall, but more commonly by a thick cactus hedge (*Opuntia sp.*), and even this defence is now often wanting. At the entrance are the huts of the sweepers, one of whose duties is to guide travellers; and on the outskirts of the village live, each in their separate quarters, the different classes of low-caste labourers. Their huts are sometimes wretched enough, yet often, and increasingly so of late years, they inhabit decent cottages of one story, built of unbaked brick and tile. In the middle of the village live the . . . owners and cultivators of the lands. Their houses, with walls of brick and tiled roofs, are usually built two and even three stories high, round courtyards opening with a gate into the street. . . . Often three or more houses have one yard in common. They front on the court, and the doors, windows, and balconies are generally ornamented with the delicate wood-carving for which Gujarāt is famous. The sides or ends towards the street present a blank wall often covered with stucco and adorned with frescoes, barbarous, indeed, in design, but brilliantly coloured and not wanting in spirit.

[1] Compare the note on Nāsik District, *Bombay Gazetteer*, xvi. 27, and for Ahmadnagar District, xvii. 48.

[2] *Bombay Gazetteer*, iv. 45, 46.

This represents the type of village in a rich country, and is above the general standard. In the Bharoch district, also in Gujarāt, the absence of the *flat*-roofed house is noticed. The *Gazetteer* describes how the villages are surrounded by trees :—'Occupying a perfectly level country, these clumps of trees, at an average distance of about three miles apart, indicate the site of these scattered communities, each having its proportion of wells and tanks.'[1] An average would give 134 houses and 509 inhabitants to each village in the district. Formerly, it is added, 'many of the villages were surrounded by walls of mud or of burnt bricks as a shelter against the attacks of free-booters,' but now only traces of such defences remain.

As a specimen of one of the coast districts I may take Ratnāgirī. Here villages seem to be compact, built in streets (paved roadways made with blocks of laterite are in use). All are shaded with belts of cocoa-nut plantation. As usual in Dravidian countries, the low-caste people are kept in an adjacent, but distinct, suburb. On the whole, it would appear that villages containing 200 to 1,000 inhabitants are the commonest.[2]

No general account of villages is given in the CENTRAL PROVINCES, except that of the total number, more than half are aggregates of houses not exceeding 200 inhabitants, and many more do not go beyond 500. The province is made up of districts variously situated as regards their physical conditions. But in general compact villages seem to be the rule, and in many, the family *garhī* or residence of the *Pātel* is more or less conspicuous in the middle.

For the NORTH-WEST PROVINCES there are more abundant materials. Compact, occasionally very large, villages are found, but sometimes the tendency is to a number of hamlets scattered about through the area of the 'village.' This depends partly on the nature of the soil, partly on other causes. In some cases it marks the gradual expansion and fission of the family groups; some branch of a large family will arrange to start a new hamlet (*majrā*, &c.),[3] which will in time become an

[1] *Bombay Gazetteer*, ii. 380. [2] *Ibid.* x. 136.

[3] *Majrā* is the Hindī form of the Arabic *mazrā*, which means a plot of land prepared for sowing.

independent village. For example, in Bāndā, one of the south-east districts of the North-West Provinces, towards the Vindhya country, I find the Settlement Officer remarking that 'where the bulk of the soil is of naturally rich quality, large villages are the rule, and the population is found collected in a single site.' He adds, that in the Bāndā *pargana* there are as many as eight large villages each with a population exceeding 2,000. Six of these, on rich black soil (locally known as *mār*), have only one inhabited site; while in the two remaining villages, in which there is 'much light and broken soil,' there are, besides the chief centres, five additional hamlets in each. In one case (Khaptihā, in the Pailāni *pargana*) there is a single village of fifteen square miles, with a population of 3,737 crowded into one central residence; while in a neighbouring estate, a much smaller population is found to have established nine villages and hamlets scattered over the area of the community. In the broken country adjoining the hills, 'the substitution of small hamlets for the single large village-site shows its fullest development.'[1] The need of manure, and the desirability of being near the fields to keep watch against animals, also affects the multiplication of hamlets.

In the OUDH *Gazetteer* (to take a very differently situated country) I find it noticed that 'the village in Oudh is not a single collection of houses. . . . The number of hamlets in any particular village varies with its area and the convenience its lands offer for building, from only one to sometimes as many as fifty [houses]. . . . The people are nowhere drawn together by the more complex wants of the civilisation with which we are familiar. Their simple huts can be run up in a few weeks on any spot which is sufficiently elevated above the rain floods, and their almost only object is to be as near as possible to the fields they cultivate. A new settler, especially if he be of high caste and rents a considerable tenement, will generally prefer to build a detached house close to his own fields. In the course of time his children and grandchildren will relieve the overcrowded

[1] *S. R. Bāndā* (Mr. Cadell's), 1881, p. 30. Other large tribal areas of this kind will be described in Chapter VI. It is not often, in such cases, that the inhabitants are collected in one village-residence.

house by adding houses of their own, and those, with the hovels of the low-caste attendants, the *çamār* and the slave-ploughmen, will form a hamlet which, if of sufficient size, may eventually attract a blacksmith, a carpenter, a washerman, or a barber.'[1]

When we read in *Sleeman's Journey* of the Oudh (Native) Government officials collecting revenue with the aid of troops and siege guns, this refers rather to the necessity of putting pressure on the Tāluqdār and other landlords in their curious forts or fortresses, which were often hemmed in with dense quick hedges of thorny bamboo, than to the villages of the peasantry.

In the PANJĀB, the varieties of climate and local situation produce corresponding differences in the villages and house-building. The mountain districts, like Kulū and Kāngrā, have their own styles of building, not at all unlike those seen in Switzerland. Wood and stone are the universally employed materials, and the roofs are covered with split slabs of wood, or, if available, great rough-hewn slates. In the plain districts compact villages, sometimes large, are the rule. But there are parts where the growth of the families has resulted in the establishment of several subsidiary hamlets. This is noticeable in the districts across the Sutlej and in the south-east. Everywhere the villages are flat-roofed, and built of mud bricks; often they are walled and gated, or otherwise arranged, so as to be defensible at least against cattle-thieves. One feature deserves mention, which is seen even in the level country. The village appears raised up on an eminence, which gradually forms in this way: the earth for the walls, both of the village and the cottages, is obtained by digging out one or more ponds or tanks, which will become filled with rain water, or possibly a spring may be started. These ponds will be the drinking-place for the cattle, and here, too, the buffaloes wallow in the hot season. They become gradually deepened as more clay is required and is dug out. As mud-houses gradually fall down by age or during the heavy rains, and are frequently renewed, there is a perpetual tendency for the house-sites to rise in level. An old-established village will thus be considerably raised, and the site must be-

[1] *Oudh Gazetteer*, vol. i. Introduction, p. xiv.

come higher and higher in the course of years, independently of the fact that, for obvious reasons, the highest ground available was probably selected to begin with.[1] It is very common to find the headmen, and others of note, having better-built brick houses, for which they have acquired the best situations. There are many local accounts of villages in districts, which it would not be possible to quote without too great a sacrifice of space.[2]

I may notice, in concluding the subject, some general statistics which appear from the Indian Census of 1891. The difficulty of fixing on anything like a unit for a 'village' in some districts, and the fact that some enumerators may have taken the administrative aggregate or circle, and others the single homestead as the unit, must of course vitiate the results to some extent; but making due allowance for this, it appears that out of a total of

[1] In the *Karnāl S. R.* (1882), Mr. Ibbetson remarks (p. 120): 'When a new village is founded, the first thing done is to dig out tanks to hold rain-water for cattle, washing, &c. The village is built on the spoil; and, as in course of time old houses fall down and new ones are built, the village is raised higher above the surrounding plain, in some of the old Nardak villages as much as 150 or 200 feet. The space immediately around the village is called *goirā*: here the cattle stand to be milked, weavers train their warp, fuel is stacked, dunghills made, ropes twisted, sugar-presses erected, and all the operations conducted for which free space is necessary. The village is generally surrounded by a mud wall and a ditch as a protection against thieves, and is entered by gates often of brick and containing side rooms in which the gossips sit when it grows hot under the huge *bar* or *pīpal* tree (*Ficus sp.*) which generally stands outside. Main streets (*galī*) run through from one gate to another, and in Rājput or other villages where the women are strictly secluded numerous blind alleys lead from them, each being occupied by the house of near relatives.' This is in the South-eastern Panjāb, but is quoted as a good account of the form of Panjāb villages in general; details naturally vary in different parts.

[2] See, for example, *Lahore S. R.* (Saunders), § 208; *Hushyārpur S. R.* (Montgomery), § 43; *Siālkot Gazetteer*, p. 33; *R. Pindi Gazetteer*, pp. 51–52; *Firozpur Gazetteer*, p. 38. In Purser's *Montgomery S. R.* pp. 52, 53, there is a very pleasing account of the villages and types of house. As to frontier villages, aggregation depends on the peculiar tribal customs afterwards described. In the *Bannu S. R.* pp. 60 ff, are some particulars, but no direct notice of the point under immediate consideration—the aggregation of residences. In Peshāwar, the villages are compact, sometimes furnished with towers of refuge (*Captain Hastings'*

close upon 714,000 villages, nearly 223,000 contain a population of 200 and over, while about 343,000 have under 200. Those exceeding 500 are, in round numbers, 98,000.[1]

These notes on the physical conditions may be concluded with a brief remark on the origin of the vernacular words for 'village.' I do not know of one that has direct reference to the grouping or aggregation of *land*. The Sanskrit *grāma* may originally have had reference to a tribal grouping of a limited number of families, as the dictionary gives 'clan,' 'community' or 'host,' 'aggregate,' as among the meanings.[2] But in the Veda the word seems chiefly to indicate the sort of fort or protected residence site into which the cattle could be driven at night or to escape attack.[3] The Hindi *gāñw*, *gām*, &c. (Panjābi *grāñw*, *girāñ*, &c.) are dialectic forms of *grāma*. The Arabic *mauẓa'*, adopted into general revenue language more or less all over India, is derived in Johnson's Dictionary from the form *waẓa'*, with the meaning of 'founding,' 'laying down.' The Persian *dih* is not explained. On the Panjāb frontier the village is often called *k͟hel*, which is simply a subsection of a clan and the considerable area of land allotted to it. I cannot speak from personal knowledge of the southern dialects, but on the west coast *taṟa* has only the meaning of 'foundation,' 'quarter,' 'street,' and not anything to do with the aggregate of lands. The common Dravidian word for village is *Ūr*, which enters into so many names, as Nellore (Nal-ūr), Vellore (Vel-ūr), Tanjore (Tanjā[v]ūr), to say nothing of Indore (Ind-ūr), Gwalior (Gwāli-

S. R. p. 20). In parts of Dera Ismail Khān, aggregate sites again appear for the reasons given (*Tucker's S. R.* § 18). For the South-eastern Panjāb, see Purser and Fanshawe's account of the large villages of Rohtak (average 2,044 acres with 1,076 persons), *S. R.*, pp. 9, 10; and some curious particulars in Channing's *Gurgāon S. R.* (1882), § 70, p. 59.

[1] *Census Report* (Parliamentary Blue Book), p. 48. The large number of villages with small populations is increased by the inclusion of small groups in the hills, &c. Mr. Baines remarks that the landlord system of Bengal has tended to break up villages and settle the tenants on their holdings; and also that, life and property being generally secure, there is a tendency to form small groups of houses on the spot, otherwise the holders would have to go far from home to reach their holdings.

[2] Vide Macdonell, *Sanskrit Dictionary*, s.v. *grāma*.

[3] See Zimmer, p. 142, as to the Vedic *grāma* or *vṛjāna*.

ūr), &c., further north.[1] The terms *upagrāmam* and *kuppam*, in the South, refer to hamlets or offshoots of villages, as *dhok* and *majrā* do in North India.

[1] *Ūr* probably referred to a fortified place or even town; indeed, the origin of the word may have gone back to the early time when some place of refuge would have been the natural centre of each 'village' group. However that may be, we find quite a group of compound words indicating village features, such, *e.g.*, as *Urdaḷāvara* (Karn.), the village-servants; *Ūrkāvaliga* (Karn.), the village-watchman; *Ūruçeruvu* (Tel.), *Ūrkoḷa* (Karn.), the village-tank; *Ūrmāniyam* (Tamil), free-lands for remuneration of the village-servants, *Ūrugauḍā* (Karn.), the village head-man.

CHAPTER III

ETHNOGRAPHICAL CONSIDERATIONS

IF, as we have reason to believe, the agricultural settlement of India began, not with the Aryan, but with pre-existing races; and if, further, we find that the Aryans, and also the Jat, Gujar, and other immigrant tribes produced the joint or landlord form of village as the result of their domination or conquest—since these villages occur chiefly in the countries subject to that conquest—it becomes important to make a general survey of the provinces, and take note of the chief elements which are found in the population of each. We shall observe in each a pre-Aryan, or at least a non-Aryan element, a mixed race, and an upper class of purer Aryan caste, which, together with some families of later origin, represents the dominant or ruling race.

A very brief examination of the subject will be sufficient; we shall not only confine ourselves to what has some bearing on land-holding and the agricultural population, but we shall also avoid all uncertain ethnological questions. These latter are so numerous in India that a prejudice may arise against any kind of ethnographic survey as affording but a doubtful basis for reasonable conclusions. But though such a suspicion may justly exist, it is possible to let it go too far, and land us in the error of supposing that nothing is really known about the origin of the people at all. There are certain well-ascertained facts of Indian ethnography, and there are inferences to be justly drawn from them; and it would be as wrong on the one hand to ignore either, as it would be to build up an argument on the more speculative elements.

There is no reasonable doubt, in the first place, about the main ethnical elements with which we are here concerned.[1] The

[1] And thus, if primitive communal ownership of land is a fact, we have a number of distinct fields of observation, in one or more of which

long-continued fusion of races which has been going on for many centuries has naturally resulted in obscuring the origin of many castes or tribes, and has left it doubtful at the present day whether any particular people or tribe should be assigned to one ethnic group or the other; nevertheless, the existence of certain distinct groups cannot be questioned. Thus, beginning with the north-east, Assam was certainly peopled by races conveniently described as TIBETO-BURMAN. Similar tribes to some extent occupied the north-east parts of Bengal; and they advanced along the outer ranges of the Himalayan Mountains and furnished the basis of the more or less mixed 'castes' which form the cultivating population of the hill districts as far at least as Kashmīr. There is equally no doubt that another people, coming from the same quarter, and conveniently distinguished as KOLARIAN, were once numerous at the eastern end of India. Nor is it of importance for our purpose whether the name is a good one, and whether these people are of an entirely separate stock. It is, at any rate, convenient to separate them, for we have something of interest to learn from the Santāl people and from the Ho and Mundā tribes surviving in Chutiyā-Nāgpur, where they are found actually alongside of Dravidian races.[1] Then, again, we have the often almost unmixed and widely spread DRAVIDIAN population of the South. It is, no doubt, a difficult problem to account for the existence of Dravidian elements in Upper India before the Aryans came; but that does not in the least affect the observations we are able to make on tribes admittedly of this group, in their present location, whether nearly pure as in the South, or more mixed in the Dakhan and Central India. Then we have the ARYAN population, and with it many mixed races or castes claiming Aryan origin. Lastly, we have the Jat, Gujar, and other races who followed their steps, but only to a limited distance beyond

we ought to find at least traces of such a system. If we find it neither among Tibeto-Burmans, Kolarians, Dravidians, nor Aryans, the belief must be held to be more than ever doubtful as far as India is concerned.

[1] The distinction is also evident in the Central Provinces, where we have the meeting ground of the Aryan introduced into the northern part, the Gond or Dravidian element, and also the Kolarian—all localised. (See *Central Provinces Gazetteer*, Introduction, pp. cv–cviii., and cxxv.)

the Panjāb; and we have the Moslem tribes, the result of the Pathān and Mughal conquests. We have noticed already how the physical features of mountain range, desert, and open country affected the introduction and movements of the various invading races; and how in consequence, Upper India—the country between the Himalaya and the Vindhya (from the Panjāb to Bengal), the Western Indian Districts—with part of the Dakhan, and again Southern India, have all become marked ethnographical divisions; and these we will follow in a brief series of sections. But before describing the population of each, there is one general question which, as it affects the entire range of subsequent history, had better be dealt with at once. It is almost impossible to describe the population of any single province without reference to it. I allude to the nature of the Aryan advance—partly by conquest, partly by policy and conciliation—and to the question of the probable number of the Aryans and their relations with the population they encountered.

Section I.—The Aryan Immigration

The Aryans [1] entered India at its north-west corner, and first established themselves in the hill country among the 'seven confluents of the Indus' (*Sapta-sindhavah*), between the outer and inner Himalayan ranges.[2] From this country the tribes

[1] It is quite unimportant for our purposes whether the name 'Aryan' is a good one or not; or whether it implies a greater degree of unity than ever really existed. It serves, at any rate, to distinguish the people, or connected peoples, who gave us the Vedic hymns, and who afterwards, in one part or section of their race, developed the system of law and philosophy, of statecraft and religion, which we familiarly associate with the name of 'Hindu,' and which we find described in the Sanskrit classics.

[2] Among other authorities, see Lassen, i. 617. It is usually assumed that the Aryans occupied 'the Panjāb.' Thus, to select one passage out of several that would do equally well, Zimmer, p. 1, commences: 'The main body of the Vedic-Aryan tribes settled, in ancient days, on the banks of the Indus and in the districts lying eastward of it, through which numerous streams, great and small, find their way as tributaries to the main river: it was the country of the *Sapta-sindhava*, the Panjāb of modern times.' But I submit that the description, perfectly just in itself, does not answer to 'the Panjāb of modern times' at all. No

eventually moved forward towards the plain country of Upper India. A certain number, no doubt, occupied the lower Indus Valley and Sindh. Tradition is clear on the point, and ascribes the occupation to the *Yādavā* tribe. It is certain that Sanskritic speech had reached the mouths of the Indus in very early times.[1] Thence they extended to Western India—to the portion which was open, as already explained. Another portion may have remained in the hill districts; and some may have settled in the Panjāb plains, either below the hills or close to the rivers, where settlement alone could have been possible. The rest moved eastward across the plains. The Vedic hymns, no doubt, contain specific allusions to the Panjāb plains, and to battles fought in traversing them; but they afford no certain evidence of settlement in the Panjāb plain country. The important point is, however, not whether colonies did exist or were numerous, but what influence could they have had, even if we prefer to accept their existence. For when we hear of the 'Aryan colonisation' of the Panjāb in general, it is almost always with the meaning that it was by tribes possessing the characteristic 'Hindu' caste and religious ideas. And on a hasty view of the subject, coupled with the reflection that the 'Panjābī' dialects are classed as Sanskritic,[2] it is easily concluded that the Panjāb

one who is familiar with the locality from long residence would speak of the dry mountains and occasionally fertile valleys of the Upper Indus country—the country of the Swāt, the Kābul, and the Kunār rivers, and, lower down, of the Kuram—as 'the Panjāb.' The confusion perhaps arises from forgetting that the rivers Indus, Kābul, Jihlam, Rāvī, Sutlej, &c., have a long course through the Himalayan hill-country under the same names, or partially so, that they bear when, more than a hundred miles south, some of them form the dividing streams of the real Panjāb.

[1] Burton remarked that the Sindhī language contained many Sanskrit words, both pure and corrupted, which are now unintelligible to the unlearned in other parts. Dr. E. Trumpp says that the Sindhī is much nearer to the old Prakrīt than the Panjābī, Marāthī, Hindī, and Bengali of our days (Hughes, *Gazetteer of Sindh*, p. 88).

[2] The Sanskrit element in the language is not at all conclusive of an *early* influence; even supposing the Sanskrit words are always the originals, and not themselves derived from local speech. We shall again have occasion to notice the Hindu elements in the Marāthī language and in that of Orissa, where it is practically certain that it was an influence of much later times, long after the Puranic religion and the caste system had been fully developed.

village communities are specially Aryan or 'Hindu.' This is not the case. There is no doubt that at an early date something of the nature of a split or schism must have taken place among the tribes, and that the eastward march to the Saraswati and the Jamnā rivers was not a mere question of united movement. It was only after the separation, and among the tribes settled east of the Jamnā, that the rigid caste rules and other specially Hindu institutions and ideas were established: those who remained behind, in the Panjāb or Sindh, could have had no share in them. Merely for the sake of distinction, I call the latter the 'non-Brahmanic' Aryans. The 'Brahmanic' tribes not only moved away and made the Saraswati—then an important stream, but now very much diminished—their boundary, but evidently regarded the 'Panjāb' with so much aversion that still in the days of the epic poems, the country was declared impure—'Let no Aryan dwell there even for two days.' The reason of the 'impurity' was the neglect or rejection of what were called the 'Vedic ceremonies,' and probably also the first rules of tribal separation: 'they do not conduct themselves according to the Brahmanic ordinances' (*na-hi-brāhmaçaryam-çaranti*); that is the root of the whole matter.[1] It can only mean that the Aryans of the Indus Valley, and such as remained in the Panjāb, did not adopt the strict rules and ordinances which afterwards led up to developed Hinduism, and consequently that they would naturally have had little or no 'caste' objection to mix with other races; so their separate ethnic traces would have disappeared as they have, in fact, done. We may speak, then, of early Aryan influence in the Panjāb and the Indus Valley and Western India,

[1] See Muir's *A. S. T.* ii. 482; *Mahābhāratā*, part viii.; *Karna-parva*, v. 2063-2068. 'In this region, where the five rivers flow after issuing from the mountains, dwell the *Bāhīkā*, called *Araṭṭa*; the water of it (*tad-jalam*) is called *Bāhīkā*. There dwell degraded Brahmans contemporary with *Prajāpati* [?]. They have no Veda or Vedic ceremony. The *Prasthalā*, *Madrā*, and the *Gandhārā*, &c., dwell there.' Dr. Muir puts the note of interrogation about the Brahmans; the words are not clear in the original. May they not allude to some of the earlier bards and sacrificers—already in Vedic times beginning to be called Brahmans—who, not caring to maintain the exclusiveness of the Aryan stock, were left behind and regarded as 'degraded' and unworthy scions of the race? See Zimmer, p. 189, and Lassen, i. 616.

but it would have been one thing in these countries and quite another in the kingdoms of Oudh, the Ganges Plain, and Bengal. To an admixture of Aryan blood is very likely due the improvement of some of the early races—the *Ahīr*, the *Kunbi*, the *Marāthā* of Western India, and others in the north who could not be specified with any certainty. Aryans may also have introduced ideas of monarchy and chiefship (already known in Vedic times), but probably not the 'caste' and other customs which belong to the later 'Hindu' development.

The eastward-going tribes established their new home near the sacred Saraswati and called it *Brāhmavartā*; but when they advanced further east, they acknowledged a wider region —*Aryavartā*; ultimately they passed these limits altogether, extending to Bihār, Bengal, and Western Assam, till, having reached the mouths of the Ganges they sent expeditions to Orissa, to Burma, to Ceylon (*Selam*; [S.] *Lankā*), and even to Java, where their co-sharing (landlord) villages long remained in evidence. Even among the 'Brahmanic' tribes, caste prohibitions utterly failed either to prevent a rival religion to the Brahmanic, in the form of Buddhism and its modification Jainism, or to keep the Aryan tribes from forming regular (or irregular) marriages with the people, whether aboriginal or other immigrant races. The Aryan 'high-caste' people remained everywhere as a dominant race, establishing kingdoms and local lordships, and giving rise to many village estates of a landlord character, as we shall afterwards see. Here we pass on to another question.

(2) *The Numbers of the Aryan Tribes and their Relations with the Existing Races*

The idea, as regards Upper India generally, that the Aryan races came in a vast swarm, and that they met with some unimportant, if occasionally numerous, savage races—black, snub-nosed, and illiterate, who after some more or less bloody resistance fled northward to the Himalayan or southward to the Vindhyan ranges, or to the security of the plateaux of South-western Bengal and Orissa, and left the Gangetic plain to be mainly peopled and cultivated by the rank and file of the Aryan clansmen, under the domination of their own princes and priests—such an idea is probably no longer entertained, as it once was, even by the least enterprising of readers. The inferences which must almost inevitably be drawn from a number of facts show that the existing population was by no means scanty, though it was probably localised, and settlements were separated by great stretches of uninhabited forest. Some of the tribes, too, were of a somewhat barbarous type, small of stature and black in colour, while others must certainly have been agriculturists and much more advanced. Indeed, the literary allusions to the subject are really consistent with this view, making due allowance for the contempt which Brahmanic writers would feel for the non-Aryan people in general. While swarthy and uncouth tribes might be met with in the hill country and its confines, the superior agricultural tribes would have been found in the most fertile and level places in the vicinity of rivers, and would often be isolated. It would not be difficult to collect examples of cases where cultivation and the appliances of ancient civilisation have existed within an hour's journey of the wilderness. In the ancient kingdom of Magadhā (the modern Gāyā district in Bengal), with all its importance, and a suzerainty extending far and wide, we have reason to believe that in the third century B.C. the country immediately to the south, and beginning only a few miles beyond the great Buddhist city of Gāyā, was a dense forest only scantily inhabited by nomad tribes.[1]

It is hardly possible to suppose that the Aryan armies

[1] See the admirable monograph called *Notes on the Gāyā District* by G. Grierson, B.C.S. (Calcutta, 1893), pp. 3, 4. The whole subject is also well illustrated by Mr. F. E. Pargiter's careful paper on the Geography of the Rāmāyanā (*J. R. A. S.* April 1894, p. 231). Here we have the account of the wanderings of an exile prince, who is driven by the loss of his wife—abducted by a demon enemy—to the very southernmost parts of India. The account, though highly poetical and legendary, is based, it would seem, on at least a substantial amount of geographical fact. And we find, besides the mention of non-Aryan kingdoms near the Jamnā, the mention of the vast tracts of forest beyond the Vindhyā. The plan of the poem would not admit of any specific notice of the southern (*Pāṇḍyā*) kingdom; but incidental mention is made of the fine architecture and good government of Ceylon.

could have been supported, and cities built, unless there were locally well-established civilisation, and people able to serve and aid the ruling race; and the Dravidians of Upper India, were certainly builders and also acquainted with the structure of 'tanks' for irrigation.

It is true that the Vedic literature suggests, at any rate on a cursory view of it, that the chief opponents of the Aryans were the *dasyū*, or 'enemies,' who are described in contemptuous and unprepossessing terms. It is often, however, forgotten that the Vedas only refer to the earliest stages of Aryan advance, locally speaking, and even the later Atharvan Veda only sees them at the Ganges.[1] We have also to make large allowance in such poetic literature for much imaginative exaggeration, and for a bardic licence that confused together in one detested mass enemies of very different kinds. All that is probable is that some of the characteristics which excited so much abusive eloquence may be true of the races first met with. And as we know how widely the primitive races of the same stock were extended, it is likely enough that these characteristics were sufficiently prominent. Thus it may easily be supposed that the enemies met with in the hills, and possibly elsewhere, were of smaller stature than the Aryan and Northern tribes. It is also more than probable that longer residence in India would have made them generally blacker than the more recently arrived Northerners.[2] The hill-people, *Ḍom*, and the lower orders of *Khasā* for instance, were almost certainly of this character; and we notice the same again among the *Bhīl* tribes of Mālwā.

And one other feature appears really general among the primitive races. The Dravidians, or at least the Northern groups of them, whom some would separate ethnically, were more or less flat-nosed: this is evidently the trait indicated by the Vedic epithet *anāsu*, and this feature is traceable among their descendants to this day.[3]

[1] See Lassen, i. 644, 870–72. [2] See Zimmer, p. 113.

[3] Mr. Risley, *The Tribes and Castes of Bengal*, vol. i. (Ethnographic Glossary and Introductory Essay), remarks: 'If we take a series of castes in Bengal, Bihār, and the North-West Provinces and arrange them in the order of the average nasal index, so that the caste with the finest nose shall be at the top, and that with the coarsest at the bottom, it will be

But it by no means follows that even in Vedic times *all* the people met with were indiscriminately *dasyū*. In one place these latter are expressly mentioned separately from the race called *Çimyū*;[1] we hear also of the *Kīkaṭa*, of the *Çāmbara* (who had forts), and of the *Nishāda*.[2] These are all non-Aryan tribes. Others might be mentioned, but they are not undisputed. Then there are allusions to the 'serpent' races, some of whom were Northerners, who could not have answered to the description of the swarthy *dasyū*. That some of these tribes were wealthy there can be no doubt. M. V. de St. Martin calls attention to at least one place where the 'gold ornaments and rich jewels' of the enemy are mentioned.[3] And in the epics the wealth of non-Aryan tribes is frequently instanced.

We may therefore accept it as established by a number of separate considerations, the cumulative weight of which is considerable, that the Aryans were numerous enough to be rulers and to have armies, but not more; that the indigenous people were partly barbarous and partly not; that they were localised, and that the existing settlements occupied the best parts of the country, leaving great stretches of forest and of hilly jungle-clad country either waste or inhabited only by nomad tribes. The case has been well summed up by Sir W. Hunter when, speaking of certain features of the later Aryan conquest of Orissa, he says that the history 'unfolds the Aryan colonisation of India in a new and rational light. It discloses no trace of the universal and absolute conquest by which the primitive Aryan

found that the order substantially corresponds with the accepted order of social precedence.' And he goes on to instance as grades in a scale the relics of early tribes like the *Mundā*, *Ho*, &c., who are non-Aryan, and the higher mixed races like the *Kurmī* (or *Kunbī*), and then the trading *Khatrī* and higher castes. 'Thus,' he continues, 'it is scarcely a paradox to lay down as a law of caste organisation in Eastern India that a man's social status varies in inverse ratio to the width of his nose.' This, it will be remarked, applies to Upper India.

[1] Ṛgveda, 1. 100. 18. See Zimmer, pp. 118, 143.

[2] Zimmer, pp. 31, 143. See G. Oppert, pp. 578, 579. In Puranic writings the term *Nishāda* is applied to non-Aryans generally. In the Rāmāyanā there is a king of the Nishāda, mentioned by name, and he has a fleet of boats and an army (*J. R. A. S.* App. 94, p. 257).

[3] *Étude sur la Géographie*, &c., p. 108; and again in Ṛgveda, 3. 34. 9; Zimmer, pp. 50, 116; G. Oppert, pp. 12, 13.

settlers in Northern Hindustān are assumed to have subdued the whole continent to their sway. On the contrary, it dissipates the mist which has toned down the multiform migrations into a homogeneous advance; and exhibits the natural compromises by which a small but gifted people effected their entrance among vastly more numerous races, sometimes, indeed, by force of arms, but generally by an amalgamation which the vanity of later ages has more or less disguised.'[1]

This general conclusion is curiously illustrated by one circumstance which has not, perhaps, received the notice it deserves. If it were really the case that the Aryan tribes overwhelmed and practically supplanted the original population, how is it that at the period when the Greek and later geographers began to gather their evidence about India we do not find a much greater uniformity of population and territorial rule than, commencing with Megasthenes and the Macedonian period, we actually do find?[2] The geographers all speak of India as a series of separate countries and of separately named peoples; and this is the more remarkable because we find some of them imagining that the Indian people never received any foreign immigration.[3] And it is not merely a question of different states or dynasties, for that the familiar organisation of limited Hindu kingdoms would lead us to expect; but entirely different tribes and people are named. Some of the names are still identifiable; some very doubtfully so; others resist all attempts at explanation.[4] When we come down to the journals

[1] *Orissa*, i. 242. The particular advance in question, though ancient, occurred long after the first Aryan arrival in India, and only by the time that Aryan princes had reached Eastern Bengal and the Ganges mouths.

[2] And see also pp. 104–5, where allusion is made to the Brahmanic account.

[3] For example, Megasthenes says: 'It is said that India, being of enormous size, when taken as a whole, is peopled by races both numerous and diverse, of which not even one was originally of foreign descent, but all were evidently indigenous; and, moreover, that India neither received a colony from abroad nor sent out a colony to any other nation.' —McCrindle, *Ancient India: Megasthenes and Arrian*, p. 35.

[4] This is hardly to be wondered at when we recollect that the name had first to be 'translated' into Greek writing by hearers who probably

of Hwen Thsang in the seventh century, it is the same; indeed, this writer furnishes us with still more distinct notices of the variety of peoples and languages.

If we turn to the older Sanskrit writers, to the *Laws of Manu* for instance, we find (in the tenth chapter) a whole passage devoted to 'mixed'—*i.e.* partly or wholly non-Aryan—races. Among them figure the people of *Mithilā* and *Magadhā*; and, according to the usual Brahmanic mode, the author also treats as *Kshatriya* who have lost caste, the *Oḍra* (of Orissa), the *Draviṛa* (people of the South), the *Kāmbhojā*, *Yavanā*, *Pāradā*, *Pahlavā*, and *Çakā* (or Scythian), *Çinā*, *Kirāṭā*, *Daradā*, and *Khasā*.[1] A number of these are admittedly mixed races; others are foreign races strong enough to have established local kingdoms, and to have made themselves more or less respected by adopting Hindu caste and religious customs. Such a work could hardly, perhaps, be expected to make any mention of the 'lower orders'; but there is no doubt that in many parts of Upper India the great mass of the humbler classes, though Hinduised, are of chiefly non-Aryan derivation. It is, in fact, exactly consistent with this view of a general fusion of races, which left only the ruling castes (besides Brahmans) fairly pure, that the existing distinction between high and low castes and outcastes is what it is everywhere observed to be. It should be borne in mind that besides the confessedly mixed or aboriginal but converted races received into caste and called *Çūdrā*, there are a number of doubtful castes of good physique and superior character. Such, for instance, are the *Bhuĩñhār* or *Bābhan*, who gained possessions in 'Āzimgarh and the districts of

had little acquaintance with the native dialects, and did not catch the correct sound, nor render it scientifically into Greek. Then, too, we have to allow for the mistakes of copyists, and for the still further changes that would creep in, as the old works were quoted by the later writers, in whose books they alone survive. For a good specimen of the *tribal* lists, see McCrindle's *Megasthenes and Arrian*, p. 129 ff, or his *Ptolemy* for a later list, second century A.D.

[1] See Manu, chap. x. verse 44. There are some variations in the text as to these names: Bühler reads *Çoḍa* instead of *Odra*, *e.g.* Verses 42 69, and 72 are especially noteworthy. Verse 72 relates to a possible rise in rank of the mixed offspring after many generations. Cf. also chap. ix. verses 23, 24, 149.

Bihār adjoining the eastern end of the North-West Provinces, and there formed a rather numerous caste, with a sort of inferior Rājput rank. Some believe in a Brahman origin for them.[1] The Rājput clans have at all times permitted alliances, if not regular marriages, with women of other races; and the families resulting have sometimes formed separate castes. Colonel Tod mentions a class called *Golī* or *Dāsā* in Rājputānā, originating in this way.[2] In Naipāl the late Mr. Brian Hodgson has given an interesting account of the formation of a caste—with *Kshatriya* privileges—from the union of Brahmans with indigenous women.[3] Some of these mixed races are of superior pretensions, and would not consent to rank as *Çūdrā*.[4] If other instances of superior but evidently mixed races are needed, I may refer to the Western Himalayan States, where races like the *Thakkar* and *Rāthī* are well known, and many of them are of distinctly good physique; they are certainly mixed races of Tibetan origin with a strain of Aryan blood. To these I may add the caste called *Kanet*. The *Girth* (or *Ghirath*) are probably more largely aboriginal.[5]

[1] A good account of the *Bābhan* will be found in Risley's *T. and C. of Bengal*, i. (Glossary), 28 ff.

[2] Tod, i. 159-160. Malcolm (*Memoirs of Central India*, ii. 126) mentions a class called *Soṇḍi* of the same kind. It is hardly necessary to recall the fact that in ancient literature and traditions we have repeated allusions to patriarchal sages and others who married daughters of non-Aryan race. And where concubinage was so general, mixed families would everywhere be numerous.

[3] *Essays on the Language, &c., of Naipāl* (London: Trübner, 1874,) part ii. p. 37 ff.

[4] See the remarks in *Elliott's Glossary*, i. 167 ff.

[5] It is curious that in general, where there is a considerable preponderance of the aboriginal or non-Aryan strain, the caste is an *agricultural* one. For a good account of the Himalayan races, see Ibbetson's *Panjāb Ethnography*, §§ 458, 487; and regarding the *Girth*, § 489. The *Khasiyā* form a considerable part of the Kumāon population. In the Kāngra Hills the *Kanet* are numerous, and they are in two divisions, one called *Khasiyā* and the other *Rāo*. Ibbetson (*Panjāb Ethnography*, § 488, quoting Lyall on Kulu) says that the division is traditionally ascribed to a former Rājā of Kulu, who desired to make the people more attentive to Hindu religious observances. The *Khasiyā* obeyed and received the *janeo*, or sacred string. Brahmans who gathered round the Rājā's Court were always striving to make the Hill people more orthodox Hindus and less

In a widely different part of the country the *Nāyar* caste of the West Coast affords another example of a superior mixed race. They are partly Dravidian, but with perhaps a considerable infusion of Northern—possibly Aryan—blood. At any rate, the mixture must now be considerable on account of the tribal custom of taking temporary Brahman husbands for their female relatives, and giving the inheritance to the sister's son. These proud caste-men are reckoned in Brahmanical books as *Çūdra*, yet no caste has greater pretensions to rank and ceremonial purity.[1]

All indications that can be gathered from the present ethnical *data* of the provinces, as well as all that can be gained from local traditions, combine to convince us that the Aryan (and perhaps other later Northern) races have left us an upper stratum of originally very superior quality—families of good physique, of lighter colour and with a genius for military organisation and for some of the arts; while their priestly families had a taste for the most refined philosophic speculation, as well as for religious contemplation. They originated, in fact, a religion which, including every kind of worship and esoteric doctrine in a hundred schools and sects, is more a social system made a matter of religious import by means of its ceremonial connection than anything else; and this was eagerly accepted, as it improved the social position without hindering local cults and the worship of favourite divinities. From this limited refining element also arose a not inconsiderable number of races, mixed indeed, but still distinctly superior; and then we have the great mass of the agricultural and farm-labouring population, that becomes more and more connected with the 'aboriginal' races the further we descend in the social scale.

The importance of this from the point of view of the student of land-customs is that it comports with the facts of the land tenure in general—namely, that whatever customs regarding

devoted to the local divinities. The lower division resisted these efforts to a much greater extent.

[1] Thus Dr. Day (*Cochin: Its Past and Present*, p. 316) says: 'Should a *Chogān* or a *Maknā* or one of the lower caste dare to pollute a *Nair* (*Nāyan*) by approaching nearer than the prescribed distance, he was formerly at liberty to cut him down.' Cf. Lassen, iv. 270.

land are of Aryan origin, they are the customs of a conquering race, or at least of a race which took the superior position in everything. The tenures that arose from their State arrangements and their locations of Chiefs—whether they now appear as larger landlord estates or as co-shared villages—were all essentially overlord, or at least landlord, tenures. That is quite true in spite of the fact that some 'Aryan' clans remained without any aristocratic pretensions, or developing any system of Rājā or other titled chiefs, and that they formed land-holding communities based on a peculiar method of equal-sharing. The equality was among themselves only; they would consider themselves altogether superior to their tenants, or to the lower castes generally.

(3) *Present State of Inferior Races*

It remains only to add a few words regarding the present state of various tribes or races which may be such as to suggest erroneous conclusions regarding their former history. We have to bear in mind the fact that paucity of number, present poverty, and often social depression in rank, afford no ground for positive inference regarding the original status and importance of the races, or as to the degree of prosperity and material civilisation that they had anciently attained, under wholly different circumstances. Especially is it necessary to bear in mind the effect of the introduction of caste rules, and the artificial constitution of society in grades. Nothing is more striking than the way in which we again and again come across traces of former importance among races now only found in scattered families, or perhaps still numerous but in the lowest grades of the caste or social scale. Low-caste people will be found in some cases to retain certain curious privileges, which can only be accounted for on the supposition that once a higher rank was held.[1] In one country we hear of high-caste Hindu princes receiving the *tilak*, or mark of investiture, from *Bhīl* or *Mīnā tribesmen.*[2]

[1] See G. Oppert, pp. 53, 73, and the excellect remarks quoted from Walhouse (*Indian Antiquary*), iii. 191, in a note at p. 84.

[2] As to the *Bhīl*, see *Imperial Gazetteer*, ii. 387; and see *Rājputānā Gazetteer*, i. 73. The *Mīnā*, a tribe having as many as 146 *got* or septs, though now in a reduced condition, are spoken of as the 'hereditary

When once it became a mark of respectability to be in 'Hindu' caste, the highest families, as we so constantly find, would employ Brahman family-priests and become strict observers of caste rules. Their ruling chiefs take Hindu names, and in time, their real origin being long forgotten, they are received into 'Rājput' rank, and after a few generations they are allowed to marry into the best houses.[1] Mythical heroic ancestors are easily provided for them by Court bards; and everything is traced back to some Hindu deity, or some miraculous occurrence in Puranic books. The mass of the peaceable agricultural people, on the other hand, received Brahmanic teaching, and found in the endless gradations of even the fourth caste, a position sufficiently high above the equally endless divisions of low-caste or no-caste beneath them to satisfy their aspirations. The defeated races, the irreconcilables, and those (perhaps hill) tribes who had not reached the same stage of elementary culture as the plain dwellers, did not share in the rise: they took refuge in the woods and the remoter ranges of hills, and the circumstances of such a life would not only prevent any more civilised development, but would rapidly establish nomadic and perhaps predatory habits as well as the deterioration of physique and the loss of any ideas of settled life that may once have been possessed.

If the real characteristics of some of the 'aboriginal' races are examined, it will often be found that they are by no means

guards of the States' Chief,' and 'on every succession a *Mīnā* performs the ceremony of investiture.' The author adds that the same custom prevails in several other parts of India. It was a *Bhīl* who invested *Gohā*, founder of the *Gahlōt* Rājputs, with a *tilak* made by the blood of a young *Bhīl* tribesman (Tod, i. 184). This custom is still observed, and the persistence of it is all the more remarkable that the touch of *Bhīl* blood is defilement to the Hindu Rājā, and on the other hand the *Bhīl* tradition is that the person from whose arm the drop of blood is taken is likely to die within the year.

[1] Cf. Introduction to *Central Provinces Gazetteer*, p. lxvii, for some excellent remarks from a competent witness. The Chutiyā-Nāgpur Rājās alluded to are, however, not *Mundā* but of the *Urāoñ* (Dravidian) stock: this makes no difference to the general argument. We sometimes hear of princes placing themselves ceremonially *inside cows* made of brass—in one case, if I remember rightly, of gold, which was afterwards cut up and given to the Brahmans. By going through this form they indicate their new birth into Hinduism.

so despicable. I shall only here mention the case of the *Khānd* tribe, whose customs will attract our attention hereafter, and who represent a primitive tribe, but one whose 'barbarous' character was almost solely inferred from their retention of periodical human sacrifices. The *Bhīl*, again, though driven to the hills, and for generations treated by their neighbours as outlaws,[1] have shown very valuable material in their nature; and the efforts made by Sir J. Outram and others for their reclamation have had a good measure of success. Many other outcaste people, when once freed from oppression and placed under good government, have shown themselves in a very satisfactory light.[2] This fact must not be forgotten; nor can the relative civilisation of all races be denied because of some undoubted instances where the scattered remnant is so decidedly 'barbarous' that we are obliged to infer either that they never rose above the nomadic stage, or that exceptionally unfavourable circumstances have hastened their decadence to a condition below the normal.

When, therefore, authors casually attach the epithet 'barbarous' or 'uncivilised' to the older races, we may treat their language as chiefly conventional, and seldom resting on any basis of ascertained fact or even probability. At any rate, we may be on our guard against looking at everything through Aryan or Brahmanic spectacles. The intellectual superiority of this race gave them, so to speak, the entire command of literature; so that almost everything that has passed into written form has been cast in an Aryan mould. For real history the Brahmanic writers never cared anything: early events and family origins invariably assume a mythic guise, and everything about non-Aryan races is either omitted or only noticed to glorify the conquest of the 'twice born' over the 'demons' and 'barbarians.' It is then only by a careful comparative study, by regarding the relics of original speech in the local dialects, by comparing ethnological data and local customs, and by coordinating local legends and traditions, that we can derive any

[1] The cruelty with which both Muhammadan and Marāthā Governors treated the *Bhīl* tribes may be seen in Forbes's *Rās Mālā*, and in Malcolm's *Central India.*

[2] See, for instance, G. Oppert, p. 75.

reasonable knowledge of the past. But with these aids it is possible to form conclusions which are probable, and even to extract some reliable elements out of the old Puranic and bardic fables in which gods and men, real events and impossible fictions, are mixed together in picturesque confusion.

It seems to me that just as in literature, so in discussing the origins of land-tenure there is a natural but unfortunate tendency to allow certain tribes or races to become so prominent as to exclude all care for any others. In literature it was very natural that the Aryans, with their polished Sanskrit language, their epic and dramatic poetry, their elaborate philosophy and their curiously intertwined legal, religious, and social ideas, should have been the most extensively studied. The tendency was doubtless favoured by the belief that the Aryans really had reduced or annihilated all other races, and formed the bulk of the existing population; and indeed this belief in its turn was largely due to the prominent position occupied by their literature.[1] The one has reacted on the other. It is now time to turn to Western and Southern India, and to the local traditions of non-Aryan races in India generally. The literature and folklore of the South naturally offer the greatest promise; and we may come to find that the Aryans owe much more than we have hitherto supposed to the indigenous races. At any rate, increased light will be thrown on the remarkable conditions under which the original Vedic religion exhibited such a kaleidoscopic transformation into that of the Purānā. Nor is it only the southern and western regions of India that have to be studied; the tribes of Assam and North-eastern Bengal have some institutions not unworthy of investigation;[2] and the people we call

[1] The tendency has always been marked to discover a *Sanskrit* derivation or meaning for everything. A familiar instance is in the Indian names of certain valuable products which occur in the Books of Kings and Chronicles. In the time of Solomon, circ. 1000 B.C., there is very little reason to suppose that Sanskrit words were much, if at all, in use in the south and on the western coast. Dr. G. Oppert has shown that *Dravidian* words are really the more probable originals. In Mr. J. A. Baines's Census Report of 1891, *Parl. Blue Book*, there are some excellent remarks on this subject, p. 126.

[2] We have only very slight acquaintance with details of agriculture and village life among the *Gāro*, *Khasiyā*, and other hill tribes of Assam and the north-east frontier.

Kolarian also, though the distinctive traces of them are fast disappearing.

One consequence of the almost exclusive attention to the Aryan element is that the landlord and other higher caste proprietary-tenures have attracted attention to the almost total exclusion of others. Hence '*the* village community'—meaning the jointly-owned village, *i.e.* one specialised form of village land-holding—has come to be spoken of as if it were the sole phenomenon of Indian agricultural life, and from that position it is almost inevitable to slide into the conclusion that this village-form must necessarily be primitive and universal. Whatever the truth on this subject may be, it is my hope that the considerations advanced in these pages as to the distribution of the different land-holding tribes and communities may help us to follow more easily the evidence that will be collected in the sequel as to the origin and growth of the existing village forms.

Section II.—The Population of Upper India

(1) *The Panjāb*

At the present day the Panjāb contains a variety of races, sometimes distinct in language, but oftener speaking various dialects of 'Panjābi' and Hindī. The hill districts, the sub-montane districts, the Salt Range country, the central plains, the south country of Multān, and the south-eastern districts beyond the Sutlej, are all distinguishable by their people and forms of speech. In general a Panjāb Census Table shows the names of many castes and clans not found further east, and some that go as far as the Ganges Doab; while the Rājputs (Military Aryan caste) are comparatively few and localised, and belong to later times. Whatever *early* Aryans stayed in the Panjāb must have fused completely with the population, leaving at best some faint traces.[1] The Panjāb bore the full brunt of the so-called Indo-

[1] It is true the Panjābi is classed as 'Sanskritic'; but the Sanskrit element is not necessarily due to the *earliest* Aryans, if any number of them settled there, which is doubtful. On the frontier Pashtu is spoken, and lower down on the west, Bilūchī. Beyond the Sutlej and in the south-east the dialects are more completely 'Hindī.'

Scythic irruptions, and was naturally afterwards much affected by the Pathān and Mughal conquests; indeed, Moslem tribes settled on the north-western frontier present us with an almost unique example of tribal customs of land-holding, which will occupy a large share of our subsequent attention.

The population of the hill country must not detain us. The upper classes are of later Aryan (Rajpūt) origin; and the bulk of the agriculturist tribes are mixed races, *Khasiyā*, *Kanēt*, *Ghirath*, *Rāthi*, &c., on which some observations have been made in the last section.

As to the original elements of the agricultural population of the Plains or Panjāb Proper, where the joint or co-shared village, both tribal and of individual origin, is so universal, we have definite evidence as to certain tribes met with at the time of Alexander's invasion, 327 B.C. And there is also proof of other northern incursions later than the Aryan; one, at any rate, of considerable importance *before* the Macedonian adventure, and one at least *after* it—in the two centuries immediately preceding the Christian era.

The climate and soil of the Panjāb plains are such that no very large or generally extended population could have maintained itself, except in a few districts where the rainfall is greater, or along the banks of the rivers. Any great extension of the inhabited area must have been accompanied by the invention of canals for irrigation, and by the use of wells, with some means of raising the water.[1]

Alexander found some apparently non-Aryan tribes in the Panjāb; and especially in the north, one race who worshipped the Sun and the Serpent. Of races with an evidently Aryan connection, there is only the tribe led by Porus.

A part of the population in Macedonian times seems to have already been so long established that General Cunningham was led to the conclusion that it was also pre-Aryan.[2] For serpent-

[1] In the Central Panjāb and some distance north, south, and east as far as the Sutlej, the 'Persian-wheel' is used. This appears to be a foreign introduction, but I cannot suggest a possible date for its becoming known.

[2] See the question stated in *Rep. Arch. Survey of India*, 1862-5, ii. 3 ff. Lassen also held the same opinion (i. 128). 'The Panjāb,' he says, 'as a country divided into separate states, appears equally in the

worshippers, as described by the Greeks, are also mentioned in the Veda; where we find them as hostile to, or at least outside the pale of, the Aryan tribes.[1] In Ṛgveda, 5. 31. 4, to quote a single instance, there is mention made of a tribe 'strengthened to smite down the snakes (*ahi*).' Later on, we find many allusions to the *Nāgā*.[2]

The serpent-worshipping tribe which Alexander's historians allude to was the *Takā*, who had their capital at Taxila (*Takāshila*, or in Sanskrit *Takshāçila*,[3] which is now proved to have been in

oldest Indian tradition and in the earliest competent descriptions of Western historians. Alexander found small kingdoms under their own princes in the north-west portion; and in the south-easterly parts free tribes with an almost republican constitution.'

[1] *Rep. Arch. Survey*, ii. 9.

[2] 'They [the *Nāgā*] held a very prominent position in Indian folklore, where they generally appear in human shape; and ancient writings abound with allusions to them as a people. But in the allegorical descriptions of later writers they become supernatural beings or actual serpents. . . .' See the whole article on 'Serpent Worship in India' by Surgeon-Major C. F. Oldham, *J. R. A. S.* July 1891.

There can be hardly any doubt that 'serpent worship' is connected with the North, though it spread over the whole of India in the course of time. It became associated with Buddhism, as most of the serpent-worshipping tribes of the North adopted that religion; and sculptured images of Buddhā are often found representing the saint seated under a serpent with his hood expanded like a canopy. Even in the South, it is remarkable that snake-worship is most traceable where Jainā religious relics remain (Jainism being only a modified offshoot of Buddhism). Whatever may be its real origin, snake-worship is found in various parts of India. It was carried by the Talaing into Burma (Phayre's *History of Burma*, pp. 21, 22, 33). As to its existence in Madras, see Macleane, *Ethnol.* p. 82, and Sturrock, *South Canara D. M.* i. 84, 140. And in the Central Provinces, see the curious account (from personal testimony by Mr. Hewitt) of the solemn and secret worship of the serpent (*Journ. Soc. Arts*, May 1887, p. 618), and see *J. R. A. S.* xx. part 3, 389. A curious notice of a temple with no idol in it but a snake-image, in one of the Chattisgarh districts is given in the *Central Provinces Gazetteer*, Introduction, p. lxv. As usual, the Puranic Hindu religion adopted the *Nāgā* deity, and the *Nāg-pañçamī* is now a regular and very popular Hindu festival (Monier Williams's *Religious Life in India*, pp. 323, 340.

[3] See *Rep. Arch. Sur.* ii. 10. It is often stated that *Takshaka* in Sanskrit means a snake (= *Nāgā*). The word has no such meaning. I regret to have fallen into this error in my *Land Systems of British*

the modern Rāwalpindī district. They were then a numerous and powerful people. Their chief city is described as the first of all the cities between the Indus and the Jihlam rivers, and as possessed of great wealth.[1] We hear of them also in Sindh.[2] The same race is mentioned in history as late as A.D. 900, when '*Takādeṣ*' was a province of the Kashmīr king *Sankara-varma*, and relics of them still exist in the Gujrāt district of the Panjāb and in the outer hills of the Jamū territory—localities which would be most naturally, at one time, included in a territory of which the capital was in the modern Rāwalpindī district. Their non-Aryan customs of worshipping the *Nāgā* and various other snake gods, *Bāsukdevī*, &c., as well as the sun-symbol, are detailed by Dr. Oldham in the article already referred to.[3] They introduced the written character still widely used in village shop-books, and known as the *Lande* or *Tākrī*.[4] As this is rudely cognate with the *Nāgari* character, it shows either that they had learnt it from ancient Aryan connection, or, more probably that the *later* literary Sanskrit character developed out of a ruder Northern script.

There are some other races in the Panjāb, now small and localised, who are also believed to have a very remote antiquity. Such are the *Doṇḍ*, *Sadāñ*, *Meḍ*, and *Saṭi*; but the question of their origin is too uncertain to permit further notice.

When we try to discover what tribes, if any, the Aryan invasion itself brought, we are at a loss to discover any distinct trace; this would indeed be a natural result if the early Vedic Aryans remained undeveloped as to their caste ideas. They may have

India, ii. 612. Probably the Sanskrit is a mere linguistic adaptation of *Tāk*, *Takā*, or *Tākhya*; and it is purely an accident that there is a Sanskrit word *tāksha*, which means 'cutter or cleaver.'

[1] See McCrindle's *Ptolemy*, pp. 118, 119.

[2] *Rep. Arch. Sur.* ii. 8.

[3] For some further evidence see *Rep. Arch. Sur.* ii. 10, where General Cunningham speaks of coins with a serpent-emblem, and of his belief that all Kashmīr was once peopled with *Nāgā*. There is also valuable information in *Elliott's Glossary*, i. 113. Especially important is it to note that in some ancient Tibetan (trilingual) records lately discovered and held to be of great value historically, '*Takshaka*' appears in the list of the *Nāgā* kings. See *J. R. A. S.* January 1894, p. 91.

[4] *Rep. Arch. Sur.* ii. 9.

fused with and improved some of the existing Panjāb castes whose origin is now unknown. The Hindu tradition based on Vedic allusions, is that the Yādavā (sons of Yadu) occupied Sindh, and the Ānavā (sons of Anu) settled in the Panjāb.[1] The former tradition is no doubt confirmed as regards Sindh and Western India, but the latter is doubtful. Puranic tradition, however, suggests some early return of Yādavā (Bhātī) chiefs from Sindh, and some other settlements in the Northern Panjāb and in the Jālandhar Doāb.[2] It would seem that even in Alexander's time such a reflex movement had already begun, and that an Aryan prince with his followers, returning from the East country, had formed a petty kingdom in the North-western Panjāb; for 'Porus' is a name which it seems most natural to connect with '*Pauravā*,' or one of the race of Puru, a clan which we first hear of settled near the Jamnā.

The Panjāb, however, owes a great deal, from an ethnographical point of view, to the Northern or 'Indo-Scythian' incursions already mentioned. The invasion of *circa* 515 B.C., in the time of Darius Hystaspes, was the important one which, according to Cunningham brought the tribes of *Kāthī* (Kathæi of the Greek writers), the *Ghakar* (still found in the North-western Panjāb), as well as the *Bālā*. It is also quite possible that some of the *Jat* races may have come in with an earlier (pre-Macedonian) invasion, although the bulk of their settlements are attributed rather to the later incursions—connected with the names of

[1] It is clear that General Cunningham's suggestion about the existing Āwān clans as possibly representing the Ānavā is difficult to accept. See Thomson, *Jihlam S. R.* 1883, p. 29; D. Ibbetson, *Ethnography of the Panjāb*, § 454. It has been also suggested that the *Janjhūā* or *Jhanjuā* (the spelling is uncertain) are Yādus. But this also is hardly tenable. They are Rājputs no doubt, but claim to be of the *Rāhtor* clan from Mewār. For some details as to the Puranic stories see *Rep. Arch. Sur.* ii. 14-16, 20; and see further p. 129, *post*.

[2] It may be asked how, if the Panjāb was 'impure,' Aryan chiefs of high caste, and afterwards Brahmans, would settle there. But such a prohibition would become forgotten in the course of time: the Brahmans were great wanderers and everywhere sought to extend their influence, while soldiers of fortune would hardly seriously regard the existence of such a ceremonial obstacle.

Kadphises, Kanerki, and the rest. The existence of such early Jat settlements is suggested by the mention of Alexander's meeting with tribes which had a government by councils of elders. But it is quite possible that various early 'Scythic' races may have had similar characteristics.[1]

The *Kāthī* have left their descendants, still holding villages in the Panjāb; and they extended to Upper Western India, where the province, now divided into a large number of petty chiefships, called *Kāthīāwār*, derives its name from them. They have now merged into the Rājput race generally, owing to long contact with the Aryan races from Mālwā and the neighbourhood; but their strikingly non-Aryan customs are described by Colonel Tod.[2] They were numerous enough in Alexander's time to resist the joint armies of Porus and 'Abisares'—the latter being reasonably identified as the ruler of *Abhisāra*, the then Ghakar dominion (modern Hazāra district).[3] This introduces the *Ghakar*, of whom it may be mentioned that they still hold a number of villages with much pride of origin, in the Northern Panjāb.[4]

In the Southern Panjāb the Greek historians mention the Malli and Oxydrakæ (Sudrakæ of Curtius), who also appear in the Mahābhāratā as the *Kshudraka—Mallava* (coupled together).[5] These tribes seem also connected with the northern invasions, since the Malli, who had their capital at or near Multān

[1] See *Historical Researches into the Politics &c. of the Principal Nations of Antiquity*, A. H. Heeren, vol. i. 'The Persians' (translated from the German. Oxford: Talboys, 1833, p. 310). 'When Alexander crossed the Chināb (Acesines) he fell in with other nations not living under princes but possessing a republican constitution. These Indian republics occurred in the country between the Acesines and Hyphasis (Chināb and Biās Rivers) or on the east of the province of Lahore.' The allusion, as the late Sir G. Campbell pointed out, was to the tribes, with their *panchayats* or committees of elders, such as managed Jat communities till quite recent times, and are even now by no means extinct.

[2] Tod, i. 101.

[3] *Rep. Arch. Sur.* ii. 35.

[4] There is a good *résumé* of the *Ghakar*, or *Gakkar*, history in Hunter's *Indian Empire*, 3rd ed. p. 234 ff.

[5] *The Invasion of India by Alexander* (McCrindle, p. 350, Appendix). The connection suggested of Kshudraka with Sudra (*Çūdra*) is hardly admissible.

(*Mallāsthāna*), were sun-worshippers like the Kāthī and the Bālā.[1]

A large part of our present population is, however, connected with the JAT race, and on this some remarks must be made, leaving it an open question whether our Jat communities are in general pre-Macedonian, or whether they belong to the later invasions closer to the commencement of the Christian era.

In the plains of the Panjāb these races are numerous from the Indus to the south-eastern districts. Jats are found in Sindh and also in Gangetic India and Rājputāna. They are now divided into very numerous clans, different in different parts of India. Their physical appearance and general characteristics are locally various;[2] and the generic name varies from *Jat* in the Panjāb to *Jāt* in the South-eastern Panjāb and the North-West Provinces. But although it may be said that the term 'Jat' has come rather to represent a heterogeneous class of agriculturists than anything else, it can hardly be denied that there is a real nucleus of northern tribes of distinct origin.

As far as it concerns us, for the purposes of this book, to express any opinion as to what the Jats or Jāts really are, so much may be safely said: (*a*) that the existing clans are often of mixed or altered race; that they have largely intermingled (in the long course of time) with the Aryan races, and that there is no doubt that the many *gentes* and clans are, on one side, of Rājput ancestry. Traditions about a clan springing from a Rājput who married a Jat wife, or of the ancestor being a Rājput who lost caste by eating with Jats, or adopting some custom contrary to

[1] Cunningham, *Ancient Geography*, 235, 237, and *Rep. Arch. Sur.* ii. 34. 'We know that both the *Bālā* and the *Kāthī* of the present day pay special adoration to the sun, which was the chief deity of Multān from the earliest times down to the reign of Aurangzeb, by whose order the idol is said to have been destroyed.' See also G. Oppert, pp. 78, 82, who refers to Sir H. M. Elliot's *History of India*, i. 23, 27, 35, 82, 205, 469.

[2] The names of the chief Panjāb Jat clans do not appear much, if at all, in the literature of other provinces: the Central Panjāb Jat differs much from the Sindhi Jat, and he again from the Jāt of the South-eastern Panjāb and North West Provinces. On the general subject reference may be made to Tod, i. 92; Ibbetson, *Ethnography of the Panjāb*, pp. 219 ff; *Rep. Arch. Sur.* ii. 43 ff, and Beames' *Elliot's Glossary*, i. 130.

his own rule, are too persistent and generally believed, to be devoid of truth.[1] (*b*) It is also the case that a long lapse of time and differences of climate have gradually produced wide differences among the Jats themselves, both in physique and dialect; this accounts for the dissimilarity between the Jat of Rājputāna, *e.g.*, and the Jat of the Panjāb central districts and the Jat of Sindh. But the existence of such changes shows that many generations must have elapsed, and hence it is highly probable that the first origins of the Jat clans may be dated back to the invasions of so-called 'Indo-Scythians' at the period mentioned by Sir A. Cunningham. And it is also apparent that while many of the Jats may be settled in or near the districts where they first obtained a footing—viz. in the Panjāb plains and eastwards as far as the Jamnā and the Doāb districts of the North-West Provinces, and southward to Rājputāna, it is also true that, not unfrequently, the Panjāb Jat clans in their present location represent the reflex movements of small portions of clans whose main body first settled further east or south. The suggestion that Jats and Rājputs are all one race, and that the Rājput only represents the upper or ruling families and princes of a common stock, appears to me untenable as far as *origins* are concerned, though it has *become* practically true to a considerable extent. It is certainly the case that a Rājput might sink to be a Jat by widow marriage, or by taking to agriculture under certain conditions; but the difference between the customs of the races, as well as the course of their history, shows that

[1] For an example see *Rep. Arch. Sur.* ii. 11 (on the authority of Colonel Tod), where a Bhāti becomes a Jat in consequence of eating with a Tāk or Takā chief. In the Gujrānwāla district we have many instances of clan names common to both Jat and Rājput. Such cases are also widespread: *e.g.* in the Muzaffargarh district (Southern Panjāb), Mr. O'Brien (*S. R.* p. 55), remarks: 'There is not a Jat in this district who has any knowledge, real or fancied, of his ancestors, that would not say he was once a Rājput. Certain Jat tribes . . . have names and traditions which seem to connect them more closely with "Hindustān." Some bear the Rājput title of *Rāi*, and others, as the *Saigal* and *Khairā*, though Muhammadans, associate a Brahman with the "mullā" at marriage ceremonies; while the *Puñwār*, *Parīhār*, *Bhatti*, *Joyā*, and others, bear names of well-known tribes of Rājputāna.' See also some excellent remarks in the *Rohtak S.R.* p. 20, and *Karnāl S.R.* § 195.

the progenitors of the pure Rājput clans were in India before the Jat, and that the two races were originally distinct. Nor have we any instance of a man known to be a Jat by birth raising himself (or being raised) to Rājput caste. There are two Jāt States in Rājputāna (Bhartpur and Dholpur), but they are not of Rājput rank.[1] Throughout history the Jats appear in bodies and perfectly distinct from the Hindu Rājputs; they are often in conflict with them, and, not without success, with the earlier Muhammadan emperors.

A very similar account may be given of the GŪJAR or GUJAR.[2] They are not nearly so numerous as the Jats, ranking only eighth, I think, in the list of castes as regards numerical superiority. They also seem to have a distinct tribal origin, but to have largely mingled with Rājput and other families. They must have used the Western or Indus Valley route, as well as the direct route to the Panjāb plains, as they are found not only in the Indus Valley, but in Upper Western India. There is no trace of them in the province of Bombay called Gujarāt (the Gurjarāshtra of the Sanskrit writers); but they are found in the Nāgpur districts (where Sir R. Jenkins says they claimed 'Rājput' descent); they were noticed by Dixon in Merwāra, and they are found in the Narbadā Valley and also in Northern Bundelkhand. There is a small independent State—Sāmptar, still ruled by a Gujar chief.[3] They are most numerous in the plains of the Panjāb, giving their names to the two districts of Gujrāt and Gujrānwālā.[4] They also extended to Delhi and beyond; for we find that the Upper Doāb and Rohilkhand

[1] This may seem to conflict with what is elsewhere said about some ancient royal families in the Central Provinces, Orissa, &c., being in time recognised as Rājput; but the Jat is much more modern and more distinct in race than these were, and the 'royal' families, besides being of ancient race, were always 'royal.'

[2] The word Gujar is possibly the Northern 'Tokhar' (Τόχαροι) softened into a Sanskritic form as Tusara and then Gujara. The Gujar period is connected with the names on coins familiar to collectors—Kadphises, Kanerki, Huvishka, Vonones, &c.

[3] Beames' *Elliot's Glossary*, i. 101; *Imp. Gazetteer*, s.v. 'Sāmthar.'

[4] Their location in juxtaposition with the Jat clans is curiously illustrated by the Tribal Map of the Gujrāt district given in *L. S. B. I.* ii. 670.

districts of the North-West Provinces contain many of them. So much so that one part of the Sahāranpur district was actually called 'Gujrāt' (during the last century.) Reckoning up the clans or divisions known in different parts of the country, eighty-four names are given in *Elliot's Glossary.*

To this notice of the later Jat and Gujar tribes it must be added that the frontier population has been reinforced by Pathān and Bilūchī tribes, of which more specific notice will be taken in the sequel. There are, of course, a number of other tribes, like the *Āwān*, *Kharral*, &c., which are chiefly local, and the humbler but more ubiquitous *Arāīn*, which it is difficult to classify under any head. Certain limited colonies of Mughals, Afghāns, Pathāns, &c., are due to the later Muhammadan invasions, but as a rule the bulk of the Muhammadan agricultural tribes are converts.

To summarise briefly the whole question, it may be said that, whatever early Aryan clans may have settled in the Panjāb, they were 'non-Brahmanical,' and would not long have remained distinct. There were also local Aryan kingdoms, and later settlements of Rājputs. The country was also overrun by later Northern or Indo-Scythian tribes, and was afterwards directly affected both by the earlier and later Moslem conquests. These considerations combine to explain why the strict Hindu element is comparatively slight in the Panjāb (beyond the towns), and that apart from the fact that so many clans became Muhammadan and others Sikh. Indeed, the very fact of such conversions shows how little any Brahmanical system had taken hold on the country at any early date. In the Panjāb plains there are no ancient Brahmanical monuments.[1] The Hindu law of the books is unknown, and to this day local customs of various kinds, sometimes quite

[1] Brahmanic temples of some antiquity may be found in the hill districts of the Himalaya and their vicinity, as, *e.g.*, in Kāngrā and Chambā. But I am not aware that any are so old that they must be dated back to any Aryan settlements prior to those which occurred when the Moslem conquest began to disturb the Hindu kingdoms of the plains and drive the princes to the hills for refuge. There are some vestiges of traditionally *ancient* Aryan families in the Kāngrā Hills, as will be afterwards noted.

opposed to the later Hindu ideals, are in vogue. When I say that the Hindu law is not followed, I should perhaps except town families or others whose rank or dignity of caste suggests that they should acknowledge it at least nominally. Brahmans have now everywhere secured a certain amount of respect; but where the Jat and other tribes may be called 'Hindu' it is chiefly with the meaning that they are not Sikh or Moslem.

The foregoing remarks on the elements of the Panjāb population are illustrated by the general *data* as tabulated in 1881 by Mr. Ibbetson. The chief land-owning, tenant, and cultivating, classes are thus grouped—*per mille* of the total population, including the Native States :—

1. Bilūch and Pathān tribes	56	
2. Jat	195	
3. Rājput	81	
4. Minor dominant tribes	67	(including Gujar)
5. Minor cultivating tribes	89	
6. Foreign races	21	

These six heads require a few words of explanation. No. 1 consists of the Trans-Indus (Frontier) tribes. No. 2 includes Jats of all kinds, including those so called who are tenants in the districts where Rājput and other dominant castes are land-owners. The Jats as village owners predominate in the Sikh States, in the South-eastern Panjāb, and in parts of the central districts. In the sub-montane districts like Kāngrā and the North Panjāb (Salt Range tract), Rājputs and the 'minor dominant tribes' take the place of Jats. The Rāthi and Thakkar of the Hill districts are classed with Rājputs, and the Kanet and Girth with the 'minor cultivating tribes.' The head No. 4 includes the smaller local tribes with pretensions to rank, such as the Ghakar, Āwān, Khattar of the Salt Range tract, the Dāūdputra, Kharral, and Khokar of the Western Plains, the Dogar, Ror, and Meo of the East; and the Gujar more generally distributed. No. 5 includes lesser tribes who are small owners, or tenants, &c., as Saīnī, Arāīñ, Ahīr, Mahtam. Head No. 6 consists of Shekh, Mughal, Tūrk, &c.

(2) *The Population of the Ganges Plain*

I have dwelt at some length on the Panjāb, because this province is the starting-point, so to speak, of the travels of so many immigrant tribes, and of the enterprises of conquering princes and their armies. When we proceed to the districts east of the Jamnā—to the Ganges Doāb, to Oudh, and further still to Bihār, Bengal,[1] and Western Assam, we find Aryan and mixed Aryan races in greater abundance, and the whole country at one time or another covered by a network of Aryan kingdoms and chiefships. Jats and Gujars, as I have said, are found in the upper districts of the Ganges Doāb and as far as Rājputāna. Some races, like the Ahīr and Kunbī, have evidently emigrated to these parts from Central India or Gujarāt; while there is a great number of mixed castes whose origin is largely aboriginal. Sir H. M. Elliot's work as supplemented in Mr. J. Beames' edition, is still the central authority about the castes and races of the North-West Provinces, and is easily accessible. Mr. Risley's elaborate volumes on the Tribes and Castes of Bengal are even fuller of detail. Both these works render anything more than a brief notice of certain features affecting the land-holding interest unnecessary. The main point is to notice how the original population was dominated by the superior Aryan tribes; how the Aryan chiefs afterwards suffered eclipse and the original races recovered possession, but only again to lose it finally, before the re-distribution or new location of the Aryan (Rājput) clans and chiefs which dates from the twelfth century onwards.

The Brahman tradition of the first Aryan kingdoms is so far noteworthy that it suggests no settlement of a vast population *en*

[1] The 'Ganges Plain' includes the North-West Provinces and Oudh, as well as Bengal. The 'North-West Provinces,' besides the hill districts of Kumāon, &c., contains the Rohilkhand tract (immediately east of the Ganges, and between the river and the Oudh frontier), the Ganges Doāb, Benares, and, to the south, Bundelkhand. Bengal includes a small portion of hill and sub-montane territory (Darjeeling and the West Dwārs); the northern districts (adjoining the North-West Provinces) are called Bihār, and the rest is Bengal Proper, with Orissa and Chutiyā-Nāgpur to the south-west.

masse : it represents a series of powerful princes, with their dependent chiefs and armies, establishing a series of local rulerships, and building capitals, some of fabulous extent and grandeur. Both 'Solar' and 'Lunar' princes appear as founding kingdoms ; the 'Solar' seem to have been always in favour of the Brahmans, the 'Lunar' not unfrequently became Buddhists. The 'Solar' princes of the House of Rāma, founded *Ayodhya* (in Oudh) and afterwards *Mithilā* (=Tirhūt in Bihār), also another kingdom, *Vaiçali*, near Patnā. The 'Lunar' princes are represented as descendants from Yayātī, who also is the mythical ancestor of the *Yādava*, &c., but in a separate branch, that of Puru. These founded the kingdom of *Pañcāla*, which extended north-west of Delhi, from the mountains to the Chambal River. *Hastīnapurā* was around Meerut (Mīrath), and adjoined *Indraprasthā*, the kingdom of Delhi. These two kingdoms, celebrated in the Mahabhārāta, were held, the former by *Kaurava* princes, the latter by *Pāṇḍu*. In the course of time other dynasties arose and kingdoms were formed, united, separated, and again aggregated under suzerains, in a manner which it is difficult to follow. Kanauj,[1] became a great centre of rule, and seems always to have been a stronghold of Brahmanism. We are now assured that Buddhism was not put down wholesale by the sword ; that the two creeds continued side by side, and that Brahmanism ultimately triumphed over its rival in a peaceful manner. However that may be, the Aryan kingdoms were for ever fighting with each other, and Buddhist or Jain princes are generally found arrayed against Brahmanist.

These various kingdoms were not established in a wilderness, nor were they peopled entirely by Aryans. Both in the hills, and in the sub-montane tracts in the Ganges Valley, a pre-Aryan or non-Aryan population is abundantly in evidence. Throughout the hills and extending to the *Tarāi* or moist districts at the foot of the ranges, we find races of Mongoloid connection. The *Khasā* or *Khasiya*, and *Ḍom*, are prominent, and we hear of the *Thaṭera*, and further east *Dhimal*, and some others such as *Bhoksā*, *Thāru*, of less certain origin. The mixed castes or races of the hills as far as Naipāl (just as in the States of Simla

[1] On the Ganges, in the modern Farūkhābād district.

and Kāngrā) are in all probability connected with this stock; in other words, we have a gradation of races from the tolerably pure Aryan down to the wholly aboriginal.[1] The *Ḍom* are now in a very humble position, but once they ruled over or possessed wide tracts at the foot of the mountains. Mr. Benett mentions in his *Gondā S. R.* (North Oudh) that villages still exist deriving their titles to land from grants of *Ḍom* princes.

Further down on the plains we find almost all parts of the Ganges Valley abounding in traces of the once numerous tribes called *Bhaṛ* and along with them the *Soirī* or *Suvirī* (the spelling is very various), and still further east the *Çerū*.

As to the *Bhaṛ* (often written Bhār, but the former, written with the 'burring' *ṛ*, appears more correct),[2] Dr. G. Oppert says that 'legend associates their name with the earliest Aryan heroes, *e.g.* with *Rāma* and his sons; but the *Bhaṛs* suddenly disappear from the scene, and, as far as history is concerned, reappear just previously to the Muhammadan invasion of India, at which period they certainly possessed a vast territory and were indeed the real owners of the soil. In fact, the *Bhaṛs* must have ruled over a great area of country stretching from Oudh in the west to Bihār in the east, and southwards to Chutiyā-Nāgpur, Bundelkhand, and Sāgar.'[3]

[1] See p. 86 ff. *ante* for some remarks on the quality of the mixed races in the Hills.

[2] See G. Oppert, p. 38, and authorities quoted. General Sir A. Cunningham remarks that the '*ṛ*' was characteristic of the non-Aryan races, and the Aryans in ridicule called them *barbara*, which in the Hindustani dialect is written *baṛbaṛ*. The nasal '*ñ*,' so commonly introduced into Panjābi words, is another feature attributed to a non-Aryan element.

[3] G. Oppert, p. 39. General Cunningham (*Rep. Arch. Sur.* xi. p. 67) throws doubt on the reality of some of the asserted *Bhaṛ* remains (forts, tanks, &c.) He says, though without offering any proof, that the *Bhaṛ* were an uncivilised race. As to names of places involving *Bar* or *Bhaṛ*, there is much room for difference of interpretation; though such names as *Bharaich* and *Barelī* (or *Bharelī*) are incontestable as referring to the tribe. But the existence and power of the *Bhaṛ* is too well attested to be affected by any individual case or cases. I would, also, not lay undue stress on the existence, in so many parts of Oudh and the North-West Provinces, of forts and other buildings ascribed by tradition to the *Bhaṛ*. Some of them may be due in reality to other early kingdoms. But

It is probable that the *Bhaṛ* tribes (especially in later times) became more or less 'Hinduised,' and that there was much fusion with early Aryan clans; but the tribes evidently represent, in the main, what we may fairly conclude to have been an original pre-Aryan population; and of their considerable number there can be no doubt. Thus in the *Gazetteer* of the Benares district we find it noted: 'The traditions of the whole province represent the *Bhaṛ* as once dominant from the Tarāi of Naipāl to the hills of Sāgar in the Central Provinces;'[1] and again in Ghāzipur (a district on the confines of Bihār) Mr. Wilton Oldham remarks: 'The testimony of tradition that the middle Ganges Valley was formerly occupied by non-Aryan aboriginal races is the evidence, not of one, but of a hundred concurrent traditions of all land-owning tribes in the Benares province, in Oudh, and in Bihār. The evidence is confirmed by the fact that in Shāhābād the *Bhaṛ* have up to the present day retained a portion of their vast domains. The *taluqa* of Koinda, an extensive tract in the Vindhyan Hills on the borders of the Mirzapur district, belongs to a clan of *Bhaṛ*; and their headman a few years since—Rāmbadan Singh—was a man of considerable wealth and influence. . . .'[2]

The following notice is extracted[3] from the *Mirzapur District Gazetteer*. After speaking of the *Bhaṛ* tribes as very numerous and their remains as everywhere to be found, the writer says: 'The *tanks* are specially numerous. . . . Mr. Duthoit in his memoir of *pargana* Bhaḍohī, says it is hardly possible to travel three miles in any direction without meeting examples of these, which are always to be distinguished from later works by the fact that they are *sūrajbedī*—*i.e.* having their longer diameter from east to west, while Hindu work is invariably *çandrabedī*, or with the longer diameter north and south. On the south side

there is certainly a disposition to call the *Bhaṛ* an 'uncivilised race' on very little evidence. Civilisation is a relative term, and very ancient people may be 'civilised'—for their time and place. The race that had kings and chiefs and that certainly left the remains of *some* great buildings and irrigation works, and that is mentioned in history so often, cannot have been altogether barbarous, nor do I see much indication that it differed from the Aryan in point of material progress.

[1] *N.-W. P. Gazetteer*, xiv. 102.

[2] *Memoir of the Ghāzipur District*, p. 47 (Allahābād Gov. Press, 1870).

[3] *N.-W. P. Gazetteer*, xiv. 115 ff.

of the Ganges also, the *Bhaṛ* have left wide-spread traces of ancient supremacy. Their chief city appears to have been on the Ganges bank some five miles to the west of the present city of Mirzapur. . . . This city, of which the traditional name is Pampāpura, was evidently of great extent.' The author goes on to notice the sculptures which are believed by Sherring to represent the *Bhaṛ* Rājās, 'with their peculiar headdresses and their pointed beards. . . .'

But the *Bhaṛ* were not the only aboriginal tribe which found a home in Mirzapur. In the hills and jungles of the east and south are found *Çeru*, *Seorī*, *Kol*, and *Kharwār*. The *Çeru* are now fallen, and insignificant in number, but they claim to be of Nāgā race. As to the *Seorī*, 'their traditions tell of wide dominions in Shāhābād and Ghāzipur and the adjacent parts of this (Mirzapur) district. The memory of a great conflict between them and the *Çeru*, and their final victory and the occupation of the lands of the vanquished, still lives.' The *Kharwār* are also described, and the remains (including archaic sculptures) of a great city, the capital, are alluded to.

I could multiply quotations relating to all the districts of the Agra and Allāhābād divisions as to the *Bhaṛ*; and they are still frequently mentioned in conjunction with the *Seorī* and the *Çeru*.[1]

[1] I will not attempt to discuss the question whether the *Bhaṛ* is connected with the *Bhārata* of Sanskrit writers. Dr. G. Oppert thinks the identity highly probable (see the story of the race in his book, *The Original Inhabitants of India*, p. 587 ff.). The *Bhārata* are first mentioned in the Veda (*Ṛgveda*, 3. 53. 13 and 7. 33. 6): they are a people who 'come from afar'; they fight the *Tṛtsu* tribe under *Vasishtha*; being defeated, they return eastward across the Biās and Sutlej rivers. *Viçwamitra*, the priest and bard attached to this tribe, is himself probably an Aryan, as he is the author of one of the hymns of the *Ṛgveda*. He is represented as the son of *Kuçika* (p. 590–1), and the tribe called by this name are in close relationship with the *Bhārata* (Zimmer, p. 128). He is also leader of the people, and his *gayātri*, or hymn, secures their well-being. It is this people who afterwards establish a kingdom in Magadhā. *Viçwamitra* is at first in favour with the *Tṛtsu* and their king *Sudās*, to whom, for a time, he acts as bard and priest; but a bitter quarrel ensues, and he withdraws with the *Bhārata*, and the end is the battle above alluded to. If the *Bhārata* were of non-Aryan origin they probably early adopted many Aryan customs. 'Being very numerous,' the *Harivaṁsa* says, 'they acquired great influence.' It is noteworthy that in *Ṛgveda*, 7. 33. 6, they are

I have not space to say anything of the less prominent races such as the *Āhīr*,[1] the *Gaur*, and the *Thaṭera*. In the Hardoi district of Oudh and elsewhere, I find mention of a tribe called *Pasī*, who are stated to have owned in former days an extensive domain, and who are still numerous in the district.

The *Çeru* mentioned above were a very important people further east. They dominated Bengal; and as late as the time of the Bengal sovereign Sher Shāh (*post* 1537 A.D.) we find that monarch rejoicing that his general had defeated the *Çeru* chief of Bihār.[2]

The *Çeru* belong, indeed, more to Bihār than to Oudh and the North-West Provinces, and the mention of them naturally carries us further east. Here (Upper Bengal) the population seems to have less and less of the Aryan element; the greater part of the

described by the epithet *arbhakāsah*, which Muir (*A. S. T.* i. 320) translates 'contemptible.' Zimmer (p. 128) uses the more equivocal term '*winzigen*.' Professor Macdonell informs me that the word in Sanskrit means 'puny, small.' Whether this can be taken in a literal sense to describe a stature different from that of the Aryan tribes, or is merely a term applied by victors to a conquered enemy, I cannot pretend to determine. As usual, in the later Epics, tradition found for them an Aryan origin. *Bhārata* is now a king, and the son of *Viçwamitra's* daughter *Sakuntalā*. *Viçwamitra* himself, is, however, curiously connected with the aboriginal, or mixed, races by the legend that makes his sons, owing to a curse, the progenitors of the mixed or non-Aryan races *Āndhra*, *Puṇḍra*, *Sābara*, *Pulinda*, and *Mūtiba* (*Aitareya Brāhmana*, quoted by G. Oppert, pp. 592, 593). The *Mahābhāratā* represents King *Bhārata* as conqueror of all the races of *Kirāta*, *Hūna*, *Yāvana*, *Āndhra*, *Khaçā* and *Saka*—all these including northern, mixed, and non-Aryan tribes (see Lassen, ii. App. xxiv.).

[1] The *Āhīr* seem to have a wide distribution. They occur in the South-eastern Panjāb, and in the North-West Provinces in the districts of Budāon and Murādābād (*S.R. Murādābād*, pp. 8, 9). In Mainpuri (*Gazetteer, North-West Provinces*, iv. 558) they are so numerous as to form 16·8 per cent. of the population. They are found again in the Central Provinces, which make it possible they were the *Abhīra* of Sanskrit books, and connected with the Abhiria country of Ptolemy, on the western side of India (McCrindle's *Ptolemy*, p. 140). They are divided into *Āhīr* and *Āher*, and into many minor subdivisions, some claiming, as usual, Rājput and sometimes Brahman, connection. Others assert a 'Yādu' origin, which is likely enough if their original home was Upper Western India.

[2] Beames' *Elliot's Glossary*, i. 59, s.v. *Çeru*; G. Oppert, p. 39.

peasant class is, in fact, almost purely 'aboriginal.' In the north-east of Bengal the tribes are probably much connected with the Tibetan stock and with some of those branches of it that peopled Assam. The *Kūçch* (or *Koçh*) have left a relic of their existence in the name of the Native State Kuch-Bihār. In the eastern districts, up to the sea-board, the *Magh* tribes, probably indicated by the Macco-Kalingae of the geographers, gave their name to the kingdom or country of Magadhā.[1]

These facts tend to show how small an element numerically the Aryan really was; but it was the ruling power. It is evident that while the mass of the existing population is largely aboriginal in its character, nevertheless the whole of Bengal came under the dominion of Aryan princes. Indeed, in the course of time, these became sufficiently powerful, and by means of their command of the Ganges mouths, to send out expeditions by sea, as I have already mentioned.

The country of Chutiyā-Nāgpur, in South-western Bengal, is full of interest ethnologically; and so is the hill country of Orissa, with the adjoining Tributary States; for here is the refuge ground of both Kolarian and Dravidian tribes. In Chutiyā-Nāgpur the plateau land is culturable and adapted to fixed village settlements; [2] so here we can still find the original form of village in survival. The non-Aryan races are represented by the *Urāoñ*, who overcame the (Kolarian) *Ho* and *Mundā* tribes, and who gave their name to Orissa long before the conquests of the Hindu Gajapati kings.[3]

[1] In the *Laws of Manu*, 'Magadhā' is one of the mixed *races* mentioned in Chapter X. This country, afterwards so celebrated, was very early the seat of an Aryan kingdom or overlordship. The old accounts are not easy to reconcile. Some relate that a kingdom was founded by the (Solar) *Kuçika*, descendants of *Kuça*; the Mahābhāratā speaks of a Lunar origin, or *Yādava*, if they are to be reckoned as separate, and has much to say of King Jārasandhā, who is probably a real person. Possibly, as tradition also gives Solar princes to the first kingdoms of Mithilā and Vaiçālī in this neighbourhood, there may have been some early Solar prince overthrown by the other race. Certainly Magadhā became a centre of Buddhism and was the kingdom of Çandragupta, the Sandracottus of the Western historians.

[2] See *ante*, p. 47.

[3] The distinctness of the *Urāoñ* from the *Mundā*, &c., is recognised by Dalton (G. Oppert, p. 122). See also Risley, *T. and C. of Bengal*, ii. Glossary,

SECTION III.—INDIA SOUTH OF THE VINDHYAN RANGES

(1) *The Population of Upper Western and Central India*

It will be remembered that in speaking of the Vindhyan Hills as a barrier between Upper India and the South, we noticed how, at the western end, the upper barrier ceased, and through the second or south range also a route was open, so that access could be had to the plains of Gujarāt, and thence easily to the Narbadā and Taptī Valleys and to Berār. There can be no doubt that this route was used in early immigrations from the Indus Valley and the west frontier, just as it was afterwards when Sultan Mahmūd of Ghaznī swept down on Somnāth. The population of Upper Western India, Berār, and part of the Central Provinces exhibits a considerable mixture with Aryan or other Northern races which affected both physical appearance and language. Owing to this admixture, the people of the West are very different from the more purely Dravidian races of the South; and it is, therefore, a matter of convenience to give them a brief separate consideration. Moreover, it is to be remembered that, access being from the Indus Valley by the desert and Kaçch, the immigration was very probably sustained by Northern or 'Scythic' races like the Kāthī, as well as by tribes who had the religion and language of the Vedas. And while one at least of the tribes named in the Vedas (the *Yādavā*) is prominent in the traditions both in Sindh and in the West of India, it is remembered that they belonged to the 'non-Brahmanical' section.[1] Brahmanic caste and religious ideas were not introduced till long after the

138. As to the Dravidian element in the language of Orissa, though it has been much obscured by the Sanskritic element, it is distinctly traceable (see Caldwell, p. 40 and Appendix). The history of Orissa before the Aryan rule is an absolute blank; for the earliest writers of the temple records were Brahmans, and they, of course, would not care to preserve the memory of real ancient historic events, still less to notice a non-Aryan people, even if the materials then existed. Neither the Hindus nor the Moslems, nor later still the Marāthās, really had any hold on Orissa beyond the level rice-plains which could yield a revenue.

[1] *Ante*, pp. 80–1.

Aryan settlements east of the Jamnā were in an advanced stage of development.[1]

In nearly every case tradition ascribes the Western ruling castes (that have evidently resulted from a mixture of races) either to *Yādavā* origin or to some evidently 'Scythian' or Northern serpent-worshipping stock. Most of the princely houses that conquered and ruled in these parts in the earlier days are connected with the name of *Yādu*. The *Sāmā* who reigned in Sindh, the *Jhaṛeja* (or *Jaḍeja*) and their kindred the *Bhāṭī* (who afterwards made a settlement in the Panjāb, where they are called *Bhattī*), are all *Jāduñ* (to use the dialectic form). To this day many Marāthā chiefs claim descent from '*Jadu*.' The *Haihaya* (or *Haibansī*), who are among the very earliest of so-called Aryan rulers in the Narbadā Valley, are said to belong to this race.[2]

It is impossible to find any more definite traces of the early non-Brahmanic Aryans. It is highly probable that a number of the best races—*e.g.* those collectively called '*Marāthā*' were the result of a fusion of Aryan and Dravidian blood. And the same may be true of the *Kunbi* caste, and the *Ahīr*, as will presently

[1] And so the Marāthī language was probably not developed in its present form till later times, as it is said to be 'particularly Brahmanic in all its elements and connected with *later* Sanskrit (*Indian Census of* 1891, Parliamentary Report, J. A. Baines, p. 141). The Marāthā Brahmans are a class apart—just as the Draviṛa Brahmans or the Gauṛ Brahmans are elsewhere—all missionary immigrants from Upper India. It is curious, as noted by Grant Duff (*History of the Mahrattas*, i. 25), that while the Marāthā people have great veneration for the hermit and the ascetic, they have very little for the Brahmans as a class. The limits of the Sanskritic speech, as judged by linguistic evidence, are given in some detail by Professor Christian Lassen (i. 423). But it must be borne in mind that this includes the results of the later Brahmanic influence. Along the west coast, southward, an Aryan element in the speech is discerned as far as Gokarnā in North Kānarā; while for the inland Marāthā country, a line drawn from Pūnā eastwards up to the Central Provinces, and including all the northern part of Bombay, with Gujarāt, Mālwā, &c., would generally mark the limits. Below Pūnā, the dialect varies somewhat, showing a distinct trace of the non-Aryan or original element.

[2] See Tod, i. 36, 78: if they were not really Turanian or Northern tribesmen, which is just as likely. Mr. J. F. Hewitt connects them directly with the '*Nāgbansī*' houses. Sleeman wrote a long article on the *Haihaya* princes of *Garhā-Maṇḍlā* in *J. A. Soc. Bengal*, vi. part ii. 623.

appear. But the population of Western India owes as much to Northern (non-Aryan) races as to any other. Thus one part of the country was anciently called Saurāshtra, after the *Saurā*, or *Çāwarā*, a tribe called 'Rājput,' but neither 'Solar' nor 'Lunar.'[1] Indeed, it is curious that the whole of this region is connected with the royal houses of '*Agnikulā*' descent—*Solankhi* (*Çālukyā*), *Çauhān*, *Pramārā*, &c.—tribes which so often adopted Buddhism and whose traditional birth shows that they were later and probably foreign additions to the true Kshatriyā Aryans.[2]

Other confessedly early Northern tribes established their rule in these districts, though the later conquests of Rājput houses have done much to fuse the races together. Thus, the country still called Kāthiāwār owes its name to the Kāthī. These exhibit Northern customs, such as the worship of the Sun and of Weapons.[3] The Bālā, another Northern tribe, appear also in the West; how far they may be connected with the princely house that founded Bālabhipur I will not attempt to discuss.[4] Before the eighth century we have no real history, but vague traditions of kingdoms and chiefships which disappeared, first before the incursions of later Rājputs from Mālwā and the vicinity, and finally under the effects of the early Moslem conquests.

It is very probably to these early Aryan and Northern races that we owe the presence of an element in Western and Central Indian races which distinguishes them from the Dravidians of the South.

As might be expected, in Western and Central India there are still many remnants of the non-Aryan races in the hill

[1] Forbes, *Rāsmālā*, p. 27.

[2] The tradition was that the ancestors of four tribes sprang from the sacrificial fire (Agni), at Mount Abū; and that they were miraculously born in aid of the Brahmanic cause. This the tribes did not always afterwards maintain. The Pramārā, for instance, founded a Buddhist kingdom in Mālwā; and Chandragupta and Asoka, of the Mauryā house, were notoriously Buddhist (*Central Provinces Gazetteer*, art. Nimār, p. 377).

[3] See Tod (i. 101 ff) for an account of the customs of the Kāthī, and see also the whole passage at p. 60 ff, which is curious. Colonel Tod was by no means critical or reliable as to points of date and history; but on matters of custom and legend where his own personal knowledge and experience are placed on record, his authority is as good as can be desired.

[4] See G. Oppert, p. 78.

country; and some tribes who are perhaps Dravidian slightly mixed with a Northern element. The *Kolī* tribes of the Vindhyan Hills (not to be confused with the Eastern *Ho* and *Mundā* tribes called '*Kol*') need hardly more than a bare mention. The *Bhīl* have already been alluded to, and it may here be added that they have a sort of upper class called *Bhīlāla*, whose persistent tradition is that they have a share of 'Rājput' blood.[1] In the Bombay Dakhan, scattered families of *Mahār* or *Mhār* are still found—the relics of a once numerous people—now chiefly acting as hereditary guardians of village boundaries. This circumstance has led Mr. J. F. Hewitt to suggest that the position is due to their once being associated with the land as its owners. Dr. G. Oppert says that the *Mahār* claim to have been once the ruling race in '*Mahārāshtra*.'[2] More towards the centre of the continent there are groups of non-Aryan tribes, often represented partly by humble agriculturist castes in the plains, or by primitive hill-dwellers, who have either lapsed into, or never emerged from, a half savage state. Among them are found the *Gond* races, who gave their name to *Gondwāna* of the ancient maps. They occupied the whole of the central districts up to Chutiyā-Nāgpur, and Orissa, to the east, and part of Haidarābād to the south.[3] The original *Gond* population can hardly, I think, be doubted to have had some early Northern connection. It is worth while to

[1] Within historical times powerful local chieftains of this class were met with. The Puranic literature even has a legend to account for the origin of the *Bhīl*. (See *Central Provinces Gazetteer*, art. Nimār.)

[2] And if this author's identification can be accepted, it will unite this race, locally called also *Parvārī*, with the *Mālā* and *Malli*, who appear so widely in India, and with the *Paraiyar* (Pariah) of the South (G. Oppert, pp. 21, 22, 31). The *Paraiyar* are called *Mālā* (*vaṇḍlu*) in Telugu (Caldwell, Appendix, p. 543). G. Oppert quotes Dr. J. Wilson as connecting them with the Pōruaroi of Ptolemy.

The Sanskrit writers called the Western Dakhan *Mahārāshtra*, and some have suggested that the name is from *mahā* = great; sc. 'magna regio.' But there seems no reason for such a designation, while 'country of the *Mahār*' would be in every way intelligible.'

The name now commonly used, *Gond*, or rather *Gauḍ* or *Gaunṛ*, is apparently not recognised by the existing relics of the people, who call themselves *Koitūr*. As a class the *Gonds*, in the Central Provinces, are divided into *Rāj-Gond*, who claim to be connected with the former ruling families, and *Dhūr-Gond*, who were the plebeian section.

note that we have no definite tradition even, of Gonds as rulers till quite modern times. But when the Bhoñslā Marāthās attacked Central India, Gond princes were in power. The Marāthā Rājā seized the Gond Rājā's demesne (Nāgpur, &c.), but left the less valuable and outlying districts in the hands of the original subordinate chiefs; it is, in fact, the descendants of these chiefs who still hold the land, some of the greater ones being regarded as Feudatory chiefs, and the minor ones having been recognised as 'Zamīndārs,' or landlords of estates. Besides the Gond we have also some local traditions of *Gāulī* rulers in the central districts, and of *Ahīr* chiefs, a people whose name we have already met with, and who, from the places in which notices of them are found, must have extended from the Indus mouths to the Chambal River and beyond.[1]

Of the modern population it is not necessary to say much. The northern part of the country has received many Hindu emigrants from Mālwā and the north, but only in comparatively late times.[2] The rest is still largely populated by the 'Marāthā' races.[3] I have already suggested that these are really of mixed Dravidian and Aryan origin, and their superior families may be more Aryan than the rest. The originators of the modern Marāthas completely disappear from history; and the race only reappears towards the close of the seventeenth century under Sivājī. This chief himself belonged to the caste or race, also widely distributed, called Kunbī or Kurmī. They are noted agriculturists, and as such have wandered far and wide—to Oudh, and Bengal even, in search of land-holdings. They have now no distinctive language; they are called *Kunbī* in Marāthī, *Kunabī* in the South Marāthā country, *Kumbhī* and *Kurmī* among the people of Hindustan.

[1] See also at p. 109, *ante*, as to the wide distribution of this people.

[2] *Ante*, pp. 44–5.

[3] As to the name of this people or tribe, I have preferred the form above employed to the common term *Mahratta*—*i.e. Marhaṭṭā*—which latter is not recognised by the people themselves, and means in Hindī 'robber,' being an opprobrious epithet applied by the Mughal soldiers. (See also Tod, ii. 420). At one time these races seem to have been called (for instance, in Firishta's *History of the Nizām-Shāhi Kings*) by the name of *Bargī*, or Bhargi. (See Grant Duff's *History of the Mahrattas*, i. 69).

(2) *The Population of Southern India*

Except for the openings at the western end, and to a lesser extent at the eastern end also, the Vindhyan Range served as a complete barrier confining the bulk of the Aryan conquerors, or colonists, to Upper India; it opposed any further advance to the south, at least as regards any considerable number of clans bent on conquest. It was only at a much later time, when the Aryans of Northern India had spread as far as the Ganges mouths, that adventurous princes with their armies made expeditions to Orissa and the northern part of the Telugu country. When we come to the real South—to the Madras Presidency—we are brought face to face with the genuine representatives of an almost purely Dravidian population. At the same time we find the Brahmanic religion and caste well established, and the languages to some extent—very much less than in the North, affected by Sanskritic additions.

The earliest traditions show no sign of any general immigration of Aryan clans. As Dr. Macleane[1] has justly observed, 'The view of the Aryans marching in bodies in this direction or that is supported by no facts of any sort in the case of the country south of the Vindhyans.'

It is, as I have remarked, only in the north-eastern districts that there could have been any communication of a general character with the Aryanised people of Upper India, and that, at such a distance from the Aryan centre, could only have been with people of very mixed blood. The sovereigns of Magadhā at one time extended their suzerainty further south, and other dynasties may have claimed or exercised sway in the north-west of Madras, but that is no proof of any large importation of an Aryan population.[2]

[1] *Manual* (*History*), p. 53. See also Lassen, i. 116, confirming this statement, which is, however, quite indisputable.

[2] From early times, the Upper or Telugu country seems to have been partly peopled or occupied by a race called by a name which Western geographers turned into Kalinga. The Greek geographers speak of a threefold division of this people—the Kalinga, Makko-Kalinga, and the Gangarid-Kalinga. Those living inland were connected with the name *Āndhra*, which occurs in Manu, and still earlier, *e.g.* in the *Aitareyā*

The effects actually produced upon the Southern people and the introduction of caste and religion must have been the result of a gradual intercourse, which had nothing to do with tribal conquest or with a general settlement of the Aryan people. It was effected by the individual, but repeated and cumulative, efforts of the Brahmans. In no field is their peculiar genius better displayed than in this new kind of conquest. They used no force, they did not even displace the local deities; they wove all cults into one general scheme, and made their ideals acceptable to the people, so that in time it became a mark of respectability or superiority to become 'Hindu' and to be 'in caste.' The causes which led to so ready an acceptance of the philosophical and religious teaching, but more especially of the social and ceremonial system which is the essence of Hinduism, are beyond our province: we must be content with saying that this change was effected mainly by the efforts of hermit missionaries, but was also furthered by the admission of Brahman advisers to the Courts of indigenous princes, and possibly by the occasional reception of military (Aryan) chiefs, who were welcomed as organisers of local armies and the like, and would soon establish themselves as lords of estates and territorial chiefships. Such adventurers would naturally have won their way to local rank by the romance attaching to their long adventurous journey so far south, by the mystery of their distant northern home, and by their general prowess and superiority.

Everything in the Madras country points to the existence, from the most ancient times, of numerous, and, considering the age, civilized, groups of non-Aryan races who occupied the more fertile and level portions of the country, leaving, no doubt, wide

Brāhmana. (See Caldwell, Introduction, p. 30.) The Makko-Kalinga were coast people, and probably represent the *Màgh* of Eastern Bengal and Chittagong. The Mauryan kings of Magadhā, deriving origin from one of the *Agnikulā* houses of the royal Rājput stock as reckoned by the bards, nominally ruled as far as Ganjam, since Asoka's edicts are found there in inscriptions. And a later offshoot of this dynasty founded the Āndhra kingdom during the first centuries of our era. This, however, was a military occupation only. Macleane (*History*), p. 132; and see Cunningham's *Ancient Geography*, p. 529, for Hwen Thsang's account of the Telugu country.

stretches of jungle and forest which spread over the north, and covered the hills of the centre and south. Among the jungle-clad hills, tribes, still nomad, would continue to wander, being cut off from the civilising influences to which the people of the arable plains were accessible.

Early legends speak of Āgastyā—the *Tamiẓ-muni*, or sage of the Tamulians—coming as a hermit across the Vindhyan Ranges, and by his power commanding them to bow down till his return. As he never did return (according to the Southern version), the ranges continued to be lower than other mountains to this day.[1] The names for Brahmans—*Ayyār* (fathers) and *Parpār* (overseers)—go some way to indicate the position they held as missionaries and founders of a new order.[2]

When the Brahmanic teaching at last spread widely, a large part of the population adopted Hindu forms, and were of course classed by their teachers as *Çūdra*—the only possible caste on the developed Brahmanic theory;[3] while the bulk of the humbler

[1] For the story of Āgastyā, see G. Oppert, p. 24.

[2] It is remarkable at how early a date the natural genius of the Brahman caste for a hermit life, for the discovery of places of pilgrimage, and for the location of shrines at all points of natural scenic beauty or physical peculiarity, led them to wander all over India. In the Rāmāyana we have a highly coloured picture of the hermits settled in the southern forest beyond the Narbadā River, and of the interruptions they suffered from the forest tribes. 'These base-born wretches implicate the hermits in impure practices and perpetrate the grossest outrages. Changing their shapes and hiding in the thickets adjoining the hermitages, these frightful beings delight in terrifying the devotees. They cast away the sacrificial ladles and vessels, they pollute the cooked oblations, and utterly defile the offerings with blood. These faithless creatures inject frightful sounds into the ears of the faithful and austere eremites. At the times of sacrifice they snatch away the jars, the flowers, the fuel and the sacred grass of these sober-minded men' (Rāmāyana, iii. 1, 15, in Muir's *A. S. T.* part ii. chapter iii. section iv. p. 427). When at last such hermits reached the inhabited parts, their message must have been received with something like awe from the mystery of their origin. Even to the present day, the crowds that any new Jogī, or mysterious ascetic, will draw are quite wonderful.

[3] It is curious to note that in the South the 'Sudra' is spoken of as indicating a somewhat proud superiority, in contradistinction to the 'Pariah,' &c., a feeling quite out of keeping with the degraded position theoretically assigned to the *Çūdra* in Manu. Thus, I remember reading

classes and the remoter tribes were roughly classed as out-caste races—*Paraiyar* and the like.

This original isolation of the Southern people, and the mode of their subsequent conversion to Hinduism, are reflected in the local languages, and in the additions that have been made to the vocabulary. The whole of Southern India, as is well known, is divided between the Telugu-speaking races in the upper part, with Kanarese (language of Karnāta) in the north-west; Tuluva and Malāyālam in the west, and Tamil in the south. The Tamil, Telugu, Kanarese, Tuluva, and Malāyālam are all defined languages originating as branches from a common stock. Tamil in particular has a long history; it has for centuries been divided into a classical and a colloquial dialect, and has both ancient and modern written characters. The extant literature probably does not go back beyond the ninth century of our era; but the facts about the language and its dialects show its antiquity and indicate a considerable degree of civilisation of an archaic type. The Sanskrit had no part in the earlier language, and only added its terms and forms in comparatively later times. The further we go back with the Tamil language, the freer from Sanskrit words we find it.[1] As to the stage of civilisation anciently attained by the Dravidians, Dr. Caldwell has collected evidence, from the existence of pure Tamil names, as to what they were acquainted with. It does not follow that nothing else was known, but certainly agriculture was well understood; and some arts—*e.g.* pottery—had reached a considerable degree of excellence.[2]

From many parts of the country there come indications that at least some of the tribes had a settled monarchical govern-

in some old missionary report the complaint that only 'the Sudras' could make themselves heard by the officials; the humbler classes could get no redress, &c. The distinction may frequently be met with.

[1] All these facts are stated in detail in the Introduction to Caldwell's *Dravidian Grammar*. Dr. Macleane in his *Manual* (i. *Ethnology*, 33–55 and notes) has collected a mass of information. See also Morris's *D. M. of the Godāvari District*, p. 165 ff.

[2] Caldwell's Introduction, p. 117 ff. And it is to be remembered that such proof is by no means exhaustive; for words may once have existed but become lost or superseded by Sanskrit words in the course of time.

ment. This will be further remarked on in speaking of Dravidian customs in the next chapter.[1]

In the remote past there is evidence that some of the now lowly-esteemed Dravidian races were once powerful peoples, divided into numerous clans or divisions each with its own *insignia*; and this alone shows some degree of wealth and even luxury to have existed among them.[2] 'They still cherish,' remarks Dr. G. Oppert, 'as the *Bhaṛ* and *Mhār* do, the memory of former greatness, and regard themselves as the original owners of the soil.' They retain also some curious religious privileges.[3] Their priests, the *Vaḷḷuvar*, are 'probably the representatives of the ruling class of ancient times.'[4]

It would serve no useful purpose to enter into any detail about the different races of the South. What special characteristics some of them had will be noticed when we come to describe the surviving Dravidian customs affecting land. It is here sufficient to observe that the South owes little or nothing to the Aryan element in the matter of land-holding customs. Agricultural villages organised on a distinct plan must have long existed,[5] and there is every reason to believe that the form of villages in which the several families each constitute a separate land-holding unit, but having certain bonds of local union, and kept together under the rule of an hereditary village-chief, was the original Dravidian type, and one which is most nearly and obviously related to a still existing form (of unquestionably

[1] Dr. Macleane (*Manual* [*History*], p. 113), states that 'the Dravidians were a practical people with considerable resources; in matters of Government they were—unless in the very earliest stages—under the monarchical system, with defined areas of country for the exercise of rule.'

[2] As to this, see G. Oppert, pp. 50–57. The note at p. 57 enumerates these tribal emblems; some of them, such as bells of victory, white *chaurī* (fly-flaps), white horse, ivory palankeen, golden pot, &c., indicate wealth and some degree of state.

[3] Cf. *ante*, p. 89, and G. Oppert, p. 54.

[4] Oppert, p. 69. A *Vaḷḷuva kon*, or chief, presided at the ancient assemblies of Malabār when a *Parumāl* or sovereign was elected for the country (the election was then periodical).

[5] Extensive kingdoms, with Courts, and armies, and cities, could hardly go on, or even come into existence, without an efficient provision for the regular cultivation of the soil. And we shall see *village* customs in Dravidian tribes evidently of great antiquity.

Dravidian origin), which has actually survived unchanged in the fastnesses of the Chutiyā-Nāgpur plateaux and in the hills of Orissa. This, however, is a matter the discussion of which belongs to a later stage.

Section IV.—The Present Location of Aryan (Rājput) Land-holding Communities

There is one other subject which it is necessary to deal with before directly inquiring into the different forms of village. That the Aryan communities of land-holders should be confined to Upper India, and should especially be prominent in the Central Ganges Plain, as far as Bihār, is very natural; but it is not so easily understood that the village groups and landlord estates of the Rājput domination or of Brahman possession do not occur in the sites in which the ancient settlements took place according to tradition and literature. Here and there the local belief suggests a settlement which has been more or less undisturbed, but it is rare; and in general the existing tribal and individual villages are the result of later movements—most of them dating back to the Mughal or to the earlier Pathān conquests.

From the earliest times the Aryan clans were subject to internecine feuds and wars, and the spread of Buddhism certainly tended to promote such quarrels. However much these two creeds may have existed side by side, religious differences formed at least the pretext of dynastic wars, and to these we must ascribe that repeated devastation and abandonment of the local kingdoms, and the reversion of cultivated tracts to jungle which is so noticeable a feature in the early legendary history of Upper India. And then came the Moslem invasions from the eleventh century and onwards. At no period did the Aryan princes make really common cause against the invaders; but in general, if they did combine for a time, it was only to break out into hostility again, as soon as the immediate cause of danger passed by. Various tribes were then dispersed, and, driven from the domains directly occupied by the Moslems, they sought new homes in the further parts of Rājputāna.[1] Others took service

[1] The sort of dispersion that followed these local wars and invasions is well pictured by the author of the *Rājputāna Gazetteer* (i. 39), where

under the Emperors, and were encouraged or allowed to return in more scattered parties to the provinces where Aryan kingdoms had once flourished. The Himalayan districts, too, afforded a refuge; for the original petty chiefs of those localities, unable to combine and oppose the Rājput leaders, soon fell before their attack.

The following local quotations, selected out of many, will better illustrate the subject than any further general observations. Take, for example, the Unāo district of OUDH.[1] 'Previous to the dawn of authentic history,' says the writer, 'we find a trace of Rājput dominion. . . . But the *Bisen* alone appear to have had any actual colonies, for they alone have left a distinct trace of the estates they held; the others appear to have merely exerted a nominal sovereignty over the aborigines.' The real colonisers, the writer goes on to say, were the Rājputs, who fled across the Ganges on their defeat by the Muhammadan G͟horī kings (end of the twelfth and early thirteenth centuries), and afterwards, those who, having entered the service of the Delhi Emperors, received grants of land, or took possession as adventurers.

In the northern part of Oudh (Bahraich and Gondā) we have the location of one of the great Buddhist centres. But the cities of Sravastī, Kapīlanagara, and others, perished. When, in A.D. 410, Fa Hian, the Chinese pilgrim, visited the country, Sravasti

he describes how the Rājput clans, ejected from the more fertile homes they had first selected, were pushed into the drier and less valuable parts of the present Rājput States, and into the hilly country around Mālwā above alluded to. 'When the dominant families of a clan lost their dominions in the fertile regions of the North-west, one part of the clan seems to have remained in the conquered country—here obtaining service and the landlordship of scattered villages—while another part, probably the defeated chiefs, kinsmen, and followers, went off westward and carved out another, though much poorer, dominion. . . . Having there made a settlement and built a city of refuge, each clan started on an interminable course of feuds and forays, striving to enlarge its borders at the cost of its neighbour. When the land grew too strait for the support of the chief's family or of the increased clan, a band would assemble under some new leader and go forth to plant itself elsewhere.'

[1] *Oudh Gazetteer*, iii. 452.

was in ruins and the country desolate; and when Hwen Thsang came (640 A.D.), it had still more hopelessly relapsed into forest. Bhaṛ and Thāru tribes[1] resumed possession; and there is some historical evidence that in the eleventh century Sayyad Sālār overthrew the Bhaṛ chief Suhildeo.[2] In A.D. 1226 we find a Moslem chief 'overthrowing the accursed Bhartuh'; and it is not till 1340–1450 that we find *Çhatrī* leaders again establishing their colonies in the country.

In the Gondā district, if early Aryans had ever established themselves, they must have disappeared. Ptolemy, writing in the second century,[3] names the inhabitants Tanganoi, who are apparently the *Tangana* of the Mahābhāratā, where they are mentioned as a tribe bringing a tribute of gold and horses to the King of Hastināpurā. A king, apparently Brahmanical, named Vikramādityā, was then reigning at Sravasti. I have already mentioned how, two centuries later, Sravasti was in ruins. Some attempt was made—traditionally by Sombañsi Rājputs—to colonise, but the cultivation of the district dates from the fourteenth and sixteenth centuries.[4]

Mr. P. Carnegy, whose long residence in Oudh gave him ample opportunities of knowing the facts, has stated not only that the Bhaṛ tribes held all the land in a great part of the cultivated districts, but that even the existing Aryan land-hold-

[1] The *Thāru* here appear as one of the aboriginal tribes; but I should like to call attention to the suggestion (Gorakhpur District *North-West Provinces Gazetteer*, vi. 357), that the Thāru may be really relics of an early Aryan clan, who were cut off when their brethren were expelled. If so, they must have become a very mixed race. Cf. p. 105 *ante*.

[2] The detail is given in *Oudh Gazetteer*, i. 111.

[3] McCrindle's *Ptolemy*, p. 210. It is supposed that the Tangana may survive in the Toñk Rājputs, and in certain other clans.

[4] And, summing up the history of North Oudh, Mr. Benett writes (*S. R. Gondā*, § 17, p. 6): 'Here, as in the South, the internecine wars waged by the neighbouring Çhatrī clans, and, perhaps still more, the bloody rivalry of the Brahman and the Buddhist, had resulted in the complete collapse of the old Hindu power, and, here as there, the forest gained on the cultivated plain; a scanty population was ruled by the representatives of the aboriginal stocks; the country fell an easy prey to the Muhammadans, and the Hindu system only revived at the commencement of the fourteenth century with an immigration of *Çhatrīs* from the South-west.'

ing families are of mixed descent.[1] Speaking of the absence of any marks of a continuous Aryan occupation dating back from ancient times, he says: 'I can refer to the histories of many now land-holding Rājput clans . . . but none of these declare the arrival of an army of clansmen and colonisation by the victors, with their families and kin. . . . The Oudh clans, who claim an extra-provincial origin, trace their descent to single *Çhatrīs* and not to troops of invaders. Such are the *Bais* of Baiswāra[2] and the *Rājkumār*.' After enumerating some other locally well-known clans, he shows how their origin is lost, or is traditionally attributed to mothers of the *Ahīr* and *Bhaṛ* (non-Aryan) race. 'Here,' he concludes, speaking of the *Pulwar* clan, 'we have a Hindu-Bhaṛ origin freely admitted.'

Throughout the NORTH-WEST PROVINCES similar testimony can be collected. The Rājput settlements now known are almost all the result of later movements of small bodies or clans; and frequently originated in individual adventure and in royal grants to settlers in available waste tracts. Indeed, it is worthy of remark that in so many of the districts of the North-West Provinces the Rājput proprietary bodies are locally called, not Rājput, but '*Thākur*' (lord or baron), implying that their original position was that of local lords. Throughout the districts we find that Rājput clans or single adventurers came to the place when driven from other provinces by the Muhammadan conquest. The great movement appears to have followed the overthrow of the Hindu kingdoms of Delhi, Ajmer, and Kanauj, in the twelfth century.

As a somewhat curious instance I will refer to Mr. Wilton Oldham's account of the Ghāzipur district.[3] After remarking on the non-appearance of any general ancient or primeval settlement of Aryan tribes, and that the present higher caste tenures (villages held by co-sharing families) are of comparatively modern origin, Mr. Wilton Oldham goes on to say: 'With re-

[1] In a paper in the *Journal of the Bengal Asiatic Society*, xlv. 300–302, as quoted in G. Oppert, p. 45.

[2] The Bais are descendents of Rājā Tilokchand; there are other castes of this designation, but not so descended.

[3] *Memoirs of the Ghāzipur District*, p. 67 ff. This is one of the districts of the old Benares Province.

gard to the manner in which the Hindus supplanted the "aborigines," the traditions are entitled to some credit, because they often partake of the nature of evidence against interest, or, as it is sometimes called, self-disserving evidence. Tradition generally represents the "Hindu" as coming first a solitary adventurer, and taking service with an aboriginal chief, as gradually increasing in influence, and gathering round him his kindred and other adherents, till at last, on the evidence of some real or fancied indignity, he throws off the yoke of dependence, murders his employer, and makes himself master of his "estates." There is nothing to be proud of in such a method of acquiring property, and the Rājput and *Bhūīñhār* tribes are often chary of making known their traditions till interrogated by some one who has heard them from some other source. . . .' Here we have not only a case of individual foundation of estates, but also the late date is implied: no signs of any original Aryan invasion *en masse* appear.

In another part of the country—the Bandā district—where the Rājputs are called Thākur, I find it mentioned that at the time of the first British Settlement as much as two-thirds of the district was in the hands of Thākurs, and one-fifth in that of Brahmans. The Settlement officer's remark that 'the land was in possession of the tribes which had occupied it for centuries' merely means 'for perhaps six hundred years,' when the Chāndela clan were overthrown by the Chauhān.[1]

I must specially allude to the case of the Farū<u>kh</u>ābād district, because in this, the ancient city of Kanauj was an important centre—apparently for long periods, if not always—of the Brahmanic Hindus.[2] Here we find one of the exceptional cases in which, at least in the northern part of the district, old Aryan settlers, possibly never removed, are found.

[1] *S. R. Bandā* (1881), p. 31, and see p. 61 as to the earlier Thākur clans. See also *S. R. Fatihpur* (1878), pp. 9, 10; *S. R. Allāhābad* (1878), p. 49, for similar accounts of Rājput re-settlement in the twelfth and fourteenth centuries.

[2] Kanauj, on the Ganges, was still a great city in Hwen Thsang's time, and was still such at the date of the Ghaznevide invasions, 1018 A.D. Fa-Hian mentions (fifth century) that the whole country from Mathurā up to the Panjāb was then Brahmanical; and we know that a Guptā dynasty lasted in Kanauj from 315 B.C. to 275 A.D.

Further north, in the Doāb districts, the location of the Aryan villages has been a good deal interfered with by the invasion of Jat and Gujar tribes.[1]

To conclude with some of the Rohilkhand districts, Shāhjahānpur [2] affords a typical instance. The Thākur clans are strong, especially in *Pargana* Jalālābād. Here no less than fifty-four clans are found; the Report specifies seventeen of the principal, of which I will only mention the *Çauhān*, with 8,555 members, *Çandelā* about 6,000, and the smaller bodies, *e.g.* the *Tumār*, numbering only 728. But none date back beyond the fourteenth century; and there was a settlement of the *Katheriyā* tribe as late as the sixteenth.[3] It is also remarked that though, until comparatively recently, the Thākurs were the principal landowners, 'they were the dominant class, but never formed the bulk of the population.'

I shall conclude these observations with an extract regarding the Barelī district, bordering on Oudh, as it contains a quotation which suitably summarises what I have been attempting to explain.[4] In this district Mr. Moens gives an account of each of the Rājput tribes, beginning with the *Rāhtor*, who came to the northern *parganas*, as clearers of the jungle, some ten generations back. All of them are, in fact, comparatively late historic arrivals. 'Thus,' he says, 'all the chief tribes in every part of the district of Barelī concur in stating that on their arrival they found no Rājput tribes. The previous occupants are always

[1] There is a good account of the matter, which is too long to quote, in *Cadell's S. R.*, Muzaffarnagar District (Ganges Canal Tract), p. 24.

[2] *S. R. Shāhjahānpur* (1874), § 45, p. 24. There are also some good remarks about the effect of marriage alliances in bringing about a dispersion of small groups of *different* clans, because all were exogamous, and husbands of another clan must be sought for all the daughters.

[3] The *Katheriyā* were a powerful clan, who first established themselves in the twelfth century in this part of the country, so that it was called '*Kather*.' There is a full account of their traditions in *S. R. Barelī* (1874), p. 23 ff. In the thirteenth century we find them in conflict with the Moslems; but they were not thoroughly defeated till the reign of Akbar. The most probable account seems to be that they were a mixed race, possibly connected with the original Aryan rulers of the Solar line in Oudh.

[4] *S. R. Barelī* (1874), pp. 20, 21.

either *Ahīr*, *Bhūīñhār*, or *Bhīl*, or else the land is unoccupied jungle. . . .'[1] He concludes by quoting Mr. (now Sir C. A.) Elliott's *Chronicles of Unāo*, an Oudh district, in a passage which he says is 'exactly supported by the state of things in Barelī':

'When the Aryan[2] race invaded the Gangetic Valley and the Solar chiefs settled in Ayodhyā, the natural resource for the aborigines would be to fly to the hills and find refuge in the impenetrable fastnesses girded about with the deadly Tarāi, the malarious country at the foot of the hills. . . . It has been before remarked that the mythic legends leave no impression of a large subject population existing in Oudh, but rather of a vast solitude inhabited by a scanty race employed in pasturing cattle. The scene before us at the fall of the historic curtain is an uninhabited forest country and a large colony of *Sūrajbańsī* occupying Ayodhyā as their capital. When the curtain rises again, we find Ayodhyā destroyed, the *Sūrajbańsī* utterly vanished and a great extent of country ruled over by aborigines called *Çeru* in the far East, *Bhaṛ* in the Centre, and *Rāj-Pasī* in the West. This great revolution seems to be satisfactorily explained by the conjecture that the *Bhaṛ*, *Çeru*, &c., were the aborigines whom the Aryans had driven to the hills, and who, swarming down from thence, overwhelmed the Aryan civilisation not only in Sahētā and the other Northern towns, but in Ayodhyā itself, drove the *Sūrajbańsī* under Kanak Sen to emigrate to distant Gujarāt,[3] and spread over the country between the Himalaya and that spur of the Vindhyan range that passes through the south of Mirzapur.'

The view explained in this extract seems to me to be very true in general; but I venture to think that, though there were great tracts of forests uncleared, and though the original population may have been found in detached kingdoms or scattered groups, the total amount of it was much less scanty than is supposed.[4]

[1] This tradition is curious, because each one of the tribes named is possibly a mixed race (more or less) of early Aryan connection, as we have seen.

[2] *Chronicles of Unāo*, p. 27.

[3] In Upper Western India. Here (tradition says) they founded a city and kingdom at Dwārka, and possibly originated the *Katheriyā* clan who afterwards settled in Barelī (p. 126, *ante*).

[4] See *ante*, p. 84 ff.

But more especially there is no necessity, but rather the contrary, for assuming quite so much 'flight to the hills'; for the Solar princes and their army could only have taken the rule, and established a military supremacy. Why should the inhabitants have fled at all? The conquerors would have hardly been anxious to drive out the inhabitants, at the risk of causing a famine; they would rather have been under the necessity of conciliating them, at least so far as to leave them in a position to cultivate and raise crops, without which the Aryan armies and the Court could not have been supported for long. The *return* of the aborigines is spoken of as 'in swarms'; had they fled to the hills as a very scanty and defeated body, which is the hypothesis, it is hardly likely that they would have thriven there so as to multiply exceedingly before their return, and thus acquire a force against the Aryans which originally they did not possess. I believe, as a matter of fact, that the traditional evidence we have points far more to the Aryan clans coming as a distinctly limited and ruling class, and that they subdued and came to terms with the 'aborigines,' who were already settled in the more open parts of the country, but left them very much as they were, while for a time cultivation extended and families of mixed blood multiplied so long as the Aryans maintained their supremacy. Such of the 'aborigines' as fled at all were either the immediate followers of chiefs defeated in battle, or particular clans who preferred a jungle life of independence to submitting to the Aryan dominion; the traditional evidence does not, however, suggest any extensive fighting with the aborigines at all. When, therefore, the Aryan rulers in their scattered forts and urban centres of rule were in turn destroyed by their own internecine contests, rather than by any revolt of the 'natives,' there was no need of any extensive movement to re-establish the *Bhaṛ*, *Seorī*, *Pasī*, and other tribes, in independent possession of the soil. These, however, were unable long to maintain a government, and therefore fell before the Rājput chiefs on their return, and, I suspect, not unfrequently gladly accepted their renewed rule and protection.

From what has already been said of the PANJĀB, we are prepared to find hardly any definite traces of an *ancient* Aryan domination.[1] No doubt some of the older races may be derived from a mixed Aryan stock, and this may be true in spite of the present profession of Islam and the consequent tendency to assert descent from Muhammadan ancestors. So, too, the line between Rājput and Jat is here exceptionally difficult to draw; but still there are admittedly Rājput communities ; I hardly, however, know of one in the plains that does not itself assert a comparatively late location. Around Delhi, for instance, the Rājputs are connected with the *Tūmār* (or *Tuñwār*) and *Çauhān*; both of whom are '*Agnikulā*' clans, and confessedly long subsequent to the original invasion. The *Bhattī* (this is the Panjāb form of the name, which is *Bhātī* in Rājputāna) now trace their settlement to a body which emigrated to Pindi-Bhattiāñ (Gujrānwālā district) from an earlier home in Bhattiāna or Bhātner. Near the Salt Range, *Janjhuā* settlements are found—possibly the relics of a local dominion; but the tradition they themselves have is that they are of *Rahtor* origin, coming originally from Rājputāna. In the Western plains, the *Siāl* are a late arrival; they claim to be *Puñwār* Rājputs who moved westwards to the Jhang district, and formerly to Siālkot, which derives its name from them, during the first half of the eighteenth century. Almost the only traditionally *ancient* Aryan relics are to be found in the Kangrā Hills, and possibly in the Salt Range tract of the North Panjāb.

[1] There are in the Kangrā Hills some families of *Katoçh* chiefs who are really ancient, and assert that they are older than either the Solar or Lunar princes. It is quite possible that they may be vestiges of the earlier Aryan movements. In the North-western Panjāb, the *Çib*-Rājputs, who still retain a number of villages (Gujrāt district) claim a similar antiquity, and are believed to be a branch of the Katoçh. See as to the Puranic tradition p. 97, *ante*.

CHAPTER IV

CUSTOMS REGARDING LAND-HOLDING OBSERVED AMONG THE NON-ARYAN RACES

SECTION I.—THE TIBETO-BURMAN GROUP

IN this group we naturally include the population of Burma, and in that province we are at no loss to trace characteristic customs. But in India the tribes referable to the same group seem to have been confined to the province of Assam, and to the north-eastern part of Bengal; and the customs affecting land which can be more or less distinctively ascribed to them are but few. While the Tibetan element is thus limited in the plains, it has extended more widely in the hill and sub-montane country. It has certainly formed the basis of the agricultural population, all along the outer Himalayan districts, from Darjeeling as far as Kashmīr. How far these are immigrant people coming from the north-east end of the range, and slowly advancing westward, and how far they have filtered, so to speak, directly through the hills from the Tibet plateau, it is impossible to say. Travellers will remember that beyond the Hills of Chambā and the Upper Sutlej Valley, and beyond the British districts of Kāngrā and Kulū, they come to Ladākh, Spiti, and other districts with a distinctly Tibetan population; and it is quite likely that Tibetan chiefs and Tibetan tribes may have formerly extended their rule through the hill districts, apart from any north-eastern immigration. Certain it is that the Khasā or Khasiyā people found all along the range are of Tibetan origin,[1] and that other mixed races, improved by a strain of Aryan blood,

[1] See pp. 39, 87, *ante*. The central districts about Kumāon were formerly called 'Khasdes' from this feature.

have much the same origin. Probably other races than Aryan may have made conquests in these hills. Nevertheless, we have some traditions and customs which seem to be indigenous and belong, at least, to non-Aryan tribes. In the first place, there is a tradition (both in Kumāon and Kāngrā) that the Hindu Rājās were preceded by petty local chiefs (evidently Tibetan) who had no centralized government, and so fell an easy prey to the Rājput chieftains.[1]

Speaking first of the hill districts, the absence of village-communities and the artificial formation of estates and villages, have already been alluded to; but the fact, justly as I think it may be ascribed to the physical conditions of settlement, is not entirely independent of other causes. It is a matter of racial custom that joint holding is not recognised. In Kumāon, as in Kāngrā, all the family holdings are separate and independent. A few holdings may be grouped together, but that is not the same thing as a 'village community.'[2] The case is just the same with the Simla Hill States (under their Hindu chiefs), where no artificial village groups have been formed. 'There are

[1] See the *Kumāon Collected Reports*, p. 164, and cf. Lyall's *Kāngrā S. R.* § 79, pp. 106, 107. I have already noticed the Katoçh chiefs, who may really be relics of some previous early Aryan settlement. The same is true of the Katorā chiefs in Kumāon. In this latter case there is a definite tradition that the early conquerors were again defeated by local princes; but finally the local rule was destroyed by the Rājput princes of the Chānd line, whose success is held to date from about the twelfth century. In general the Rājput chiefs date from the time when the Moslem invasions disturbed the Hindu kingdoms of the plains. Throughout these hills, it is quite possible that there may have been an early and local domination by Aryan chiefs, who after a time disappeared, and who were only at the date of the Moslem conquest replaced by more completely Hindu successors of the same race.

[2] For the Kumāon tenures see *Collected Reports*, pp. 129, 130, 132, 283, 329. See also Lyall's *Kāngrā S. R.* p. 62, which also contains some interesting tables showing how far the foreign element is represented among the land-holding classes. Thus we find Brahmans represent 18 per cent. of the land-holders; pure Rājputs only 6 per cent.; Rājputs of the second grade (*i.e.* partly mixed), 15 per cent.; the more completely mixed races—superior Çūdras, Thakar, Rāthi, and Kanet—37 per cent.; inferior Çūdra, 19 per cent.; tribes outside caste altogether, 2 per cent. All who have become Hindus adopt the joint succession, so that each farm will often be shared between relatives (average two shares to a holding).

no village communities,' writes Colonel Wace; 'each squatter held direct of the State. . . . To this day a land-holder (*zamīndār*—the term is used only in the literal sense) will speak of holding his *pattā*, *i.e.* grant or lease from the Rājā. The holdings are aggregated in circuits called *bhoj* mainly for revenue and administrative purposes.' [1]

In the inner ranges of the Kāngrā district we have, however, an interesting survival which has apparently come down unchanged, in that remote locality, from old times. In certain *Kothīs* (old administrative divisions) of Bangāhal, the dwellings are in clusters on the hill-side wherever there is space enough, and shelter, and a supply of water. The cultivation is provided for by taking up such patches or larger areas in the vicinity as can be terraced or made into fields. Each such area is called *sīr*, and every household has a holding called its *vand*; this implies a right to an equal portion in every *sīr* attached to the group. But these several plots are not, therefore, divided into as many fields as there are households. To ensure equality, each *vand* is held to consist of 'several small plots situated in every corner of the *sīr*.' When any patch of cultivation is destroyed by a landslip or other mountain accident, the custom is to redivide by lot what remains.[2] These *vand* were not ancestral shares of a family, for the households in the hamlet were independent, and not even of the same stock. Possibly, however, in ancient times they may have had something of the character of clan or tribal allotments. On the death of the holder, the *vand* was not divided among his sons: the youngest son stayed at home to succeed his father; the eldest and other sons went to the chief's army or to service, or started new households and obtained their *vand* elsewhere. In the Kulū subdivision a very similar custom is still noticeable. I must add also Sir J. B. Lyall's own comment on this custom.[3]

'Such a tenure,' he says, 'I believe to have prevailed from very ancient times in the countries far back in the Himalayas which border Tibet, or have at one time or another been included in that

[1] Wace's *Simla S. R.* 1883, § 8.

[2] Lyall's *Kāngrā S. R.* p. 35. The lots are cast (*phoglu*) with dried goats'-droppings duly marked.

[3] *Ibid.* p. 120 ff.

empire. Every family or householder had its holding or share of one; but such holding is not in the shape of an ancestral or customary[1] share of the fields round the hamlet, but rather in the shape of an arbitrary allotment from the arable land of the whole country. . . . All the arable lands seem to have been divided into lots, each lot being of presumably equal value, and calculated to be sufficient to provide subsistence for one household.'

After mentioning that in the course of time lots became unequal, and new plots were added on from the reclaimed waste, and by sales, &c., the author continues:

'The original of it seems to be that each head of a household was entitled in return for rent, tax, or service due from him to the State or Commonwealth [might we not say as a member of the tribe or clan—in the stage probably then prevalent?] to a lot or share of arable land sufficient to support one household. No man wanted more land than this, as, shut in by these high mountains, land was a means of subsistence, not a source of wealth. The lot being calculated to support only one family was not meant to be divided, and, with the house to which it was originally attached, was handed down unchanged from generation to generation. If a holder had several sons, those who wished to marry and live apart would have to look out for separate lots, and the paternal house and land would pass to one son only.'[2]

When the earliest Rājās established their rule in Kulū, they superimposed on this system one that recalls the arrange-

[1] In making this reference to 'ancestral' and 'customary' shares, the author is thinking of the principles which are found to govern the sharing in the joint-villages of the plains. It will be noticed that he refers to Kulū as probably at one time belonging to Tibet, just as some of the inner districts do to this day. This would of course give a more directly Tibetan origin to custom than the mere fact of the ethnic connection of the Khasiyā and other hill people with the Tibetan ethnic stock, which is what I have chiefly relied on.

[2] A very similar custom prevailed in Kulū. In this valley, as elsewhere, the right in the soil having been assumed by the Rājās, the private right or idea of hereditary ownership is now centred in the family house; and the Kulū saying is '*zamīn Rāi kī, ghar bāi kī*' ('The land is the Rājā's, the house is the father's') (*S. R.* p. 120). The adoption of the Persian word *zamīn* in this proverb shows that it only dates back to times when the Moslem languages had to a certain extent influenced the speech of India and penetrated to the hills.

ments we shall describe in Assam. The system was known as *jeolā-bandi*, and consisted in dividing the agricultural population into classes—one that was liable to military service and the other to menial service. The holder of land in the former class was allowed a portion of his land free of taxes (*barto-jeolā*) in return for his service; while for the rest he paid revenue (*hāñsili-jeolā*). The menial holdings were known as *çati*, and paid no revenue, except the labour or services required.

At present we have no other information about Himalayan tenures. Naipāl would be doubtless an interesting sphere of inquiry, but it is not a very accessible one; and I have found no specific information about the small portion of British territory around Darjeeling.

Leaving the Himalayan districts, we next turn to ASSAM, where we find some races of Tibeto-Burman stock almost unchanged, especially in the hill country; while the valley population, originally of the same ethnical character, has become much mixed and subject to Hindu religious and other influences. The Hindu system of caste and religion, in fact, completely displaced the earlier Buddhism, which itself must have been a foreign importation. The local dialect, Assamese, is a comparatively recent modification of Bengāli. Local traditions, and even written records, exist. From time to time the names of kings are capable of verification. From the remains of ancient temples, and still more ancient fortified cities of great extent, it is evident that traditional history is so far correct in asserting the existence of organised States from a remote period. And then came a time when Aryan or semi-Aryan chiefs had extended their dominion from the Ganges Valley as far as the western portion of Assam. The Aryan names, Kāmrūp, Brāhmaputra, and others similar, are relics of this contact. It is fairly certain that Assam was anciently divided into several, or many, small kingdoms, and that after the time of Buddhā, the Western kings adopted the Buddhist faith.[1] As might be expected, the western districts

[1] This is doubtless referred to when the Annals (written by Brahman authors) speak of the kings as *Asura or Dānava*, terms applied to 'heretics.' A good account of ancient Assam will be found in the *Calcutta Review*, xlv. 510, reprinted in 1884. This is followed by a further article about the ancient religion, which is more speculative in

are often found united under one ruler, whose sway extended as far westwards as Bihār or even Gorakhpur on the confines of Oudh. These Buddhist princes felt the effect of the Brahmanic struggle for ascendency and were ultimately overthrown.[1]

A distinction appears to have been early recognised between the west (*Kāmrup*) and the north and north-eastern part of the valley (*Uttarkol*). It was the latter that was most thoroughly Tibeto-Burman as regards its population. One of the most important immigrations was that of the *Boro* (or *Baḍa*) tribe,[2] which had several subdivisions. A *Boro* kingdom existed near the modern Sadiyā. The *Meç* and *Kāçāri* tribes, who will presently be mentioned, are probably branches of this race. The name 'Assam' (*Āsām*) is most probably traceable to (the *Boro*) *Hā-çom*=the low or level country; while the *Boro* word for water (*dai* or *di*) has remained in the names of rivers—*e.g.* *Dai-hang* (the Dihong of the maps). Under the *Boro* rule 'tradition states that the country was thickly populated, and reached a high state of civilisation. It was divided for the purposes of Government administration into numerous districts; and the executive consisted of a body politic, selected from the most wealthy and respected men in each division. The King exercised but a nominal control over the deliberative assemblies.'[3]

character, and the chronology is confusing. The name of King Bhagadatta, well known in literature, figures largely; he was a Buddhist, but his successors became Hindus in the ninth century.

[1] It is curious to observe how the traditions represent the oppressed Buddhists as seeking refuge through the hills as far west as Kashmīr; and, at least at one time, we hear of a prince ruling over Kashmīr leading an army into Assam. There are scattered remnants of these once ruling houses still existing under the name of the *Kultā* or *Kulitā* caste. A certain number, now Hindus, are in the Assam Valley. But two small colonies made their way to South-western Bengal, which has been a refuge ground to several tribes. One is now in the Native State of Bonaigarh, the other in the Sambalpur district of the Central Provinces. The name *Kulitā* is supposed by some to mean *kulā* (family), *itā* (gone or lost); but these Sanskritic derivations are open to not a little suspicion.

[2] In Bengal and Assam the 'ŏ' is generally the result of the dialectic pronunciation of the 'a' in the Sanskritic alphabets. Thus Bhagadatta is pronounced Bhogodott, and accordingly so written by some authors.

[3] Quoted from the article referred to above. Perhaps we might put it in a little less 'modern' administrative form if we said that the country

It seems characteristic of Tibeto-Burman races that they have a number of separate local chiefs, who in many cases have no cohesion and no centralised control, so that in the course of time they fall under the dominion of some conquering prince. And even then the sovereign seems always to act in concert with a council of the chiefs. Thus in Naipāl to the present day there is a State Council of twelve nobles.[1] The old Burman State had also its *Hlut-daw* or council of chiefs, and we may well suppose its origin in a tribal form of government.[2] Nor was the rule of these north-eastern tribes confined only to the upper part of Assam, for as late as the fourteenth century, when the last of the Hindu dynasties was overthrown before the Muhammadan King of Gaur (Bengal), we find a *Meç* tribe ruling in Goālpārā, and also tribes of *Koç* or *Kūç*. Their rule was destroyed in the end of the fifteenth century. The memory of it still survives in the little State of *Kūç-bihār*, in North-eastern Bengal. The *Kūç* still form the chief constituent in the population of the Western Dwār districts, though at the time of the British occupation of that country they had fallen under the oppression of their neighbours, the *Bhūtiyā*. The *Meç* tribe also musters strongly in the district of Goālpārā. Of the *Kūçāri* we shall hear subsequently. But while these tribes were still ruling, an energetic race—as it must once have been—the *Aham* or *Ahŏm*,[3] was making rapid progress. They established

was, as so often observed, divided into districts or areas, probably connected with the clan-divisions or clan-chiefs' jurisdictions, and that the elders and wealthier men formed councils for the control of internal affairs, while a king or head chief had a general supremacy.

[1] The Gorkhā rulers of Naipāl were Aryan (or semi-Aryan) conquerors. They would doubtless, however, find it politic to adopt local or indigenous forms of administration.

[2] At one time in the early Assam history we hear of a rulership of the *Bāra-bhūiyā*, which *may* only mean 'twelve chiefs,' during a time when the supremacy of a king had been destroyed by war. Others have supposed the term to refer to the temporary rule of a race called *Bhūīñyā*—one of the many Dravidian races, relics of which, with this name, are still found in some parts of Eastern India. The matter is, however, too uncertain to call for further notice.

[3] It is sometimes said that Assam (*Āsām*) derives its name from 'Aham;' but the derivation is unlikely; though the local dialect would easily soften an *s* into an *h*, it is held that the contrary change here

themselves at first in the extreme north-east; but it is impossible to fix a date for their arrival, which indeed was probably gradual. They ultimately extended their rule over the whole valley, and about the thirteenth century we begin to have something like an historic record. The Aham princes were able to withstand the Muhammadan power: their rule, in fact, lasted down to our own times.[1] The race was completely non-Aryan, but their princes ended by adopting Hinduism; not, however, till the close of the sixteenth century. The Aham still number some 180,000, though now mingled with other castes.[2] From an early time they had a king, and a number of 'nobles' who bore distinctive titles. It is stated in most of the accounts of Assam that I have seen, that the Rājā as conqueror assumed the right in the soil of his dominions; but this does not appear to me necessarily to be inferred from the facts. The King had, however, other and far more curious pretensions, which seem characteristic of Tibeto-Burmans. He organised the whole of the subject-population into groups, so that he might exact military service, labour, and supplies, from all, rather than demand an over-lord rent from the soil, which, as cultivation was extremely sparse, would have been less profitable.[3] The grouping was carried out in this way. Every male above sixteen years of age was designated a *pāik*. Each group of three *pāik* formed a *got*—observe the adopted Aryan term for a

requisite, would be dialectically impossible. Altogether, the *Boro* name given above (p. 135) is more probable.

[1] As usual with such dynasties, the end was brought about by intestine decay and family feuds. The interference of the Burman sovereign was invoked by one of the rivals, and the Burman rule, one of great cruelty, was for a short time established. As it is graphically expressed in a petition presented by certain inhabitants to the British Government, 'the country fell into the hands of the Burmans, and the people into twelve kinds of fire' (Mill's *Report on Assam*). The Burmans were driven out by the British in 1824.

[2] The whole population consists of *Aham*, *Kūç*, *Meç*, *Kāçāri*, *Çutiyā*, and a considerable admixture of Hindus from the west. Sir W. Hunter observes that the 'Assamese' are by no means strict in caste ideas, and that intermarriages are common.

[3] Not that he took *no* revenue from the land; only it was not the chief thing as it was elsewhere.

family or minor clan. One person in each *got* was always to be available for service, not only in the army, but in supplying carriage, collecting wood and grass, and, if a craftsman, contributing of his handiwork; or he could be called on to aid in executing public works. The Aham rulers left abundant traces of their zeal in providing tanks for irrigation, as well as other monuments. It will be observed that this obligation to service was not serfdom; there were large bodies, probably of the 'inferior' and conquered tribes, who were actually serfs or slaves, and were employed in the cultivation of lands to which they were attached—lands held by the Rājā or his chiefs, or by the religious grantees, who became numerous when the princes adopted Hinduism. In order to facilitate supervision and to ensure the due rendering of the service, the *got* were further aggregated into larger bodies called *khel*: 20 *got* went to a *khel*.[1] It became the practice for the several *khel* to subdivide their duty; one undertaking the supply of wood and grass, another of fruit and betel-nuts, and so on; so that it became customary to speak of 'the wood and grass *khel*,' the betel-nut *khel*, &c. The *khel*-service could be assigned: *e.g.* to the King's wife, or to a relative. And when land was granted to a Brahman, the service of certain *khel* was granted with it, besides the serfs belonging to the land.[2] The working population, thus organised,

[1] The terms used are modern dialectic forms which, perhaps, once had older indigenous equivalents, just as we find the Kol, Gond, and other races now using, in connection with their own customs and institutions, terms which they borrowed from the Hindī. The use of the term *khel* is somewhat remarkable, but perhaps it is only a coincidence of form. It may be compared with the Santāl and Kolarian term *kīlī* for a sub-division of a tribe. There is a Persian word *k͟hel*, which properly means a troop of horsemen and then a tribe. This *may* have gained currency in India. On the north-west frontier the village groups are called *k͟hel*—sections of tribes. In Berār the term *k͟hel* was formerly used in connection with joint family holdings.

[2] It may be worth while to notice that this method of obtaining supplies for the Court was not unknown to the Aryan princes. In Manu (vii. 118) we hear of the Rājā assigning to certain district officials as their perquisite 'such food, drink, wood, and other articles as by law should be given each day to the King by the inhabitants of a village.' It is also noticeable that in the Simla Hill States, and, indeed, throughout the hill country, certain of the lower castes had to give a certain number of

was subject to a corresponding series of officials. Over each *khel* was a *Barā*; over 100 *got* (*i.e.* 5 *khel*) was a *Saikyā*; and over 1,000 *got* was a *Hazārī*. In order to provide for the support of the people, each *pāik* was allowed a plot of land for his house and garden (*bārī*) : on this only a small 'hearth-tax' was payable annually. Each also held a small allotment of arable land (called *goamatti*, said to mean 'body-land') amounting to about 2⅔ acres, which was held free of charge.[1]

I have not been able to trace any similiar organisation under the kings of Burma. But the latter were sometimes of Aryan descent, and the historical conditions were different. A nearly similar organisation was, however, imposed on the *Kūç* and *Meç* tribes by the conquering *Bhūtiyā* in the West Dwars. The individual holdings of land (there called *jot*) were made to pay land-revenue; each small cluster of houses was headed by a *pradhān*. Over several of these groups was a *siyāna*.[2] Over these, again, was a local collector; and finally a chief of the district aided by a deputy.

In the Cachār district of Assam we are introduced to an interesting variety of the *khel* system. Cachār is now known principally as a district of tea-planters; its native population is miscellaneous, largely made up of settlers from the hill country around it. It fell under the dominion of a ruling house of the *Kāçāri* tribe as late as the eighteenth century.[3] One of the

days' unpaid labour (*begār*), and, at the harvest, special offerings of maize, &c., to the Rājā, independently of the regular revenue dues. The obligation to work and service was, in fact, imposed by many conquering rulers in India, in one form or another; the demand being, as a rule, confined to the lower-castes or out-castes. It was carried to great lengths in Kashmīr, as the recent account of the country by Mr. Walter Lawrence shows. Cf. also H. E. Seebohm, *The Structure of Greek Tribal Society* (Macmillan, 1895), p. 115 ff, showing similar customs among the ancient Greeks, the Persians, and even the Israelites.

[1] It is said that the *goamatti* was neither hereditary nor alienable, and that it was regarded as the property of the State or ruler.

[2] The reader will note these terms as reappearing in Kumāon, where the population was so largely Tibeto-Burman in origin.

[3] I may repeat that the *Meç*, *Kūç*, and *Kāçāri* are believed to be branches of one tribe. Indeed, it has been thought that the term *Kūç* was only invented to distinguish those *Kāçāri* who adopted orthodox Hinduism. The *Kāçāri* families dominated at one time a considerable

Rājās became a Hindu by the process, not unknown elsewhere, of placing himself and his son in the body of a cow made out of copper; of course they became '*Rājbansī*,' or 'Royal' Hindus, and claimed rank as Rājputs. The *Kāçāri* kingdom, as usual in this group, included a number of chiefs under the Rājā (called in the books *Bar-man*, perhaps *barā-mānus* = great man). The land-holders were grouped into *khel*, and the Rājā had the right to demand service and supplies for the royal household, from the *khels*. As, however, the kingdom was a new one, it was obliged to deal gently with the cultivators. By that time the neighbouring province of Bengal had long been paying the State-revenue in cash, and doubtless this example was followed in Cachār. For this purpose each *khel* formed a *jointly responsible* body, the responsibility being, for a lump sum, assessed on the *khel* as a unit or whole. A headman called *mukhtār* (agent) was appointed to each, and a number of *khel* united had a *rāj-mukhtār*, or superior representative, with the State officials,[1] and the group of *khel* so represented formed a *rāj* or *rāij*. The joint responsibility for the revenue was in fact a measure of protection against internal inquisition by petty officers of the State, with their frequent opportunities of levying fees on individuals. A lump sum, whether high or low, was (necessarily) fixed, and, on the official representative producing that, there was much less pretext for further interference. The responsibility was worked by means of a custom called *ghasāwat*. If anyone failed to pay, unless some richer neighbour would make good the arrear and take over the land, the whole body contributed the amount and took the land. If a whole *khel* failed, then the *rāj* was answerable and took over the village land. It is quite certain that the system had nothing to do with joint-ownership

portion of Assam; and the district which now distinctively bears their name could only have been a lately occupied southern territory taken when the tribes began to be pressed by other competitors. The earlier kingdom extended much more into the hill country. The last *Kāçāri* Rājā died in 1830 without heirs, and the country became an escheat to the British Government. The neighbouring state of Tiperah (*Tṛipura*) has still a ruler of *Kāçāri* descent.

[1] These names of course are purely modern. *Mukhtār* is the ordinary Persian word for an agent or attorney.

such as exists in a North Indian village: none of the groups had any tribal or family connection; they were miscellaneous and recent settlers. It is at best uncertain whether the joint system was imposed by the ruler or voluntarily adopted. I think the latter the more probable. It is remarkable that in one of the northern districts of Madras (Cuddapah) a similar system, which could have no connection with Assamese customs, prevailed under the name of *vīsabadī*: there the villagers clubbed together to manage the whole of the lands, and to meet the revenue charges, on the joint-stock principle—each undertaking a certain portion of the area against a fixed fraction of the assessment.[1] The fractions were the series known to Tamil arithmetic ($\frac{1}{8}$, $\frac{1}{16}$, &c.; *vīsa* = $\frac{1}{16}$). In both cases I suspect we have a voluntary device which had nothing to do directly with customs of any particular race; but the matter deserved some mention, as showing how an appearance of common ownership may be misleading if its origin is not inquired into.

In themselves, the Assamese land-holdings are always purely individual, and are based upon the right of first clearing; unless, indeed, they have arisen, as in the case of some larger estates, by the direct grant of the ruler.

There is no word for 'village' in Assamese nor in the older local dialects; the revenue term *mauza* has been introduced solely for administrative purposes, and is used, in a quite local and special sense, to indicate a circle of holdings under one petty official charge.

It will be permissible to make a rapid sketch of the modern land-holdings which have arisen out of this previous state of things. The province of Assam is treated in effect, though not called so officially, as *raiyatwār*. The only exception is where some of the larger purchasers of waste-lands, or grantees and others, have become landlords or proprietors, or where certain of the larger land-holders were acknowledged as landlord-owners under the Permanent Settlement of Bengal, which extended to some of the districts. There are only some cases in which any-

[1] See Munro's Minute in Arbuthnot's *Sir J. Munro*, &c., ii. 360. See also *Godāvari D. M.* p. 314. This plan was accompanied by a rule that any co-sharer who thought his share was too highly rated might offer to exchange it with another; the details cannot be here gone into.

thing like a village group is formed, although there are parts of the country where there is no physical peculiarity to prevent it. The genius of the people evidently does not lead them to any union; and the holdings are completely independent. In some parts the assessment is still made annually; but in others, settlements for a period of years have been found possible; here especially, as cultivation increases, village-groups will probably be consolidated, but in a *raiyatwāri* form.

In the country known as the Bhūtān-Dwārs there is a noticeable tendency to form what will become small landlord estates rather than villages. I find an interesting article on this country written shortly after its annexation at the close of the Bhūtān war.[1] The individual farmer or cultivating settler is called *jot-dār*, or holder of a *jot*—a term frequently met with in Bengal for the individual holding, whether (locally) as proprietor or (more commonly) as tenant-farmer.

'The whole of the land,' says the writer, 'at present being held in detached farms, has a very marked effect on the arrangements of the population, and . . . there is scarcely a village to be seen from one end of the Dwārs to the other. The plan adopted is for every holder of a *jot* (cultivating lot) to establish his homestead on the most eligible site for building on, within the limits of his *jot*; and around the *jot-dār's* house those of his dependents cluster. . . . The size of these homesteads varies, of course, with that of the *jot*. Some contain as many as forty or fifty houses (*i.e.* cottages), whilst others have not more than six or eight; but in all, the same characteristics prevail: the *jot-dār* is the head of the little community and is looked up to as the master over all; it is he who manages the affairs of the whole *jot*, lets out the lands to his under-tenants, and retains what he chooses for his special use. His word is law; he is, in fact, a little patriarch living in the midst of his family and dependents, whose influence for good or evil is felt by every member of the society.' The whole country is dotted over with these separate homesteads.

[1] *Calcutta Review*, vol. xlviii. (January 1869). The two portions forming the Eastern and Western Dwārs (or Duārs) have been attached respectively to Bengal and to Assam. The Eastern Dwārs form part of the Jalpaigūri district; the Western, of Goālpārā.

I am not aware of any local peculiarity which would discourage the 'village' formation; but apparently it is not here in the nature of the people. It often happens that one man owns more than one *jot*: in this case he lives on one, and lets the others out either to some substantial tenants (*çūkanīdār*, or *mūlandār*), who agree with him for a yearly rental in cash, or to poorer people (called *parjā* or *raiyat*), who, in fact, somewhat resemble metayers, receiving plough and oxen from the *jotdār* and giving him one-half or even two-thirds of the produce in kind.

It would be impossible to leave the description of Assam without some allusion to the *hill tribes*, who from their remote situation have been much left alone, and probably retain the customs of their ethnic group much unchanged. In the northern hills are the *Ākā*, *Daphlā*, *Mīrī*, and *Abar* tribes, at the western end, and the *Mishmī* at the eastern. In the central ranges south of the valley proper, are the *Gāro*, *Khāsī*, and *Nāgā*. In the hills on the south-east are the *Kūki* or *Lushai* tribes. We have but little definite information about their land-customs; but this is owing partly to the nature of the country, which lends itself chiefly to shifting cultivation;[1] but there is evidence of some method of tribal allotment by which the various clan groups have their own 'beats,' doubtless indicated by natural limits of valley, ridge, and stream. I have been told by persons of local experience that within the last thirty years the men of one group in the Gāro Hills would turn out in war array to resent any encroachment on their land or pasture ground. It will be borne in mind that the origins of these tribes are in some cases very doubtful. In the central hills, for instance, there are tribes whose language is not to be classified in the general group; and it would seem that some considerable tribes unconnected with the rest of the group found refuge in these hills.[2] In general there is a very loose cohesion; separate chiefs of territories are recognised, some with very little authority over the minor or local chiefs of villages or ultimate clan-groups. Under such a state of things there must always be a natural

[1] See *ante*, p. 52.

[2] See Census Report, 1891 (*Parliamentary Blue Book*), p. 137.

tendency for the chiefship to remain in certain families, and for a chief of energy to enlarge his pretensions and become a sort of Rājā over a number of others. Or, on the other hand, it is not difficult for some neighbouring foreign chief to compel a number of his neighbours to submit to his suzerainty. We should like to know for certain on what principle the groups forming villages are separated. Fixed hereditary ownership of land is hardly possible, at least until the clan begins to adopt some customary principle modifying the shifting cultivation, or *jūm*.

Sometimes the village groups are placed so as to crown the tops of separate hills, and each is securely stockaded. The frequency of clan feuds and the malarious character of the valleys would combine to account for this. The *Nāgā* clans, for instance, live in stockaded villages : they acknowledge a sort of chief over a clan or group of villages ; but he is not hereditary, and apparently his authority is not strong. But in the north, I find it noted that among the *Mīrī* (a branch of the same stock as the *Daphlā*, *Abar*, and *Ākā*) the chiefs *are* hereditary ; and it sometimes happens that one of them acquires sufficient influence to establish a kind of lordship over a considerable area.

In the southern hills, the *Lushai* (or *Kūkī*) are said 'markedly to differ'[1] from the others, inasmuch as the clan chiefs are not only hereditary but are all taken from a certain 'royal stock.' Captain Shakespear, who read to the Society of Arts the interesting paper referred to in the footnote, has described how the chiefs are selected from one or two families in different parts of the country. Each village has its own chief also, and is located independently on the top of a hill. Some groups are large enough to have 200 to 800 cottages. An incompetent village chief is removable by the voice of the villagers ; or rather the villagers will desert the chief and build a new village (the bamboo structures are easily replaced) on another site. Each chief (I am not sure if this refers to *village* chiefs) is advised by one or two men called by a local term signifying 'old man,'[2] or by the borrowed (Hindī) term *kārbāri*. Property, Captain Shakespear informs us, belongs to the family, not to the indi-

[1] See *Imperial Gazetteer* (2nd ed.), xiii. 530, and *Journal Soc. Arts* (January 1895), xliii. 167 ff.

[2] Cf. the *siyāna* (= wise man) already mentioned.

vidual members; and the family 'lot' for *jūm* cultivation (hill rice being the chief crop) is worked by all the capable members together. Without this co-operation such cultivation would be impossible. Fixed fields seem to be unknown. In some parts, however (as among the *Chin* tribes), Captain Shakespear notes that the village-site is located not on the hill-top, but on the slope, so that a local stream can be laid on to fields terraced for rice cultivation. Here we have the beginnings of permanent land-owning.

The central hills (*Gāro* and *Khāsi*) have this difference, that the inhabitants have more intercourse with the level country both to the north and south; and in the *Khāsi* Hills we have a strange tribe, settled as already noted. We are not surprised to find that the chiefs ruling over a group of villages sometimes adopt the title of Rājā. But the Rājā's authority is small, as everything is decided in the village assembly under the village chief; and contiguous villages will cause their chiefs to assemble to discuss a matter that interests several of them in common.

I have come across an interesting article on the *Khāsi* Hills.[1] The author states that these hills were divided into twenty-three petty 'States,' each having its own 'Rājā.' This chief, however, has but little authority, except in administering justice; he receives a small revenue or tribute in kind from traders and others, and has something from fines; there is no regular land-revenue, as there is but little permanent cultivation. As usual, public business is decided at a meeting called in the name of the Rājā; and in each village any matter of local dispute is decided by such an assembly in the village.[2] The proceedings

[1] *Calcutta Review* (Reprint of 1884), vol. xxvii. September 1850.

[2] See article alluded to, p. 24. 'The village is assembled by warning given the previous evening. The crier goes out at an hour when the people are likely to have returned home, and, placing himself at some suitable spot where he is likely to be heard, he attracts attention by a prolonged unearthly yell, and then delivers himself of his errand: "*Kaw!* Thou a fellow-villager, thou a fellow-creature, thou an old man, thou who art grown up, &c., thou who art great, thou who art little! *Hei!* in his own village, in his own place! *Hei!* there is a quarrel! *Hei!* because there is a contest! *Hei!* to come to sit together! *Hei!* to come to deliberate together! *Hei!* ye are forbidden! *Hei!* ye are stopped to draw water then, to cut firewood then! No *Hei!* to go to work then! No *Hei!* to

are opened by the village priest, and witnesses are heard. The chief at the end states what he thinks about the matter in dispute—'making at the same time a hearty appeal to the assembled villagers—"Is it not so, my young, energetic ones?"' To which they respond unitedly, 'Yes, it is so, young energetic ones,' and the matter is thus settled. It will not fail to be noticed how prominent the idea of assemblies is in all the races of this group. We shall, however, find similar assemblies, both local and tribal, to be a feature of Vedic life among the early Aryans.

It is to be hoped that, with regard to these tribes and the Shān and Karens in Burma, we may have more definite information as to how the tribal, or clan, and village, areas for cultivation and for general occupation, are determined on. So much only can at present be said, that some such allotment is apparent, and that the tribal stage, with the feeling of equal right to a share for each household or family or individual, as the case may be, is recognised. Community in property, except for the necessary co-operation of all hands in a family or household for forest-clearing, can hardly be looked for.

We may now turn to BURMA, where we expect to find the most characteristic exhibition of the customs of the group we are considering. The population is, as a whole, scanty. It is only, in fact, in certain districts in the rice-plains or valleys of the great rivers that the cultivation is continuous in area and the people fairly numerous. There are no jointly-owned villages on the Indian model; but villages of the other type are everywhere found, and there is a tendency, I am told, for families of the same descent to settle together. In Burma it is quite possible that elements of custom of diverse origin may be found; there is of course the Mongol element (Sai or Shān) strongly represented; but there is reason to believe that some tribes, known as Talaing, were Dravidian and came from the South of India. They call themselves *Mūn* or *Mwūn*. There was also a small Aryan element.

descend to the valley then! *Hei!* now come forth *Hei!* the hearing is to be all in company! *Hei!* the listening attentively then is to be all together! *Hei!* for his own king! *Hei!* for his own master! lest destruction come, lest piercing overtake us! *Kaw!* come forth now, fellow-men!"'

In early times, but at a much later date than the Burman annalists place it,[1] some Kshatriya prince and his followers made their way, by Manipur, into the upper part of the Irāwādi Valley, and founded a kingdom at Tagong, on the Irāwādi, and afterwards one near Prome (*Tharē khetara*).[2] Another group appears to have entered Arakan, which was not difficult when once Aryan influence had extended as far as Eastern Bengal and Chittagong. That such adventurers would be pure Aryan is, however, very unlikely. The Aryan element was Buddhist not Hindu, and its Pāli language affected both names of places and the language generally; but the Aryan people readily fused with the Mongoloid.[3]

As to the Mūn or Talaing, their chronicles have been so largely destroyed that little is known beyond the fact that the Irāwādi delta and Martaban were anciently colonised from the East Coast of India. Talaing is apparently connected with *Tilinga*. The race is now represented (in a distinctive form) in Siam better than it is in Burma.[4] The various Tai or Shān irruptions mentioned by Phayre need not occupy our attention. The overthrow of the Aryan dynasties was probably due to them. It is only needful to remark that there is nothing to show that there were no Mongoloid inhabitants in Burma previously; or that Aryans, or Talaings, were the first settlers of all.

The Indian element, whether Dravidian or Aryan, can only have been comparatively small. It is not possible to trace any Burmese custom to either source. The Burman kings had 'Royal lands,' *i.e.* lands specially set apart to furnish an income to the Court; but this, though a Dravidian institution,

[1] See Lassen, ii. 1047 ff, and Phayre's *History of Burma* (Trübner: Oriental Series), p. 3.

[2] This name Lassen thinks a modification of the Sanskrit *Sṛi khetra*. See Phayre, pp. 10, 11, note.

[3] 'The Indian settlers,' says Phayre, 'gave to them (the indigenous Mongoloid people) and adopted themselves, the name of *Brahmā*, which is used in the Buddhist sacred books for the first inhabitants of the world. The term has survived in the form *Mrāmmā* (generally pronounced *Brāmā*). This term is evidently the origin of the entirely Anglicised forms, Burma, Burman, or Burmese.

[4] Phayre, *History*, p. 28.

is also found among other early races of Tibetan origin when they had Sovereigns and Courts. The joint succession of the heirs to property is not necessarily Aryan; if it were, it would have become general in Burma through the influence of the Buddhist religion which spread over the country. Only one Mongoloid feature we notice, the tendency for the country to be divided under a number of local (probably clan) chiefs; these, when falling under some superior royal house, are regarded as subordinate, but are conciliated with local titles, or form a Council of State. Where there is a powerful sovereign like Alompyā or Anawrahtā, the kingdom is held together and extends its sway. When the reins of government fall into feeble hands, the dynasty perishes and the independence of the local magnates is reasserted.

Cultivation in the *hill country* of Burma is by the shifting or temporary method (*taungyā*); permanent rice lands and orchards are found in the level valleys only; we have no evidence, traditional or other, of any tribal settlement or allotment of lands. The early kingdoms, as I have said, relied rather on the possession of 'Royal lands' for their revenue, than on a system of land-revenue collected in kind, for the latter cannot be effective unless there is a fairly continuous area of cultivated territory. The kings did indeed exact a 'rice land-tax,' but whether this was very ancient there is no means of knowing; it never formed (even up to the date of the Burmese war) the real staple of the royal revenue, as the land revenue did (and still does) in India.

There is not, as far as I am aware, any real word for 'village.' The term *kwin* (otherwise written *queng*) is said to mean 'level ground'—*i.e.* rice cultivation as opposed to the temporary clearings on the hill slopes beyond. But though the various holdings are always independent, and nothing like a community of land or joint-holding of an entire village is known, the holdings are in compact village groups, and the dwellings also are placed together, often on the banks of one of the numerous creeks or streams which so often serve also as boundaries between the *kwin* groups. Thus, without violence to terms, the *kwin* can be called a 'village.' There is always the probability that such groups settled together originally on a clan basis; and we are not surprised to find *two* local headmen, one chosen by the villagers themselves, and one (*kyedāngyī*) appointed by the State, to look after the revenue and administrative matters. I have found no mention of any staff of artisans, serving only the one village, hereditary, and specially remunerated by free holdings or grain fees, such as we meet with in all Indian villages.[1]

Land has at all times, in Burma, been so largely in excess of the population to till it, that we may reasonably believe the first settlements to have been very much by choice—each group of settlers taking land as much as, and where, they pleased, but keeping together to a certain extent, both for safety against wild animals and against hostile incursions, as well as for society. The land is registered as the property of one man; and when he dies, his sons, and also the widow and daughters, succeed jointly according to Burmese law. If the holding is large enough, it will simply be divided into separate holdings for the several members of the family; if it is too small, the house-father will arrange before his death for one or two members to take the land and the others his moveable property; or one member will possess and work the whole holding and pay rent to the other sharers, or will buy out their interest. The Burmese idea of right in land is, as might be expected, solely based on first occupation and the labour of clearing. The later Burmese kings, at any rate, established the usual principle asserted by conquerors, that they had a superior right in all land; but this was consistent with a practical hereditary right of private holding; and the seizure of occupied land was always looked on as an act of oppression.[2] So strong was the right in private

[1] In modern times, the land revenue system is in effect a *raiyatwāri* system; the *kwin* has become regularly demarcated, mapped, and registered as the geographical village division, which is essential to all our revenue systems (at least where great landlords are not dealt with). And there are now civil and police headmen, and accountant-surveyors to keep up the land records.

[2] See *L. S. B. I.* iii. 403, 404. The Burmese law originally recognised seven modes of acquiring land: (1) allotment by Government officers; (2) gift by the king; (3) inheritance; (4) gift; (5) purchase; (6) clearing the virgin forest; (7) 'prescription' (as we should call it)

land, that when it was mortgaged, no limit of time was allowed to bar the right of the 'owner,' or his heirs, to redeem. I have already given some account of the interesting phenomenon of a transition state, in which temporary *taungyā* clearings are passing into permanent ownership.[1]

Our information about rights in land as understood among the hill tribes of Karens and in the Shān States is very limited. There are probably fixed territories indicated by natural features of hill and valley, in which the different clans and family groups have their several locations in which the *taungyā* cultivation is practised over the suitable slopes taken in rotation. Among some Karen tribes I find it noticed that the bamboo dwellings are adapted to the method of living, so that there is no difficulty in abandoning one site and erecting a new abode. The houses, in fact, are like long barracks with a single entrance at the gable end. In these, several connected families live together, forming a sort of house-communion under the control of a family elder or headman.

Among the Shāns, while the *taungyā* form of cultivation is practised by tribes in the hills, there is an abundance of permanent cultivation of palm-groves, gardens, and rice fields in the level valleys and plains. Everywhere the organisation of agricultural society seems to be very similar to that of Burma; and the 'villages' are local clusters of families each with its own headman: a number of these 'villages' are united under the jurisdiction of a local chief.[2] One of the reports I have seen alludes to the difficulty of settling terms of protection or of relation to the British Government as regards trade or frontier affairs, because there is no really responsible authority over the territory to deal with. Here and there some chief of greater ability or energy will take the lead and maintain a kind of suzerainty for a time. It is obvious that a number of petty and loosely held local chiefships must always tend to fall under

or adverse holding for ten years with the knowledge of a former possessor, who did not interfere to assert his own claim.

[1] *Ante*, p. 55, and *L. S. B. I.* iii. 506.

[2] There is a charmingly written paper describing the Shān States, by Colonel Woodthorpe in the *Journal Soc. of Arts*, xliv. 197 (January 1896). But this gives no direct information about the modes of land-holding.

some other authority. Hence it is that we see the Karen and Shān States some independent and some acknowledging the control of Burma, China, or Siam, as the case may be.

In conclusion, it may be observed that, as regards India, these North-eastern races have become so mixed, and so altered by the adoption of Hinduism, that there is now but little in the way of distinctive custom to mark them. When they first settled in India, their stage of social progress was evidently a tribal one; and that resulted in the formation of small groups of families and a certain local dominion of chiefs of territories. These from time to time are aggregated under the rule of some prince or dynasty strong enough to keep them together. No kind of community of ownership is traceable; but it is highly probable that every member of a clan considered himself, and was generally acknowledged, to have a right to a share in his clan-territory, and to the use of the pasture grounds. Right by occupation and first-clearing seems to be the general (as it is the most natural) basis of title in a country where every acre has to be won from the primeval jungle under considerable difficulties.

SECTION II.—KOLARIAN CUSTOMS

There is really no need for a separate section under this heading, except to contain a notice of the surviving and apparently unchanged customs of the *Ho* and *Mundā* tribes (so called *Kol*), who found refuge in ancient days in the plateau-land of Chutiyā-Nāgpur, and to include some customs of the *Santāl* people in Bengal. These are distinctly non-Aryan customs; and they seem also to differ from the purely Dravidian customs also to be found in Chutiyā-Nāgpur, in Hill Orissa, and in the South. They are accordingly described under a separate heading, but merely for convenience, and without any intention to formulate any opinion as to how far Kolarian races are ethnically distinct on the one hand from the Tibeto-Burman group with whom they have a certain amount of affinity,[1] and how

[1] This curiously appears in small matters—*e.g.* that the Tibeto-Burmans make no use of milk, nor do the Kolarian. In point of language I am informed that the speech of the *Ho*, *Mundā*, and *Santāl* tribes has points

far, on the other hand, they may be connected with some of the more northern-dwelling Dravidian races, which Dr. G. Oppert proposes to call the 'Gaudian' branch. Nor need I enter on the question of the affinities of certain hill tribes such as the *Kurkū* or the *Baigā*, since, being almost nomadic and living by the chase, we have but little to learn about land-holding customs among them.[1]

In this group, I will, however, mention the *Bhīl*,[2] as a portion of the race has locally settled down to agricultural life in the Vindhyan country; and here we see the outlines of a *tribal settlement*. 'In the Udaipur State,' says Sir W. Hunter,[3] 'they are now settled in little hamlets, each homestead being built on a separate hillock, so as to render it impossible for their enemies to surprise a whole village at once.' By 'village' is meant a group of such separate homesteads, which is called *pāra*, or *parra*.[4] The groups are small, and separated by the cultivated and waste lands held by each. Each has a chief, called *Tarvi*. In a tract sixty miles by ten (from Mandu as a centre) in Mālwā, it was found that there were 112 *pāra*, each on the average containing nine huts or cottages, with four or five persons to each dwelling. There seems also to be some larger clan-grouping, but this is not clear; and the Bhīls acknowledged a chief of their own, who called himself by the Hindī title of *Rāwat*.[5]

of contact with that of the *Khāsiya* hillmen of Assam, and that of the *Meç* in North-eastern Bengal. See *J. R. A. S.* xx. part iii. 329; Cunningham, *Anc. Geog.* p. 506.

[1] These tribes in the Melghāt Hills are in a very primitive condition, and are described as very dark-skinned and with Mongoloid features. Even if they are of the same stock as the *Mundā* (compare Colonel Dalton's description of these latter quoted in Cunningham, *Anc. Geog.* p. 507), we are quite familiar with the circumstance that races of the same stock, ethnically speaking, may be now in very different stages of civilisation.

[2] Following the *Census Report of* 1891, p. 147 (Parliamentary Blue-book).

[3] See Hunter, *Short History, &c.*, p. 43, and *Imp. Gazetteer*, ii. 388.

[4] Malcolm, *Memoir of Central India*, ii. 53, 54, and 184. In Appendix XIV. C, the author gives a sort of census of the *pāra* and their population.

[5] Some of the families may have a certain admixture of Aryan blood See p. 114, *ante*.

Turning next to the east side of India, the interesting feature of the Chutiyā-Nāgpur districts is, that they afforded a safe refuge to Kolarian tribes who have remained to some extent unchanged. The Kolarians also came in contact there with tribes of Dravidian stock, and accepted their rule, when the latter, pressed in their turn by enemies, found their way into the same fastnesses. The 'Kol' appear to have had no centralised government, but a loose cohesion of clans under chieftains; and the clans, again, were subdivided and grouped into village communities of a special form.

On the north-east of Chutiyā-Nāgpur, again, we find the tract called the 'Santāl Pergunnahs,' from its being chiefly peopled by another tribe, the *Santāl*, also marked by Kolarian customs. The settlement of these latter in this locality dates only from the eighteenth century, when they were driven by the oppression of the Marāthās from their former home in Orissa.[1]

The 'Kol,'[2] says Mr. Hewitt, 'still form the bulk of the population in the east of Chutiyā-Nāgpur; but in the west they have been deprived of the best lands by the Gond and Urāoñ (Dravidian) invaders, whose superior organisation made them permanent rulers of the country.' The British districts of Hazāribāgh (with Lohārdagā), Singhbhūm, and Mānbhūm, are largely peopled by *Mundā*, *Larkā* (or *Ho*), and *Bhūmij*, respectively. 'The Ho adds Mundā,' says Mr. Hewitt, 'who now hold what must have been very early settlements of the race in their progress westwards from Arakan and Burma, have . . . maintained themselves as a separate and distinct people from

[1] The *Santāls* found the central hills of their new home already occupied by wild Pahāria, or hill-people; but there was ample room in the lower hills and valleys, into which the Pahārias did not venture. Article quoted, p. 401.

[2] Mr. J. F. Hewitt was Commissioner of this division and knew the people well; while his after experience of the more Dravidian population of the Central Provinces gave him opportunities for comparing and contrasting their customs. He has written an interesting article on Chutiyā-Nāgpur and its people (*Asiatic Quarterly Review*, April 1887, p. 396). The chief tribes are *Ho* and *Mundā*. There are others—the *Sāoñt*, *Rautia*, &c., but their numbers are few and their affinities little known. The *Bhūmij*, or *Bhūiñjyā*, are said to show certain marks of Dravidian origin.

the earliest times.' The Ho of Singhbhūm have always remained independent; and though Urāoñ and other immigrant tribes settled in the Mundā country and took the rule, 'tradition says that they were admitted peaceably: they imposed their own organisation on the Mundā villages of the west, and left those of the east undisturbed.'[1] The Rājās of the States formed in Chutiyā-Nāgpur were in fact Gond or Urāoñ in origin; others in the neighbouring States are called 'Nāgbańsi'—a Hindī name given to royal families of non-Aryan (probably mixed Dravidian) origin, and meaning sons of the Nāgā or Snake. Some of them have since been admitted to Rājput rank.[2] In fact, the loose tribal organisation of the Kolarian tribes invited the assumption of sovereignty by any neighbouring chief whose family had attained sufficient dignity and power.[3] Of the other States of Chutiyā-Nāgpur, Sirgūjā (and with it Jāshpur) is occupied by Gonds and Urāoñs.[4] In the western hills we find a separate Kolarian tribe, the *Korwā*, having the characteristic tribal organisation by *totems*; one part of them are still nomadic, but others are beginning to form more

[1] Quoted from *Journ. Soc. Arts*, xxxv. 620. The Urāoñ were a Dravidian people (see p. 110, *ante*), whose name is preserved in 'Uriya'—'Orissa' (= *Uṛā* or *Oḍra-des*).

[2] In the *Central Provinces Gazetteer* (Introduction, p. lxvii.) mention is made of 'the Mundā Rājās of Chutiyā-Nagpur;' but the Rājās themselves were either Urāoñ or from the Gond country. See also *Journal As. Soc. of Bengal* for 1866, xxxv. part ii. 16. An inscription as old as A.D. 1073 shows the Rājā of the Bastār State as 'Nāgbańsi,' though now the chiefs are accounted 'Rājput.' As to the advancement of the Nāgā chiefs to Rājput rank, see some good remarks in the Introduction to *Central Provinces Gazetteer*, p. lxiv. ff.

[3] I am not aware of any instance of a certainly Kolarian clan giving rise to a ruling house. It is probably by a mistake, originating with Dr. Buchanan-Hamilton, that the *Çeru* or *Çīru* are sometimes called 'Kolarian.' They certainly furnished rulers for a somewhat extensive kingdom in and about Bihār, but it is fairly certain that they were Dravidian—possibly connected also with some other northern foreign race; they were originally snake-worshippers, which Kolarians were not. Ultimately, of course, the still surviving remains of the race became Hindu (Beames' *Elliot's Glossary*, s.v. 'Cheru'; and *Journal R. A. Soc.* xx. part iii. 354).

[4] In Sirgūjā State the Dravidians form 40·1 per cent. of the population, and the Kolarians 21·5 per cent. (*Imperial Gazetteer*, s.v. 'Sirgūjā').

permanent cultivating settlements. Mr. Hewitt notices one interesting point, which is that in this transition stage, though the families of the same *totem* make their dwellings together, they have as yet *no fixed boundaries to the incipient villages, nor any village-headmen.* At the same time the *clan* territories are defined and well guarded, and there is an hereditary chieftain over each.

The separation of the several Kolarian tribes must have been of long duration, since the dialects, though radically connected, are distinct. The *Ho* tribe is divided into minor clans called *kīlī*, which are numerous, each having its own name. The Santāls are also so divided.[1] The more settled tribes have villages in which the groups were (at any rate originally) formed by families with the same *totem.*[2] The 'unions' of villages or clan-territorial divisions of the country were called by some word which has survived locally as *parhā*. Each such *parhā* contained from ten to twenty-five villages, and had a chief called *mānkī* (and by other names locally). Unless these chiefs became united in subordination to some 'Rājā,' they remained independent and hardly in a sufficient degree of relation to form a confederacy; though it seems that they met in assemblies to confer on any matter that concerned several of the *parhā* in common. The *parhā*, or union grouping, is still traceable, and on festival occasions each one exhibits its own flag with the distinguishing device or *totem.*[3] The *parhā* chief is not always hereditary, though he is so among some of the tribes.

[1] *Journ. Soc. Arts*, May 1887, pp. 621–2. And see Dalton, *Ethnography of Bengal* (Calcutta, 1872), p. 151 ff. The names of the Santāl clans are believed to have meanings—perhaps names of the animals selected for the *totem.* One only is so recognised with reference to existing speech; but the names may have been gradually corrupted. The clans are so far exogamous that a man of one *totem* has to seek a wife in a family of a different one. See also Risley, *T. & C. of Bengal*, ii. 230 (Glossary).

[2] See *J. R. A. S.* xx. (1889) 330, where Mr. Hewitt remarks on the absence of the *village* priest, and that the villages in one group or union are served by the same priest, who goes on circuit and propitiates both the village deity and the *desaulī*, or territorial deities.

[3] *Journ. Soc. Arts*, xxv. 622; also Risley, *T. & C. of Bengal*, ii. 105, Glossary.

Each separate group of families or village had its own headman, known as *mūndā* among the *Ho* and *Mūndā* tribes, *mānjhī* among the Santāl, and *sirdār* (a later borrowed Hindustāni word) among the Bhūmij.[1] In the more settled Ho and Mundā districts we find the village-headman quite a permanent institution; and there is a village-priest also, though not hereditary. There are some other village officers, but these were probably added at a later time by the ruler, for the purpose of control and for facilitating his revenue collections. When a permanent cultivating settlement was made, and the jungle was cleared, a grove (*sarnā*) was left as the sacred abode of the village gods; but the grove has often dwindled to a single tree.

It is worthy of remark that this idea of a village sacred tree or grove is not confined to the Kolarian tribes, though it may have originated with them in the remote past. It is noticeable among the Southern Dravidians (*e.g.* the *Devara-kādū*, or sacred groves of Coorg). True it is that the circumstances of Eastern life in all the provinces of the plains would make a grove or a large shady tree almost a necessity of existence where any place of public meeting was required; but this alone would not account for the idea of sanctity connected with the tree; and we find that in the provinces where the country is barer, the planting of a tree is an essential feature of the village foundation. In the dry and almost treeless plains of the South-eastern Panjāb, among a totally different class of people, we shall notice a custom of driving in a stake (*moṛī*), cut from a particular kind of tree, at the foundation of a new village, and how very lucky is the omen if the stake should be induced to strike root and grow into a tree; a result which would only occur with certain species and under favourable conditions.

But to return to the Kolarian village. The headman is the person to allot the lands within the area, and to settle any

[1] This is perhaps owing to the circumstance that in Mānbhūm and Barābhūm districts the Bhūmij have so frequently become *ghātwāl* or frontier militia and wardens of the marches under the local ruler; hence they have become familiar with the modern military title *Sirdār* (= troop-leader).

dispute as to the location of a family. As each village begins to outgrow its limits, small hamlets (*ṭolā*) are formed outside, in the waste, but still consider themselves as portions of the parent-village; for the headman is temporary and acts in concert with the original *mundā*.[1] He only attains separate rank, and the office becomes hereditary in his family, when the hamlet has developed into a separate village.

The villages of the Santāls have been picturesquely rather than fully described. Tribal areas, like the *parhā*, are recognised, and are under a chief now called *parganait*: his functions are chiefly social, and he gives his sanction to all marriages and consults with the village elders on occasion. All the families have their separate holdings, and the headman settles any dispute; the stage of society is purely patriarchal.[2] As the Santāls have only moved within a century to their present home, every village must have been founded separately under a *manjhī*.[3] Accordingly, the spirit of the original head of the group (*manjhī-hanan*) is worshipped in the village sacred grove, and the existing *manjhī* derives his hereditary authority from him. But there is a second headman (*pramānik*) described as a 'deputy.' Both these officers are aided by an 'executive,' *jag-mānjhī* (also with a deputy), who sees to the actual execution of orders and the routine business, while the *manjhī* sits and issues the orders, and, as Hunter adds, only 'interferes on great occasions.' The *jag-manjhī* seems also to act as a sort of censor of the morals of youth; and his control lasts till they are married.[4] Each

[1] *Journ. Soc. Arts*, May 1887, p. 621.

[2] *Annals of Rural Bengal*, i. 217 ff; and see Risley, *T. & C. of Bengal*, ii. (Glossary), 234.

[3] I write this word as I find it. I am not really aware whether it is *manjhi* or *manji*, and whether the *a* is long or short (*a* or *ā*). Wilson gives *mānjhi*, but then he identifies it with the Hindī word of the same form, meaning steersman of a boat; so does Risley, who also says that *mundā* is Sanskrit. I should like to feel sure that these words and others of the kind are not much older than Sanskrit, and that they were not given to the literary language from an older dialect.

[4] The Santāls, like other Kolarians, do not adopt the plan of keeping all the youth of the village together—the males in one house, the girls in another. This is a Dravidian custom.

village has its watchman and its priest (*naiki*) to scare away evil spirits. The *pramānik* was specially concerned in seeing that there was an equable distribution of land, so that all the families might share and share alike, and not that one set should monopolise all the good land and leave the bad to the rest. It will be observed that there is no appearance of any joint-ownership among the village bodies: the 'title' to land is by occupation and clearing, under the direction of the tribal authorities; and the only idea of right in the uncultivated jungle is that it is within the territory of this or that *parhā* and cannot be encroached on by another.

A few words may be added about the organisation of the Kolarian population by the Rājās of frontier States, to form a militia to protect the passes. This has perhaps its points of resemblance to the organisation made by the Aham rulers (in Assam) of the subject people into groups for service. In Chutiyā-Nāgpur the plan had this advantage, that it conciliated the people by allowing a free holding of land to each man according to his grade; and at the same time it utilised the superior knowledge they must have possessed of the byways and intricacies of so difficult a frontier. In organising the force, it is evident that natural clan-divisions and grades of authority were made use of, as being already familiar. The lands held free on what is known as the *ghātwālī* tenure in certain British districts originated in this way: the Rājā's rule has passed away, but the holders of land still remain, willing to perform frontier duty if required, but clinging to the privileged holding of land. In Bengal such tenures were common along the 'frontier' between the hill country and the plains of Bīrbhūm and the Ganges Valley: similar tenures are known in Berār and elsewhere. In Chutiyā-Nāgpur the rank and file of the militia (so regarded) are largely 'aboriginal' tribes, though some of the upper grades of officers may be of different race. In the absence of any survey and record it very naturally happens that the area of privileged lands increases beyond all bounds, and the Rājā's revenue is seriously threatened. Such a complication had arisen in Mānbhūm between the local chief and his subjects. A British officer was deputed to settle the matter and determine what lands were *ghātwālī*, or privileged, and what were not so.[1]

The rank and file of the clansmen (locally called *çhuār*) were grouped for service in small companies under petty officers called *digwār*—*i.e.* guide or way-shower. A number of these were again subordinate to a superior officer, the *sirdār ghātwāl*. But in the *land-holding* arrangements for the remuneration of all grades we see something of the natural (tribal) grouping. Each village had a headman called *sirdār*, who was, in fact, the *mundā* already spoken of. Then a union or group of villages is called '*tarf*,' and the union-chief is '*sirdār ghātwāl*.' This latter officer, however, is one of the Rājā's creation, and he sometimes gives himself great airs of rank and dignity. But in fact he was found to be ousting or replacing another official called *sadiāl*; and at first various questions were raised as to what the real position of this latter officer was. There seems to be no reasonable doubt that in fact he was the indigenous chief, or *mānkī*, of the union; but in order to secure a preponderance of the Rājā's authority he was rather overshadowed by the *sirdār ghātwāl*, though still left with certain privileges and perquisites.

SECTION III.—THE DRAVIDIAN GROUP

Though the Dravidian races are very numerous and have formed the basis of a large part of the existing population, and though they are represented by existing languages having a very distinct structure of their own, yet there has been nothing in their history or circumstances to prevent their progressive alteration and their fusion with other races, whether Aryan or Kolarian. But, more than that, the gradual but complete adoption of Hindu caste and Hindu customs has had a very great effect in obliterating the traces of earlier distinctive Dravidian tribal law or custom. The principal object of our remarks in this section is, therefore, a limited one; it is to endeavour to eliminate such vestiges of custom among confessedly Dravidian peoples as can be traced back to early times, before the Hindu

[1] Mr. H. Risley, B.C.S. His elaborate Report to the Board of Revenue, Bengal, full of interesting details, is dated December 20, 1883.

influence was felt. These vestiges are more numerous than they are in the case of Kolarian tribes, but they are still somewhat scanty. The country around Chutiyā-Nāgpur and Hill Orissa—the refuge-ground, as I have called it, of early tribes—has also preserved to us the Dravidian village in what there is every reason to believe to be its original form. And there are a few other localities in which we find ancient Dravidian races evidently in varying degrees of progress; and here again customs regarding village life and land-holding have to some extent been preserved. But Dravidian custom must necessarily have had a much wider influence than these special localities indicate. The main bulk of the population of India below the Vindhyan Hills was confessedly Dravidian, and there can hardly be any serious doubt that the Central and Southern Indian *raiyatwāri* village, marked by the existence of an influential hereditary headman, and by the method of allotting free lands as the special privilege of the village chief and the accountant, as well as to remunerate its hereditary staff of artisans and servants, is the direct descendant and surviving representative of the old Dravidian form of agricultural settlement.

It will be desirable, in the first instance, to give a brief *résumé* of what has been said as to the position of the Dravidian group of races in India. We observe that north of what I have called the Vindhyan barrier we have now few, if any, traces of *distinctively* Dravidian custom. The Aryan population has there dominated, and has impressed its character and language on the whole country, so as to leave, it is true, a very large amount of the aboriginal element in the population, especially in the humbler castes and classes, but little of what can be proved to be non-Aryan custom. And not only Aryan invaders, but other northern races like the Jat and the Gujar, have had a large share, especially in the North-West, in modifying original conditions. Nevertheless, there is reason to believe that extensive Dravidian races were once to be found even in Northern India. For this we have no direct explanation to offer. We know nothing of how such Dravidians came, and whether they entered by a route (like the Indus Valley) which would give access both above and below the Vindhyans, or whether they spread from south to north, or *vice versa*. The long course of time, and the absence of any apparent opposition to their spread, may have combined to make the diffusion of this stock on both sides of the Vindhyans possible. All we can perceive is that Dravidian races in the North have gradually fused with, and merged into, a general 'Hindu' population, losing all definitely separate languages or dialects. Even below the Vindhyā, where the Dravidian element is far stronger, we find a distinction between the modified Dravidian type of the upper part of the peninsula and that of the South. For this we can only partially account. In the upper West of India, however, there is reason to believe that the introduction of an Aryan element—and very likely a Scythic element as well—has been the cause of the difference. Indeed, we meet with some curious local traditions which connect some of the (mainly) Dravidian peoples of the central region, such as the Gond, with the North.

At the eastern end of the Vindhyan country, as in Chutiyā-Nāgpur, the Dravidian races have become intermingled with the Kolarian, and to some extent with races of Aryan origin, when these latter ultimately reached Orissa and the North of Madras—an event which, naturally, could not have occurred till comparatively late historic times.[1] When we pass below this Western and Central belt of modified Dravidian tribes, we find the South occupied by almost unmixed Dravidian peoples speaking their own languages; and, though these ultimately adopted Hinduism, it was by the efforts of individual Brahman missionaries and possibly the occasional adventures of Aryan princes, not by means of any general Aryan immigration or extensive fusion of races.[2]

Among these different Dravidian tribes and peoples it is evident that civilisation had made progress in varying degrees.

[1] For instance, by the time the (Hindu) Gajapati kings occupied the plains of Orissa, they had developed the Puranic religion and a State organisation such as we find in Rājputāna.

[2] It is to be remembered that it is quite possible for the language to be much affected, consequent on the complete diffusion of religious and caste ideas, without any very extensive admixture of the people, and certainly without going back to any very remote period. The Orissa language is very Sanskritic in character, yet no Aryans came there till the days of the Gajapati kings. The same is true also of the Marāthī language. (See p. 112, *ante*.)

There was frequently a strong tribal organisation and government, and we shall see southern kingdoms established in an apparently civilised form in very ancient times. Vast ruins of forts, tanks, and other works show that the Dravidian people were builders ; agriculture flourished among them, and it is impossible to suppose that the regular institution of villages, unions of villages, and territorial divisions, of which evidences meet us everywhere, could have had no existence until Aryan teachers came and introduced them. But in so vast a congeries of people it is not to be expected that there should be any uniformity as to custom, or as to the stage of civilisation attained. We find in some places tribes much more developed than in others. The physical features of the country had probably a good deal to do with such differences. Some tribes would have been dwellers in the hills and so been less accessible to civilising influences. Others would have inhabited the broad and fertile plains, where, the difficulties of clearing the jungle once surmounted, everything would have been favourable to the development of wealth and to the growth of the art of government. Whatever the cause, the fact of the difference cannot be doubted. The best races were civilised, and had cities and armies and a monarchy ; the lower races must have either fallen back, through defeat, subjection, and poverty, into a stage which we must call half barbarous, or have been isolated and never raised above a stage of society, which was primitive rather than uncivilised. Nor must we forget that after centuries of local war, and, later on, of foreign conquest and internal feud, as well as of social and religious revolution, many changes, both in advance and in retrogression, must have occurred. Tribes may now appear enslaved or in the lowest rank, that once were important and wealthy. If, as appears to have been the case, the adoption of Hindu caste rules was, in earlier days, the road to success, many tribes who clung to independence and refused conformity may have found themselves losers—forced back to a roving hill life and nomadic cultivation, or sunk to be the helots of races which marched more with the times. It is not surprising, then, to find that distinctively Dravidian customs can now only be found in certain limited localities where circumstances tended to preserve them. It will be well to examine first the tribal, and ultimately the monarchical, organisation, as it can be traced in Dravidian countries, and then to describe what are more specifically Dravidian land-customs, including the form of village settlement.

The Dravidian Tribe and its Developments.

Of a very early tribal organisation, the Kāndh clans[1] afford us a still surviving example; and, from traces of *tribal* territories and subdivisions found in all parts of the South it is only reasonable to conclude that a similar organisation was once general. We also have some indications of the way in which patriarchal government developed into the monarchical.

The Kāndh tribes had long ago separated. One section simply merged into the low-caste population of the plains; another allowed itself to be absorbed in the militia system of a neighbouring Rājā; while a third section, which acknowledged the suzerainty of a neighbouring Hindu ruler, retained practical independence and its own patriarchal constitution.[2] In some respects these latter clans represent very primitive ideas: witness the practice of human sacrifice, only abolished in our own times; in others they exhibit certain marks of advancement—a strong family organisation of an earlier type than the Hindu joint-family, and well-defined customs of social life. It happened that one principal section of the tribe inhabited a part of the country represented by the Bod and Āthmālik States, and by what was once the Gūmsūr State, near the Mahānadī River, now in the Ganjam District of the Madras Presidency. The rebellion and misconduct of Gūmsūr in 1835 led to the suppression of

[1] The name is variously written, as Khond, Kāndh, &c. The tribe will not be confused with the 'Gond,' from whom they are distinct, though ethnically of the same stock. Dr. Macleane has collected a great deal of the information about this people (*Ethnology*, i. 36–51). There is more than one dialect of Kāndh speech; the language is distinct from that of the Gond tribes, and has a resemblance to Tamil and Telugu.

[2] 'This section,' says Sir W. Hunter (*Orissa*, ii. 72), 'wrung from their Hindu neighbours the position . . . of free allies. A system of military aids, homage, investiture of the tribal chiefs and patriarch by the Rājā, and other feudal incidents, sprang up as the superior civilisation of the Hindu prince more and more exerted its influence.'

the State, and consequently the Kāndh population was brought under direct British administration.[1]

The Kāndhs regard war *and agriculture* as the only business of life; they despise trade and money concerns of all kinds. The families form connected village-groups; of these we will speak presently. These village areas are the locations of groups of families united in a larger clan-territory, now called by the borrowed Hindī name *muṭṭhā.* This is evidently the territory of some clan-division, which we also see as the *nādu* in so many of the other districts. Each village has its chief, and the *muṭṭhā* has its chief, called *abāyā.* When there is business which concerns a number of villages, the village chiefs meet in council under the presidency of the *abāyā.* Just as the head of the eldest family in the village is the village chief, so the head of the eldest family in the whole clan-territory or *muṭṭhā* is the *abāyā.*[2] The general supremacy of the various *muṭṭhā* has now passed to a Hindu sovereign; or, in the part of the country I am describing, to the British Government; but in former days it would seem that the heads of clans would meet in council to settle matters of such wide import as to interest the several clans in common. There is another similar tribe called *Bhūyā*, or *Bhuīñyā*, in the Keūnjhar State; but they have lost their original language and now speak Uriyā. They have accepted the supremacy of the Hindu Rājā, but it is curious to observe that they couple this with an assertion of their own independent title to the soil they occupy, which they maintain by insisting on the right to instal the Rājā (putting on him the *tilak* or mark of sovereignty)—a right which they have again and again maintained by obstinate wars.[3]

[1] They found a sympathetic superintendent in Lieutenant Macpherson, whose efforts in helping the tribes, and putting a stop to the sacrifice of aliens to the Earth Goddess, are justly appreciated in Sir W. Hunter's *Orissa.* It is to Lieutenant Macpherson's reports that we are chiefly indebted for our knowledge of details. Sir W. Hunter has rightly attached much importance to the customs of the Kāndhs, and the full account in vol. ii. of his *Orissa* makes it unnecessary for me to do more than notice those points of custom which have a direct bearing on our subject.

[2] Each *muṭṭhā* has a priest of the *Domnā* tribe for the whole territory. This recalls the Kolarian *Baigā* priest.

[3] Cf. *ante*, p. 89. An account of the matter will be found in Hunter's

Here we have tribes with no monarch of their own, and consequently—even with their strong feeling for independence and tribal union—obliged sooner or later to place themselves, or fall, as the case may be, under the protective suzerainty of some foreign ruler.

In Chutiyā-Nāgpur, on the other hand, the Dravidian chiefs developed a more centralised rule; and here we find the usual model—a central territory held by the Rājā or greater chief, and outlying domains governed by lesser chiefs in a sort of feudal subordination. The ablest military leader among the chiefs is usually entrusted with the frontier marches. We can still trace the site of the central demesne and its capital at Pātkum, in the Mānbhūm District.[1] The outlying chiefships were Dhālbhūm, Barābhūm, &c. These chiefships at one time fell under the suzerainty of the Haihaiyā princes in the Upper Narbadā Valley, but were not much interfered with. Descendants of the ancient chiefs still held the country when the Permanent Settlement of Bengal was made, and they were recognised as 'Zamindārs,' or landlords of their territory, paying a fixed land-revenue, or rather tribute.

All around this part of the country we have a series of Native States, and some chiefships not of sufficient rank to be 'States,' but recognised as 'landlord' estates with special terms of Settlement. Towards the west, beyond the territories of the Urāoñ chiefs above mentioned, are the lands of Gond chiefs and others, who were originally 'Nāgbañsi.'[2] It is not known how ancient the

Orissa, ii. 114 ff. There are some interesting remarks about the *Bhuīñyā*, in the State of Bonai, in Mr. Hewitt's article above quoted (*Asiatic Quarterly Review*, April 1887, p. 404).

[1] Hwen Thsang had visited this country, then called Kirana-Suvarna, in the middle of the seventh century. He found the people 'honest and amiable,' and notes 'that they loved learning exceedingly and applied themselves to it with earnestness.' General Cunningham supposes the capital to have been at Barābāzār; but Mr. Hewitt, with better local knowledge, points out that this place is not near the Subanrikha River, as the traveller says the capital was; while Pātkum not only is so placed, but at Dalmi Village in the neighbourhood, vast ruins of an ancient city still exist.

[2] The Rājās and chiefs in time became Hindus and of course Rājputs; the Nāgbañsi descent, of which they were once proud, and the snake-

Chutiyā-Nāgpur chiefs really are, nor when the idea of a monarchy was developed. In the case of the Gond dynasties of the Central Provinces, they did not emerge to notice till quite late times, and were overthrown by the Marāthās. Seeing the very ancient establishment of some form of kingdom in the Narbadā Valley, both in the lower valley and in the upper part at Garhā-maṇḍlā, it is always possible that the Dravidian chiefs copied the institutions of their neighbours of Aryan or northern origin. In any case, it is not easy to feel satisfied that these Urāon and other chiefships, though certainly Dravidian, were the result of a development unaided by example from without. Mr. Hewitt, however, to whose local knowledge great weight must be attached, thinks they were wholly indigenous.

We turn naturally to the more celebrated southern dynasties connected with the names of *Pāṇḍyā*, *Çerā*, and *Çoḷā* (*Çoṛā* or *Shozhā*),[1] which in early times extended over the greater part of Madras. The former was in the south (Madurā, &c.); *Çerā* (or *Kerāla*) was in the upper-west; and Çoḷā extended over the whole Tamil country. They were known to the Greek writers three centuries B.C. In this case an indigenous origin can hardly be doubted, even if it be true, as it well may be, that the name *Pāṇḍyā* is derived from an Aryan prince. The other kingdoms have not even this asserted for them.[2] Indeed,

symbol which they once engraved on their signet-rings, have gone out of fashion (see *Central Provinces Gazetteer*, Introduction, p. lxiv.).

[1] *Çoḷā* is spelt with the peculiar Tamil letter which is poorly represented by 'ḷ'; some think it better represented by 'zh' or a liquid 'ṛ'—hence we sometimes find 'Shozhā' written. The *Çoḷā* and *Çerā* kingdoms are mentioned in inscriptions of Asokā (*circa* 250 B.C.) *Pāṇḍyā* was known to Megasthenes and Strabo. In vol. ii. of the *Southern Archæol. Surv. Rep.* there is an account of these dynasties by Mr. Sewell. For an estimate of their antiquity see Caldwell's *History of Tinnevelly*, pp. 26, 27, and Nelson's *D. M. of Madurā*, part. iii. Professor H. H. Wilson's sketch is well known (*J. R. A. S.* iii. 199).

[2] It is quite possible that some wandering Aryan adventurer of the *Pāṇḍu* House may have obtained a ruling position in the South; and the capital, Madura, may thus be connected with the Sanskrit name of Mathurā. See G. Oppert, p. 98, as to the popular tradition and worship of *Pāṇḍavas*. Even if an Aryan prince did obtain the rule and give his name (or rather his patronymic) to the kingdom, it does not follow that the form and constitution of government were Aryan, or that it was the first essay of the kind in the South; such, indeed, is in every way unlikely.

given the strong tribal organisation which marks the Dravidian races, to start with, it is a most natural development that either in time of war with neighbouring tribes, or by the action of personal ambition, some chief of commanding ability should have taken the decided lead, and persuaded or compelled others to act under him. That a chief thus exalted above his fellows should sometimes be a foreign adventurer coming with all the glamour of his romantic journey, as well as his personal superiority, and probable military skill, would be in no way remarkable. All over India we are familiar with the manner in which princes have gained the rule over provinces or States with which they have no connection by birth, and in which they have no strong clan-connection or support. I will only add that South Indian history has always shown the turbulent power of independent local chiefs, who evidently trace their origin to tribal chiefs of the *nādu* or local division of territory. In the days of peaceful tribal government such chiefs act in concert, and the *nād-kuṭṭam*, or territorial assembly, maintains its influence; but soon the chiefs are forced into more or less unwilling submission to some superior, or to the suzerainty of some (possibly foreign) dynasty; in that condition, they are scarcely heard of, but when the dynasty is overthrown they throw off all restraint, and resume their freedom, very generally becoming oppressors of their people. All over the South we find these chiefs with the title of *nāyak*,[1] or *pālegārā*, and the like, who, after the overthrow of the southern dynasties, became emancipated from all control. The result in modern times has been curious; for, when the provinces became British at the beginning of the century, a Permanent Settlement on the Bengal model was ordered; and, had these various local chiefs appeared in peaceable possession of their estates, and had they accepted the inevitable as the Bengal

[1] *Nāyak* (*Nāyakku*, Tam.; *Nāyaḍu*, Teḷ.) is *said* to be a Sanskrit word. Caldwell (*Gramm.* Introduction, p. 29) refers these chiefs to 'the descendants of those soldiers of fortune by whom the Pāṇḍyā and Çoḷā kingdoms were subverted.' But in truth there is no occasion to come to any late event for the origin of local chiefs; under whatever local name, the *nayak* or *pālegārā* are among the earliest Dravidian institutions. Even in the days before the colonisation of (what afterwards became) Arcot, tradition shows the ancient Pallava territory divided into twenty-four *kuṭṭam*, each under its own chief.

chiefs did, they would one and all have been recognised at least as dignified landlords, with only a moderate permanent land-revenue or tribute to pay; and the prevalent tenure of the greater part of Madras might now have been that of considerable land-lord estates or properties. But, so long had these petty chiefs been accustomed to turbulence and to unchecked indulgence in local fighting and marauding expeditions, that they could not settle down to a new position; consequently, they revolted, and for a time carried on what have been dignified with the name of 'Polygar wars' in the southern Presidency. The result has been that they have disappeared—all, in fact, but a few of the greater chiefs, to whom the above description has no application, and a very few of the lesser ones.

There is one curious example of the growth of a Dravidian monarchy, and the subsequent conversion of local chiefs into landlords, which deserves mention. In Malabār, on the west coast, we know that the population was made up of various immigrant races from the South and other parts, including, in time, a colony of Brahmans.[1] The ruling tribe which furnished the chiefs was called *Nāyar*.[2] The country and its language are Dravidian. There is a somewhat fabulous local history called the *Kerālolpati*. Of Brahmanic authorship, it is written to glorify the caste, whom it represents as the original owners of the whole land! But through the legendary matter runs a vein of real

[1] Who must have been a comparatively late addition, as they came with developed caste and Puranic religious ideas, and so must have represented a time when the Aryan settlement in the Ganges Valley had long been consolidated.

[2] The Nair of books. *Nāyar* is the plural of *Nāyan*. Mr. Logan derives the name from the Sanskrit *Nāyaka*. It is quite possible that the original name may have been different, and that this was adopted later with the Hindu caste. The whole details are to be found in Mr. Logan's *Malabār District Manual* (2 vols., Madras Government Press, 1887), which, in spite of some untenable theories about the origin of the *Nāyar* claims to landlordship, is full of interesting information. The *Bant* caste of South Kānara has had an almost exactly similar history. It is curious to observe that in this district, which adjoins Malabār, the date of the arrival of Brahman colonies can be fairly well fixed, and it does not occur till about the eighth century of our era. (*South Kānara D. M.* i. 145).

tradition which is often supported by other evidence.[1] Practically, it seems that in Malabār the Brahmans were content with a great measure of influence, while the Nāyar chiefs were the military and ruling class—just as the Khsatriyā Rājās and their Brahman counsellors became a feature of the Hindu polity in the North.[2]

What is important for our purpose is that this country was also from early times divided into districts called *nād*. The *nād* was at a later time subdivided into *deşam*, which was a matter of military organisation, each *deşam* having its quota of men to send to the army. Traditionally, four of these *nād* had the pre-eminence, and the group of their representative chiefs formed a council to govern the country. But the plan was not successful. Next we find that for a time a head chief was elected for three years; but, this also failing, an assembly was held to choose a king from the neighbouring country of *Çerā*. (*Kon* was the more ancient title of the king.) This elected king was to hold office for twelve years.[3] It is not necessary to pursue the history in detail; the time came, as might be expected, when the overlord, by this time entitled *Parumāl*, established himself for life. At last the dominion broke up, when, as there is historical ground for believing, one of the kings became a convert to Islam and determined on a pilgrimage to Arabia. Curious enough are the legends telling how, before his departure, he distributed his territories; but they do not touch upon our point, and must be left aside with the remark that, though certain territories were

[1] For example, the legend suggests that the Brahmans were troubled by the 'Snakes' (Nāgā, or Dravidian) races, and came to terms with them. Malabār was once converted to the Jain religion, which seems in the South to have so often replaced the Dravidian snake-worship, as Buddhism did in the North.

[2] The *Nāyar* could only be *Çūdra*, and are so ranked in the Brahmanic caste-system; but they are great caste purists, and regard themselves as of very high rank with reference to the many grades below them (see p. 88, *ante*).

[3] Dr. Day (*Cochin Past and Present* [Madras, 1863], p. 42) mentions that at the end of the twelve years the proper course was for the king to commit suicide, or at least to retire into a hermitage. Dr. G. Oppert (p. 69) mentions that the *Valluva kon*, or chief of the *Valluva nād*, was president of the elective council or assembly.

aggregated under one head, the general condition which ensued was the resumption of local rule by a number of independent, and doubtless rival, chieftains. The lapse of years only aggravated the weakness of such a system, and the chiefs fell before the attack, however short-lived, of the Mysore Sultāns. Out of the ruins ultimately arose the claim of the *Nāyar* chiefs and their descendants to be *janmī*, or hereditary landlords of the territories they once ruled—a claim which was admitted by the British Government, though under much misunderstanding of its real history. This landlordship, however, as usual, rather affected the legal status of the subordinate tenures than changed their form. Though not directly connected with our subject, I may be permitted to mention that these tenures arose out of a system of 'fiefs,' or service-holdings, which were provided for the minor chiefs and yeomen of *Nāyar* caste, under the greater land-holders, or *janmīdār*, as they were called. Each of the subordinate holders had his land on permanent tenancy on condition of paying a cash deposit for the use of the superior or territorial chief; the interest of this sum was the equivalent, wholly or in part, of an annual rent. Such tenures were naturally not understood by British officers of the late eighteenth century; they accordingly were supposed to be a sort of 'mortgage-tenure' *which the landlords had a right to redeem*; and thus the position of the subordinate holders was materially lowered. Originally the idea of 'mortgage' arose out of the fact, not only that the tenant paid a sum of money to the landlord, but there were customary rules for revising the terms on the death of the landlord or at certain recurring periods.

But to return to the monarchical organisation. Though a central government was established, the *nād* divisions long retained their importance. We continue to hear of a great council of 600 chiefs of *nāds* assembled from time to time.[1] This institution, in fact, lasted down to a late period, for in 1746 we find a British officer reporting: 'These Nairs, being heads of the Calicut people, resemble the parliament and do not obey the

[1] See Logan's *Malabār D. M.* i. 88, 89. It was probably a united assembly of the chiefs of the 150 *taṛa*, or family groups, for each of the four leading *nād*.

King's dictates in all things, but chastise his ministers when they do unwarrantable things.'

The earlier Dravidian plan seems to have been not to give a general produce-share or land-revenue to the chief or sovereign, but to assign[1] 'royal farms' or lands, cultivated by slaves, for the support of his dignity. We shall notice the same plan, on a smaller scale, in the *mānjhihas*, or lands for the chief, set apart in each village of Chutiyā-Nāgpur. The same institution appears also in the little kingdom of Coorg, where the *panniya*, or royal farms, were still recognisable at the British Settlement.[2] In the Chutiyā-Nāgpur States we see further how the chiefs became dissatisfied, or unable to live on the original provision, and how they imposed the contribution of a share in the produce on other lands, exempting only the priest's lands and those of the original settlers and privileged families who furnished the hereditary village-officers.

Whatever, then, may be the antiquity of the monarchical form among the Dravidians, and its claim to be pre-Aryan in point of origin, it is evident that from the remotest times a division of the country—evidently marking the territories of different clans under their chiefs—was a universal feature. And this prepares us to expect that some minor subdivision inside the *nād* was equally ancient.[3]

Dravidian Village-organisation in Orissa

Turning now to the *village* as found among Dravidian races, I will revert first to the less advanced members of the race, and describe the Kāndh custom as regards the *village*, as I have already done on the subject of tribal-organisation. The tribe, or

[1] See Logan's *Malabār D. M.* i. 223, 225.

[2] Coorg, it may be mentioned, is another instance of a country held by a number of proud independent chiefs of *nāds* without much coherence; and so they fell under the power of a foreign Rājā, who reduced the Coorg chieftains but left them their lands on permanently favourable terms, constituting the *jamma* tenure of Coorg.

[3] In the early attempts to settle the 'Jaghire' territory about Chingleput in 1795–9 we find a class of people still surviving called *Nātvār* (Nauttwar of the Reports; see *Mirasi Papers*, p. 8). These were certainly *nāduvār*, chiefs of the old *nād* divisions. Cf. the *Nāduvār* of Kānara.

rather the clan, is first subdivided, it will be remembered, into *muṭṭhā*, which I may call the minor-clan group, each descended from a common progenitor.[1] Each *muṭṭhā* territory contains a number of hamlets or villages. We have no direct information, as usual, as to what caused the various families of one *muṭṭhā* to separate themselves into smaller groups. But, however formed, these villages represent small aggregates of independent families, kept together not by any holding of land in common, but by some connection of *totem* or for some other clan reason, and under the control of a hereditary chief who was always, unless specially incapacitated, the head of the eldest family in the group.

The stage of progress represented by the Kāndh tribes does not place the family in the same position as the Hindu joint-family, where ancestral land is regarded as the joint property of the whole body, and the house-father is merely the representative, and is strictly limited as to his power of disposal of any part of the ancestral estate.

Among the Kāndh, the head of the family alone owns the homestead and all the land attached to it. His sons continue to live with him even after marriage; so that there is a sort of house-communion, and all share in the family meal prepared by the mother or—I suppose, possibly—the grandmother. The sons have no property during the father's life; it is only on his death that they will divide the land equally, daughters receiving no share, on the ground that they are unable to defend their possession.[2] The eldest son alone, unless incapacitated, succeeds to the chiefship if the father is village-headman. There is no trace whatever of each family having a certain fractional share in the entire village area, still less of any common ownership.[3] There is no evidence as to what was the rule or principle of allotting

[1] Macpherson's Report, quoted in *Orissa*, ii. 72.

[2] The father's brothers succeed in default of direct descendants; and, in default of all heirs, the land is divided among the other families of the village.

[3] This is expressly stated; see *Orissa*, ii. 72. Other Dravidian customs are noted, from Dalton's *Ethnography*, in Dr. Balfour's *Cyclopædia* ii. (Art. Kandh), such as that the youth of both sexes are separated, the males having their own club-house, in which they sleep at night; all the girls are kept in a separate dormitory under charge of a matron.

lands to each family, or even to each clan. It is observed that the clan, or rather the minor-clan (=*muṭṭhā*) was recognised in its *locale* simply by priority of occupation; and within the *muṭṭhā* it would seem that sometimes the boundaries of each village were fixed and the waste allotted to each. Throughout large tracts, however, the villages had practically no boundaries whatever, and a Kāndh could claim any unoccupied land within the tribal area; that means, I understand, within the limits of his own *muṭṭhā* or immediate clan territory.[1] Within the village areas, again, it seems that each family simply took out of the abundant waste[2] just what piece of land suited its means and requirements to clear and cultivate. Evidently a strong abstract idea of property in land had not arisen; land became property when it was cleared and occupied; while it lay waste it was hardly regarded as 'property' at all. No doubt, however, the entire area of land held within the *muṭṭhā* location was regarded as a territorial possession, so that a hostile tribe trying to encroach would at once be driven out. Land once occupied and cleared was not only regarded as heritable property, but it could be sold by calling witnesses and informing the *muṭṭhā* chief; this was done, not to gain his consent (so Lieutenant Macpherson informs us), but to secure the transaction being known.[3] The farms or homesteads forming a village-group are not closely placed together; they are, however, so far in a group that there are recognised servile castes or hereditary menials, blacksmiths, potters, herdsmen, and distillers, who 'hang about the outskirts of the village or live in a separate row of huts assigned to them.'[4] Thus in some parts

[1] Macpherson's Report, quoted in *Orissa*, ii. 210.

[2] In 1841 it was reported that only about *one-eighth* of the Kāndh territory was in the occupation of individuals, so that there must have been ample room for any settler of the clan to take up what he would, and acquire his 'title' by occupation and first clearing.

[3] The sale is completed by the vendor leading the buyer to the hamlet where the field lies; and, calling together five husbandmen of the place, he delivers to him a handful of earth and publicly receives part of the price. I find a similar form of land transfer mentioned among the Coorgs.

[4] This is still the characteristic of Madras villages generally (see p. 68, *ante*).

the Kāndh village or hamlet consists of two 'streets'—one a double row of family houses with a barrier at each end; the other a row of inferior huts for the servile families. In other parts the hamlet consists of a row of houses with the menials' huts clustered at one end. In other hamlets, again, the 'patriarch's' house is in the centre, near the sacred tree, which was always either left when the clearing was made, or was planted on the establishment of a new location.

The village chief has no special holding of land in virtue of his official headship; nor do I gather from the authorities that there are any village officers connected with the 'Rāj' and concerned with the collection of the Rājā's dues or with the extension of cultivation. This happens in later times. The clan chiefs of all grades have no special remuneration beyond their personal holdings, though they receive occasional free-will offerings. Their authority is solely derived from the family and clan connection and eldership.

West Coast Land-Tenures

We may now turn to the west coast districts, about the government of which we have already spoken. Here there are no village groups, and we have a totally different result of Dravidian customs. There seems here to have been, in very early times, some differentiating cause at work, because we have already, in the comparatively narrow space between the mountains and the sea, two different dialects, the Malayālam and the Tulu; Kanarese[1] also appears in the north, and the Coorg (Koḍagu) dialect may be reckoned as separate.[2]

Whatever may have been the original form of independent land-holding, we have now to take note of the Dravidian custom

[1] Kanarese, or the language of Karnāta, more properly belongs to the north-west corner of the Madras plains—Bellary and the neighbourhood. It will be remembered that, by a strange freak of accident, the term 'Carnatic' has become applied to the *east* coast; really the Karnāta district was in the north-west.

[2] There is no doubt that India shows many instances of the readiness with which dialects become localised when there are any physical features of mountains and rivers to separate the people. In the Himalayan valleys it is quite surprising how the dialects differ one from the other, especially as to the vocabulary—the names for different objects.

as affected by the adoption of caste, and of the joint-family idea which may have come from outside. Then, too, the whole country was dominated by local chiefs and their followers, with the result that when their rule passed away their estates became landlordships with a number of subordinate tenures which represented the 'fiefs' or holdings of the minor chiefs and yeomen of the military caste, as I have above described. There being no village-groups in the west coast country, the interior organisation of the *janmi* estates was peculiar, and depended on the strong sense of union which the Nāyar families possessed. The basis of the territorial organisation, coming down from very early times, was the *nād*, and every *nād* contained a number of Nāyar family groups called *taṛa*,[1] while Brahman groups were called *grāma* and the inferior castes by other names. The lands belonging to each *taṛa* were not, I understand, necessarily contiguous or even in the same jurisdiction. The group of blood relations forming the *taṛa* is the *taṛavāda*. Owing to causes which cannot here be gone into, the principle of the matriarchate prevails, and the members of the *taṛa* are *as many of the descendants from the common ancestress as remain united*. The *Nāyar*, and other families of rank, prefer to remain undivided; and the common property of the whole *taṛavāda* is managed by the *Kāraṇavar*, or elders of the group. The *taṛavāda* can at any time be completely separated into a number of new groups, but only when all consent. As long as they remain undivided, every member, male or female, *has an equal share in the common property, though no one can claim to have that share separated off*. This family union does not prevent the members having the practically separate enjoyment of property and of the isolated fortress-like houses, or rather premises, so picturesquely described by Mr. Logan. For each member who has his or her separate family house, with the fields around it, forms a branch called *tāvaḷi*; only the theory is that the partition is not real till a legal deed has been executed by the whole body.[2] This association, it will be observed, is very different from the Aryan joint-family, in which, apart from the fact that the descent is patriarchal, the several members have larger or smaller shares

[1] See *Malabār D. M.* i. 82 ff., 131, 133, 154–4.

[2] See especially *Malabār D.M.* i. 153.

according to their place in the table of descent. The *taṛavāda*, in fact, is a small 'minor-clan,' sept, or *gens*, which recognises its continuing bond of union by blood as a matter of dignity, and has some at least of its property undivided.[1] But, in reality, the plan of separating off the residences and the fields attached to them (*tāvaḷi*) prevents the theoretic community of family property from being practically inconvenient. The less dignified castes, who have also the Hindu idea of the joint-estate, carry out partition without objection. 'The process of disintegration,' says Mr. Logan, 'goes on continually, except among the highest classes, who pride themselves on maintaining a large common stock.' I should not fail to remark that the 'common stock' must, in any case, be maintained, under the Malabar custom of inheritance, I had almost said, automatically. This kind of joint estate is quite unique, and could not occur in any community with different customs of inheritance. For, as each male member of a *taṛavāda* dies, his share, as well as any property he may have separately acquired, *must*—unless he has gifted it away in his lifetime—go to the whole family, for *he can have no direct heirs*; his children inherit, not from him, but in their *mother's taṛavāda*.[2]

To the north of Malabār lie the two districts of Kānara (Kānnaḍa). These appear to have had much the same kind of tenure as Malabār; only that, being nearer or more accessible to the neighbouring States, they had fallen much more completely under the power of the 'Hindu' dynasties. At one time Kānara formed part of the *Kērala* or *Çerā* (Dravidian) kingdom, and then seems to have been conquered by Kadamba kings; in time it was prosperous under the rule of Vijayanagar and Bednūr, and finally came under the Mysore Sultans. 'Prior to

[1] Where some members of the group have some hereditary local dignity (*sthānam*), it is customary that a portion of the joint property should be made over, for life only, to that member for the support of his position.

[2] The *taṛavāda* in no wise resembles the joint-village of the North Indian *pattidāri* type; but as a group it has points of resemblance to the *khel* or minor clan of the north-west frontier in which common relationship is acknowledged, and the equal right to a share in the tribal property; only that in this latter case the share is nearly always divided out in a separate lot.

the introduction of Brahmans under the auspices of Kadamba kings in the eighth century,' writes the author of the *South Kanāra D. M.*, 'the early agricultural population of Tuluva seems to have held a subordinate position to the *Nāyar* or *Bant*, who were military adherents of the chieftains who ruled as feudatories of an over-lord, who in his turn recognised some more distant suzerain.'[1] In fact, the original separate holdings all over the district were gradually aggregated into lordships, under *Bant* castemen, who were possibly of the same origin as the Malabār Nāyar.[2] As usual, when the chiefship decayed, the families clung to the lands as owners; and the principal kind of hereditary estate, held by *Bant* and also by Brahman castemen, was the *mūlāvarg*, the estate going back to the 'root' or 'origin.' Owing to various causes, the estates became somewhat broken up, and so consisted of various plots scattered through several of the local aggregates of holdings (*māgane*) which do duty for villages. They are held by undivided families; and the same rule of inheritance by the sister's son (here called the *aliya-santana* custom) prevails as in Malabār. The term *varg* seems to be derived from the registers kept up under the early kings; a considerable estate of several plots would occupy a whole page in the palm-leaf books.'[3]

These superior holdings, which correspond to the *janmi* of

[1] *South Kanāra D. M.* i. 54, by J. Sturrock (Madras: 1894). North Kanāra is described in *Bombay Gazetteer*, vol. xv.

[2] They are *now* quite distinct. The Malabār Nāyar have adopted certain limits beyond which their caste will not permit them to dwell.

[3] This word is derived, according to *South Kanāra D. M.* i. 118, from the Sanskrit *varga*, which is said to mean 'a leaf.' The writer of the North Kanāra memoir (*Bombay Gazetteer*, xv. 182) interprets it 'account.' But the Sanskrit *varga* means neither; it means 'kind,' 'class,' or 'category,' and is rather a term of art (used in grammar, philosophy, &c.), and so is unlikely to have come into use in connection with tenures—unless, indeed, it was locally adopted with some special meaning. On the other hand, many Arabic words found their way into use with the Mysore assessments, and very likely before that—*e.g.*, *waidegeni*, a tenant on special contract (Arabic, *wa'da*), and *mauje*, *majre* (*mauza*, *mazrū*). It seems possible, then, that the word is really from the Arabic *warq*, which *does* mean a 'leaf.' Some of the records spoken of (locally called *kaddatam*) were perhaps seen by Sir T. Munro as late as 1800, but they have since perished (*D. M.* i. 94, 95). It is curious to observe that the superior

N

Malabār, have, as might be expected, numerous sub-tenures, which really are exactly on the same footing as the *kānam* holdings of Malabār. The *mūlgēnī* is the subordinate (military caste) holding under the *mūlāvargdār*. It is permanent, the rent cannot be raised; and the amount of rent is sometimes reduced with reference to a fee paid in advance, the interest of which is equivalent to a portion of the rental.[1] Ordinary tenants are called *çāligēnē*, or if with a specified term of years, *vaidegēnē*.

In short, the *original* Dravidian agriculturist holdings, of which it can certainly be said that there was no community or joint-holding in villages, were overborne by over-lord tenures, with their connected fiefs and minor holdings. Under these, the original inhabitants became serfs or, at best, tenants. The joint ownership of the superior estates themselves seems very

hereditary character of the *varg* was never lost. Similar independent holdings that have been established on escheated or abandoned lands are distinguished as *sirkārgeni varg*—*i.e.* established under the authority of the Government. Though in every way as secure and as valuable, they are not *mūlā*, or vested with the magic of high-caste 'inheritance.'

[1] See *South Kānara D. M.* p. 131. I cannot understand why the Board of Revenue in January 1818 should have written that the *mūlgenigar* was a class unknown in Malabār. In reality the tenure was exactly that of the *kānakkārar* in Malabār, only that in the latter country the details of tenure forms were better preserved, the country having been less subject to changes by foreign intervention. Extravagant ideas of the position of the 'landlords' were, however, early entertained; and, as was not unnatural in 1792, English ideas of tenure were largely imported nto the discussion. As already stated (p. 170), the holdings of the subordinate classes of Nāyar came to be regarded (and treated) by our early English officials as 'mortgages'—with which they really had nothing to do. Mortgages, as such, are well known in Malabār, but are quite distinct. This idea of 'mortgage' not being attached to the Kānara *mūlgeni*, the two tenures were supposed to be different. But the Board themselves acknowledge the payment of the fee or *premium*, and in fact state all the features which show the real identity of the two tenures. Both were in origin not contract tenancies, but subordinate 'fiefs' for the minor ranks under the greater owners who held the *varg*, or estate in chief. The *mūlgēnī* holding was originally not alienable; it seems probable that some of its early features had become lost in Kānara, while they survived in Malabār, and that thus the tenures came to be distinguished.

likely to have been due to the adoption of Hindu caste; and it would certainly tend to keep up the position and the dignity of the families; while the peculiar customs of inheritance would help to maintain the joint-estate in the manner already alluded to.

Dravidian Villages in South-western Bengal

Leaving the West Coast, as the home of so many curious tenures in which Dravidian custom has been only partially preserved, we pass to the other side of India—to South-western Bengal, where we have a survival of the Dravidian *village*-formation, and one which indicates a somewhat more advanced stage than that which the Kāndh village represents. The Dravidian form of village, as we see it in the Chutiyā-Nāgpur districts,[1] was apparently based on the Kolarian model, but more consolidated and better organised. Here we find the grouping of families, and their settlement in compact village sites under their own officers and provided with a staff of artisans and menials resident and entitled to their regular remuneration. We have definite village boundaries and arrangements for the extension of cultivation. Agriculture was always esteemed, and the strongest attachment to landed-property is manifested.[2] In every village there seems to have been a more or less distinct plan or method of location, and of allotting the different holdings. First, there was set aside an allotment of land (*manjhi-has* shortened to *majhhas*), which, as its name implies, was for the support of the chief of the district (not village). Another land division, or *khūnt* (this is a borrowed Hindu term), was assigned

[1] See pp. 153, 166, *ante*, where an account is given of the Dravidian occupation of these districts.

[2] Mr. J. F. Hewitt remarks (*Journ. Soc. Arts*, xxxv. 622, May 1887): 'The feeling of proprietary right in the lands held by their forefathers was, among the families with privileged right, stronger than among the Kol. Members of these families believe firmly in the indefeasibility of their rights; and I have met Urāoñ cultivators who have lived all their lives and held land in villages beyond the limits of their own country, who named to me the villages where their forefathers had owned lands which they had never seen, and believed firmly in their right to return and claim a share in the lands should they wish to do so.'

to the hereditary headman or chief of the village, *mundā*.[1] A third lot went to the *pāhan*, or priest, and was called *pāhanai*.[2]

The families who represent the first settlers and original 'first clearers' of the soil are distinguished as *bhūinhār*, and are regarded as privileged in various ways: the family of the hereditary-headman always belongs to this number.

The rest of the ordinary, or non-privileged families and settlers (possibly of later date), have land allotments suitable to their requirements; but these were in former days periodically redistributed, so as to give each holder his turn at both the good and bad. An exception was made in favour of certain holdings which were, for special reasons, regarded as permanent: for example, those (now called *jalsūzan*, *i.e.* water-providing), for which the cultivator had laboriously constructed a small reservoir by damming up the angle of some ravine, and so supplying irrigation for his terraced rice-fields on the hillside. When new settlers were to be admitted, the whole of the holdings of the moveable class were redistributed, in conjunction, no doubt, with all the new holdings proposed to be created out of the waste.

When the princes of Dhālbhūm and its dependent States were well established, they introduced a change into the villages; the old 'chief's' lands (*majhhas*) were naturally appropriated to the use of the King; and a second headman, called *māhato*, was appointed to look after the Rājā's interests; accordingly, another special allotment of land (*māhtoāi*) had to be found for

[1] From this title of the headman it may suggest itself that the village had been originally established by Kolarian *mundās*.

[2] The *pāhanai*, or priest's, land was curiously organised; it was subdivided into three fields to make provision for a triple order of worship. First, there was the *bhūt-khetā*, or provision for the local spirits (*bhūt*), and the divinities of the village (*gāoñ-devatā*), whose abode was in the sacred grove or tree belonging to the village; next, there was a field for the *deṣaulī*, or deity of the whole district (*deṣ*)—that is, the deity whose influence was conterminous with the clan-territory under the chief (*manjhī*); thirdly, there was the field called *dālīkātārī*, or land for the service of the earth god (or goddess ?)—the general object of worship. Naturally, in after times, as the people adopted the Hindu faith, the *pāhan* tended to disappear, and his holding diminished or else lapsed into the form of some revenue-free holding by the Brahman who took his place.

his support. And yet another group of fields was set apart; for it became the rule to allow what were called *beṭkhetā*, or lands held free of payment, for the maintenance of the cultivators and labourers who tilled the 'royal' lands.[1]

But the time came when the requirements of the Rājā's Court could no longer be satisfied by the produce of the *majhhas* lands; possibly it was because the princes had in many instances granted or assigned these lands to cadets of their own family or as rewards to other persons. Whatever the motive, the custom soon arose of also levying a *share of the produce*; the share was taken on all lands that were not privileged as belonging to the deities, or to the *bhuīṅhār* families, or to the village officers. It became the practice to designate all land which was thus made liable to the grain-share by the term *rājhas*. When the days of the native rule passed away, and the Rājā's descendants were recognised as feudatory chiefs, or in other cases as 'Zamīndārs,' the *majhhas* lands (if not already assigned or alienated), became the 'Zamīndār's' special holding, while the *rājhas* lands became the ordinary rent-paying *raiyat's* lands. The older *bhuīṅhāri* lands, under the theory of the landlord Settlement, fell into the category of 'tenant' lands also, and that without any legal provision for maintaining the privilege of the holders. This gave rise to many troubles and to more than one local rebellion; for the older families had, as I have observed, strong ideas about their ancient rights; they could not, and justly so, conceive how the Zamīndār representative of the former ruling houses could be entitled to destroy old customary rights and privileges, merely because he had become 'landlord.' In the end our Government directed a special Settlement to be made, and enacted a law designed to preserve the tenures—viz. the 'Chutiyā-Nāgpur Tenures Act' of 1869, supplemented by the local 'Tenancy Act' of 1879. The *bhuīṅhār* families are now exempted from any further increase of their 'rents.'[2]

[1] In other cases we find the 'royal lands' cultivated by slaves or serfs. This was the case in Coorg; the foreign (*Haleri*) Rājā there assumed the right to the *panniya* lands throughout the province, and had them tilled by slaves. These Rājās also levied a land revenue, in kind, in addition.

[2] I will only add that there have been differences of opinion about the value and sufficiency of the legal provisions enacted. I have been told

I shall not at this stage offer any remarks as to how the Dravidian and other pre-Aryan institutions naturally produced the existing *raiyatwāri* form of village; such remarks will be more suitable in another place, when we come to consider the connection of the tribe, or the tribal stage of society, with the village grouping of land-holdings. But I may notice how easily in the midst of such villages special lordships might grow up, and how in such a country as Malabār, for example, the exceptionally 'aristocratic' joint-families, or *taṟavāda*, kept united by pride of caste and ceremonial purity, might have produced landlord-villages, held 'in common' or undivided, had not the features of the country and other circumstances been unfavourable to the formation of such village estates.

But it will be observed that nothing in any Kolarian or Dravidian custom as such, suggests a *joint* tribal holding of village or other areas; nor does it show a village owned in shares by a particular group of families. Indeed, the joint-family does not yet seem to be in existence. It is only when we come to the Nāyar families who have adopted caste and the Hindu law that we find their families keeping together and avoiding partition as lessening their dignity.

that protection was not carried far enough, and that in some cases the claims of the interested persons had not always been correctly understood. It is only right to mention the fact, but I cannot go into any argument on the subject. The whole of the details above given are derived partly from Mr. Hewitt's papers and partly from various official reports and correspondence relating to the Tenancy Act and the recording of rights under the Tenures Act.

CHAPTER V

THE ARYAN AND LATER CONQUERING RACES AND THEIR CONNECTION WITH THE LAND

In the last chapter, endeavouring to discover specific customs characteristic of the early tribes over whom the Aryans obtained dominion, we could only light upon fragmentary evidence; we find indications afforded by occasional survivals in exceptionally favourable localities, and we can take note of the general agricultural and social condition of parts of the country which are known to have been peopled chiefly by non-Aryan races. We are entitled also to draw certain inferences from a number of incidents—each perhaps small in itself—which, combined, produce a conclusive effect on the mind. It is hardly possible not to conclude that while the earliest settlements were in village groups, they did not represent bodies of men owning the land in common. If there was any general prevalence of the idea of a unit estate, or village held in shares at all in the manner of existing joint-villages, we should surely have some trace of it; but there is none. Nor does the 'Hindu' joint-family seem to have been known at first; we only find it among the higher Dravidian races, when they had taken, as they did almost with vehemence, to caste ideas and pride of religion. Once more, we cannot help noticing that the village of separate holdings is characteristic of the countries where the old or non-Aryan races were most widely spread, and were least disturbed. If, moreover, we turn to the indications afforded by the Aryan literature, we cannot help noticing that, whether in Manu, or the *Jātakas*, or any other, when the village is alluded to, it is the *raiyatwāri* form, with its hereditary 'headman.' And in all the traditional evidence we have of the early Rājās and their mode of government, the villages are clearly groups of individual free cultivators, and not co-sharing lords of a petty manor. How, then, did the Rājputs (Aryans) get their joint-villages? What notions had they about property in land? As we have observed what we could of non-Aryan custom, so we may try and trace what is specifically Aryan. And then Jat and other races have established 'joint' villages as much as the Aryans, so that we must go on to see what further influence these later tribes have had on village land-holding.

Of the effects of the Aryan settlements in India itself in the earliest period, we have no real evidence beyond certain scattered allusions in Vedic literature, and some faint local traditions. We can fairly surmise that the chief feature of their conquest was the establishment of local kingdoms or chiefships. We also remember that one part of the Aryan tribes—that connected with the Panjāb (or north-west Himalayan) Hills, the Indus Valley, and the upper part of Western India—was separated from the others, so that these 'non-Brahmanical' Aryans, as I have called them, had no part in the later development of caste and of all the peculiarities of the 'Hindu law.' One result of this would have been that such tribes would mix more readily with other races, and with the superior tribes of the pre-existing populations, while very probably infusing into them something of their superior energy and organising power. It does not seem likely that the earliest Aryan settlers had yet any such definite forms of land-holding as to produce any great changes, except in so far as the erection of a local lordship is a change; such Aryan settlers of the humbler order as took to farming would in all probability form villages on the pattern they found existing. The more striking institutions which we associate with the name 'Hindu'—the quasi-feudal system of Rājputānā, the old ideals of monarchy still traceable in the existing Hindu States, the Puranic religion, the law of the text-books, and the complete establishment of caste, these are all due to the Aryans settled, beyond the Saraswati and the Jamnā, in the Ganges plain. When we come to later and more settled times, under the influence of the Hindu system, the actual knowledge we have of Rājput and other similar tribally and individually founded villages, comes from local traditions, bardic legends, and sometimes from family histories, called *baṅsāvalī*.

In the attempt further to describe specific Aryan (Hindu) customs of village-tenure, and the customs of the other Northern tribes who followed their footsteps and made Northern India their chief home, we shall find that the best illustration will be derived from actual examples rather than from general and abstract description. Nevertheless, a chapter must be devoted to the discussion of some general matters of Aryan custom. In the first place, we have often been told that there is a specially *agricultural caste* among the Hindus ; and this has, perhaps, tended not a little to spread the idea that Indian village institutions are essentially or mainly Aryan. This question of caste in relation to land-holding should be elucidated. Then, too, we shall in our subsequent allusions to specific village histories continually mention the *clans* of Rājputs, and the establishment of Rājput monarchies and chiefships ; so that it is essential to give a brief account of the constitution of the older Hindu society and its government—as far as it bears on the land question. Lastly, we have some indications, in Hindu texts and elsewhere, of the general ideas held regarding property, and especially property in land, and these it will be well to consider. A final section on the effects of the settlement of post-Aryan tribes and of the Moslem conquest can also most conveniently be included in this part of the work.

SECTION I.—ARYAN CASTE IN ITS RELATION TO AGRICULTURE

Everyone who has opened an Indian Census Report knows into what a multitude of *castes* Indian society is divided ; the system became so well established, and it coincided so easily with distinction of race and clan, that, in a certain sense at any rate, it became applied to Sikh and Muhammadan people as well as those called 'Hindu.' These castes are the growth of centuries. They have, in fact, multiplied, divided and again sub-divided times without number. Difference of caste, implying the general inability of one to eat, drink, or smoke with the other, and making intermarriage out of the question, has arisen, partly out of religious distinctions, partly out of racial or tribal differences, and still more out of hereditary crafts, occupations, and modes of life.

In the Vedas we only see the beginnings of such a system. But long before any idea of religious and ceremonial distinction was developed, the tribes appear to have recognised a certain 'classification,' which, in fact, became the foundation of the caste-system.

There were, from the first, priests, or rather singers of those sacred hymns and invocations, the proper use of which had the greatest effect in securing victory and abundant spoil. And the course of adventure which the advancing tribes were pursuing could not fail to bring into prominence the warrior class[1] —especially those noble and distinguished families which gave birth to the natural leaders of the clans, and which afterwards furnished the Rājās and chiefs who arose out of the earlier tribal organisation. These two classes grew into the 'twice-born' (Brahman and Kshatriya) castes. Both, from the first, had the least possible connection with agriculture, except as over-lords of the soil and receivers of shares in the produce.

Setting apart these two chief castes, all the bulk of the people are merely spoken of collectively as *Viç*, which later became *Vaiçya*—*i.e.* 'the (Aryan) common people.[2] Every invading army or colonising nation, however, comes with a host of camp followers and inferiors, probably of various origin; among the Aryans some had apparently been admitted at least to the outer-courts of the community, and had conformed to Aryan customs. Accordingly, as the settlement progressed, so another (fourth) group came to be distinguished. Perhaps one of the tribes early admitted within the Aryan pale may have originally had the name of *Çūdra*; or it is possible that some of the camp-followers, or serfs, were called by this name.[3]

But no sooner were Aryan tribes settled in India than mixed

[1] King Alfred in his Saxon translation of Boethius remarks: 'Unless their are priests, soldiers, and workmen—*gebedmen*, *fyrdmen*, and *weorc-men*—no king can show his craft': quoted in F. Seebohm's *English Village Community*, 3rd ed. p. 183.

[2] See Zimmer, p. 214.

[3] That the fourth group was an after addition will, I think, be

races began to grow up. In fact, the Aryan influence extended as much by mixed marriages, alliances, and conversions, as by direct conquest. Before long the converted aboriginal and mixed races acknowledging Hindu customs, alike required a new name; they became fused into one general class, and were called *Çūdra*. The races who were not received into the pale at all remained 'out-caste.'

These broad divisions soon came to split up into many groups, and into subdivisions innumerable, and the old general names remained chiefly in books, and were used as generic terms rather than as actual caste-names.

The military caste of the older organisation is now represented by a few of the higher families, who still call themselves *Kshatriyā*, as well as by the mass of 'Rājput' clans [1] and castes, some of, perhaps, 'Indo-Scythian,' and others of more or less mixed race. The bards early recognised thirty-six 'royal' houses, which were divided into 'Solar' and 'Lunar' branches, but included the later 'Fire-born' (*Agni kulā*) houses,[2] as well as, if Colonel Tod's lists may be trusted, some Northern

admitted. The name *Çūdra* occurs but *once* in the Ṛgveda and that in the *Purushasūkta*; but this *maṇḍala* is, I believe, held to be a late addition to the original. See Caldwell, Introduction, p. 111 ff, and Zimmer's note on Ptolemy's *Sudroi*, p. 435; and on the subject generally, Zimmer, p. 204 ff.

[1] It is curious that, as a *general caste-name*, *Khsatriyā*, or in the Hindī form *Çhatri*, has almost disappeared, except as presently noted. It is commonly said that the large caste of *Khatri*, the shop-keeping and trading caste, derives its name from the Sanskrit *Khsatriyā*. I believe this to be doubtful, for why should the other form, *Çhatri*, *also* survive? The military, or royal caste, is now usually called *Rājput* (= sons of the king), and in some places, generically, *Thākur*, barons or lords of the soil. But it is curious to note that as the *Rājputs* have in so many cases descended to the peasant rank, and become mere landholders in villages, cultivating their own fields, the higher families disdain the name. In Oudh the chiefs always call themselves *Çhatri*, and would be insulted if told they were *Rājput*. So it is in Kāngrā (Ibbetson, *Ethnography*, § 456); the near descendants of the ruling chiefs returned themselves in the census as *Çhatri* or *Kshatriyā*, to distinguish them from the *Rājput* peasantry or cultivating landholders.

[2] This later addition is very remarkable, and points distinctly to an extension of the 'military caste.' See p. 113, *ante*, and Tod, ii. 408–9, and i. 82.

princely houses—the *Kāthī*, *Bālā*, *Hūna*, &c. To these divisions belong all the multitude of Rājput clans of the present day—the *Çauhān*, *Tumār*, *Rahtor*, *Solankhi*, *Pramāra*, and many more whose names will occur in the sequel. Others, like the *Jādu*, *Jhaṛejā*, and *Sammā*, are probably still older, and connected with the earliest (non-Brahmanical) Aryans. The Brahmans have also split up into a number of distinct branches, many of whom are quite strangers one to the other, and are looked upon as inferior by the rest. Some have descended so low as to take to cultivation. All the rest of the people, the original *Vaiçya* and the *Çūdra*, have long ago been classified anew into hundreds of castes largely dependent on trade or occupation, some of them being more nearly Aryan, and the vast majority being mixed, or more approaching the 'aboriginal' races.

That originally the Aryan tribes were a pastoral people is generally admitted. But a people occupying, even for a time, a country like that beyond the north-west frontier, consisting of mountain lands and intramontane valleys, could not possibly subsist without growing cereal crops; and we are not surprised to find several allusions to agriculture as essential to life in the earliest Vedic hymns.[1]

These allusions to agriculture in the Ṛgveda are often introduced only by way of metaphor or simile; and there is no description of any form of land-holding or mode of settlement for agricultural purposes. The modes of tillage known seem to have been of quite a primitive character; but in many respects the same character attaches to the implements as well as the methods in use at the present day. It seems that as the Atharvan Veda represents a later stage of Aryan progress, so the allusions in the book indicate a somewhat more extended

[1] *Kṛshṭī*, the Vedic word for 'people' in general, is connected with *kṛshī* = cultivated land, and *karsha*, a plough (Zimmer, p. 141). But this merely shows that the general notion of mankind living by the produce of the ground is very ancient. From the way in which the phrase *pañça kṛshṭāyah*, the 'five people or tribes,' is used, it is evidently synonymous with *pañça-janāh* or *pañça mānava*—*i.e.* the nation at large (see G. Oppert, p. 577, note). It does not necessarily lead to the conclusion that the early Aryans were naturally agricultural by habit, rather than pastoral.

or advanced agriculture. It is here alone, for example, that we hear of ploughing, evidently in the open fields and heavy soil of the Gangetic plain, with yokes of six and eight oxen.[1] It is here also that we hear of the iron ploughshare (*pavīravanta*). This, however, does not imply more than the primitive plough still in use. The plough—in two chief forms, one heavier and the other lighter—is to this day made in the rudest manner; and the share is only a pointed cap of hammered iron covering the spike of wood which digs the furrow. As soon as the art of hammering the soft and excellent iron which abounds in the Himalayas became known, the preparation of this iron cap or point would be among the simplest discoveries.[2] So, too, the mention of water-channels (*khanitra*, Ṛgv. 7.49.2) does not indicate any advanced artificial irrigation works; it is just such a natural diversion of a stream in a valley as can be seen in abundance all along the Haro river in Hazāra, for instance, or in fact anywhere in the mountains where a stream is led on to the fields, and sometimes carried along the hillside for some distance.

There is no specific mention of the crops grown; the words relating to the 'grain' are of general import only. It is clear, however, that though nothing is stated as to who cultivated the land, whether the tribesmen, or serfs, and subject people, there is no indication that agriculture was despised, as it afterwards was. From several passages we gather that the plough as the producer of food was thought of importance; and in one place the singer, apparently addressing people in general, urges them to leave idleness and gambling with dice, and attend to their fields and to getting food. We shall have to speak of the Vedic *grāma*, or village, in another connection; but there is not the least suggestion that it is a group of land-holdings held in common, or in any other way. But the idea of fields, owned by some one, seems familiar, from the allusion found to measuring

[1] *Ath. Veda*, 6.91.1; 3.17.3.

[2] The Sanskrit *pavī* evidently implies only such a rude iron tip or point as is in use at present; for the word also is used for 'spear-head.' A rude process of smelting iron (in a malleable form) at a low temperature by charcoal, is evidently of great antiquity in the Hill States and in many other places.

the fields with a staff of reed; and to there being bare strips or balks (*khilya*) left between the fields.[1]

So far, then, as the early Aryans are concerned, agriculture appears to have been in no disrepute; nor can we learn whether it was the business of any particular tribe or class. It is probable that the very fact of settlement would have effected a sort of natural division of labour and adjustment of suitable occupations. Some of the tribes or families would take to agriculture, and these would form the majority of those who remained stationary when the rest moved on. Naturally, therefore, the farther the Aryans moved into India, the more would the advancing body be composed of Brahmans and fighting tribes, and the more disposed these would be to relegate agriculture to the humbler classes, and to the conquered 'aborigines' and the mixed races who so soon sprang up and multiplied.

Whatever may be the true date of the *Laws of Manu*, we have no earlier literary mention of agriculture, after the Vedic hymns. In Manu we are already in times of settled royal government. The kingdom is internally organised into administrative divisions under appropriate officers. The *Vaiçya* (the term is now applied to a caste) is represented by the merchant whose business is with trade and with buying grain and other goods; he is regarded also as the owner of flocks and herds. 'The cultivation of land' is only casually thrown in among his permissible occupations as a subsidiary matter. And even so, the expression used seems quite possibly to refer to agricultural land-holding, not as a personal occupation, but as a means of employing capital. At the present day the *Khatri* and *Baniya* (traders and money lenders)—the most non-agricultural Hindu class in the country—are eager to buy and to hold land as an investment. Thus in the 'Laws' we read, 'to tend cattle, to bestow gifts, to offer sacrifices, to study [the Veda], to trade, to lend money and to cultivate land'—are the 'duties assigned' to a *Vaiçya*.[2]

[1] In Ṛgv. 1.110.5, the divine artificers (*Ṛbhū*) are spoken of as measuring 'as a man measures a field with a staff of reed' (*Rohrstab* in Grassman's translation). In Ṛgv. 10.142.3, in a hymn to Agni, the bare strips or balks are mentioned.

[2] *Mānava Dharmaṣāstra*, chap. i. p. 90. G. Bühler translates 'assigned'; Sir W. Jones makes the Glossary addition 'or permitted.'

The author has indeed little feeling for agriculture, as in another place[1] he says that 'some declare that agriculture is something excellent; [but] that means of subsistence is blamed by the virtuous; [for] the wooden [implement] with iron point [the plough, *i.e.*] injures the earth.' The idea that the *Vaiçya* is *the* agricultural caste *par excellence* is quite without foundation. Indeed, in spite of the employment of the term in Manu, *Vaiçya* did not generally come into use as a caste-name at all. There is no general caste so called, although locally some unimportant groups may be found calling themselves so, for want of a more distinctive name.

What is perhaps stranger still, the *Çūdra* caste, though it must, in the times we are referring to, have come to include a large body of settled cultivators of mixed as well as of non-Aryan race, is not treated as a specially agricultural caste, nor is there any allusion to ploughing or farm labour. And although the laws of Manu may deal more with ideals than with actual facts, still it is very remarkable that agriculture should not have been specially attributed to the *Çūdra*[2] unless,

In chap. ii. p. 31, we are told that a *Vaiçya's name* should be connected with wealth: in chap. v. p. 37, mercantile business seems to be the object of his life. So in chap. viii. p. 113 the *Vaiçya* witness is to be sworn 'by his kine, grain, and gold'; if he were essentially an agriculturist, attached to his land as Indian villagers notoriously are, surely the ancestral acres would be a much more natural object to swear by. So in chap. x. pp. 79, 80, agriculture is just mentioned as a means of livelihood—when necessary; but trade is the most commendable for a *Vaiçya*. Cf. also chap. ix. pp. 326, 327, 330, where the only direct indication of a *Vaiçya's* interest in agriculture is that he ought to be 'acquainted with the manner of sowing seeds and with the good and bad qualities of fields.'

[1] *Ibid.* chap. x. p. 84.

[2] Of a *Çūdra* it is said, Manu, x. 99, 100, 'if he is not employed in waiting on twice-born men,' he may principally follow such mechanical occupations as joinery, masonry, or the various practical arts, as painting and writing, by which he may serve the twice-born. I have not found any text which speaks of a *Çūdra* agriculturist. The *Çūdra* of the 'Laws' appears rather to be regarded as the lowly camp-follower of the higher Aryan castes—but still within the pale; he is not treated as what he really was, or very often was, an aboriginal tribesman who had accepted Hinduism, or a half-blood.

as seems probable, the then existing agricultural communities were largely, and indeed essentially, non-Aryan or of mixed descent, and therefore beneath the specific notice of Brahmanic authors. Nor can it be said that this proves too much; it does not exclude the practical certainty that a large number of the humbler ranks of Aryans took to agriculture, or at least to farm management, with the aid of aboriginal and other races as their tenants and labourers. But it was just these humbler Aryan clans that were most likely in time to fuse completely with the original population. To summarise our conclusions, it may safely be asserted that all the upper classes of Aryan origin had little feeling for agriculture, and that India does not owe to them either the introduction of settled cultivation or (directly) any particular policy or principle of land-ownership. To this day castes with some pretensions, though they may have been reduced to the necessity of cultivating their own lands, are usually in the position of proprietary co-sharers, or at least privileged tenants under greater landlords. The position is well stated by Sir W. Hunter when he says: 'We know that the Aryan invaders never penetrated in sufficient numbers into India to engross any large proportion of the soil. That throughout five-sixths of the continent the actual work of tillage remained in the hands of the non-Aryan or Sudra races, and that even at a remote time husbandry had become as degrading an occupation in the eyes of the Aryan conquerors as the tending of sheep was to the Mosaic Pharaohs.'[1]

SECTION II.—THE ARYAN CLAN-ORGANISATION AND THE 'HINDU STATE'

If we make a general survey of the existing Aryan (Rājput) land-holding communities in Upper India, and remember the fact already explained,[2] that the present allocation is due to an extensive redistribution and resettlement which occurred long subsequently to the original establishment of Aryan chiefs around Delhi, in Oudh, and in the Ganges Valley, we are

[1] *Orissa*, ii. 206. [2] *Ante*, p. 121 ff.

struck by one notable circumstance. Some of the Aryan agricultural communities appear in a still purely clan and family stage, and have always remained democratic in their constitution.[1] Otherwise, the *Kshatriyā* class usually developed a monarchical system; and this system appears in some cases constructed distinctly on *clan-lines*—that is to say, the 'Patriarch,' and sectional chiefs become 'Rājās,' and Thākurs or 'barons' graded in a kind of 'feudal' order. But very often also there is a single royal house or a single chiefship, which is quite unconnected with any clan-gradation, or with the presence of adherents of the same clan.

Both the *clan-organisation*, and the monarchical system as producing *the Hindu State*, are intimately connected with the history of village tenures. It is to the *clan-organisation* of the Aryan tribes that we owe the features of those Hindu land-holding communities of the joint type, but which had nothing to do with aristocratic origin or territorial rule. It is also ultimately to the *Hindu State system* that we owe a large part of those greater landlord estates—the Zamīndāris, Taluqdāris, and other forms of general over-lord tenure—with which this work is not directly concerned.[2] But it is also to the same development, whether in the more perfect form of the Hindu State or in the mere local lordship of adventurous knights and scions of noble houses, that we owe many *village communities* of Aryan connection.

It is, then, a matter both interesting and important to trace back the Aryan polity to Vedic times, and notice how (1) its clan-system was organised and (2) how the prominence of the Kshatriyā or warrior caste has led both to the perfect 'clan monarchies,' as I will call them, such as we see in Rājputāna and elsewhere, and also to those rulerships and chiefships in Oudh and elsewhere founded by single individuals without any clan connection at all.

(1) The earliest Vedic accounts, though showing only the

[1] There are some excellent remarks on this in the district article 'Hardoi' in the *Oudh Gazetteer*, ii. 40.

[2] For the sake of clearness I omit, at present, all mention of the Muhammadan dynasties, which in fact copied or adopted the Hindu system and thus gave rise to similar tenures among *their* descendants.

germs of the *caste* system, always represent the Aryans as consisting of differently-named tribes, and as having divisions and subdivisions of tribes and clans, each headed by its appropriate grade of chief. We are also prepared to expect that this patriarchal or social tribal system will be in part modified by a military organisation; and the two together may be the source of some confusion in our minds.

The main groups or tribes in early Aryan times are described by the term *janāh*, and the clans or larger branches by *viç*.[1] There is one passage in the Ṛgveda (2. 26. 3) which specifies the entire series of the divisions. The favour of the Father of the Gods, it tells us, is to be sought by sacrifices, &c., that wealth may be acquired through the tribe, the clan, the minor clan, and the families; or, as Zimmer translates: 'Wer den Vater der Götter für sich zu gewinnen sucht . . . der erlangt Beute und Reichthum durch die Männer; durch Stamm (*janena*), durch Gau (*viçā*), durch Verwandtschaft (*janmana*), durch Familie (*putraih*)'[2] Here we have the *tribe* or whole, then the *clan* (Gau = *viçā*), then the *minor-clan* (Verwandtschaft = *janman*)—*i.e.* the wider kindred or body of related families that have still some connecting link, whether or not they have settled together in one village,[3] and lastly the close kindred—the existing single family—whatever may have been the customary limit of descent.[4]

There are various grades of leaders and chiefs; the *grāma* we have already heard of as a cluster of buildings or fort of refuge,[5]

[1] In the bardic records (and the *Çāran*, or bard, is a great personage in Rājput Courts) the whole tribe was called *kulā*. The *kulā* divides into *çakhā*, or clans, and the clans into *gotra*, or *got*, which are septs or minor clans. In ordinary (non-royal) castes that had a tribal basis, popular use has adopted the Arabic word *qaum* for the whole 'caste' and *got* for the clan. Thus a man is described as *Qaum* Jat, *got* Sidhū, meaning a Jat of the Sidhū clan. Sometimes there is a further division of the *got* into *al*. The Hindī word *al* is traced to the Sanskrit *āvali*, or *ali* = a line or row. There is also an Arabic word *āl*, which has a somewhat similar meaning = progeny, &c.

[2] Zimmer, p. 160; Ṛgv. 2. 26. 3.

[3] The learned author thinks that *janman* refers to a 'village community ('Dorfgemeinde'); but there is, as I shall afterwards show, no authority for this whatever.

[4] This question will be discussed when we speak of the tribe and the village, Chapter VI.

[5] Zimmer, pp. 141, 142.

and the leader or commander of such a place (*grāmani* or *vrāja-patī*) is apparently connected with the disposition of the quota which each centre of residence contributed to the clan forces ;—as Zimmer puts it, he is the 'Anführer des Heerbannes der bestimmten Ortschaft.'[1] The clan has a chief called *Viçpatī*. Over the whole there is a *Rājā*—such a rank at least is frequently mentioned; but the Vedic *Rājā* appears very different from the autocratic ruler of later times. The office was hereditary, but sometimes apparently elective.[2] No regular revenue or tax is yet levied—in a stage of society which is still a continuous war-like campaign—but contributions and gifts are offered, and enemies are made to pay tribute. The king also, as such, receives a share in the booty gained by a successful foray.[3] The *Rājā* is evidently not independent of some great popular assembly; and affairs seem generally to have been managed by councils of the tribe—of the clan, or of smaller groups, for more than one distinct term is used. The *sabhā* appears to be the council of the minor-clan, or other limited group; the *samitī* would be a larger gathering of the clan or tribe[4] over which the king presides—rather, however, as *primus inter pares*.

(2) Out of such a social stage we pass quite naturally to the later *monarchy*. The tribal organisation has to be strengthened for war, or ultimately for the domination of a conquered territory; a greater degree of power in the king, and of military obedience and loyal service on the part of the chiefs, become a necessity of success. The king himself rules the central territory, and the chiefs take charge of districts all round; the frontier most exposed to danger of any kind being entrusted to the one who, as *senāpati*, or captain of the host, has the greatest military skill.

The land-revenue arises in the same natural order. When

[1] Zimmer, p. 171.

[2] *Ibid.* pp. 159, 162. Possibly elective out of certain suitable families only. In Ṛgveda, 10. 124. 128, there is mention of the clans (*Gaue*, as Zimmer translates) electing the king.

[3] Zimmer, pp. 166, 167.

[4] *Ibid.*, p. 174. We shall see afterwards how this idea persisted in Rājputāna, where the chiefs considered themselves the 'brethren' of the Rājā, and often asserted their right to be consulted, which the Rājā was apt to forget.

the king is peaceably established, he finds cultivation going on in villages of the aboriginal races, many of whom have accepted his rule with very little if any opposition; the humbler ranks of his own followers also take to cultivation, and it becomes a natural plan for each to give a share of the grain produce to the sovereign or the local chief, as the case may be. Outlying tracts subdued, but not occupied, will pay their tribute also, in whatever form is most convenient, to the Royal Treasury. The system of taxation was soon extended further, for we find the trading and artisan classes organised into recognised guilds, each with its own head; and by this means a contribution from the non-agricultural classes was secured.[1]

When we come to the times represented by the Laws of Manu, the 'manner of the kingdom' is already well known; and there is no detailed description of it. The Rājā receives his regular grain-share, and has officers to supervise its collection. Naturally (for the Brahman must be exalted), the council of chiefs has disappeared into the background, and the Brahman ministers are the ostensible advisers. But this more nearly represents the individual monarchy than the tribal form, where a sufficiently complete clan, with its greater chief and heads of minor clans were engaged in the government of a territory. When we see the 'Rāj' established on this clan-basis in Rājputāna, we observe how an important post is assigned to every chief within the clan, and with it an oath of service is exacted and a formal recognition of the Rājā's supremacy.[2] This is something different from what Manu contemplates.

Bearing in mind the limited object with which this account

[1] I may be permitted to observe that in towns this 'guild' system of tradesmen and merchants still exists; and if we had boldly made use of it in our first efforts to establish an income tax, there might have been less friction; for it is a matter of obvious justice as well as of ancient custom, that non-agriculturists should contribute as well as the owners of land. What caused the unpopularity was the attempt to enforce a European mode of levy—an inquiry into profits and incomes, and a very useless and nominal examination of shop-books. It might have been unscientific, but it would have been far more practical, to assess the different 'castes' or trade guilds, &c., in lump sums through their *çaudharis*, as they were afterwards called.

[2] We have, fortunately, the valuable assistance of Colonel Tod's

of the Hindu State is introduced, I do not propose to give all the *minutiæ* of the really ancient organisation of Mewār and other early kingdoms. It will be enough to say that in the complete or clan ' Rāj,' the rank of Rājā [1] is given to the head of the chief family of the eldest branch : thus, the chief is still addressed as '*Bāpjī*' (revered father). Under him the heads of the lesser clans and families will have graded titles—*Rāo* (or *Rāv* in Western India), *Rāwat* (or *Rāwal*), *Thākur* and others.

The Rājā's demesne was the central, and usually the richest, part of the country, and each chief had a territory round [2] it; while the lesser chiefs, who could not be so furnished, held special

Rājasthān, originally published in 1827 and since reprinted. Colonel Tod is no doubt uncritical, and his linguistic and other deductions are of little value; but for all matters of custom and observance, of which he had intimate personal knowledge, his authority is first-rate. His love of analogies often leads him to absurdity. Hence he is too fond of identifying the Rājput system with the feudal system of Europe, to which, no doubt, it has *some* resemblance. As an instance I may quote his allusion to the *minor* holding, on military service, of what he calls a ' hide ' of land. The native term *çarsā* means the leather or hide bag used for irrigation, and referred probably to the area of land watered by one *çarsā*. Obviously it had no kind of connection with the ' hide ' in the English manorial system or with European feudal tenures. The etymology of ' hide ' is not understood (Seebohm, *English Village Community*, p. 398; Stubbs's *Const. History*, 5th ed. i. 79); but it can have no similarity with the *çarsā* of land in India.

[1] The title varies, but it is usually *Rājā* or *Rānā*. *Mahārājā* is a complimentary addition. *Ādhirājā* is sometimes coupled with the latter, and where not merely a bombastic title it properly implies ' suzerain ' over a number of other States. For it will be remembered that one of the most frequent features of Hindu States, especially those *not* on the clan system, is that they are combined in confederacies, and united under the hegemony of some great emperor like Asoka or the sovereign of Kanauj. The Chinese pilgrim in the seventh century saw the State barge of Kanauj being drawn by eighteen minor Rājās. This confederacy did not imply any interference with interior State affairs, only with general defence and offence. *Çakravartī* was another title applied to a ' suzerain ' Rājā.

[2] This was often pictorially represented as a flower with open petals round a central disc. See, for instance, p. 1 in Cunningham's *Ancient Geography*, where the Map of India, A.D. 550, according to *Varāhamitra*, is given. The whole is represented, on this ideal, as a central domain with subordinate kingdoms lying all round it.

offices with assignments of Revenue or other means of support, within the central demesne.

The Rājā's demesne has come to be universally described by the Arabic word *Khālṣa* (or *Khāliṣa*), which has supplanted any older indigenous term or terms. The Sikhs also adopted the word, first as representing the consolidated territory belonging to the whole of the Sikh confederacy, and afterwards as meaning the 'State power' unified under their great Rājā Ranjīt Singh. The Mughal emperors employed the term to signify the whole of the lands paying revenue direct to the Treasury, as distinguished from the territory available to be held 'in *jāgīr*'—*i.e.* on assignment of the local revenue, to certain great chiefs or officers of State (*Mansabdār*).[1] This was evidently an adaptation of the Aryan model.

To return to the Hindu 'Rāj.' Where there were no geographical features that invited a natural division of territory otherwise, the chief's portions were frequently allotted by counting up groups of villages. The full estate was most frequently the *çaurāsī*, or group of eighty-four villages.[2] Smaller estates, or even subdivisions effected for any family or local reason, were *beālisī*, or tracts of forty-two villages, or *çaubīsī*, tracts of twenty-four. It is only necessary to add that the traces of this division always, as far as I know, indicate the remains of some rulership, or at least of a local barony or over-lordship of some kind, and never the mere clan-settlement of cultivating landholders in a 'democratic' group.

The Rājā and the chiefs each collected the revenue in his own territory; the chiefs paid no revenue to the Rājā, but

[1] Colonel Tod does not give any Hindī name for the 'demesne' even in the case of the ancient dominion of the Rāṇā of Mewār. I have some reason to think that the term *kot* may have been applied, or perhaps *maṇḍalam*.

[2] Some interesting information regarding vestiges of old *çaurāsī* divisions in various parts of Upper India will be found in Beames' *Elliot's Glossary*, (s.v. '*chaurāsī*'). In the Statistical Account of the Gorakhpur District, North-West Provinces (*N.-W. P. Gazetteer*, vi. 436), I find this term used, not with reference to a number of villages, but to an extent of circuit in *kos* (= 1½ mile.) Thus a certain Rājā's territory was a circuit of eighty-four *kos*, enlarged to a *satāsī*, or circuit of eighty-seven *kos*; and so with the lesser divisions.

helped him with aids in time of war; and the chief's heir paid a 'fine' on his succession; when also he did homage and received investituro from the Rājā.[1] The early rulers made no claim to be owners of the soil; there is not a trace of such a claim in the Mānava Dharmaṣāstra or in any other ancient text.[2] In Rājputāna we find, for example, the oldest and most dignified of the rulers only claiming as his State-right, what was described by the three words '*Ān, dān, kān*'—*i.e.*, as Colonel Tod explains, his right to allegiance and military service of all grades; his right to the land-revenue share (*bhog*) and other taxes (*barār*), including supplies of grass and wood or the equivalent thereof (*khar-lakr*); and his right to royalties on mines.[3] No doubt this right included, as elsewhere, the power to dispose of waste and unoccupied land in the demesne.

It is frequently the custom of writers on Indian subjects to speak of this system of chiefs in subordination to a Rājā as 'feudal'; but it is forgotten that really it differed from the feudal system of Europe in being as much dependent on clan-relationship as on anything else. The safety of the State and success in war alike demanded the loyal allegiance and obedience of every clansman in his grade and place: otherwise, the chiefs remembered that they had as good a right to the *pāt*, or feudal estate, as the Rājā had to his 'Rāj.'[4] In neither case did the

[1] In Mewār the *pattāit*, or subordinate chiefs, were numerous enough to be ranked in classes (Tod, i. 127). The fourth and lowest consisted of the *Bābu*, or younger branches of the Rājā's own family, who received life grants for their subsistence.

[2] The question of State ownership of the soil is dealt with in the next section.

[3] In Mewār there were some valuable minerals (see Tod, i. 128). *Kān* = mine, is a Persian form, but connected with the Sanskrit *khānī*.

[4] Colonel Tod has given some interesting appendices of original documents illustrating this. One of them sets forth the grievances of the *pattāit*, or vassal chiefs, of Deogarh, against their *Rāwat*. The petitioners give him the correct title, Deogarh being a State of secondary rank; in the reply the chief styles himself *Mahārājā*. The chiefs remind him that when the State was founded, their territorial allotments were made out as much as the *Rāwat's* own. They complain of his assuming to make grants to outsiders within their estates; and of his listening to the advice of foreigners instead of allowing them (the chiefs) to form his Council.

allotment of territory have anything to do with the actual ownership of the soil; the chiefs' territory and the Rājā's were alike in that respect.[1]

A similar system of a Rājā and his 'vassal' chiefs with appropriate allotments of territory all round, appears in the account of the Hindu kingdom of Orissa as given by Sterling. It was adopted in its essential idea, though not in detail, by the Sikhs; and its features may be traced in the States of Simla and Kāngrā.

But obviously the system in its completeness depends on the presence of the whole clan and its branches. And when we remember by what strange adventures and by aid of what singular freaks of fortune many local rulerships were gained, it is not surprising to find a single chief without his clan, or attended only by a small following. The whole of India furnishes us with examples of Hindu States[2] which at one time or another had rulers or Rājās of some princely Rājput house, and perhaps not one other chief of the same family in his territory. OUDH affords us many examples. Thus, for instance, of the northern kingdoms, Gondā, Atraulā, &c., Mr. Benett writes:[3] 'The *Rāj* rested on a

[1] So little was the 'fief' connected with ownership in the land, that there was a time, in Mewār at any rate, when the fiefs were moveable. (Tod, i. 146):—'I need only mention that as late as the reign of Rājā Singhrām the fiefs of Mewār were actually moveable, and a little more than a century and a half has passed since this practice ceased.'

It is also hardly necessary to add that the *working* of the system, and the degree to which the Rājā was really chief ruler and the vassals really subordinate in their own estate, depended on the energy and character of the Rājā himself and the general *morale* of the whole clan. With a weak ruler, the tendency for the local chiefs to assert complete independence would soon become marked, especially as the clan-feeling grew weaker, as it must do in the course of time.

[2] It will be remembered that the States were always comparatively small, and constantly changing. When we hear of great Hindu empires or extensive kingdoms, it is always that the 'Emperor' was the head of a great confederacy of smaller States, reproducing on the larger scale the idea of the 'Rājā' and his 'barons.' They were held together by the slenderest threads; the sending of an embassy was enough. It was only thus that it was possible for Asokā, for instance, to be nominal head of an empire extending at one time from Afghānistān to Ganjam. See Grierson's *Notes on the Gāyā District*, 1893, p. 102.

[3] *Gondā S. R.* p. 37 ff.

purely territorial basis. . . . Every *Rāj* was confined to a definite tract of country, enclosed in a ring fence by recognised boundaries, and applied to every inch of land within those boundaries. . . . To suppose that it was in any way connected with the idea of clanship is a mistake. . . .' The author goes on to instance the territory called Khurāsa, in which, though a numerous *Çhatri* clan (*Bisēn*) held properties, the Rājā was a *Kalhaṅs*, he and his immediate family being the only members of the clan in the territory. Many similar cases could be quoted. There was thus no opportunity for any feudal baronies; or perhaps there might have been one or two adjacent territories which acknowledged a dependence on the Rājā, but that was all. The minor members of the Rājā's family (*çhotbhaiyā*) would then be provided for by grants or assignments of revenue or territory within the *Rāj*. The 'Rāj' is essentially a territorial dominion, one and indivisible; and, properly speaking, the Thākur or 'Baron's' estate is also indivisible. But in the latter case, in former days at any rate, partition was not always avoided. I have even met with instances where a Rājā's kingdom has been formally partitioned among his heirs. This, no doubt, is exceptional, as the rule of primogeniture most commonly applies to the public or territorial estates of Rājās and ruling chiefs. The subject of primogeniture will come before us again at a later stage,[1] and need not be further considered here. Hindu States were nearly always of small or at least limited size.[2]

It may not be out of place to add that in the movements and turmoils of the Rājput disruption occasioned by the Moslem invasions—and probably it has been so at all times—a great number of local chiefships have been established in a very informal way, and ruled without any attempt to adopt what I have described as the more regular features of the Hindu monarchy. We find small parties of Rājputs settling down in a place and

[1] *Post*, p. 304.

[2] It was the small States, ranging, in the Trans-Ghāgrā districts, from 100 to 1,000 square miles each, that afterwards formed the principal basis of the Revenue divisions or *Taluqās* formed under the Muhammadan government of Oudh. I need hardly also allude to the thirty-two small States in the Simla Hills; all are held by their separate Rājā or Rānā; and only in some cases are there one or two dependent 'baronies' attached to the State.

establishing a rude kind of 'barony.' If the leading chief afterwards attains to some power and reputation, and to an extensive domain, he will probably assume, or receive from the emperor, the title of Rājā. Such dominions were autocratically, but not unkindly, governed in old days. But they were very unstable, and were exceedingly liable to be broken up by family quarrels and to go to pieces.

Section III.—Aryan Ideas of Property in Land

It has been incidentally mentioned that the idea of separate fields measured with a reed appears in the Ṛgveda. This shows that the principle of appropriation was not unknown at that early date. But from all that we know of the results of the Aryan invasion, the chief agent in producing varied forms of land-tenure must have been the introduction of a number of separate centralised governments, with the opportunities that they afforded for the growth of over-lordships, whether extending to considerable estates or to single villages. The humbler Aryans no doubt settled down to village life either in independent democratic communities or under village or other local lords; but, as tradition and history are more concerned with the deeds of the military and ruling classes, the prominent subjects of attention are the founding of royal capitals and the establishment of monarchies. These are varied with many incidents of local adventures, of estates gained by grant, or by what were in fact mere marauding expeditions. Everywhere we hear of little groups of Rājputs, under efficient leaders, seizing on and extending territorial possessions. Nor do we forget the case where no monarchical development occurred. Even in those Aryan villages that were always held by cultivating fraternities from the first, the co-sharers, 'democratic' though we may call them, and having no pretensions to any noble rank, still regarded themselves as holding the land on a superior tenure extending to the whole area of their possession, in a way that we do not observe among the humbler *raiyatwārī* communities. And it may be convenient to add that the same feeling of superiority and of union was evinced by the Jat, Moslem, and other clans who later formed similar settlements of joint-villages.

In the case of Aryan clans or individuals establishing a territorial *rule*, their original practice was only to take the lord's share of the produce, without directly affecting the cultivating tenure of any existing holders. If, then, on the loss of the ruling position, the families became actual owners of the land, under the toleration of some new conquering ruler, we may be sure that the ownership would be of a 'superior' character. In the larger estates, the great landlord would still regard himself very much as if he were still a Rājā. He would be a great over-lord and rent-receiver, without interfering much with the actual soil tenancy. If the resulting estates were scattered villages, the bodies of 'inheritors' would become still more the immediate owners, perhaps themselves cultivating the land; but there would still be the pride of descent, and that sense of superiority which in India depends much more on caste and birth than on appearances of wealth or forms of occupation.

Aryan land-holding, in the case of all the higher castes, had thus a natural tendency to the landlord form. Otherwise, we have no evidence whatever that the Aryan mind conceived any *special form of village* as such. The same physical conditions and tribal ideas of family grouping that operated in all cases, equally invited the Aryans to form 'villages'—even where they were not taking the lordship of villages already established. But their peculiar position and sense of superiority led automatically to a difference in the *internal* constitution of those villages which were held by the higher castes.

When we come to speak, in the next chapter, of the *origin* of the joint-village, we shall discuss the kind of tribal feeling which gives rise to a sense of joint-ownership in some form or degree; and we shall consider the nature and effects of the joint-inheritance as producing what is called common ownership in the joint-family of the original over-lord. It will be sufficient to notice here that the purer Aryan clans exhibit both principles; they had a strong sense of union in the clan, and of the right of all the clan members to share alike in the common acquisition of territory; they also had the joint-family.

As to the earliest ideas of land-holding among the Aryans,

in the state of movement and constant warfare which the Vedic hymns represent, we do not find any direct or even covert allusion to any system of sharing the land conquered or occupied.[1] If anything of the kind had existed, it is hardly possible that it should have escaped all mention.

What, however, is still more to the purpose, is that there is no mention in the much later *Laws of Manu*, of anything like a joint-village or an area of land held 'in common.' This is the more remarkable because the joint-inheritance principle *is* fully asserted ; and so it would follow that if a father became the owner of a whole village, and was succeeded, say, by four sons and six grandsons (representing two other sons deceased), the whole village would naturally be held by a 'community' of ten co-sharers. But the 'village' as a form of tenure depending on a co-sharing constitution, such as is now observed in Upper India, is nowhere mentioned by the author or authors.[2] The *grāmam*,

[1] Zimmer once or twice speaks of the 'Dorfgemeinde,' but this is rather by way of using a current form of speech; for there is no Vedic evidence that 'communities' were formed by 'village' bodies in any sense at all, far less as connected with land-owning. In the passage above quoted from the Ṛgveda (p. 194, *ante*), giving the different divisions of the tribe, we find mention of the *Verwandtschaft*=*janman*. Zimmer (p. 160) remarks that this is 'evidently' (*deutlich*), a village, because the inhabitants of the village were originally of a single family or kindred. I submit there is nothing 'evident' about it; the statement about the village is derived from the conventional belief on the subject and is based on no evidence whatever. All that the term (*janman*) implies is that there was a group of connected single families held together by some tie of descent, so as to be recognised as one of the groups into which a tribe was subdivided, possibly having a central residence or fortress. As to community of property or of land-holding, nothing of the kind is so much as hinted at.

[2] Although it is again and again represented by our books that the 'village community,' meaning one with a *collective* ownership, was known to Manu. I have more than once gone carefully over the latest and best translation (Dr. G. Bühler's) without being able to discover the smallest trace of any such allusion. M. de Laveleye's statement (*Propriété primitive*, p. 66), that 'the mention of the "communautés" in Manu did not suffice to enlighten the English lawyers' as to the joint-village, is perhaps thus explainable! The fact is that until 1795 (when the Benares province was to be settled) English administrators had no opportunity of coming across any jointly owned villages at all; and the significance and

or village, is referred to; and, as it must have then been a well-known, if not already ancient, institution, it is perhaps not to be expected that any description should be given. The code contemplates the king as receiving his revenue-share in kind from each village; and there are district officers in several grades having jurisdiction over ten or twenty, or one hundred, villages; and there is the plan of granting to such officers an assignment of the land-revenue share on one or two or more 'ploughs' as an official remuneration. The village thus referred to is that which corresponds to our *raiyatwārī* form, with its hereditary chief or headman; the latter, as I have remarked,[1] being the characteristic feature in which the joint-village is naturally wanting. Moreover, we shall see presently that the *Mānava* idea of right in land is apparently confined to a primitive and natural one based on the feeling that labour expended on the first clearing of the virgin waste gives a claim to the continued enjoyment of the 'lot'; and this comports rather with the *raiyatwārī* idea of village holdings. Nothing is said of the ownership of a whole village in shares, or of the general lordship of a whole village being granted by the king. Possibly the time had not yet come when such grants (to cadets of the Royal house, or to persons deserving of a reward) were common. More probably, to my mind, in the author's time, such grantees or other over-lords were not yet regarded as *owners of the soil*, or their heirs as forming a body of village co-proprietors; they were still merely the assignees of the royal revenue and perquisites—'lords of the manor' and nothing more; in other words, the position of the superior family had not yet developed into that of a 'village community,' with an acknowledged *ownership in the soil* in any shape, but was an *over-lord right* not regarded as in itself inconsistent with the still subsisting, permanent, and original, right of the village-cultivators as clearers of the soil.

As regards a general idea of title to the soil, or property in land, I am not aware of any direct declaration on the subject earlier than the mention of it in the *Laws of Manu*; and this.

peculiar nature of them was not realised till 1803-1820, when the administration extended to the North-West Provinces, the home of this form of village.

[1] *Ante*, p. 10.

again, appears to be consistent with very early tribal ideas in India.[1] We do not, of course, expect to meet in Sanskrit literature with any juristic analysis of ownership, or of the theory of 'possession,' or a 'just title,' or of the nature of the rights and enjoyments which cluster round ownership; these are refinements of Western jurisprudence. But the writer in the 'Laws' plainly refers, not to his own ideas, but to what he understands to be the ancient opinion, when he says that 'sages who know the past call this earth (*pṛthivī*) even the wife of Pṛthu; they declare a field to belong to him who cut away the wood, or who cleared and tilled it, and a deer to him who owned the arrow which first struck it.'[2] Certain attributes of 'private

[1] Colonel Tod, for example, records the saying of the soil cultivator in the ancient State of Mewār, that he had so close a connection with the soil that he was like the *akhāi dhūbā*—the *dhūb* grass that could not be eradicated; and he asserted his right in the oft-repeated saying—

Bhogrā dhan-i-Rāj hu
Bhūmrā dhan-i-mājh hu.

'The Revenue share (*bhog*) is the king's property [or wealth = *dhan*]; the soil is my property.'—Tod, i. 424.

Something of the same idea is perhaps expressed by the Kashmīr proverb (right acquired by labour and skill bestowed), '*Yus kariḥ gonglu sui kariḥ krāo*'—'He who has ploughed the land shall reap the crop,' a rule, alas! for centuries overridden by despotic rulers in that valley. (See Walter Lawrence's *Kashmīr*, or his shorter and charming paper in *Journal Soc. Arts*, April 1896, xliv. 491.)

[2] Laws, chapter ix. v. 44. The Glossary of *Kullūkā Bhaṭṭā* explains 'eradicating the stumps' by the addition 'who cleared and tilled the land.' The text is:—

Pṛthor-apīmam pṛthivīm bhāryām purvā vidoviduḥ
Sthān-uççhed asya kedāramāhuḥ çalyavatomrigam,'

where *kedāram* is a field or cultivated land in general.

I observe that in one of the reprints in Professor Ashley's series of *Economic Classics*, Richard Jones, in his *Essay on Rents* (App. vi.) falls upon this passage and ridicules Colonel Tod for applying it to Mewār (*ut supra*, Tod, i. 424), or taking it as a declaration of fact when it is 'mere allegory.' But Jones (writing before 1830) had very little information, even at Haileybury, about Indian tenures, and he was completely taken up with the idea that land had at all times been regarded as State property in India; so this assertion of private right was a stumbling-block to him. It may be well, therefore, to mention that the passage in Manu is quite reliable. It occurs, it is true, casually, in con-

ownership,' as we should say, are also alluded to—for example, the sale of land by a formal process; and an imprecation is denounced on one man who should wrongfully sow seed in the field of another; rules for settling boundaries are given, and the fencing of fields is alluded to.[1]

There is no reason to suppose that in the time (whatever the true date may be) represented by the *Laws of Manu*, the claim of the king to be owner of all land was as yet asserted. Nothing of the kind is mentioned in the Code or in any other ancient text. But the fact of the king having a share in the produce naturally put him in a position to exercise a degree of control, the limits of which, in fact, depended on his own sense of what

nection with an argument about the right to a child begotten on a woman by a man other than her husband; and the writer, no doubt, merely introduces his statement about land as an *illustration* or *argument from analogy*. But the whole point of his case would obviously be lost if the illustration itself were not a statement of fact, and one which his readers would recognise as such. There is nothing whatever metaphorical or fanciful about the text; it is a plain statement of a principle of ownership, and obviously the ancient commentator also treats it as such. It is consistent with all we know, in other ways, of early Indian land-owning; it is consistent with everything else that Manu says about the subject. There is, of course, no regular chapter or formal section on land-ownership in Manu; such a thing could not be looked for.

[1] The right by 'first clearing' appears in various guises in India. Indeed, in early times, when cultivators were scarce in proportion to the arable land, any reasonable ruler must have discovered the importance of fostering and extending cultivation and attaching the cultivators to their holdings. The same principle (right of the first clearer), Colonel Vans Kennedy informs us, is admitted by all the Muhammadan jurists (see, for example, the *Hidāyā*, written about A.D. 1152, Hamilton's Translation, 4 vols. 1791, book xlv.; referred to in *L. S. B. I.* i. 229). Even at the present day nothing is commoner in Northern India than to hear tenants claim occupancy rights on the ground that they are *būtāmār*, or took part in the *būtā-shigāfi*, as the popular phrase is—*i.e.* in clearing the jungle. Here, from the general growth of over-lord claims, the cultivators are very often in the tenant class, but the sense of permanent right on the basis of first preparation of the soil is the same.

It will also be observed that in places where the periodic redistribution of allotments was customary, it always ceased to apply, or never applied in the locality at all, where the holdings were irrigated, or were made culturable by some exceptional expenditure of labour or capital on the part of the holder.

was right. It is not surprising that, as a matter of history, the claims of the Rājā, or the State-right, if we prefer so to call it, soon became consolidated and intelligible. We have seen how the Mewār Rājās spoke of their *Ān*, *dān*, *kān*; and it became a recognised attribute of the ruling power that, as a matter of custom, it had the combined right to the share of the produce, the right to the waste, and the right to tolls and transit dues. This aggregate of rights was from early Muhammadan times spoken of as *the Zamīndārī*. Later on in history, when the continued invasions and local wars brought about a frequent succession of new conquering princes and marauding chiefs, and when, at the break up of the Mughal Empire, the deputies over the great provinces assumed independence, the temptation to increase the share demanded from the husbandmen, and to enlarge the pretensions of the ruler generally, was irresistible. The old State-right, or 'Zamīndārī,' was magnified into a general superior ownership of the entire domain.[1] This natural pretension of conquering princes received a further impulse from the Moslem invaders, who not only had all the ideas of superiority natural to conquerors, but added to them the religious zeal which supposed that the faithful were the natural 'inheritors' of the wealth of infidels. All over India, the rulers, whether Moslem or Rājput, had thus no lack either of motive or opportunity for establishing their virtual ownership of the soil of their territory. But in practice, it is only just to remember, the better class of even foreign conquerors never conceived of their rights as

[1] The earliest notice I can find is about 312 B.C., where Megasthenes is describing a *land tribute* as well as the *land-revenue share*, which Chandraguptā, King of Magadhā, made the people pay because 'all India is the property of the Crown and no private person is permitted to own land.' This may have been merely an erroneous inference from the particular local obligation to pay 'land tribute.' And Chandraguptā was a conqueror of alien race. Lassen (ii. 726) also remarks that Megasthenes was in error. This must certainly be held to be the case as regards any *general* assertion of the Rājā's right in land at so early a date. It was at a much later time, possibly when the Buddhistic princes had been generally defeated, that the Brahmanic writers invented the story of Parasu Rāma having conquered the whole earth and presented it to the Sage Kasyapa (*i.e.* to the Brahmans), who allowed the Kshatriyā ruling chiefs to manage it for them.

necessarily antagonistic to the concurrent, hereditary, permanent, and long-established right of the older cultivators of the soil.[1]

Whatever may have been the precise date to which the right of the State to be considered superior owner of the soil may be carried back, it is certain that no ancient Hindu authority can be quoted for it; nor is it consistent with the genuine principles of the Muhammadan law. On the other hand, by the beginning of the eighteenth century, and in some cases of conquest long before that, all the rulers of the Muhammadan States, and all the local Rājās who were conquerors and mostly foreigners, were found *de facto* to claim the superior ownership of every acre of their dominions. And this right is asserted by the Native States to the present day.

It is often stated in books that 'the Hindu law' recognises the State ownership of the land; but it will invariably be found that the only authority for this is an implied, and occasionally an express, reference to what the author apparently did not know to be a purely modern Hindu law digest known as Jagannātha's.[2] The compiler of this work, who collects and comments on really

[1] The feeling in favour of the protection of the husbandman seems to have been noticed in early times. It is reflected in the Statement of Megasthenes as epitomised by Diodorus (McCrindle's *Megasthenes*, &c., p. 41), that husbandmen were exempted from fighting and 'devote their whole time to tillage; nor would an enemy coming upon a husbandman at work on his land do him any harm.' And again (p. 33): 'Among the Indians . . . by whom husbandmen are regarded as a class that is sacred and inviolable, the tillers of the soil, even when battle is raging in their neighbourhood, are undisturbed by any sense of danger.' He adds also that the land is not ravaged with fire nor the trees cut down.

The fact is that all settled rulers, not mere marauders under the necessity of plundering while they could, have recognised that security to the cultivator means in the long run the best revenue. Even the Marāthās did not altogether forget this. The harshness of native rule is usually inferred from the heavy revenue demand, or the excessive share of the produce; but it is forgotten that the demand was not enforced except in the most elastic manner, and that pressure was relaxed at once in a bad season. The European principle is a low rent and punctual, inexorable, payment. The Oriental rule is the largest possible claim and only take what you can for the season.

[2] *The Digest of Pandit Jagannātha Tarkapañçānana*, translated by H. T. Colebrooke, 3 vols. (Calcutta, reprinted London 1801). The work

ancient texts sometimes with great skill, is, in this matter of asserting State ownership, reduced to writing some remarks of his own, while he *does not attempt to quote a single ancient text* in support of them. He was probably aware of the fact that the soil in Bengal and other States had, at the date of his writing, long been *de facto* subject to the claim of the State; and, although he had no authorities to give in support of such a claim, he thought it necessary to conform his opinion to the actually existing practice.[1]

When once the Rājā attained to a superior lordship of the whole soil, all grantees and others deriving their title from him would naturally have *their* pretensions enlarged; and these they could the more easily realise, because they were in closer managing connection with the land than the Rājā at his capital, acting only through his officials, could ever be. Hence we soon find the ancient 'right by first-clearing' in many cases put aside or overshadowed by a new claim of conquering tribesmen, or adventurous settlers and grantees, who spoke of their conquest right or over-lordship as their *wāriṣi* or *mīrāṣī* right or as their *wirāṣat*.[2] There is frequently good reason to desire

was compiled towards the end of the last century at the suggestion of Sir W. Jones.

[1] He attempts to get out of the difficulty (i. 460) by alluding to the myth of Parasu Rāma and his gift, and saying that the land became the 'protective property' (whatever that may be), successively held by 'powerful conquerors' and not by 'subjects cultivating the soil.' The compiler allows that the 'subject' acquires an 'annual property' (!) on payment of the land revenue, and that the king may not give the land to anyone else for *that* year. He seems to think that, unless there is a special agreement otherwise, the king *may* turn out any owner from a field if anyone else offers to pay him a higher revenue. The whole passage is, however, so vague that it is hopeless to extract any reasonable meaning.

[2] All being connected with the Arabic *wirṣ*, *wirṣa* = inheritance. It is curious to notice how these Arabic terms have become general. Among the Panjāb frontier tribes, of course, the use of the term *wirāṣat* for right in the soil is natural because the tribes are Moslem. But in the Dakhān and Southern India *mīrāṣi* became everywhere used for the landlord or superior right in or over a village. The term came in with the Land Settlements and careful assessments of Malik 'Ambar and other ministers under the Muhammadan kings of the Dakhān. It was the policy of these kings to confirm or resuscitate the families that had obtained over-

some euphemistic term to account for the successful acquisition of a village or other estate; and when the title has actually descended to later generations, it is spoken of proudly as 'the inheritance.' It will invariably be found that, wherever we have this term applied, it is always in connection either with some originally over-lord right (which has in time ripened into a proprietorship in the hands of a joint body of heirs), or with some special privileged ownership or permanent superior title. The clans who were agriculturists as well as conquerors, like the Jats, do not use the term so much; perhaps because they combine in themselves both the right resulting from first establishment of cultivation and also the right of conquest or successful acquisition. Moreover, a large number of existing Jat communities were peaceable settlers.

There is one aspect of the changes resulting from Aryan over-lordship which is worthy of special remark. This is true not only of Aryan clans but equally of the Muhammadans, Marāthās, Sikhs, and sometimes Jats. I allude to the fact that wherever some royal grant has issued, or some other special interest in land has been created or assumed by conquest, we are not unfrequently presented with the spectacle of a series of

lord rights in the villages of their dominions, and make the Revenue Settlement with them for the whole village. Whenever a man speaks of land as his *mirās*, he means that he has a superior sort of right as being descended from one of the old over-lord families, or as having purchased such a title in past days. But as the Revenue Administration of the Mughal emperors and also of the Muhammadan kings of the Dakhān was the only business-like, tolerably systematic administration known, its principles were generally copied; and the Perso-Arabic terms employed became generally diffused even in Marāthā and Hindu States.

The only place where I have seen *wārisī* adopted by Hindus and used of a *secondary* kind of right, is in the hills of Kāngrā and Simla, where the Rājās were themselves the superior owners, but where they respected the permanent, hereditary, and, to a limited extent, alienable right of the land-holders, and called it *wārisī*. Here perhaps the meaning is that the holding is *hereditary*, just as the modified form *maurūsi* is applied to what we should call the 'occupancy tenant' classes. This seems the more likely because in the level (outer) Talukās of Kāngrā, where regular villages were formed, the title of the proprietary families is described by the term *mālikī*, or ownership, not as *wārisī*. See Lyall, *Kāngrā S. R.* § 17, p. 20; and Barnes, *S. R. Kāngrā*, § 133 ff.

rights or interests *superimposed* one on the other. In parts of the Panjāb, for instance, we may find villages with three such interests. There is an original body—possibly once independent settlers and first-clearers of the soil. They have now so completely acquiesced in the 'tenant' rank that there is no further question of any possible change. Over them will be found the general co-sharing body, who represent the 'proprietary' interest in the village; only, in the cases alluded to, they are not quite free, they are called *adnā mālik*, or owners in the second degree; for over them another co-sharing family has obtained the overlord position as *'alā mālik*, or superior proprietors. Now, under the *régime* of British law, all these interests have been preserved and defined, and stopped from going any further; so that in all probability the *adnā mālik* are the virtual owners, and the superiors are only entitled to some fees or rent-charges, or to have the benefit of the waste, &c. But had things gone on without interference, the time would probably have come when the 'actual proprietors' would have also been completely reduced to the grade of tenant, and the 'superiors' would have claimed the entire landlord-right. The same sort of thing is often seen in the greater landlord estates, where every shade of right, from a mere claim to a nominal manorial due or fee up to a complete managing right over the land, can be observed.

Even at the risk of seeming to wander away from my direct subject, I may pause to explain how it was that these complicated rights could be in practice given effect to, and how they could exist together without interminable confusion. They grew up under a social stage in which an extremely vague notion prevailed as to *ownership in the soil*, although a feeling of 'right,' in some sense, existed, and the utmost attachment to an old family location was evinced. Up till quite late historical times, the most complicated interests would be dealt with in terms of *sharing the actual produce*. The old Oudh kingdoms afford a good illustration. And in the case of Gondā we have once more the benefit of an exceptionally good account by Mr. W. C. Benett.[1] 'The produce,' he writes, 'is the common property of

[1] *Gondā S. R.* p. 48.

every class in the agricultural community from the Rājā to the slave. No one is absolute owner any more than the others; but each has his permanent and definite interest.'[1] And again: 'The basis of the whole society is the grain-heap, in which each constituent rank had its definite interest. There is as yet no trace of private property, whether individual or communal; the rights which bear the nearest resemblance to it being the essentially State-rights of the Rājā.'[2] I have quoted the words as they stand; but they must be understood in connection with the context and all that is further said about the independent hereditary right to the separate family holdings. The words do not really imply that there was any ignoring of a specific interest of each holder in his hereditary land. What is meant is that no one conceived of his hereditary right as setting up an exclusive title to the enjoyment of the whole of the produce of the land tilled. It comes to this, that a claim to a certain share of the *produce* is the tangible element and apparent symbol of right rather than any theory of *soil* ownership, whether individual or collective. It will not be supposed, *e.g.*, that all the grain from all holdings was thrown into one common heap, and that, after first deducting the dues of the headman, the watchman, the *paṭwārī*, the carpenter and so forth, the rest was formed into two heaps, of which the Rājā took one and the rest was equally allotted among the cultivators—share and share alike. Every holding collected its own grain-produce, and after setting apart the share of village officers and artisans, and then the Rājā's share, the rest went entirely to the several land-holders. The cultivating holder's share was not, therefore, in any way independent of the extent and advantages of the particular holding or the amount of labour and skill expended on it.

[1] It is interesting to notice that in Bastī, a district once forming part of Oudh, where the grain distribution was found still in full force, the grain heap is actually spoken of as '*pāṅçoñ-māl* (= the property of five: *i.e.* that in which an indeterminate number of people have an interest). See Hooper's *Bastī S. R.* 1891, p. 39, where there are curious details about the grain division.

[2] Referring to the fact that around the Rājā's right to his share in the produce there clustered a number of other rights which were recognised and had the character of permanent property at a very early stage, see p. 208, *ante*.

From quite another part of the country I may quote an actual instance which came under my notice judicially, and which shows how complicated interests can be settled in terms of sharing the produce—interests which would be the despair of the jurist attempting to define them scientifically, in terms of *landed* right. The case occurred in a village near the Jihlam River, North Panjāb. There was first an old cultivating group—possibly representing the original clearers and settlers, who may once have had independent rights. But long ago another superior-caste family (whether by a Rājā's grant or by some forgotten act of conquest or usurpation, it is now impossible to say) had acquired the ownership and formed *the* village community as a co-sharing body; they claimed the whole estate, and the first group were unmistakeably their tenants with whatever privileges. So far we have the ordinary type of a joint- or landlord-village—in this instance apparently grown up over an earlier cultivating group. But in Sikh times some enterprising person with the necessary capital observed that, if a canal-cut were made in the alluvial soil, from the river, it would bring water to the village and greatly enhance the productiveness of the land as well as render it secure against failure of wells or of the monsoon rains. This person applied to the local governor and obtained a grant to carry out his work, he being given an assignment of a portion of the Government revenue share. As the work largely increased the harvest outturn, no one felt the charge very much ; the extra share was, in fact, paid without diminishing the Government heap from what it had been before. But the capitalist had thus acquired a permanent interest of some kind in the entire village. But there was yet another interest : it happened that a shrine of some sanctity existed within the village area ; and some religious mendicant or other similar applicant besought another assignment of produce to enable him to provide for the up-keep of the shrine and worship thereat. His request was granted, and thus another permanent interest—called a *mu'āfī*—was grafted on the village estate. Practically the whole of these various interests were provided for by dividing the grain heap. Before the canal-maker came the produce was divided between the owners, the cultivators, and the Sikh governor. When the canal grant was made, and later on the *mu'āfī*, do not suppose that the grantees would simply get a part of the share which the governor's officers were carting away. The grantees were both of them regarded as having some kind of permanent interest in the whole village; and both of them would go to the official headman, and the grain shares of all would be adjusted by bargain and compromise. Doubtless, if things had continued as they were, under Sikh administration, one or other of the 'over-lords,' as I may call them, would have got the upper hand, and made all the rest his 'tenants'; but the British rule came, crystallising the rights into recorded forms, and preventing further aggressions and decays and changes, and all the four interests of tenant, joint-owner, canal-grantee, and religious-grantee, became stereotyped and defined as best they might.

One other instance I will quote from the Kāngrā Hills, where we have already noticed the assumption of soil ownership by the Rājās and the consequent position of the actual land-holders as what we may call 'Crown-tenants.' Such land-holders often have tenants, some of a permanent character called *opāhu*, under them; the *opāhu*, in fact, probably represent an older stratum of cultivating right, and belong to families over whom, in some cases, the *wārisī* was established. This gradation of right from the Rājā to the cultivating tenant is, as usual, expressed in terms of a division of the produce. The *opāhu* tenant accordingly describes his position thus: 'My superior, the *wāris*, is the owner (*mālik*) of the lord's share or first half of the grain (*sat*), and he has the (*thīkā*) duty of paying the Rājā's revenue; I am owner of the cultivating holder's share (*krat*) or remaining half, as well as of the (*kāsht*) business of cultivation.'[1] 'Ownership' is not in the soil, but in the shares of the produce, and in the 'business' of cultivation or of paying the revenue.

SECTION IV.—THE 'INDO-SCYTHIC' OR NORTHERN TRIBES: THE MUSSULMANS

Long after the Aryan kingdoms had been founded, other tribes, as we have seen, from time to time followed the steps of the first invaders, and established themselves sometimes as rulers,

[1] Lyall's *Kāngrā S. R.* p. 62.

sometimes as colonists, in Upper India. The most important of these races, from an agricultural point of view, are the Jats and Gujars. They, too, are among the most prominent of the founders of villages and of *villages in the joint-form.*

It is not surprising, then, what with Rājput clans, Jats, Gujars, and other more or less closely connected races, all of whom had pretensions to superiority, and many of whom had the most complete *tribal* organisation, there should be varieties of joint-villages, whether tribal, 'democratic,' or held by the joint descendants of 'aristocratic' founders, as the prevailing tenure from the Indus to Benares.

The Jat and Gujar are especially largely represented, by original village foundations over extensive tracts, in the Panjāb. The Gujar were more pastoral, and perhaps for a long time continued to feed their cattle in the great prairie and jungle areas of the Panjāb Doābs before they took to settled agriculture. We find the Jat village settlements to be among the most strongly constituted; often there is a considerable clan feeling, and not unfrequently much pride of descent from some noted ancestor, to be found among them; and there is always a co-sharing or joint-claim to the whole village area. Sometimes we find Jat settlements on areas much larger than the 'normal' village. As a matter of fact, it is highly probable that the Jat villages represent both the clan settlements or settlement of 'democratic' colonising groups, and also the estates of dignified leaders or chiefs, very likely of half Rājput origin, whose descendants form the existing communities.

The internal constitution of the Jat and other tribal villages is, in fact, very much the same as that of the Rājput. But I am rather inclined to believe that the true *bhaiāchārā*, or method of equally-valuated holdings, is a Jat, or at least not a Rājput, principle. I could not, however, say this with any confidence; and in the sequel we can without difficulty describe the different kinds of joint-village without separating Rājput from Jat or other owners. Whatever religion these Northern races may originally have had, they are now either nominally Hindu or Mussulman; except, indeed, where some of the finest clans have swelled the ranks of the Sikh confederacy. It may be conveniently here mentioned, that while the tribes are nominally Hindu or Mussulman, they have, in the Panjāb at any rate, adhered to a customary law of their own. Their rules of inheritance, their customs of adoption and other kindred matters, differ considerably from the Hindu law of the text-books; nevertheless, the customs are such as tend to keep up the idea of the *joint-family property; and hence it is that their forms of joint-village are so similar.* In fact, Jat custom recognises the 'joint-family' quite as strongly as the Hindu law does, though in a less elaborate form. There are many great and lesser clans of Jats whose custom is not entirely uniform; but all agree in the feeling that ancestral land belongs to the whole family. I cannot venture on a detailed examination of the customary rules;[1] but I may mention that the idea of joint-right to ancestral land is indicated by the customary limitation of the 'house-father's' power of alienating it. Concurrently with this, the power of defeating the expectation of collateral agnates, in the case of a sonless owner of land, by making an 'adoption,' is much restricted. The succession is strictly agnatic, and females take no share.[2]

There is one subject, however, which I have hitherto purposely kept in the background in order that it might not seem to complicate the discussion of the really important elements of joint-village origin, the Aryan and the Jat custom. I refer to the Moslem conquests and to the effect they may have had on village tenures and on ideas of land-holding generally. The strange thing is that they had so little *direct* effect. Their dominion, of course, introduced many grantees and other superior holders of estates, whose descendants remain to this day. It was to the Mughal supremacy that the country owed the introduction of something like a regular system of

[1] Nor is this necessary after the work of Mr. C. L. Tupper, who has collected in his *Panjāb Customary Law* a number of the tribal codes, to which he has prefixed valuable introductory essays. Still more recently, a small but excellent book, giving the *judicially decided points* of customary law as far as they relate to ancestral land, has been brought out at Lahore by Mr. Justice Roe and Mr. H. A. B. Rattigan (*Tribal Law in the Panjab.* Lahore: *Civil and Military Gazette Press*, 1896). This also contains a good preliminary essay on the subject of the customary law in general. (See *Asiatic Quart. Rev.* July 1896.)

[2] The widow is allowed to retain land, on a life tenure only, as representing her husband, when there are no sons.

land-revenue administration; and with that system a number of new and sometimes convenient terms for tenures and other matters connected with land-holding became current. But the very fact that a conquest, or rather series of conquests, which occupies such a prominent place in Indian history, and which developed the land-administration so extensively, should have had so little effect on the land-holdings, at least in the villages, is in itself somewhat remarkable, and makes it all the more necessary to explain why it was so.

The chief features of the Moslem conquest are easily remembered. We may pass by the Arab invasion of the eighth century of our era, which only affected a part of Sindh and the immediate neighbourhood. As far as India is concerned, we have first the series of Pathān dominations, and then the Mughal. The Pathān period commenced with mere raids or plundering expeditions. Sultān Maḥmūd of G͟haznī was in fact a knight-errant, actuated partly by religious zeal, partly by love of adventure and plunder. For more than a century the princes of his House had no wider dominion in India than the Panjāb, or rather the western part of it. But with the twelfth century invasions began to have more lasting results under the successful efforts of the G͟horī kings. From that time successive colonies of Turkī, Pathān, and early Mughal families were introduced into India; but they were mostly soldiers, and when they did settle here and there in agricultural villages, they seem to have adopted the habits of their neighbours, or observed their own purely tribal methods of dividing the lands occupied. In most cases there is little to distinguish their villages from settlements of other adventurous or conquering tribesmen; but one series of settlements on the Panjāb frontier will furnish us with interesting material for future consideration.

The chief result of the success of the first or pre-Mughal emperors (1152–1525 A.D.) was to establish, besides the central kingdom of Delhi, other independent Muhammadan States in Upper India, of which Gaur, or Bengal, is perhaps the most prominent.[1] Further south, the Muhammadan kingdoms of the

[1] It is curious to observe that the geographical features which influenced the first Aryan movements also affected the Moslem invasions. Some of them, taking the Indus Valley line, were directed to Gujarāt and

Dakhān arose out of the disorders at Delhi after the time of 'Alāu-d-dīn Khiljī. A successful general (Zafr Khān), in the usual Indian fashion, set up as an independent prince; and though the single kingdom afterwards split up into five, the period of dominion was not an unhappy one for the country (A.D. 1489–1688).

The full establishment of the Mughal empire of Northern India may be dated from the reign of Akbar in 1556. The Revenue Settlement of this emperor, effected under the direction of Rājā Todar Mal, has become famous. It will be observed that though the Settlement was, locally at any rate, accompanied by something like a survey, or rather a rough chain-measurement of holdings, it had nothing to do with any inquiry into landed rights, or with securing titles, as the British Revenue Settlements undertook to do. It propounded no State policy or new theory of rights in land. It settled the amount of revenue, with reference to the crop and kind of soil: the amount was collected village by village, and there was no tendency to interfere with the existing tenures, either by definition or modification. Akbar's dominion was extended southward to Ajmer and to the northern part of Bombay known as Gujarāt; but the Muhammadan kingdoms of the Dākhan beyond were not interfered with till the evil genius of Aurangzeb, in the latter part of the seventeenth century, moved him to seek their destruction—and his own. The Marāthā power, in fact, rose upon the ruins of both, and would have probably removed every vestige of Moslem rule south of the Vindhyas if the State of Haidarābād, which as usual originated in a governorship or dependency of the empire,[1] had not been preserved by the events of the French and English struggles for supremacy.

From the land-holding point of view, the Mussulman element in India is represented first by a number of colonies of early Moslems, the relics of the Pathān empire; and these had very

the Western Dakhān, the Vindhyan Hills not opposing an advance (p. 43, *ante*). The later invasions proceeded from the passes more to the North-West; and Upper India — including Bengal — was the chief scene of their success. When the Mughals attacked the South, it was by means of the passes through the Vindhyan barrier, at a comparatively late period.

[1] Whence the title the *Nizām* (= *Nawāb-Nāzim* of Ḥaidarābād.)

little sympathy with the later arrivals in the train of Humāyūn and his successors. As the result of both empires, but chiefly the later one, many individual Sayyad and other dignified Moslem families (some with pretensions to religious sanctity) rose to local influence and obtained estates or received grants of villages. Thus we have a number of landlord estates, and over-lord estates, and some village-communities of Moslem tribes, as I have already stated. By far the strongest Mussulman element in the agricultural population consists of tribes and families already settled—Jat, Gujar, Rājput, and others, who adopted the Moslem creed. But neither the original Muhammadan invaders (and with them we may for this purpose include our Panjāb frontier tribes) nor the local converts, though often fiercely religious, had any knowledge of the Muhammadan law; nor, indeed, if they had, would they have been likely, as landholders, to follow it accurately. The Muhammadan law of inheritance, which is the branch that would most nearly concern land-holding families and communities, evidently had its origin among a people whose chief wealth was in camels and merchandise, or even houses in towns; it is ill adapted for those whose attention is before all things concentrated on their ancestral land. As a matter of fact, the Moslem land-holding villages and tribes in Northern India very generally follow what I may fairly call the general agricultural custom of family land-holding,[1] more or less modified by features derived from the Muhammadan law—such as allowing shares to daughters (until marriage). In other words, the joint-family system is observed; there is an equal inheritance of all sons and grandsons, &c. (agnates), in their grade of descent; the same degree of restriction is placed on the alienation of ancestral property, and even more objection is felt to adoption, by a sonless landowner, of anyone who is not either a near agnate (with consent of the rest) or a resident son-in-law.[2]

[1] It is only the greater families, chiefs, and persons of religious pretentions, that attempt to follow the *shara'*, with its complicated rules of sharing and its exclusion of one grade of descent by another, and its allowance of shares to females. The villagers usually follow their own custom and imagine that it *is* 'the Muhammadan law.'

[2] The 'resident son-in-law,' *khāna-dāmād* (P.); *ghar-jawāī* (H.), is

No wonder, then, that Muhammadan joint-villages are not very different from Hindu or Sikh villages of the joint type, and that where they are purely tribal villages their mode of settlement and sharing the land still assimilate them in class to the ordinary joint community type.

The indirect influence of the Muhammadan systems of administration has, however, been not inconsiderable. In the first place may be mentioned the general introduction of names and terms connected with land tenures, which have had a gradual tendency to fix ideas and crystallise forms, although in themselves these words and terms rarely imported any new ideas. The Moslem governments, in fact, everywhere adopted the customs they found ready, and the old things were called by new names. For example, the royal rights—to the revenue share, to the waste land, and to other levies and taxes—were collectively called the *Zamīndārī*; the royal demesne—itself derived from the old clan ideas of territorial division—was called *Khālṣa*. Hereditary rights (of the superior families) were called *mīrāṣī*, but no change was implied in the nature of the right. The revenue system was simply the old indigenous system, not really affected by Muhammadan law theories of the tax or *khirāj* imposed on the conquered, though the name is made use of. The change introduced by Akbar from payment in kind to payment in money was one which was inevitable; it was made by Hindu States as well. Indirectly the change affected village life a good deal. As long as the old grain-share system lasted, the management was necessarily very much what we may call *raiyatwārī*, and the tenure of the village lands was secure, since the headman and the whole body of cultivators managed the business together; and the concern of the tax-gatherer was not with the nature of the holdings nor who held them, but with the quantity of grain he might (on one or other of the methods of estimating it in use) successfully demand as the generally known total

virtually a form of adoption. A sonless land-owner will take into his family a child, or a youth, and if he gives satisfaction will marry him to his daughter on the understanding that he is to succeed as heir to the land. Sometimes the marriage takes place at once; oftener the 'son-in-law' is taken as a child, and the father defers the formal acknowledgment and betrothal till he sees how the boy will turn out.

produce of the village. The grain was brought to the village threshing-floor, and was divided, as we have seen, so much to the menials and artisans, so much to the king, and the balance to the cultivator. But the cash revenue not only demanded a survey and record of holdings, but it led to a calculated total demand from the village, which had to be realised without much regard to individual rights. Especially was this the case when revenue-farming became a general practice. It was out of this system that the fabric of the Bengal landlords' estates grew,[1] at the expense of the old village constitution; and where farming went more by single villages, the control of the manager seemed to convert itself into virtual ownership, with equal facility—always supposing the decadence of the Central Government and the consequent relaxation of detailed local control. The farmers, once established, left their families to inherit and to share the village lands among themselves. In the south country, the system of farming—though adopted by the Mārāthās, did not lead to the general establishment of landlordships, because it was efficiently, and indeed mercilessly, controlled by its adopters. But of all the varieties of tenure that grew up locally, fewest of all are due to the operation of the Moslem systems of land-administration.

In Madras, the Moslem power was never really established, except as regards the short-lived dominion of the Mysore Sultāns in the West, and of the Nawābs of the Carnatic (and Karnūl)—dependencies of the Haidarābād State. These insecure and tyrannical Governments destroyed much in the case of individual rights, but created nothing in the way of new tenures. The occasional joint-villages that have survived, or that once existed, south of the Vindhyas, do not owe their origin to Moslem rule.

[1] Though it must not be forgotten that the landlords were not *all* originally mere Revenue farmers. A number of local hereditary Hindu Rājās of the old *régime* had been subdued and converted into tributaries, and were regarded by the emperors as the 'Zamindārs' or managers of their estates. It was very probably the example set by the management of these territories that suggested the appointment of capitalists and others to farm the revenues of large tracts, and so to found landlord-estates, where there were no hereditary Rājās.

It may also be said to be one of the indirect effects of Moslem conquest that Hindu Rājās fled into the hill country, and there produced the changes that we have mentioned; also that Rājput chiefs and Rājās, and sometimes whole clans, were removed and dispersed, and set upon new adventures, and often owe their over-lordship in new homes to the encouragement or the grant of the emperors.

But it will be remembered that the dispersion was almost as much the result of feuds and internecine quarrels among the Rājput clans themselves as it was of the imperial victories. From the end of the twelfth century, the inability of the clans to unite ensured the defeat of the Tumār, Rahtor, Chauhān, and other leading Hindu powers of the day.

One other effect on tenures, though it is a more doubtful instance, may be stated. The principle that the conquering ruler became the owner of all land, and that the local cultivators became only his *raiyats*, or subject-tenants, may perhaps be said to have originated with the Muhammadan invaders. At any rate, the claim received a great impulse from the Moslem theory that the property of 'infidels' became the right of the conqueror. The theory, it is true, was in strict law largely modified by texts which virtually secured the property of all who submitted and lived in peace and obedience; but conquerors were apt to seize the principle and forget its limitations. It may be justly said, however, that we have some evidence of Hindu conquerors adopting the same pretensions before Moslem times; and at least it is uncertain whether the Hindu Rājās of the Hill States, for instance, were influenced by ideas learned from the Moslems in establishing their claims to the land, which their successors adopt to this day.

The embarrassment of the British Government on succeeding to a *de facto* but not *de jure* claim to all land, and the existing theory of State ownership in all Native States, may, on the whole, be fairly regarded as a legacy of the Moslem conquest.

If I were dealing with the history of the revenue administration, it would be necessary to take notice of the Marāthā administration, at least in the districts where it was firmly established. But from the point of view of village-tenures it requires little or no attention. Whatever effect it had was to break down individual rights, and to charge with imposts tenures that had before been free. As a rule, the Marāthās were far too keen financiers to allow their revenue-farmers to remain long enough in possession to establish themselves as owners. That result happened either when there was no control, or when, as in the first days of British rule, the position of village co-sharers was misunderstood. As a matter of fact, the *Khot* estates in one or two of the Bombay coast-districts are almost the only 'estates' that have arisen out of Marāthā revenue-farming.

CHAPTER VI

THE TRIBE AND THE VILLAGE

SECTION I.—PRELIMINARY OBSERVATIONS

A CHAPTER on the relation of the tribe to the village will hardly need any preliminary justification.

If physical circumstances invite the grouping of cultivators into more or less compact bodies, and cause them to arrange their cultivated fields and grazing grounds in a ring fence, it is also true that there must be something more, which determines what households shall thus settle or keep together; if there are limits other than those of available space in the contemplated village, we ask what are the limits of relationship which determine the several groups? Next, it is evident that if we are right in believing that pre-Aryan races had established villages and permanent cultivation in very ancient times, it is a necessary conclusion that such settlements took place under purely and primitively tribal conditions of life. Indeed, as we reviewed in Chapters IV. and V., the whole series of races —the TIBETO-BURMAN, KOLARIAN, DRAVIDIAN, ARYAN, LATER NORTHERN, including our latest arrivals of MOSLEM TRIBES ON THE PUNJĀB FRONTIER, continual reference to their *tribal* condition was made. The evidence, in the case of the earliest tribes—now long mingled with the general 'Hindu' or 'Muhammadan' population—is naturally scanty. We see, however, certain survivals and remnants, all of which point to the earliest village settlements having been formed as subdivisions of some wider *clan-area*. Indeed, in some cases the clan-territory is much more definite than the village. The KOLARIAN villages of Chutiyā-Nāgpur, including those of the *Santāls*, the DRAVIDIAN villages in the same neighbourhood, the *Kāndh* villages of Orissa,

—all are on a tribal basis. When we come to the ARYAN and later tribes, we still have much evidence of tribal life. As might be expected, however, we soon begin to find a stage of more rapid progress, and with it inevitable diversity; we cannot expect to find that *all* the villages resulting from Aryan, Jat, and other later races are connected with the tribe. For one thing, it was only a limited number of the Aryan clans who never developed monarchical ideas, and who settled without Rājās or chiefs of territories. Most others seem to have become monarchical very readily. It is true that at one time the monarchy itself was constructed on clan lines. But many kingdoms were ruled by individual princes, and in them clan institutions tended to become modified and gradually to disappear. The development of the Hindu State was, in fact, one great though indirect cause of a large number of non-tribal villages.

It will be remembered, then, that while tribal-villages are sufficiently numerous and important to demand a separate chapter, we shall also have to devote another chapter to an almost equally large class of non-tribal villages.

Speaking first of the villages connected with clan-settlements and arising as subdivisions of distinct clan-territories, one thing strikes us, and that is that the earliest settlers seem to be connected with a form of village in which there is no joint-ownership, but only the aggregation of individual or household possessions, the title to which is based on the labour expended in clearing the land and making it fit for the plough. The later clans, on the other hand, appear always to have some stronger cohesion, some sense of superiority and conquest, which produced at least the appearance of collective ownership in their settlements.

Those who have a strong *a priori* inclination to believe in the universal existence of collective-ownership among early tribes may be disposed to doubt the possibility of the *raiyatwārī* or separate-holding village emerging from tribal conditions of life; and no doubt the matter will call for our further consideration hereafter. Meanwhile, the fact remains that the *raiyatwārī* form of village prevails over the districts occupied by non-Aryan tribes and clans, and that it was the Aryan and later tribes—who may be called 'superior'—that developed villages in the joint form. I shall here be pardoned for repeating the warning that 'the joint form' does not imply one single principle or cause of collectivity. The 'jointness' of clan or tribal villages is something practically distinct from the 'jointness' of villages the owners of which are co-heirs and descendants of a single founder or grantee. And these again are distinct from villages united by association, or aggregated in some other way—neither tribal, nor by descent from the individual.

The mention of the *raiyatwāri* village as in origin tribal, and of *some* of the joint-villages as also tribal, may seem to produce some kind of cross-classification of villages in general. But a short table in the footnote will make the matter clear.[1] For, reverting for a moment to our initial distinction between *raiyatwāri* and *joint* villages, the real fact is that of joint-villages only a certain portion are connected with the tribe; while of tribally-originating villages, only a portion exhibit features of joint ownership. The table in the footnote also enables me to call attention to a distinction which it is desirable to make in the 'tribal' section of our joint-village class. It is easy to understand the fact that, when an area of country is found to be occupied by a clan or a tribe, that result may have come about in either of two ways—(1) the whole clan or tribe, already existing in sufficient numbers, may have conquered or occupied the site and proceeded to divide it among themselves; (2) or the clan may have gradually grown up on the spot, the first occupation of a considerable area having been by a single family (with its dependents and followers), and these, having multiplied in the course of many generations, have now formed

[1]

Tribal origin	Raiyatwāri village.		[N.B.—*Modern* villages in this form may of course occur apart from any tribal connection.]
	Joint-village, 1st division.	1.	Established by clan already formed and numerous.
		2.	Established by *clan* gradually growing up on the spot.
Non-tribal origin	Joint-village, 2nd division.	1.	Arising out of the joint inheritance in succession to *individual* founder.
		2.	Some form of voluntary association.

a clan, and to some extent retained the clan connection. Sometimes it is not certain which of these two things really happened. But in most cases we shall see that the 'clan-expansion' areas have certain features of their own. However that may be, it is not difficult to discern the marks of a *clan-connection* which can be distinguished from that of the mere *family*; and where that is so, we are justified in treating the village, for the purposes of study at any rate, as in the 'tribal' class.

Before proceeding further to inquire into the structure of the tribe, and how this structure affects the possession of land and the formation of villages, I should like to allude to the manner in which this question of 'the tribe and the village' has been dealt with in some of our more valuable books of reference. In his excellent volumes on 'Panjāb Customary Law,' Mr. C. L. Tupper has called attention to the difference between the explanation of origin of the village (regarded as a group of families with an aggregate land allotment) suggested by M. de Laveleye and by Sir H. S. Maine respectively.[1] M. de Laveleye thought that the tribe or clan, regarded as already grown up from the single family in which it necessarily originated, began with a sort of indefinite common ownership of the whole territory occupied by it. This was probably when the clan was in a pastoral stage, during which agriculture was only beginning to be adopted: it then sufficed to apportion the lands destined to cultivation, in lots that were only temporarily assigned to the different households. In the course of time the regularly cultivated land was more permanently divided into parcels; but even in this stage the land is regarded as the 'collective property' of the clan, because 'it returns' to the clan 'from time to time, so that a new partition may be effected.'[2]

Sir H. S. Maine, on the other hand, considered that the village groups were either bodies of actual kinsmen, or groups in which time and circumstances had caused the relationship to be forgotten, so that 'the merest shadow of consanguinity survives' and 'the assemblage of cultivators is held together solely

[1] See the dissertation (p. 7) prefixed to vol. ii. of *Panjāb Customary Law*.

[2] Quoted from *Primitive Property* (Trans.), p. 4, as cited by Mr. Tupper.

by the land which they till in common.'[1] In short, the joint family begins the process; and this expands, first into the larger family—such as the house communion—and finally into the 'village-group.' The remarks already made will have suggested that there is no occasion to make any choice between these two opinions or to regard them as in any need of reconciliation. Both contain a good deal of the truth; and they are not opposed, for the simple reason that, perhaps unconsciously, each writer is describing a different kind or division of the 'joint-village.' Given the *whole clan* settling ready made, as on the Panjāb frontier, or a small family expanding on the same spot into a clan—*e.g.* the 'cultivating fraternities' of Jats, which we shall presently describe in the Mathurā district—and still acting on *tribal* principles, M. de Laveleye's description is perfectly correct, except that his idea of 'collective ownership' may be somewhat different from that which we may finally prefer to accept. Given, on the other hand, the joint-village arising out of the multiplication of kindred of *one individual founder*, and *not on any directly tribal* principles, then we have the village as described in the passage from Sir H. S. Maine. That, I am convinced, is the real explanation of the difference; and it will be remembered that both authors were under the unfortunate impression that *all* villages in India were in essential features the same; and they did not think of the broad and fundamental distinctions, such as the little table in the note to p. 227 calls to mind.

It will be observed that neither in their suggestions regarding origin, nor, as far as I can discover, in any other connection, does either of the eminent authors afford any solution to the question how the divisions of clans, and of families under the joint constitution, are regulated, or how they originated. The illustrations which are collected in the sequel bring into prominence the existence of such divisions; and they are evidently on a uniform principle.

Where we have the earliest tribes to deal with, it is not surprising that we have only limited traces of such details, and that further study is almost impossible. But when we come to

[1] *Early History of Institutions*, pp. 77–82.

the Aryan, Jat, and other clan-settlements of later times, the divisions of clan and family are most prominent, and we may reasonably hope to discover the principle on which they proceed. We have also to consider what is the connection which the clan and its divisions have with the land; how far do they own it collectively, or individually, or 'own' it at all?

Before dealing with these two questions, it will be well to call attention to the existence of certain territorial divisions which can be traced in almost all the provinces, and which indicate the location of clans and tribes. By this means we are provided with a certain unit area connected with clan life, as a sort of starting-point from which our further inquiries may proceed.

1. It is certainly a noticeable feature that in almost all parts of inhabited India we can trace the existence of distinct territorial areas or jurisdictions, indicating the primary or secondary divisions of a tract of country occupied by a clan or tribe. As the feature is equally noticeable in the southern districts, where the *raiyatwārī* form of village prevails, the fact, reinforced by other direct evidence, compels us, as I have already remarked, to include the *raiyatwārī* village as properly belonging to the tribal class. Each such separate area seems to mark the location of a separate clan, possibly itself a section of a larger tribe. It must be added that the most early clans appear to have been *totemistic*, or at least to have had distinguishing marks or insignia.[1] The boundaries of these clan-areas were fixed, even when internal divisions were imperfectly defined; and respect for them would always be enforced. Among the Kolarians we have noticed the *parhā*, or union of villages, probably the earliest example of tribal areas. It is rarely safe to trust to mere similarities of sound, but it has been suggested that some old word (resembling *parh* or *pir*) may be the origin of the official

[1] I have noticed this among the Kolarians and Santāls as well as the Dravidians (pp. 120, 155, *ante*). Among the Aryans also distinctive banners and symbols were well known. Possibly some of the 'monograms' on old coins may have some connection with the clan symbols. The *Nāgbansi* families formerly marked the serpent *lunette* on their seals; and the use of the sun, the lion, the *kaṭār* or dagger, fish, &c., employed as royal or as tribal emblems, is well known.

pargana division adopted by the Mughal Government.[1] All over the South of India we have traces of the *nādu* (cf. also the *muṭṭhā* among the Kāndh tribes), which was often a sort of 'county'; and in some places there is a clearly surviving tradition of the purpose of this division. Thus in part of Madras known anciently as the *Tondaimaṇḍalam* we find first a number of *kuṭṭam*—the name probably indicating the 'fort' which was the seat of the territorial chief; each of these primitive territories was afterwards reorganised into *nādu*, and each *nādu* contained a number of villages (called *nattam*, *i.e.* the village site). The chief of the *nādu* was called *Nātthān*. In Malabār we have evidence of how these *nādu* divisions were governed by the *nād-kuṭṭam*, or assembly of representative elders out of the family groups, or *taṛa*, of the ruling class, in each *nādu*; these have been already described.[2] All over Northern India, again, we have clear indications of clan-areas, under the names of *taluqa*, *'ilāqa*, and *ṭappā*, or *ṭhapā*. Local illustrations of this peculiarity will occur repeatedly in the sequel. Here my object is to call attention to the fact that, such divisions being the natural consequence of tribal-life, they appear all over India and among all tribes, the oldest and most primitive as well as the latest and more advanced; and they have often lasted after the tribal stage had passed away. For this survival there are two reasons: first, when the clans themselves adopted the monarchical form of government, or were conquered by territorial chiefs, these clan-divisions everywhere became the natural landmarks for defining the jurisdiction of kingdoms and of chiefships such as those

[1] It is curious (see p. 152, *ante*) that among the Bhil a similar term—*parrah*, as Malcolm writes it, is used for the little cluster of separate home-steads or the hamlet, and not apparently for any larger aggregate of these hamlets. A somewhat similar term appears again among the Bilūchi tribes (p. 245, *post*).

[2] See p. 170, *ante*. The word *kuṭṭam* (Wilson's *Glossary*) means both an 'assembly' and also a 'fortified place or group of houses.' So that we find it applied both to the division of territory protected, so to speak, by the chief's fort or capital, and also to the assembly of the representatives of the families in the *nādu*. Some account of *Tondaimaṇḍalam* will be given in a subsequent chapter. The first *kuṭṭam* division was due to the Pallava tribes; that into *nādu* and also villages was effected by their successors, the Vellālar colonists.

of the *pālegāra*, who assumed dominion over *nādus* in the South.

In many cases (as, *e.g.*, the Panjāb frontier and the cultivating fraternities of the North-West Provinces and the Panjāb plains) the *'ilāqa* or *ṭappa* is still occupied by a number of villages *all of the same clan*, and has been utilised as the basis of modern surveys and records of rights. We may also find occasional instances of similar areas which at one time became a Rājā's territory, but which ultimately formed a kind of clan-estate or community of cultivators composed of the descendants of the once ruling house whose power had been broken.[1] In nearly all cases it will be found that old clan-areas, whether or not they became Rājā's territories, have ultimately formed the basis of the administrative and land-revenue subdivisions of districts; and that is why the '*pargana*,' the '*taluqa*,' and other such ancient subdivisions are remembered to the present day.

2. But clan-territories clearly indicate the existence of clans; and all we can discover of the earliest clans leads us to believe that they were not unorganised hordes, or collections of individuals; they were invariably organised on some principle.

It is evident, in the first place, that every large clan has certain primary and secondary main divisions, to one or other of which every existing family belongs. Even in the village which originates in a single family we may remember to have noticed divisions called *pāttī*, *thok*, &c., which are in fact groups based on the same principle as the clan divisions. In either case distinctive names are attached to these divisions, but not to any others; because they represent the first branches, or degrees of descent, from the founder of the clan, or of the individual village, as the case may be. And there is something which makes these main divisions proceed up to a certain point and then stop; so that subsequent families belonging to one or other of the established groups do not again form further groups under new designations.

It is a matter of principle which, I think, will readily be

[1] More commonly the *individual* members, remnants of such houses have formed separate village estates; but there are cases of what now appear as clan-areas of village proprietors, formed in this way.

accepted, that there is a certain aggregation of descents from an ancestor or founder which constitutes (up to a known limit of blood relationship) a 'family'; there is a further connection allowed to subsist between the different 'families'—less direct than family union, but extending much wider—which is in fact the lien of the 'minor-clan.' These ties seem to depend on natural feelings common to human nature, and therefore to be found in all tribes. The survival of the clan-stage in India is certainly marked by (*a*) a limited but practical union of the whole clan settled in one place; (*b*) the recognition of a 'wider-kindred' forming a 'minor-clan' or something similar; (*c*) a 'close-kindred' forming the 'family.' What determines the limits of these groups?

We may pass over the fission of a great *tribe* into separately named *clans*. Such a fission must necessarily take place when numbers increase very greatly. And it is a matter of accident, and of circumstances of location, whether a generic designation for the whole tribe is kept up, or whether the several clans have in fact become separate tribes.

But inside the clan there is almost everywhere observed a further grouping into what I may call *minor-clans* or septs. Perhaps there is more than one such subdivision; finally, the last of such acknowledged groups is made up of the single *families* or households.

Now let us take, merely for the purpose of comparison and illustration, such a standard as the Welsh tribe, which has recently been examined by Dr. Seebohm.[1] Speaking first of the grouping of the *people*, not of their mode of ownership, we find (1) a close-kindred or group of immediate relations recognised, and also (2) a 'wider-kindred.' The former answers to the family, the latter very much to the minor-clan. Outside that, again, is the general group of the clan, still held together by the common lien of loyalty to the chief and of obligation to general

[1] The opportunity for studying the Welsh tribe was almost unique, for it happened that shortly after the Conquest the Normans completed *extenta*, or surveys for revenue purposes, and these display in several cases the tribal constitution of the people. These 'extents' can in turn be compared with statements of the Welsh codes and other documents; and thus the conclusions drawn will be tested independently by both authorities.

service and defence, as well as by certain customs of co-aration and common pasturage. In Wales the close-kindred was called a *wele*, or *gwely*; it consisted of the purely natural group of the individual clansman, and his father, grandfather, and great-grandfather; direct inheritance went no further. And this group of close-kindred would naturally also suggest a wider group; but I will quote Dr. Seebohm's own words. 'The eldest living ancestor, as chief of the household occupying the principal homestead or *tyddyn*, and seated by the ancestral hearth, might well live to see growing up around it a family-group extending to great-grandchildren. On the other hand, looking backward to his own childhood, he might well recollect his own great-grandfather sitting as head of the household at the same hearth, just as his great-grandchildren would some day hereafter remember him. Thus the extreme natural reach of the knowledge of the head of the household might cover seven generations. Finally, if family tradition went back two stages further than actual memory, thus it would embrace the larger kindred to the ninth degree of descent.'[1] In fact, the kindred to the seventh degree came to be a recognised limit of natural direct connection; and this was reckoned as the 'wider-kindred,' while for certain purposes only, in Wales, it was extended to the ninth degree. Now, whether the precise number of degrees is the same or not in all cases, the idea of the thing is perfectly natural. Dr. Seebohm has justly pointed out that in another tribe, as widely different as that of ancient Israel, exactly the same thing was recognised. This is apparent from the narrative in the Book of Numbers regarding the trespass of Achan. The perpetrator was discovered by casting lots and successively narrowing down the area of choice: first the whole clan of Judah[2] was taken; then the minor-clan of the Zarhites, the ancestor of which, Zarah son of Judah, was of course long dead—

[1] *Tribal System in Wales*, p. 84.

[2] We commonly hear of the 'twelve *tribes*,' perhaps because they were the *great-grandsons* of Abraham, and thus on the death of their father (and all before him) they divided and began afresh; and as they were established in a new country, where there were no pre-existing areas already named after the first generation, each of the twelve began a new οἶκος—a new close-kindred which would expand again in the same way.

this was the 'wider kindred.' Then the close-kindred or 'house' was indicated. And here for the first time an individual name appears; Zabdi is mentioned personally as probably the oldest living, or, at all events, personally remembered, head. He is not called a son of Zarah; for all we know there may have been more than one degree between him and the founder of the whole minor-clan called 'Zarhite.' Zabdi's son is Carmi, and he is taken; and finally Carmi's son Achan, whose own sons are still children. Zabdi, in fact, is the great-grandfather and head of the '*wele*.' A precisely similar state of things is observed in the account of the selection of Saul son of Kish to be king (1 Samuel x. 21). The tribe or clan of Benjamin comes first; then the minor-clan of Matrites, and then the family of which Saul is the adult son. Moreover, from chapter ix. we gather that the 'Matrites' included *seven* degrees back to great-grandfather's great-grandfather—Kish, Abiel, Zeror, Becorath, Aphiah, and an unnamed 'Benjamite, a mighty man of valour,' probably Matri himself.

And these are not the only indications we possess of these features of clan, wide-kindred, and close-kindred, for which I have claimed universality, and which explain to some extent the divisions of the clan-territories, as well as of some of the village groups in India. Mr. Hugh E. Seebohm has followed up his father's inquiries in Wales by an examination of the Greek tribal system,[1] and he shows not only that the same basis of connection and separation existed in ancient Greece, but he has also drawn illustrations, with great care, from the 'Laws of Manu,' as showing the same ideas among the Brahmanic Aryans. With them, the sacrificial cake and the libation of water being essential funeral ceremonies in the *family*, we find the degrees of kindred measured by the right to offer the one or the other.

The text of the 'Laws'[2] prescribes that the cake is to be offered to three ancestors and the water to three; the fourth in descent is the offerer, and the fifth has no concern with the oblations. That is to say, three ancestors—*i.e.* to the great-grand-

[1] *On the Structure of Greek Tribal Society: an Essay* (Macmillan, 1895).

[2] Chap. ix. 186, compared with v. 60 and iii. 5. See H. E. Seebohm, *op. cit.* pp. 51, 52.

father upwards from the surviving householder who offers the gift—receive the *cake*; and three, upward again—*i.e.* to great-grandfather's great-grandfather—receive the *water* libation. So that the existing householder offers the cake to his deceased father, grandfather, and great-grandfather. But then the householder may live to see his son, grandson, and great-grandson, who can also join with him in offering the cake; so we read in the fifth chapter that the relation of the *sapiṇḍa* ceases with the *seventh* person; and it is within this degree also that a man of the twice-born classes is debarred from marrying a woman of the family. The water libation degree (*samānodaka*) is stated to extend as far back as there is community of family-name or recollection of descent. In Wales this was held not to exist beyond *fifth cousins*, and that seems practically to have been the, limit meant by the 'Laws' in the passage of the sixth chapter, where the *fifth* degree is mentioned as relating to the water offering as well as the cake.[1] All are *sapiṇḍa* who offer to the same ancestors, so that a large circle of relatives is included; while the immediate family extends in each group to the great-grandfather. This at once suggests the household (*οἶκος*) and the related kindred (*ἀγχιστεία*) of the Greeks, or the Welsh *wele*, and the wider-kindred, and also the Israelite arrangement of kindred. When in such widely different regions we come across this same distinction, we are justified in believing it to be universal and springing out of a feeling common to all early tribes, and founded in human nature itself.

The same principle of division appears also in the rules regarding the marriage relation. It will be remembered that, while

[1] Mr. Seebohm used Burnell's translation. G. Bühler's is the same. It is plain that the groups would be moving downwards with the death of each grade, and, as Mr. Seebohm says, 'at no time would more than four generations have a share in the same cake offered to the three nearest ancestors of the head of the family.' The same idea of the three degrees is emphasised in a text of the *Mitāksharā* (*Vivahāra khāndham, Mātrikā XXXII.*), as quoted by Ellis in his *Memoir* on the South Indian villages. The text speaks of the enjoyment of property by direct ancestral descent, and the Commentary adds: ' . . . descent from three direct ancestors, namely, the father and the rest [grandfather and great-grandfather], is termed direct ancestral descent. And the reason of this is, as *Kātyāyana* says, that memory does not extend beyond this degree.'

all Indian *tribes* are endogamous to some extent, so that, for regular marriage, a Rājput or a Jat always chooses a Rājput or a Jat and so on, yet also the *clans* are mostly exogamous, for a man of one *got* must choose a wife out of another clan or *got*.[1] Now, it appears that as long as a real, not merely a remote or traditional, common ancestor is remembered, the man and the women are not regarded as in groups sufficiently distinct to intermarry.[2]

If we apply these principles of division to the clan, we see how they explain to a large extent such groups as we observe, for instance, among the Panjāb frontier tribes. We find a whole *tribe* (or small nation) occupying a country called generically its *'ilāqa*. Each *clan* is represented by a *ṭappā* area. And the clan is again subdivided into large groups, which I may call incidental, as they are due to the fission *per stirpes*—sons of an elder wife being distinguished from sons of a younger, or of a concubine. These sections are called by personal names, and often have the syllable *-zāi* added. They are not distinguished by any generic name; for convenience I will call them sub-*ṭappā*. Within each 'sub-*ṭappā*' we find a number of (still large) groups called *kh̲el*. In some cases the *kh̲el* itself is subdivided into a series—viz. into *kandī* and finally into *thal*. Within these final subdivisions come all the existing 'houses' or 'families.' These acknowledged divisions seem to me essentially, and allowing for local and minor variations, to depend on the universal three grades of original descent. The whole *ṭappā* represents the common *great-grandfather* of the original family; the sub-*ṭappā*, his sons, or in some cases grandsons raised to the rank of

[1] The Mughal and other Moslem tribes form an exception to this rule.

[2] See some good remarks in Ibbetson's *Karnāl S. R.* § 186 ff, and compare the cases noted in the *Rohtak S. R.* p. 21. Thus, for example, in the Rohtak district the Jat minor-clans—*Ahlāñ* of Dighal, *Auliāñ* of Sāmpla, *Birmā* of Gubhāna, *Mārī* of Madhāna, and *Jūñ* of Çhoçi—are all known descendants of four sons of one ancestor; and they do not intermarry; they form minor-clans and not clans, and are not sufficiently out of the bonds of 'wider kindred.' Compare also the case of the *Nohwar* and *Narwar* Jats in the *Mathurā S. R.* p. 33. 'Memory,' it will be remembered, according to the Hindu lawyers, ran to 100 years, or the *three* generations spoken of. Custom and law are here at one. Cf. *Laws of Manu*, iii. 5.

sons;[1] these are the *grandfathers* of the original series. Then the *khel* are their sons—the fathers of the primary group. If there are *khandi*, or a further subdivision of the *khel*, they represent a new or secondary series of kindred and families, including all the tribal population existing at the time of location.[2]

As the tribal or clan division depends on the grades of descent in the first or progenitor family, so it will be found that a village on the *family* basis, also divides itself into primary and secondary groups according to the grades of the first founder's family. Take the case of the joint-village derived from one original founder or acquirer. As I have already mentioned in Chapter I., the primary division of a village in the *pattidārī* form follows the three degrees, with the fourth as the head of the existing households. Thus:—

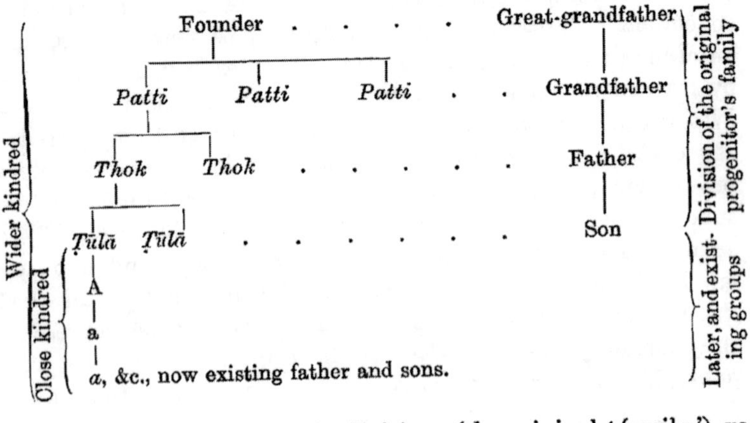

After the *ṭūlā*, the main divisions (the original 'family') go no further. The sons, grandsons, &c., of the *ṭūlādār* (head or progenitor of the *ṭūlā*) are the existing close-kindred; and only if they were to move off and found a new estate somewhere else

[1] Cf. the case of Ephraim and Manasseh, Genesis xlviii.

[2] It is exactly the same if we apply the Pathān names to the Israelite. The whole tribe or nation is Israel, and its *'ilāqa* Palestine; but the actual units are the *ṭappā* Judah, Benjamin, &c.; and, in the case above quoted, the sub-*ṭappā* or *-zai* division is the Zarhites; the *khel* Zabdi; and the *kandi* Carmi, whose son Achan and his wife and children, beginning a new series, represent one of the existing households in the *kandi*.

might we have the elder commencing a new group as founder, and his sons furnishing the *patti* division, and so on.[1]

Referring to Chapter I.,[2] it will be observed that the same thing occurs in the *bhaiāchārā*, or equal-sharing fraternity, often occupying an area much larger than an ordinary village. This estate is divided into groups as above according to the members of the *original* family in three descents. After that, the fifth and subsequent degrees all take equal shares or lots according to their actual requirement. In the ancestral-share form (*pattidārī*), the fifth and subsequent degrees still adhere to the proper fractions according to the law of inheritance. And it is this difference that marks the two kinds of village.

3. We have now to connect these groups of kindred with the land on which they are settled. It has already been remarked that in tribal settlements 'villages' are not always formed. In every case there is the division of the territory; sometimes, if the tribe is large, into clan territories and other large primary allotments. In the case of the *raiyatwārī* districts, we know that clan areas were formed, and these appear divided further into compact villages, though we cannot explain how. We have already found reason to include all the later tribes—Aryan, Jat, Moslem, &c., as alike forming village groups with a joint constitution; and it is certainly true that we can discern a strong tribal union which has enabled the Land-Revenue Administration to treat the villages (or whatever forms anything like a village) as jointly responsible for the revenue. How, then, is it possible that tribal custom can comport both with purely individual (*raiyatwārī*) holdings, and also with such apparently joint-holding customs as the frontier tribes, for example, exhibit?

It will be seen from the examples presently given that, in reality, the joint-holding of these tribal groups is of a limited and peculiar kind. Indeed, at first sight we might be tempted to deny the existence of any real common-holding, and so to do away with the distinction. It is quite true that there is no case on record in which a whole tribe possesses a large area really held in common; nor, indeed, does any considerable section of

[1] As to the different local names for the divisions, see p. 31, note.
[2] P. 32, *ante*.

the clan so hold. Sometimes we find large primary divisions made on the ground, such as I have above enumerated. In other cases such divisions do not appear, or have long been completely forgotten, and the whole area is divided ont directly into household shares—so many 'ploughlands,' or something of the kind, to each. In the case of the clan growing up on the spot from a small initial group, there may or may not be primary divisions; if there are, the division was made while the family was still small; in any case, all the family holdings are allotted; very often they have been added on, one by one, as the numbers grew. Where, then, it may be asked, does the holding 'in common' or jointly come in? In the first place, the smaller groups constituting in some sense a large 'family,' often hold jointly among themselves, being relatives within a certain limit, acknowledging a rule of joint-inheritance and the institution which we call 'the joint-family.' And there is in these joint tribal villages a wider species of union over and above that; of it I will speak immediately. These features produce a real distinction between the *raiyatwāri* and the later tribal villages; and the difference appears to me essentially to depend on the different constitution of the *family* as regards its right over the land held.

Ownership of property does not depend on universal sentiments like those which produce the liens of close or wider kindred. It is true that the sense of right to a thing in virtue of labour, time, and wealth expended on producing it is, if not a purely natural, at any rate a very widespread sentiment, and it may be accompanied or reinforced by a sense, also natural, of right as member of a tribe, to share with the others what all have together acquired, and perhaps fought for. But further development of custom depends on the conditions of life; and we see cases where the *land* is hardly regarded at all, but the irrigation water is the real object of customary right, or where rights are centred in the grain-heap at harvest. Let me once more refer, for illustration, to the case of the Welsh tribe and its family group, or *wele*. As long as the head of the group lived, the property in the homestead, and all other rights, vested in him. Whatever partition took place was informal and for convenience only: the various adult members of the family would, indeed, enjoy their several homesteads and crofts and their cattle; but no new theoretically separate 'properties' or 'estates' were formed till the final separation after the completion of the course of descent and the commencement of new '*weles*.'[1] It was owing to the circumstances of the situation that separate land-shares were not allotted on the ground, and that co-aration and the division of the harvest was the custom.[2] If the Welsh family had been in the habit of taking and managing a separate holding of the tribal land, it would have been very like the *raiyatwāri* family as it appears in early India.

Sufficient attention is hardly perhaps paid to the fact that all 'families' are not, in ancient tribes, constituted on the model of the Hindu joint-family; and not only so, but that early Dravidian and other non-Aryan tribes do not, even in India, appear to have known the joint-family, at any rate before they became 'Hindus.' The early *Kāndh* tribes, to take a definite instance, show a form of family in which the *patria potestas* is complete, and in which the head of the family is the sole owner during his life; there is nothing of that inchoate right of the sons as soon as born, and of the inability of the father to alienate ancestral property without consent of the family, and so on, which mark the 'Hindu family' not only in the theory of law-books, but in the actual custom of certain local tribes.[3]

It appears to me that the joint-family, with its limitation of the power of the head, who, in fact, only takes the place of a sort of *primus inter pares*, is a later elaboration—however old in itself—of a time when, after long settlement and regular government, the law has developed and the tribal stage is passing, or has passed, away. Perhaps the sense of clan-union, which must long have lingered among the 'twice-born' classes, found its echo in this joint-family. Moreover, Hindu law, and the custom[4] of

[1] Seebohm, *Tribal System in Wales*, pp. 89, 95.

[2] *Ante*, p. 50.

[3] Dr. Seebohm notices this distinction. See *Tribal System in Wales* p. 95. I venture to think that an examination of the older Sanskrit law-texts would show that the limitation of the power of the house-father was much less in early times than it afterwards became, when the joint inheritance law was elaborated, and so much affected the idea of the family constitution.

[4] *Ante*, p. 210.

the Northern conquering and energetic tribes, both proceed from people who have much pride of race and strong ideas of rights 'by inheritance,' and of *equally representing a noble or heroic ancestor who was the founder of their fortunes* and the object of their worship. It is quite possible that the absence of joint ownership in the family marked a condition of tribal society in which no strong sense of union was evoked by the conditions of life. Probably the first settlers found but few human enemies to contend with, or were not subjected to any circumstances that tended to supersede the purely patriarchal rule. More it would not be justifiable to say; but at least it is a geographical fact that the *raiyatwāri* form of village survives most completely where the settlement (in any numbers) of Aryan, Jat, Gujar, Moslem, and other conquering and 'superior' tribes took effect least. The joint-village is, in fact, conterminous with the range of Aryan and later conquests, or with races which have developed the joint-family. Wherever we find such joint or shared villages, either surviving or once existing, in the South, it is always in connection with some explainable circumstances of local overlordship, or special colonising privilege.

In thus endeavouring to account for the *raiyatwāri* form of village as arising under early *tribal* conditions, I should like to repeat that it is quite possible that originally the villages may have been held by subdivisions of clans—real groups of kindred—and that a feeling of tribal union may have once existed which now cannot be traced. If we were to take away from a frontier village in the Panjāb the sense of tribal union, the actual tenure would be hardly distinguishable from the *raiyatwāri*. If it is true that the head of the non-Aryan family was sole owner of the holding, the fact would have tended to concentrate and fix the sentiment of ownership as arising out of the original occupation and laborious clearing of the soil. It may be added that this also may help to account for the absence of any idea of a joint proprietary claim to a certain area of the waste adjoining each village. The villages being widely scattered through a great area of waste generally subject to the clan, the land not cleared and merely grazed over was regarded as 'common'—merely in the same sense that the air, or the water of a river or lake is common.[1] The idea of 'property' did not attach to 'unwrought,' uncleared land. Accordingly, when the looser tribal government gave way to the rule of a Rājā, whether by conquest or by commendation. it became an easily established custom for the Rājā to dispose of the waste as he pleased. It is well, too, to remind ourselves that all this is not a mere question of theoretic possibility; it is based on some actual survivals, which, though local, almost necessarily indicate a more general custom in early times. It is only necessary to refer to such well-preserved indications of early village forms as those of the Kāndh tribes, or the Kolarian and Dravidian settlements in Chutiyā-Nāgpur. We there have evidence not only of the tribal constitution of agricultural society and of the formation of village-groups, but also of the absence of collective ownership. There is no 'joint-family,' there is no co-aration, nor any holding 'in common.' True, there is equal division among the sons of a deceased owner, but that is not the 'joint-family'; it is only one feature which perhaps marks the beginning of such an institution. We have not now much evidence that the families in the Western or Southern *raiyatwāri* villages are connected by clan ties, or that groups of villages of the same clan are found contiguously.[2] It is the different idea of the 'family' that is at the root of the distinction between the non-Aryan villages and those of the later tribes.

But, besides the joint-family, the later tribes also exhibit a kind of union beyond the circle of the immediate co-sharing relatives, which in the nature of things we can hardly hope to find evidence of among the scanty relics of the older Kolarian and Dravidian tribes that alone survive. All the Northern tribes as well as the Aryans evidently had a strong sense of general unity and cohesion; there was then a feeling that when a territory was occupied it was the acquisition of the whole body, so that all were equally entitled to share in it, and that its maintenance and defence was the common concern of all. It was this feeling perhaps, among the frontier tribes, *e.g.*, that causes

[1] See *ante*, pp. 10, 11.

[2] It will be remembered, however, that this question has not been studied. On this subject, and on the causes of the miscellaneous nature of *raiyatwāri* holdings, see pp. 18, 19.

the *per-capita* principle of sharing to be so much commoner than the rule of allotment according to the varying shares of the law or custom of inheritance. And this sense of equality also doubtless led to ready acquiescence in the tribal custom of allotting the holdings for a term of years only, so that they might be exchanged, and each group get its turn at the good or bad—the more or less advantageous and convenient farms. I do not see how this feeling can be said to imply a 'common ownership' in the face of the always separately assigned holding and the definite share which is understood to exist. In the same way, the retention of the waste area undivided is a matter of convenience only, as I have more than once explained. Whenever any portion of tribal land that would under ordinary circumstances be divided out is not so, it is always under exceptional and explainable circumstances; and even then the definite shares are well known. But the conditions of tribal security also demand that the various groups and sections shall acknowledge a union for the purposes of defence, and this includes a joint liability for taxes or other charges which have to be met. For example, the frontier tribal villages would find it quite natural to accept the joint liability for the Government land-revenue, under the North-West Provincial system; and it is largely owing to this fact, and to the consequent adoption, for these villages, of the nomenclature and forms of record employed by the revenue system in question, that they have been identified with the 'joint-villages' of another kind—those in which the co-sharers are really heirs of one man.

Section II.—Tribal Custom as exhibited in the Panjāb Frontier Districts.

In the frontier districts of the Panjāb a number of Pathān and Bilūchī tribes, professing the Muhammadan faith,[1] have established themselves, and remained more or less undisturbed, all within known historical times—some within the last two or three hundred years, others even as late as the last

[1] To which they were converts under the various Khālifs. See Bellew, *The Races of Afghānistān* (Calcutta, 1880); also D. Ibbetson, *Panjāb Ethnog.* § 390–3 for Pathān, and § 377–9 for Bilūchī.

century. They are all fighting tribes: they found, however, only a limited opposition from human enemies, and a large part of the country was virgin soil when they occupied it. The arable land is mostly dry and open, both hilly and level, but with no tropical jungle to contend with. Sometimes, but locally, the soil is fertile; more often it requires artificial irrigation before it is cultivable at all, except in seasons of unusual rainfall. The tribes are wholly non-monarchical, and if they have submitted in general to the suzerainty of some neighbouring State, or some greater local chief has succeeded in making himself a territorial ruler, that does not alter their internal constitution. We see clearly the clan, with its greater chief; minor clans, with their chiefs; and again smaller groups, each with its own head. Blocks *of land* smaller than the *khel*, and such as we should call 'villages,' are by no means always found; among the Bilūchī especially, the family shares are so many portions of the general (and still considerable) *khel* territory, and a few families live together in small hamlets. And in most cases the smallest group that has a name indicating a recognised subdivision of a clan seems too large to call a 'village.'

The chiefs, as a rule, have no pretensions to be owners or even governors of the whole territory, as the Hindu Rājās were. They had no territorial 'revenue,' only their own share of the tribal possession; though it appears that in some cases, at any rate, a special share of the land was reserved for the superior chief (or *Khān*).[1] And generally there must have been some provision for the support of the patriarchal position. Mr. Ibbetson, in the work cited in a preceding note, has fully gone into the history of the Pathān and Bilūchī tribes. It is only necessary here to say that the Bilūchī tribe is called *Tumān*, and its chief *Tumāndār*. It is divided into clans (*pāra*; cf. the Kolarian and Dravidian *parhā*), the clan chief being called *Muqaddam*. The minor-clans are *phallī*. The clans are all descended from one ancestor; and the subdivision or minor-clan is the 'wider kindred' from the same head.

The Pathān tribe is said to be more homogeneous than the Bilūchī. The Pathān and the Bilūchī, however, both recognise the custom of *hamsāya*—the 'neighbour' (of some other race)

[1] See, for instance, the *Peshāwar S. R.* § 589.

taken under the tribal 'shadow' or protection. Thus the non-tribal artisans and menials of the hamlets speak of themselves as belonging to the tribe which protects them. Among the Bilūchī, whole sections of foreign clans have been adopted as clans of the tribes, under the custom of *hamsāya*;[1] but the custom is not carried to such lengths among the Pathāns.

The Pathān tribe usually, but not always, has a *Khān*—the head of the *Khān-khel*, or eldest house of the eldest branch; and each clan and minor-clan has its *malik*, or head. 'The chief,' says Mr. Ibbetson, 'is seldom more than their leader in war and their agent in dealings with others; he possesses influence rather than power, and the real authority rests with the *jirga*, a democratic council composed of all the *maliks*. It is needless to say that all the districts are found to be divided into *'ilāqa* and *ṭappā*—the distinct areas and sub-areas of each clan and minor-clan.

It is a misfortune that the tribal areas have all come under, not only the revenue administration of the North-Western system—which is quite capable of being worked to suit them admirably—but under its forms of record, and especially under a vicious nomenclature entirely unsuited to them, and invented really for villages of another character. It is simply misleading to classify the frontier-villages in a mass under such headings as *zamindārī*, *pattidārī*, or *bhaiāchārā*, unless of course where some area has become the property of one man, or of his heirs jointly (*zamindārī mushtarka*), or where some portion is really divided throughout on fractional shares, as among descendants of one original owner (*pattidārī*). *Bhaiāchārā* they all are, *in the sense* that they are governed by the 'custom of the tribal group or brotherhood'; but unfortunately the word *bhaiāchārā* has got so misused in the Panjāb as to have lost its *distinctive* meaning.[2]

An example taken from the Peshāwar district will at once

[1] See, for example, the cases reported by Ibbetson, § 380.

[2] This use or misuse of official terms is the subject of an appendix to Chapter VIII. I will only here say that any village, no matter of what form, so long as it is shared on some plan other than the ancestral system, or is held in severalty, is called *bhaiāchārā*, depriving the term of all meaning except the negative one that it is not *pattidārī*.

serve to show the way in which the clans are divided. The Yusufzai country had become the 'heritage' of four sons of one MANDANR.[1] If we accept the first genealogy, it would be supposed that these four sons would be the heads of four clans. But as a matter of tribal arrangement, the clans actually recognised are five, as we perceive from there being five *ṭappā*, or clan-territories. No *ṭappā* is called after MANNO, the eldest son, but no less than four of the *ṭappā* are allotted to his four *grandsons* (the sons of Utmān and Usmān), while only one *ṭappā* is called after RAZR, and that represents not only Razr but also his two brothers. It is curious that the supposed son Manno should be effaced entirely by a number of grandsons; and that there should be only one clan-area among the remaining three sons together. I feel sure that the real origin of this was the different mothers, and the probable disparity of their rank. In

[1] *Peshāwar S. R.* §§ 199 and 226 ff. The 'tree' is given thus:—

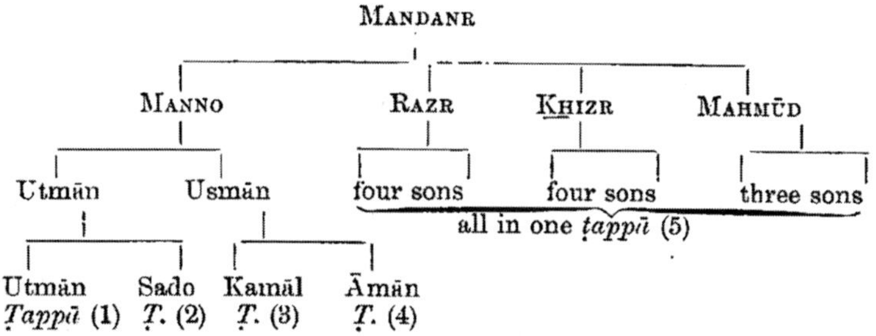

Another genealogy, which seems much better to justify the *actual* territorial allotment to the several branches, is also referred to (*S. R.* note to p. 92).

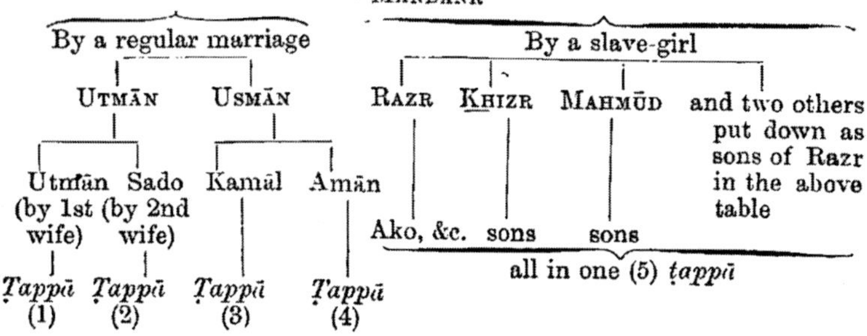

this tribe, too, the custom of *parunai-vesh* prevails—*i.e.* that all the sons of one wife, however many, share with those of another, who may be fewer, *per stirpes*. There is also the possibility that in some cases the grandson was more distinguished in war or otherwise, and so may have supplanted the father. Thus the two sons of Utmān, besides being separated (owing to the different mothers), are each given the dignity of a whole *ṭappā*, whereas normally they would have shared one between them. However that may be, the *ṭappā* divisions actually stand :—

<table>
<tr><td>1.</td><td>Ṭappā</td><td>Utmānzāī</td><td rowspan="2">Sons of UTMĀN</td><td rowspan="4">These two are grandsons (or more probably sons) of the founder</td></tr>
<tr><td>2.</td><td>,,</td><td>Sadozāī</td></tr>
<tr><td>3.</td><td>,,</td><td>Āmānzāī</td><td rowspan="2">Sons of USMĀN</td></tr>
<tr><td>4.</td><td>,,</td><td>Kamālzāī</td></tr>
<tr><td>5.</td><td>,,</td><td>Razr</td><td colspan="2">RAZR and other sons of founder (together)</td></tr>
</table>

Thus the whole *'ilaqa* is first divided into *ṭappā*. Next, some of the *ṭappā* are divided into intermediate areas for which no distinctive designation is provided; they are spoken of as *daftar*, which means any group of lands in general, but the local name still ends with *-zāī*, as if they were 'sub-*ṭappā*.' This intermediate division is due to the separation of the groups of offspring from different wives—*e.g.* *Ṭappā Kamālzāī* is so divided: the terms *Mishr-rānīzai* and *Kishr-rānīzāī* merely mean 'of the elder (*Mishr*) queen (*rānī*)' and 'of the younger or lesser (*Kishr*).'

The *Razr* division is a very large one, and is subdivided for another reason, because it includes several brothers of *Razr* (or perhaps they are his sons.)[1]

A diagram will make this plain ; it of course has no pretensions to represent any geographical fact, or the relative size of the different divisions ; it is literally a diagram.

The word, or rather termination, *-zāī* is derived from the Pashtu *-zoe* and means 'son'; while *khel* is the Arabic word meaning 'group' or 'company.' It is said that these terms are used 'indifferently for the larger and smaller divisions.'[2]

[1] These are also marked by the termination *-zāī*. In one case it appears to be *-khel*, but I am not sure that the personal name was not *Akokhel*.

[2] *Tribal Law in the Panjāb* (Roe and Rattigan. Lahore 1895), p. 4.

DIAGRAMMATIC ILLUSTRATION
of the
'ILĀQA OF MANDANR

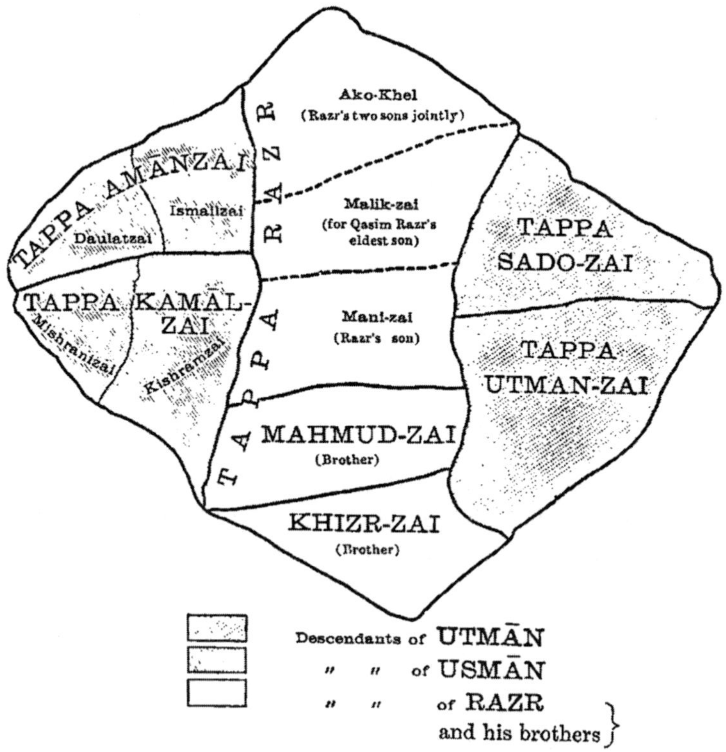

N. B.—Each of the divisions shown above is again divided into *khel*: *e.g.* T. Utmanzai is divided into forty-one such, of which four are occupied by *hamsāya* (colonies of other tribes).

But I venture to think that though in practice this may be so to a considerable extent, there is more properly a difference, and that *-zūi* indicates the larger groups from one of the 'sons,' or first main branches in the table of descent, and *khel* the secondary branches. If that is so, then the *'ilāqa* may be indicated as the tribal area; the *ṭappā* marks the greater clan; the 'sub-*ṭappā*' (or territory with the name-termination *-zūi*) also marks an intermediate division large enough to be called a sub-clan;[1] while *khel* is the still considerable group, the minor-clan or 'wider-kindred.' For the examples seem to indicate that the *khel* is too large to consist of only the immediate relatives within seven degrees (or some similar limit); the sub-sections of the *khel* correspond better to the 'close-kindred.'

As regards sharing the *land*, the *tribal* or *clan* authorities appear to have effected only the main (or primary and secondary) allotments of territories and sub-territories. Apparently the *khel* groups arranged themselves as they pleased. But about this I am doubtful. However the *khels* may have been allotted, it is usually the case that each has a considerable area; and it depends on circumstances whether there is one village-group, with its one residence for all its households, or whether separate hamlets are formed, or both.

In any case, the principal territorial areas were made large enough to accommodate all the then existing descendants—*i.e.* to give everyone a *share* on one or other of two principles, (*a*) that of counting every head (man, woman, and child), and giving to each existing household the number of equal shares it contained, without respect to gradation; or (*b*) that of regarding the table of descent, and giving larger or smaller shares, according to the number and degree of the existing kindred;[2] though whether this sharing according to grade is carried out *all through* is not so clear.

It very often happens that the individual shares are made up of separate specimen strips of each kind of soil, scattered through the whole *ṭappā* or *daftar* of a subdivision group. In

[1] And often separated because of the difference of mothers—first wife and second wife, or perhaps legitimate wife and inferior.

[2] Cf. H. E. Seebohm, *Tribal Society in Greece*, pp. 65, 66.

that case compact areas for further subdivisions of the body are impossible. The collections of families that cohere from some general rule of wider-kindred form the *khel*; and many *ṭappūs* are at once divided (on the ground) into a corresponding number of *khel* areas. As these are large and contain much waste, when the families expand, new hamlets are started, more land is broken up, and in time the hamlets grow into independence; and thus a *khel* splits up into a series of what are more like ordinary '*mauza*.' In some cases no subordinate divisions of the land *en bloc* occur, but the whole *ṭappū* (or even the whole *'ilāqa*) is at once allotted into a great number of single or household shares. In others, on the contrary, there are so many sub-sub-divisions (if I may so say) that the Revenue authorities are obliged to club several together to get a manageable unit of assessment and general control.

The materials for illustrating these frontier tribal settlements have been in part collected, and accompanied by interesting remarks, by Mr. C. L. Tupper.[1] And there are also some further Settlement Reports now in print and available for direct quotation. I shall select typical instances from the frontier districts of Hazārā, Peshāwar, Kohāt and Bannū, and the more westerly districts (which also extend further southwards) of Dera-Ismaīl-Khān and Dera-Ghāzi-Khān. In none of these do we find that the definition of small or limited *village*-areas, as such, is part of the tribal procedure of location or allotment; where they have come to exist, it is under later influences. We find that procedure essentially confined to the major-groups and sub-groups; and then attention is paid to the actual unit shares. Everywhere the people exhibit their sense of the natural aggregation, up to a certain limit, of kindreds; they also show the strong influence of the feeling that the superior right of the clan or clan-division to the whole area is unquestionable; and that every member of the clan has a right to his due share of the territory won by

[1] *Panjāb Customary Law*. Especially in vol. ii.; and as regards the custom of redistributing periodically the several shares, in part ii. of vol. iii. But some Settlement Reports have since been printed. It is only necessary to remark that Mr. Tupper throughout uses the term *bhaiāchārā* in its official sense, including *all* kinds of villages which are not on the *pattidārī* principle, or held by sole landlords.

the common exertions of the group. The shares are, as a rule, divided out from the very first; only the grazing land or the waste is left in common. More rarely, part of the arable land is also left undivided, though the shares are known. The custom of exchanging holdings (where it was applied) must have tended to keep up the feeling of a sort of general clan ownership, which, however, was not inconsistent with independent right to the household share. The exchange was, in fact, evidently invented to secure equality. The joint responsibility for taxes, &c., is accepted by the whole *khel*, but not, so far as I know, by any larger group united.

The HAZĀRĀ district is occupied by clans who for the most part do not date back, in their present location, beyond the eighteenth century; they drove out or subordinated the weaker families whom they found in the country. 'The right thus asserted or acquired,' writes the late Colonel Wace, 'by the strong over the weak was popularly termed *wirāṣat* or *wirṣa*; and its possessor was called *wāriṣ* (*Angl.* heir). In fact, as stated by Major J. Abbott in some notes left by him, the *wāriṣ* is the last conqueror.'[1] In the centre of the district are four *'ilāqa*—(*a*) Mangal, which was the joint holding of two clans or groups, Mansūr and Hasāzāi; (*b*) Nawāshahr was the holding of the Mansūr alone; (*c*) Dhamtaur of the Hasāzāi alone; (*d*) Rajoyā of the Sālār. All were subdivided into groups which afterwards served to form villages. The *status* was much disturbed under the Sikh rule, and several of the villages have fallen into the hands of 'a motley gathering of occupants of all classes.' A periodical redistribution of shares was formerly the custom.

But the PESHĀWAR district much more completely illustrates our point. 'The main divisions or tribes[2] have each a separate tract of country generally known by the name of the tribe

[1] See *ante*, p. 210, as to the use of these terms of Arabic origin. Among the frontier tribes, being Moslem, the use is not surprising. Mr. Tupper compares the *Geerften* (inhabitants of the village) under the old Germanic law and the *Erfgenamen* in the Saxon provinces of the Low Countries, who were the people in the 'mark' who possessed a *whare* or share in the tribal 'inheritance.'

[2] Captain Hasting's *S. R.* 1874, p. 84 ff.

now or originally occupying it; for instance, . . . the *ṭappā* Mohmand. . . . In each main tribe there are groups of families or branches of the tribe which, owing to their numbers or close coherence, have become distinct subdivisions.'[1] The traditionary origin of the territorial position is simple. A certain chief—Shekh Mali—made a *taqsīm*, or partition of the whole country, which commenced with the counting up of the requisite number of shares to provide one for every separate man, woman, and child in the tribe. According to the total numbers so obtained for each main subdivision, suitable areas were marked out. The allotments of general territory were apparently only roughly discriminative of soil qualities. Thus in the Yusufzai country the main divisions were for the branches of Mandanr's descendants (they were a Yusufzai tribe):[2] each got part of its territory in the hill country, part in the level. As a matter of fact, the people themselves afterwards altered this, and the Mandanr branches came to hold the whole of the plain country. The areas were taken by drawing lots. The chief's partition went no further than the main divisions or subdivisions;[3] nothing was said about 'villages' or *khel* inside the territories. I have already discussed the formation of the first great divisions; now we shall see how the further division comes about. An actual case will best illustrate what was done. The Yusufzai country is dependent on rainfall for its tillage, and a special internal allotment of the *ṭappā* was adopted. The people themselves divided the *ṭappās* into *khel*. From the records I notice that many of the *khel* areas contain each a more central group with its site for residence, and also several subsidiary (separately named) hamlets. Some 'hamlets' consist of a group of holdings on some peculiar kind of soil, as they are distinguished by the description *sholgira* (=rice growing) or *maīra* (ordinary dry loam). In the Muhammadzai *ṭappā* in the neighbouring Hashtnagar tract, there is a regular subdivision into eight large *khel*, each having a central residence group and several hamlets.

[1] See p. 237, *ante*. The allusion is to the *sub-ṭappā*, or intermediate division of the first great blocks.

[2] This is the *'ilāqa* of which a diagram is given.

[3] As in the diagram on p. 249.

Another mode of division appears among the Gigiāni clan or tribe. They first of all made their *whole area* into thirty-six allotments called *kandi* (the word we shall meet with again but not necessarily in the same sense). Each *kandi* is a mere local area adopted for division purposes, and doubtless for distinguishing the different kinds of soil. Each should contain one hundred individual and equal shares. Then the *khel* groups of families were provided for, either by their taking one or more whole *kandi* to the extent of the number of single shares their counting demanded, or else taking the due number of shares scattered through several *kandi*.

Next as to the internal arrangements of the *khels* inside the *ṭappā*. It will be observed that, whatever the size of the *khel* and the number of households composing it, the group may again have some further subdivision. Regarded as a group of families, it is subdivided into *kandi* (all households in the *kandi* have the same patronymic),[1] and sometimes the *kandi* are divided once more into *thal*, before we come to the (perhaps numerous) single households. Just as the *khel* group has a chief called *malik*,[2] so each *kandi* has its *malik*. And the *kandi* tend to set up separate residence-sites, each with its own little prayer-mosque, and its *hujra*, or guest house, in which, by the way, all the unmarried youth of the section sleep together. The land of the *kandi* or of the *thal* group always includes as many *bākhrā*, or *brākhā* (= shares), as there are *individuals* in it.[3]

If the arable land to be allotted into shares is variable in

[1] This, I presume, makes the *kandi* a 'close-kindred,' like the Welsh *wele*; and if it happens to be very large, or for some special convenience, it may be again divided into *thal* (Captain Hastings writes *tal*), just as the *wele* might be divided into *gavell*.

[2] The clan-chief is *Khān*, sometimes with the Arabic title of *Arbāb*. The next major-division chief is also *Khān*.

[3] The individual share is sometimes locally *pūchā*, and not *bākhrā*. The *S. R.* does not explain what the difference is. But, referring to the *khel* of the Muhammadzai *ṭappā* in Hashtnagar above alluded to, I notice that the four northern *khel* are divided into 6,000 *pūchā*, while the other four are composed of 480 *bākhrā*. It must be remembered that with these final shares the numbers are counted often to suit the clumsy methods of division where any system of vulgar or other fractions is unknown.

quality, the clan authorities will arrange a number of circles or series, called *vand*, consisting of the 'good,' 'middling,' 'indifferent' soils, or distinguished in some other way. Then the groups of sharers will have to take their lands partly out of each series.

Where the land depends on irrigation, this scattering of holdings over several soil-divisions is not observed. But in any case, in spite of the soil-classification, inequality in the holdings is not altogether eliminated. So a system of periodical exchange or redistribution (*vesh*) was long followed. Indeed, at first, the entire *ṭappā* divisions were exchanged. But this general exchange must have proved so inconvenient that it was naturally the first to fall into disuse.[1] The exchange of single holdings also gradually ceased when the effects of years of individual labour and cultivating skill began to tell, and individuals became attached to their fields; and when, moreover, a long period of peace made settled possession more natural. The 'village' areas, regarded as smaller groups within the *k͟hel*, are thus brought about by the gradual action of circumstances; but the tribal-grouping of families and the recognition of different degrees of kindred is really what originates it.

The *k͟hel* groups are sufficiently distinct to attract to themselves the usual local staff of village hereditary servants and menials,[2] or more than one according to size and subdivision. The *Peshāwar S. R.* notices the weaver, potter, carpenter, blacksmith, cotton-cleaner, sweeper and grave-digger, barber, ballad singer (*Dūm*),[3] and a Hindu *dharwāi*, or grain-weighman. There is always an *imām*, or priest, for the mosque, and some menials still called *g͟hulām*, or 'slave,' descendants of former captives in war or of purchased slaves in old days. These menial and artisan classes always intermarry with their own caste; they 'trace no origin, nor are they able to call themselves of any tribe or clan.'[4] They are often remunerated by small holdings of rent-free land.[5] Every *k͟hel* has it *jirga*, or council of elders

[1] *S. R.* §§ 201, 202.

[2] Cf. p. 16, *ante*.

[3] *S. R.* § 29. May it be that this Dūm caste indicates by its name an origin from the Dom—one of the 'aboriginal' hill tribes?

[4] *Ibid.* §§ 211, 212.

[5] In Yusufzai there are some 75,000 Gujar herdsmen, whom the late

(*mishr*), or elders of houses, and chiefs of the group, or of the *kandi* or section. They are referred to on 'all questions of custom and matters affecting the village society.' I find no trace of any 'holding in common,' or any co-aration; the lots are counted up and separated, from the first settlement of the tribe: the waste is undivided because it would serve no purpose to allot it.

In the KOHĀT district a very similar form is observed, and the terms used are also identical.[1] Thus the Bangash clan or tribe has four *ṭappā*, called Upper and Lower Mirānzāi, Samīlzāi, and Bāizāi respectively. Each is divided out into sub-sections, which are here mostly in compact blocks; and nothing remains as common of the whole clan. The '*-zāi*' territories were partitioned further among the *khel*, but the allotment only took account of the total number of single shares in the whole group. Thus the *ṭappā* 'Upper Mirānzāi' reckons as 1,250 shares. Of these, 500 are supposed to belong to the *Darsamand khel*. The *khel* people themselves will not always apportion the area in just that number of household-shares; as a matter of fact, the theoretical lot of 500 *bākhrā* is actually held in 347 holdings.[2] It is interesting to notice that, in the case of the Bāizāi *ṭappā*, a cash assessment imposed through some ruling chief about two centuries ago[3] caused the old share-list to be superseded; a new number of *bākhrā* was arranged, so that each should represent one rupee of the total assessment; and now shares are frequently spoken of as so many 'rupees.' In this *ṭappā* the distribution of land in compact blocks among the sections is not carried out; for the soil varies, and there is one portion, near Kohāt, which has exceptionally good springs; so each section has got a portion in the spring-watered area, and the rest of its lot, some here, some there, scattered about over the *ṭappā*.[4] The *vesh* or ex-

Dr. Bellew believed to be the descendants of one of the Indo-Scythian tribes who were settled in the country before the present clans occupied it. They are exclusively keepers of cattle by occupation, the other clans having claimed all the land as a possession.

[1] *Kohāt S. R.* 1884.

[2] See note, p. 254, *ante*.

[3] *Kohāt S. R.* § 182.

[4] And in that case the outlying blocks are made over to groups of tenants.

change was also customary. The word *vesh* is here, as often elsewhere, applied both to the process of the exchange itself and to the recognised series of areas of different soil-character according to which the holdings are made up. The exchange is here *within* the *k͟hel* only; first one entire sub-section exchanges with another, and then the families within the sub-section exchange among themselves. But the most important point to notice is, that lots or household-holdings are not here assigned, as they are in Peshāwar, by *khulāvesh*, or counting up every head in the clan or in the *k͟hel*; at least, that rule only applies to some parts. Here a *standard number of shares* for each section and sub-section is maintained, whether the actual households are, afterwards, more or less.[1] The custom of periodic exchange lasted here for a long time, and is not yet entirely extinct. In Upper Mirānzāi it was not possible, on this account, at the first Revenue Settlement, to make field maps for the villages; but the Report of the last Settlement notes that the desire of the holders to reap the benefits of their own labour and improvements has tended to put an end to the custom. In this district, too, there was a custom of having certain *qabza* (=possession) lands which were

[1] *Kohāt S. R.* § 183. The principle of ancestral shares, as compared with the *khulāvesh*, or equal shares *per capita*, is easily illustrated. Suppose a *kandi*, or sub-section of a *k͟hel*, called after an ancestor X. His three sons, A, B, C, represent the *thal*, and *a*, *b*, *c*, *d*, *e*, *f* are the individual sharers.

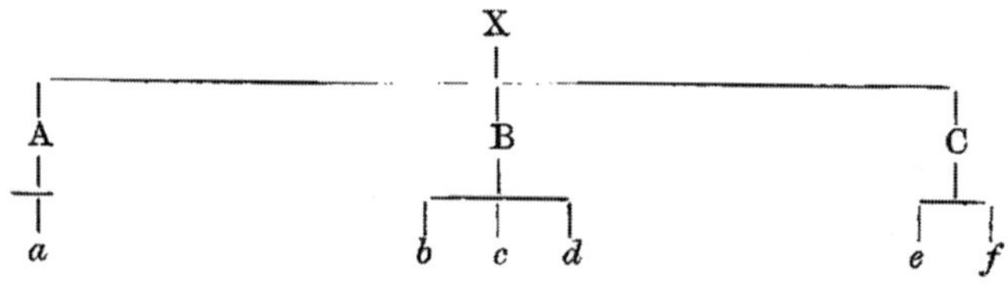

Let us suppose that the *kandi* owns a standard number (sixty) of the shares as originally constituted. Each *thal* would then have twenty shares. On the death of A, his one son *a* would inherit the whole twenty; the three sons of B would get B's twenty shares between them, or six and two-third shares each. If after the death of A, B, and C a redistribution were made on the *khulāvesh* system, *a* would not get the whole twenty shares of A, and so on; each one of the sharers *a*—*f*, would have an equal proportion of the whole—*i.e.* ten shares each.

held permanently, on what grounds is not stated, and excluded from the lands subject to the customary periodical exchange.[1]

Both in Peshāwar and in Kohāt there are special rules for sharing the water of streams used for irrigation. Space prevents me from going into the details, but the rules serve to emphasise the way in which the lands are grouped, and show clearly the division of *khel* into *kandi* and *thal*. There is a water channel for the whole *khel*, and this branches out into distributories for each *kandi*, and then again into channels for each *thal*. Within the *thal*, the fields, or plots ridged to retain the water, are made of the same number as the *bākhrā*, or individual shares included in the *thal*. It will be observed that this system of fixed fractional-shares of a given total, which is adhered to all through the grades of descent, is in principle very like the *pattīdāri*, of which the typical form occurs in the case of the village derived from an individual founder. And the system was further maintained by the fact that, the *irrigated* land being alone regarded, and being of equal value throughout, the shares of the Government revenue were, without injustice, fractions corresponding to the water-share fraction. In former days, if anyone casually cultivated some of the unirrigated land, there being no map, notice was not taken of it; payment was made according to the strictly kept shares in the *ābī* or irrigated land. But under more modern arrangements this area of appropriated unirrigated land comes under measurement, and it is then discovered that one sharer holds, and has perhaps made profitable, a good deal more land than another; under these circumstances, an adjustment will probably be called for, and payment distributed according to the acreage actually held.

In the district of Bannu there are four distinct clans. We will notice that called the Bannūchī, who settled about five hundred years ago. Here we see that, as so often observable, the *ancestral* division of the clan guides the distribution of the land-shares up to a certain point only—*i.e.* the termination of the original close-kindred. The clan is divided into main

[1] This seems to resemble the *bocland* of the Anglo-Saxon tenures—land held by some special title outside the usual or old customary folk-tenure. See Stubbs, *Const. Hist.* i. 81, and the reference to Lodge's *Essays on Anglo-Saxon Law* in the note.

sections, and these into sub-sections, all families in the latter having a common patronymic.[1] 'The traditional accounts of the Bannūchi,' says the Settlement Officer, 'respecting the original division of the country among themselves on ancestral shares, and the sub-sectional apportionment of land and water *within the limits of each main share, in proportion to the amount of canal excavation work done*, are in all probability true.' Here, as a rule, there is no *vesh* or exchange: it would not suit a state of things where each holding is permanently created by means of its channel for watering. It is interesting to notice that another clan, the Niāzāi, came to their location (in the 'Īsākhel Tahsīl or sub-district) in alliance with some Jat clan, and that on apportioning the territory they gave the Jats an *'ilāqa*, such as they had for themselves. Both clans made their main division on ancestral lines; here the first division of the *'ilāqa* is *tal*, or *thal*); that is again subdivided into *darra*, and that into single shares or *lich*.

Among the Wazīrī it is worth while noting how some of their territories are said, euphemistically, to have been 'acquired by purchase.'[2] They have no general custom of exchange; but in certain *families* the entire holding is redistributed, not after fixed periods, but occasionally—perhaps on the death of some leading member or head of a household, by means of a temporary partition.[3]

In the Marwat country we have another example in the Marwat clan (a branch of the Niāzāi, but coming to the district at a later period), where the periodical redistribution is either still practised or has only recently been given up. Here the rule of providing a share *per capita* throughout the clan prevails.[4]

[1] *Bannu S. R.* § 128, p. 123.

[2] *Ibid.* § 129. 'The fiction of sale seems to have been invented at some time after the seizure of the land in order to save the honour of the weaker side, and enable spoiler and spoiled to live together in peace.'

[3] This, it will be remembered, was the custom of the Welsh tribes; the final partition was only made among the second cousins of the *wele* group when the father, grandfather, and great-grandfather were all dead.

[4] *S. R.* § 136. This is spoken of as a 'communal' or collective form of tenure because of the periodic reallotment; and in *Panjāb Customary Law*, ii. 22, Mr. Tupper speaks of the tribe holding its

In the Dera Ismaīl Khān district, along the West frontier, we find quite a notable variety of tribes with somewhat different customs; most of which tend to show how little the village, as a separately defined group of land-holdings, still less as any kind of unit of property, has to do with the organisation of the tribal stage. The country, too, is physically diversified; there is a wide tract on the edge of the Western hills (*Damān*),[1] where the cultivation is carried on in terraced and embanked fields moistened by the mountain streams or springs. There is also the light-soiled, open country of low hills between Shekh-Budīn and the Indus River, partly cultivated by aid of hill streams, partly depending on rainfall. There is also some flat alluvial land along the river; and, lastly, the inland tract of dry land partaking of the desert character of the South Panjāb. In this district, too, we find instances of villages where a landlord family (*'alā mālik*) has obtained the superiority over the actual soil-owners (*adnā mālik*). This is, however, beyond our immediate object. Among the instances of *clans* occupying distinct tracts, we have the interesting case of a large area in the Damān, some forty miles long by twelve to sixteen broad, colonised within the present century by a tribe of Bhitāni.[2] The clan has divided into three main territorial groups. It is here noted that the residence-sites are small clusters of mean cottages and huts, hidden away in hollows; and that caves in the rock are often used as dwellings. The cluster of such dwellings is called *kirrī*; in the level country a *kirrī* will contain the dwellings of

'ilāqa 'jointly.' I am unable to see here or elsewhere any real 'communal' ownership. Nor do I know of the smallest piece of evidence of a frontier tribe holding jointly for a time even. The whole plan seems to consist in an immediate several allotment of major and minor shares. Where these depend on the individual labour and expense of providing canal irrigation, the allotment is permanent; otherwise it is first made as equal as possible, and a redistribution is provided for with the evident object of quieting jealousies, and preventing the stereotyping of inequalities in the holdings.

[1] Mr. H. St.-G. Tucker always writes the word with the final ā long; I imagine the word to be the Persian *dāman*, meaning 'skirt' of the hills. Perhaps this is a dialectic variation. I have followed the printed Report.

[2] *S. R. D. I. Khan*, 1884, § 250.

families belonging to different share groups. Each clan-territory is here divided into a large number of (usually compact) plots, called *nāla*. Each *nāla* is held by a 'number of families generally closely connected by birth.'[1] Within the *nāla*, each individual family or household seems to have no defined or allotted share, but each took what land its numbers or means of tillage suggested; and some land usually remained undivided for future occupation when required, and meanwhile for the common grazing. When there is water for irrigation, there is a rude arrangement about 'turns' in taking the water.

Still within the Damān region, the Gūmal Valley tenures only call for notice on the point that here the rice-lands are cultivated jointly; but the practice has nothing whatever to do with any idea of common ownership; it is merely for convenience, first, because the money is thus raised to pay the autumn (*kharīf*) instalment of the land-revenue; and next, because this 'strengthens' or prepares the land for the spring crop, which is managed entirely by the separate owners. The Kundi tribe, also in the Damān, demands a passing notice. Its land is held in two large 'villages,' and lies in two portions, north and south of a stream, and distinguished as the Nikannī and Prādu lands respectively. In the Nikannī the whole area is divided *per capita*—*i.e.* into a number of equal (single) shares or *daddī*, one being allowed for every man, woman, and child; the holding of them was formerly subject to periodical exchange; and the last occurred, among the Amākhel division, in 1852.[2] The Prādu lands seem either never to have been so treated, or to have been variously acquired by purchase 'or otherwise' in separate holdings.

But the most interesting tribes are those of Pathān origin in the northern part of the Tahsīls, D. I. Khān, and Kulāñchī.

[1] It is worth while noting, as showing how administrative arrangements may affect forms of tenure, that at the 'summary' or preliminary Settlement every *nāla* was treated as a separate *mauza*, or survey village. But this proved inconvenient; for the *nāla* are sometimes small, as might be expected from the variety of numbers in each 'close-kindred.' So now each entire clan area is treated as a single large village; and, as above noticed, they are three in number—Dhannā, Tattā, and Wraspūn.

[2] *S. R.* § 267.

The Gundapur tribe occupy a territory, here called *ḥad* (=boundary), of 462 square miles. The tribe have associated strangers with themselves from time to time; and now all are, by a fiction, supposed to be of the same descent. They are divided into six larger sections, or *nāla*.[1] In some *nāla*, all the sharers have the same patronymic, in others there are several groups. Exchange of holdings once existed, but has died out. The original settlement of the tribe, then in a smaller number, was at a village called Rori, which, being dependent on irrigation from a permanent stream, was divided out for the first settlers into so many *kashā* (=water cuts).[2] The shares are now 352 in number; they have lost their original owners, having been gradually bought up by the K͟hāns, or chiefs of major-sections. The rest of the tribal territory is watered by hill torrents.[3] This is *not* divided into separate larger groups corresponding to the six tribal *nāla*, but at once into 36,000 *daddī*, or single shares. Each of the six tribal *nāla* above mentioned owns 6,000 of these

[1] The hereditary chiefship is properly in the *nāla* called Brahimzāi; but, as this group suffered defeat some 200 years ago, the right was transferred to the Hamrānzāi (*S. R.* § 275).

[2] It appears to me from the remarks in § 278 that originally the rights in the Rori irrigated portion were solely rights of water; the soil seems hardly to have been allotted or regarded as property at all, except as far as each year's cultivation required; for in order to allow of fallows the water was taken to one part one year and to another the next. *Now* that the shares have passed by sale into the hands of chiefs, the cultivation is done by tenants; and, the area to be cultivated as a whole for the year being arranged, the land is divided into strips for as many 'tenants' as are counted, and a corresponding water supply is given to each. The owners distribute the whole of their rent-receipts from the entire area, according to the water-shares.

[3] This is called *dagar* cultivation; the water, which occasionally rushes down the dry beds during the rainy season, is let on to the embanked field and allowed to soak in. There is a good account of it by Mr. Yates, M.I.C.E., in *Journ. Soc. Arts*, June 1895, xliii. 702. The embankment is raised from three to ten feet high, and is made by aid of bullocks and a short stout board; as soon as one field is filled with water, the stream passes on to the next. Sometimes two soakings are given, but the soil, moistened by the gradual percolation of the mass of water, raises the crop. *Kālāpānī* (=black water) irrigation is from a *permanent* clear or dark stream, as opposed to the muddy silt-laden and purely temporary rush of the torrents formed by rain on the hillside (*dagar*).

shares. And there may be recognised divisions holding, say, 2,000 shares, and then further subdivisions.[1] A large part of the territory was actually divided out; but one part is not. This I regard as instructive, for it throws light on the question of the supposed prior 'joint-holding' by clans and sections, and which appears to me to be more or less imaginary. On one occasion, the tribe was pressed for money (in a time of war with the neighbouring *Mīāñkhel* tribe). Ordinarily, whatever was needed was raised by a levy of so much per share or *daddī* held. Under the necessity for full and punctual payment, it was agreed to set apart a certain territory south of a certain stream, and called the Prādu tract, in which everyone who failed to pay *should lose his shares and transfer them to the person who paid on his behalf.* Thus many tribesmen, besides their proper shares in the other divided area, have acquired special numbers of shares in the Prādu. Whether owing to this cause or to some other, several 'large villages' in the Prādu are still held undivided; so that the tribesmen are all entitled each to $\frac{1}{36000}$ share in them; and these undivided lands are called *tummani* (=*tumānī*?) or 'tribal' lands. The report contains no information as to how these 'tribal' lands are actually cultivated and enjoyed. There is no suggestion that the produce is thrown into a common stock and divided afterwards, or that the proceeds are taken to pay part of the land-revenue. Even if we can speak of this very exceptional area as held 'in common,' it is so under circumstances that can hardly entitle us to take it as a sample of an *earlier and general* method of tribal-holding.

But whatever the true facts may be, the landed rights of tribesmen must be somewhat complex. Thus a man may have his own divided share in his own *nāla*; also some share by transfer in the Prādu, some shares which have come to him by purchase or inheritance, and some share in the 'tribal' land;

[1] As the Gundapur had no knowledge of 'vulgar fractions,' they had an awkward system of altering the shares, while always keeping the memory of the real number. If, for instance, a section with 2,000 *daddī* was grouped into 7 equal sub-sections, as the 2,000 will not divide exactly by 7, they altered it to 700 *kaççā daddī*, so as to give each 100, which were equal to 285$\frac{5}{7}$ real shares. This detail can, however, be further seen in § 278 of the *S. R.*

and as 'in each case the lands in which they acquire these complicated rights are scattered over a tract of country 400 square miles in extent, it may well be believed that it is almost impossible even for an intelligent Gundapur to grasp thoroughly the nature and extent of his proprietary rights.'[1]

The Mīāñkhel tribe (with whom the Gundapur were mentioned as having been at war) have two large clan-territories, called Drāban and Mūsāzāi. They would require no particular notice here but for the fact that the tribesmen are not cultivating possessors but landlords living in towns, and leaving the lands to be managed by Jat and other tenants, who form their own villages and groups, having nothing to do with the tribal arrangements of the owners. The Drāban lands are either irrigated (*nālīñ*) or 'dry' (*mankat*). The territory of the former kind is divided into 77 'water-shares,' called *nāla*—*i.e.* watercourse; the latter is divided into 80 shares, called *man*. These shares occur as blocks scattered over the area as a whole; and each clan-section may own several such. Every section will have some irrigated and some dry land, each dependent on its own principle of division. But once more we find certain lands (here called *wanda*) held as '*bocland*' outside the customary share system. The Mūsāzāi lands are somewhat similarly held, except that the irrigated *lands* are not divided; the shares in the *water* here form the basis of right. A certain area, fit to be cultivated, is selected for the year, and the parts of it to be taken up by each section or group of the water-sharers are settled by lot. The sections are called *būlī*, and each contains so many *dharra*, or single shares (water-shares).

The last instance I can give is that of the comparatively civilised tribe of Bābar. They can all read and write.[2] Those living in the plains number about one thousand. 'They are very democratic, and exceedingly jealous of any member of the tribe trying to exercise authority over them.' They are divided into two main sections—*Mahsand* and *Ghorākhel*.

Mahsand forms four sub-sections, and *Ghorākhel* eight. The former hold four *būlī*, or sectional shares, and the latter eight *nīmakka*, or half-shares; some of the land is dependent on rain,

[1] *S. R.* § 279. [2] *Ibid.* § 315.

and some on *kālāpānī*[1] irrigation. But these shares will be subdivided differently, *according as they refer to the land or to the irrigation water.* Thus, as regards land, each *būlī* and each pair of *nīmakka*, being half-shares and treated in pairs, are subdivided into equal lots (*khulā*) for every head in the tribe. But the same shares, treated in terms of *water*, are different; the water-shares of each member, which are not necessarily equal are counted in '*rupees, ana*, and *tāt*.' The *būlī*, &c., regarded as a group of men, is subdivided into *gundi*, a term, I take it, cognate with the *kandi* above mentioned; and the total numbers of lots, for the whole of the *gundi* of the several *būlī* and *nīmakka*, is at present 1,721; the number actually held in each section and sub-section varies. The land of each is not in one place, but scattered about. Some of the groups still hold their shares jointly among their own members, who are relatives. The water-shares are worked in complete independence of the land-shares; the owners select each year the area which can be conveniently watered, just as if the *land* had no known owners or sharers at all; the land-share is, in fact, in abeyance as long as the irrigated cultivation lasts.

The southernmost frontier district of DERA GHĀZI KHĀN partakes more of the nature of the desert country in the South Panjāb, and the physical conditions under which cultivation is possible affect the forms of tenure.[2] In the *Sindh* lands (those near the river), and in the level plain, the tendency is to establish separate 'wells,' or homesteads irrigated by a small cut taken from the river; and the right in land depends on the labour and money expended on making the area culturable. Here also we find that over-lord families ('*alā mālik*') have won established rights over certain *ḥad*, or areas of country, and take a variety of rents and dues from the cultivators and 'inferior proprietors'; with these matters we are not now concerned. In the Pachād country—a tract with light dry soil and low hilly contour, skirting the Sulaimān Range—we have once more the tribal system. Here, too, the cultivation is in embanked

[1] I have explained *kālāpānī* in a note at p. 262, *ante*.
[2] See p. 65, *ante*.

fields watered by occasionally flowing hill streams or torrents.[1] Tradition points to the tribal land having been originally divided out by the chief (*tumāndār*) of the tribe.[2] 'Each member has held his lands ever since in complete independence.' It is interesting to notice the indications of ideas of right in land, as enshrined in certain common local terms. Thus land held on the tribal-shares is called *pat-çīr*; and a share acquired by gift among a number who have combined to provide irrigation for new land is called *dak*. In the country of wells, a plot acquired in virtue of sinking the well is called *sil* = brick—*i.e.* title derived from the structure. So we have the rather ominous tenure of *ghaṣab*, or land obtained by forcible seizure; and there are some others.

Section III.—Clan-Villages and 'Cultivating Fraternities' in Upper India

The tribal-settlements just described are quite unique in their peculiarities. Nothing exactly like them is found elsewhere in India. Nevertheless, we can see that certain features of the tribal organisation—the separate areas of clan sand sections, the desire for equality, and the general tendency to adopt a distribution of shares *per capita*, at least after certain main divisions based on the original ancestral descent are passed—these features reappear in all tribal and clan settlements as far as the *land* is concerned, though with local variations. The distinction also between the close-kindred and the wide, or more extended, kindred, as regards the groups forming villages or forming the clan-population of larger areas, is an equally universal feature of the tribal-stage. We have therefore to include within a general class of 'tribal- or clan-villages' a great many more besides those specialised as the 'frontier clan-villages.' But we shall expect to find the best instances of such villages among the tribes of Upper India, in the plains of the Panjāb, in the North-West Provinces, and in Oudh. As a matter of fact, we are able to gather a number of examples from the

[1] Fryer's *S. R.* p. 77, and see note at p. 262, *ante*, regarding *dagar* cultivation.

[2] Among Bilūchis, *Tumān* is the tribe.

less familiar tribes, Ghakar, Āwān, and the like, in the Panjāb; and again, as connected with non-monarchical Aryan clans, and with Jats and Gujars, both in the Panjāb and beyond it. In the first place we frequently come upon groups of villages (and sometimes large areas which have only recently broken up into villages) distinguished by bearing the designation of *ṭappā*, *'ilāqa*, &c., and we usually find them to be held by groups of families of one clan. But though some of these groups are not more than, say, two to five hundred years old, and others date back as far as that re-distribution of Aryan settlements of which we have spoken,[1] many are still old enough to make it doubtful what was the original method of their formation. On the Panjāb frontier we had no doubt about the settlement representing a clan *already formed as such*. In the cases which we are now to consider, some may doubtless be recognised as coming under the same head. But in the majority of cases it is evident, or at least is probable, that though *now* there is a clan occupying a contiguous area, the origin was in a small family—perhaps no more than one or two brothers with their sons and some followers, who, finding a wide area of land at their disposal, managed to retain possession of the whole, and have now filled it with the multiplied families of their descendants, in such numbers, and retaining such a general connection, as to form a clan.

In these cases it is very likely that the areas covered by the holdings were only called *'ilāqa*, *ṭappā*, &c., at a later period, and possibly for the first time by the Mughal Revenue-officers. I do not think it possible to separate the two cases completely; and an incomplete attempt to separate them would be worse than frankly taking them together as they come, and leaving the reader to see which origin he thinks most probable in each instance. This difficulty is regrettable, because there may very probably be some difference between the manner in which a clan ready made, so to speak—having its branches and kindred already complete—will occupy and allot a conquered territory, and that in which the gradually growing houses and kindreds will spread over it. But in both cases there is one thing that separates such settlements from purely individual foundations, at least in the greater number of instances. They always exhibit some

[1] Page 121, *ante*.

traces of clan union throughout the area, and rarely or never follow the *pattīdārī* principle of sharing: many of them also exhibit a peculiarity in the mode of allotting the land equally, and of valuing the several holdings for the equal distribution of burdens and charges. In these cases we have no evidence of any custom of redistributing or periodically exchanging the holdings; indeed, in the case of a clan gradually growing up on the spot, it would not be likely. We have a small settlement at first, and, as each new family grows up, the additional land requisite for its support is allotted, or perhaps is simply taken up out of the general area without any formal process whatever, and without reference to fractional rights, only to numbers and actual requirements. The whole area gradually becomes covered by the household holdings, within the original main divisions. Naturally, then, the later formed holdings would not be exchanged with the older.

There is, indeed, one other case in which villages may appear to constitute a clan-settlement, when really there is nothing of clan-sentiment in the tenure. It is when a Rājput, or similar rulership, has gone to pieces, and the members of the defeated family and its relatives have managed to cling to a sufficient number of holdings, all pretty close together locally; and so now, having multiplied into village groups, they may suggest a clan origin. Should such an origin be true in any case, however, *where the bhaiāchārā tenure*, in the true sense, *is also observed*, there will certainly be very little harm done if it is included as virtually a clan-settlement. But where in such cases the several villages are composed of families holding on the *ancestral fraction* or *pattīdārī* tenure, then they will most properly be excluded from the present section.

To summarise these remarks briefly: in all the cases included in this section we shall notice (1) not only the contiguity of a number of villages, all of one clan, and covering a considerable area, while in some cases the clan-area is not really divided into villages at all; but (2) we shall find the same desire for equality, so that the customary method of sharing gives to each household whatever land is necessary for its actual numbers; only it takes care that each holding shall contain a similar proportion of the good, bad, and indifferent soils, and that a plan of equal sharing of burdens, in proportion to the holding, shall be followed. It is to groups of this character that the Settlement Officers of the North-West Provinces more especially apply the term 'old cultivating fraternities.' The 'collective' ownership appears here also to consist in a sense of general union arising from the natural bond of kindred, leading to the acceptance of a joint responsibility for the Revenue-charge, in a sense of general clan- or family-right to the whole area, and to any undivided waste within it, and, most of all, in a feeling that every member has an equal right to share and share alike. The whole group of holdings is never, as far as my observation extends, held 'in common,' at any rate after the families have expanded beyond those first grades of descent which have fixed the major and secondary divisions of the whole area.

The actual forms in which the allotment of the land is made are the following:—

(1) The whole area is divided at once into separate single holdings. Major and minor groups of relations may exist, but are not indicated by divisions of the area.

(2) The whole area is divided into large blocks (sons of founder), and these into secondary and tertiary divisions (grandsons and great-grandsons). The later divisions often cannot be compact, by reason of the holdings being made up of plots distributed over the different soil areas. After the last separately designated division, all the later and existing families appear to take *per capita* according to what they want, as long as any land remains available.

(3) The whole area was retained undivided; a central or parent village represents the cultivation of the original family. All round, new hamlets have been added on, which gradually 'ripen' into separate villages till the whole area is taken up.

In Nos. 1 and 2 'villages' gradually separate, but under accidental circumstances, and often under the influence of modern survey and revenue arrangements.

(1) *Illustrations from the Panjāb Districts*

We proceed to pass in review the various districts which give examples of this tenure, commencing with the Panjāb and proceeding eastwards.

The first occurs in the JIHLAM district, along the banks of the river of that name. In one part are tribes of Ghakar, Āwān, and Jhanjūa; the latter are Rājputs, and probably established a sort of territorial rule, and their villages are the usual result of the decadence of that dominion; the further mention of them is therefore reserved to a later section. The Ghakar seem to have despised agriculture, and their settlements show the village residence of the tribesmen, and separate settlements of other cultivating castes, forming hamlets (*dhok*, *çak*, &c.) in the neighbourhood. There are several clans or branches, each with its own name, and the chief seats or mother-villages of each clan are generally called *mandi*. Of these there are now six generally recognised in the district.[1]

In the Chakwāl Tahsīl of this district we have five *'ilāqa* of three tribes of doubtful origin—the Mair, Kasar, and Kahūt. The first named possess two tracts, Haveli and Bādshāhāni, in the centre; the Kasar have two in the north, Bubyāl and Chaupeda, and the remaining one is the Kahūtāni. Their tradition is that their forefathers came from Kashmīr, or rather from Jamū, with the Emperor Bābar, and that they received this, at the time uninhabited, country in grant.

Still more remarkable is the case of the small tribes of Lillā, Phapra, and Jālap, believed to be allied to the Jat stock. They inhabit each 'a well-defined area in the plains below the Salt Range, and none of them is ever found outside its own boundaries.' The territory of Lillā is described in the first Report (1864)[2] as forming one single 'village,' now broken up into four separate parts; and it appears that the whole area of 22,000 acres has been populated by a clan growing out of the household of a single ancestral settler.[3]

[1] *Jihlam S. R.* 1883, p. 28.

[2] Quoted in Tupper, *Cust. Law*, ii. 29.

[3] Unfortunately in neither of the excellent *Jihlam S. R.* is any detail about Lillā to be found. No notice is taken of what the shares in land are, or how they were allotted. More information is also needed about the other great areas mentioned in the text—*e.g.* Lawā is an Āwān settlement, with four or five rival *çaudharī*, or chiefs. It is marked by strong factions among the co-sharing clansmen, who certainly have all of them separate holdings. That this is a '*bona-fide* single *estate* held by one joint and undivided body' is simply incredible. Probably it merely

The Āwān locations are even more in point. This tribe, consisting of peasant proprietors, is always reckoned as such, and not among the *sahu*, or 'gentry.' They occupy the whole of the Tallāgang Tahsīl, being distributed over large clan-areas. Lawā contains 135 square miles; Thohā-Mahram-Khān, 86 square miles; and Kandowāl, in the dry part, or *thal*, of Pind-Dādan-Khān, has 27 square miles. In Lawā there is one chief residence site (*ābādī*) containing 5,000 inhabitants; but there are several 'hamlets' also. This large village-site, as well as the great area maintained as a 'single estate,' is attributed to 'the homogeneous farming population with a large share of democratic equality.' In fact, however, the 'estate' is to some extent the result of physical conditions, for the land is dependent upon the rainfall, and the tables show that in the *whole Tahsīl* only only about 2,600 acres of land are protected by wells. The country is 'upland, of broad, gentle undulations,' with light sandy soil on the crests and loam in the hollows. Under such conditions, the area of each holding is necessarily large, and is naturally uniform in advantages. The land ploughed up for spring crops is kept separate from that used for the *kharīf*, or autumn crop; and the latter also can only be worked part at a time, because the rest is exhausted (*budhī*), and must lie fallow.[1] Each 'ploughland' is, therefore, allowed to consist of *nineteen acres*; and the large combined area of separate individual household shares, each of so many 'ploughs,' is better suited to the sentiment of the people and the conditions of agriculture than a number of separate villages of the average size. The Āwāns must have been for a long time in occupation, since in the days of Abu-l-Fazl, one of the *mahāls*, or official divisions of the Sindh Sāgar Doāb Sirkār, was called the '*Mahāl Āwānān*.'[2] It is certainly a clan-settlement; but the evidence leaves it doubt-

means that the area was not divided into *villages*, and that, though the individual family holdings are enjoyed in severalty, the whole body did not object to be regarded, from the revenue administrative point of view, as a single jointly responsible estate, owing to the general clan feeling which disposes the whole to unite against outsiders, however keen may be the feuds within.

[1] *Jihlam S. R.* Compare pp. 52, 90, and 106.

[2] *Ayīn-i-Akbari*, ii. 323 (Jarrett's Trans.).

ful whether it was occupied by a clan already formed, or whether the present numbers have resulted from gradual growth out of an original small group.

In the next district of GUJRĀT we have a Rājput dominion of a Rājā and chiefs of the Chib clan and a surviving group of village-estates. These do not belong to the present section. But the district at large shows signs of genuine tribal locations; one portion of it being known as the *Jatātar* and another as *Gujar*.[1]

In the course of time there has been some admixture of *Āwān* and other villages, but the general features of the tribally occupied tracts are still discernible.

'The Jats and Gujars are subdivided into a great number of families each called by its own name, which is generally that of some ancestor who became in his time so powerful, or otherwise noted, as to leave his name to his posterity. It would not appear, however, that any new divisions have been separated off from the main stock for the last one hundred or one hundred and twenty years. . . . Most of the clans number but few families, sometimes owning but a single village. But to this there are some notable exceptions among the Jats. The *Varāich*, *Tārar*, and *Gondal*, clans are very strong and hold a superior status.'[2]

In the neighbouring districts there is a still greater admixture of villages; but clan-groups may still be discerned as colonies, of *Bājwā* Jats in Siālkot, of *Āwān* clansmen in others. In Gujrānwālā there is a group of eighty-one villages of the *Çāttā* (Rājput) clan,[3] all in this instance proceeding from the foundation of one original adventurer who had emigrated from his home further East; and there is a large group (106 villages) of the *Bhatti* tribe, around *Pindi-bhattiāñ* as a centre.

Leaving, however, this part of the country, and coming to

[1] In my *L. S. B. I.* ii. 670, there is a map showing the Gujar area coloured *pink* and the Jat *green*; I take it the district name Gujrāt is really 'Gujar-ātar,' like the term Jatātar.

[2] The *Gazetteer* (2nd edition) *of Gujrāt*, p. 60, &c., gives a very good idea of the number of clans and their pretensions to descent from all sorts of grandees.

[3] There is a more detailed account in *L. S. B. I.* ii. 672.

the region between the Biās and Sutlej rivers, we find in the JĀLANDHAR district many Jat tribes divided into *got*, or clans, and *al*, or minor-clans. 'But,' writes the Settlement Officer,[1] 'large tracts of country each occupied by villages of one *got* are not found here, as they are in other parts of the country. The nearest approach to such a state of things is met with in the Philaur Tahsīl, where there is a cluster of *Sihotā* villages about *Kuletā* (*Barāpind*) itself a very large estate belonging almost entirely to this clan.[2] The Rājputs, of whom the *Ghorewāha* clan is the most numerous (nearly 9,000), are found in the tracts nearer the hills; their villages are only partially aggregated. Here we have the tradition of a growth from a very small origin. Two brothers came from Rājputāna on a pilgrimage to a sacred place in the lower hills (*Jawālamukhi*). Meeting with the Pathān king *Shahābu-d-dīn Ghorī*, they presented him with a fine horse, and in return the monarch gave them a grant of as much land 'as each could ride round in a day.' Each brother selected one side of the river Sutlej; one threw his spear (*selā*) where the village of *Selkiāna* now is, and the other his bracelet (*kangan*) at *Kanganwāl*, to mark the limit reached. The family gradually expanded,[3] and the branches and sections were indicated by the terms *çhat*, *makān*, and *muhī*, which I have met with nowhere else.[4] Mr. Purser points out the impossibility of the dates and other details of the tradition; but its general circumstances, and the origin of the landlordship in a royal grant (growing into a set of villages jointly owned by groups of the clan), are very probable. There are other Rājput clans of the same kind. Passing over certain groups of Āwān and Gujar, I will only mention that a tribe of *Arāīñ* (or *Rāīñ*) make up about one-seventh of the agricultural population; they are divided into fifteen *got*. They have many scattered

[1] Purser's *S. R.* 1888, p. 73 ff.

[2] The *Sihotā* Jats are 2,392 in number. Several clans are considerably more numerous, but they are found in scattered villages.

[3] One brother returned to Udaipur, leaving the other in lordship of the whole estate. Mr. Purser suggests that the *çhat*, of which there were nine, marked the shares or lordships of the leading men, and the *makān* were inferior territories.

[4] At least as regards the series of terms. The Chibs in Gujrāt call their clans *mūī*, or *mūhī*.

villages, but in some parts there are also connected groups.[1] Their tradition is that they were once Hindu Rājputs, descendants of Rāi Jaj, ruler of Sirsā, in the South-eastern Panjāb, and that they became Moslems about the close of the twelfth century; the name is said to be derived from the title 'Rāi' borne by their ancestor. Another numerous tribe, the *Sainī* (14,000), also trace their origin to a few ancestors who came from their home in Mathurā (North-West Provinces) in defence of the Hindus against the first Moslem invasions, and they multiplied in their new home. As regards the district generally, Mr. Purser remarks that the existing village bodies are not able to trace their descent very far; only 355 villages out of 1,324 are remembered to have been founded for twelve or more generations.[2]

Crossing the Sutlej river, it will be sufficient to take three typical districts—Lūdiāna, Rohtak, and Karnāl. Excellent reports of each exist, and the writers have gone fully into the tribal question.

In the LŪDIĀNA *S. Report*, after some interesting remarks on the alteration of the Jat type caused by difference of mode of life, occupation, and location, Mr. Gordon Walker[3] writes: 'To the east of the district, and especially in the Samrāla Tahsīl, the multitude of *got* (*gentes*) among the Hindu Jats is a very remarkable feature. Not only do adjoining villages belong to different *got*, but inside each village will generally be found two or three sections (*patti*) of distinct origin.' This is accounted for by the manner in which the country was colonised. In the history of each village it will be seen that the founders came in comparatively recent times from different parts of the country and belonged to different *got*; they united merely for convenience, the vague tie of belonging to the same general tribe being sufficient. In the south and west of the district, on the other hand, we do find that the Jats in some instances settled in larger homogeneous bodies. The reason for this apparently is that in the eastern parts the imperial authority was always strong enough to protect its subjects, who settled down in small village groups as they came; while in the west it was less felt,

[1] *S. R.* p. 82. [2] *Ibid.* p. 85.
[3] *S. R. Lūdiāna*, 1884, pp. 45 ff, 79 *seq.*

and people of one tribe had to collect in large contiguous villages for protection. For example, the *Gharewāl* Jats had a group of fifty villages near the town of Lūdiāna.[1] The *Gil* Jats have a group of forty villages in the Jagrāoñ Tahsīl. They commenced as a small body, some 200 or 300 years ago, coming on an uninhabited space (the *Jangal 'ilāqa*). Among the smaller clans, the *Bhandher* own ten or eleven villages in the *Malaudh 'ilāqa*, all grown out of the descendants of one settler, who left his home because he was regarded with disfavour by the family, owing to his being the offspring of a mixed marriage. There are some *old* Rājput villages; and they mostly keep up at least the form of the 'ancestral' shares as descendants of one founder.[2] The Jat and the other villages spoken of all show the sense of *clan* organisation; there is aggregation for social comfort and for defence; but there is no pretension to descent from some common ancestor or the maintenance of ancestral shares. The object is for all the families to have their equal share; and the land is divided out in *hal*, or 'plough-lands,' a number being assigned to each family in proportion to its strength. The size of the *hal* varies with the character of the soil, being, as usual, the area estimated to be ploughed by one pair of oxen.[3] Nor are the holdings in one block, but (as usual in the genuine *bhaiāchārā* or clan-fraternity method) 'the original distribution is generally most elaborate, the whole area having been divided into blocks according to quality, and each sharer getting his portion in each block—*i.e.* the number of *hal* for each family consisted of specimens of each kind of soil, good, bad, and middling. These shares are observed in the division of any culturable waste, and in apportioning the *malba*, or joint expenses, of the village community.[4] They are not now made

[1] This *got* affords an instance of what has been stated about Jats (p. 99, *ante*); their tradition is that the founder was a Rājput prince—Rājā Rikh, who lost caste by marrying a Jat woman. But from this 'royal' descent the *got* is still regarded as superior among the *sahu*, or gentry. The *Gil* are similarly descended.

[2] This will usually be found to be the case where the founder had some pretensions to territorial rank or nobility.

[3] *S. R.* p. 80.

[4] See p. 25. The fund to meet these common expenses is made up of certain rents and profits from the waste area, from *atrāfī*,—a sort of house-

use of in paying the land-revenue, which is met by an appropriate acreage rate on the area actually possessed by each.

The ROHTAK district deserves mention, as it is in this part of the country that successive Settlement Officers, from Mr. (afterwards Lord) Lawrence in 1844 to Mr. Fanshawe in 1879, have noticed the perfect preservation of the 'village communities'—*i.e.* in the co-sharing or joint form. There are 511 'estates' in this small district, and they are also compact geographical *mauza*. They owe their compactness to the fact that they are the result of the gradual fission of groups of close-kindreds as, one by one, they branched off from an original centre. Each starts a fresh hamlet, which ripens into a village, and is really held by a compact body of kinsmen. We have, in fact, the converse of what the frontier tribal-territories exhibit. *Here* we have the case of a clan expanding on the spot from a small centre, and so building up groups of close-kindred, whose holdings are defined one by one as they are taken up and naturally form villages; *there* we have the clan already existing and dividing the land among the whole body, village groups being little thought of. Out of the 511 villages, Jats, forming 12 chief and 137 minor clans, own 366. Some Afghān settlers, Brahman grantees, and others, hold villages; and the Ahīr have 26 villages.[1] 'The most noticeable point,' says Mr. Fanshawe,[2] 'is the grouping of the villages of each tribe or subdivision of a tribe in one spot. This is due in most cases to the surrounding villages having been separated off and founded from a central mother-village. . . .' Hindu Rājputs are found in the south-east of the Jhajjar Tahsīl and the centre of the Rohtak Tahsīl; the Ahīr are round Kosli, and so on. The Jats show the same features; the *Malik got* is settled round Ahalāna, Khānpur-Kalān, and Bhaiñswāl-kalān, and so on. Village groups so constituted must have taken time to grow up, and we are not surprised to learn that they are of older foundation than usual. Jat

tax on non-proprietors, artisans, &c., and *dharat*, a fee on weighing grain sold in the village, and from anything else that comes in from a common source of profit.

[1] See p. 109, *note*. The Ahīr figure considerably across the Jamnā, in the North-West Provinces.

[2] *S. R.* part ii. p. 18, § 17.

villages were established before Sultān Mahmūd's invasion early in the eleventh century. Here also the Jats profess Rājput origin, and to have come from the south.[1] The Report gives in detail the history of several such village centres. The *Dahyā* Jat, for example, have their villages along the north-eastern border of the Sāmpla Tahsīl. Their ancestor is Mānik Rāi, a Rājput *Çauhān* clan who lost caste by marrying a *Dhankar* Jat woman. His son was Dahlā, corrupted into the clan name *Dahyā*; Dahlā settled in Barona twenty-seven generations ago, and from his one original village all the others have branched off. I might repeat the same sort of story almost indefinitely for each of the other centres. The process of growth is that, as the family increases, the new households clear additional land out of the general area, and the hamlets are at first considered only parts of the mother-village, till at last they grow big enough to have entirely separate establishments; and thus a whole *ṭappā* of villages is acknowledged.[2] As to the original constitution of the entire area, it does not seem to have been divided into any primary sections according to the divisions of the original

[1] It is, in fact, in this district that the tradition occurs which has misled some writers. The Malik Jats say they are Rājputs, and come, not from Ghaznī, in Western Afghānistān (which is sometimes quoted as a proof of the western origin), but from 'Garh-Gajni,' somewhere on the Dakhān frontier. I may suggest merely that, as the proper name of these Jats is 'Ghātwāl,' they may have derived the clan name from being originally Rājputs holding some frontier hilly territory (*ghāt*) in the region of the Mahi or Arāvālī hills, or some neighbouring locality in the Vindhyan country.

[2] Mr. Fanshawe quotes some remarks of the late Sir G. Campbell in the *Cobden Club Essays*, where the author repeats the formula, at that time unquestioned, about the tribe or the village body holding the land 'in common' first of all. Mr. Fanshawe remarks that Rohtak exemplifies this. I venture to think that it directly contradicts anything of the kind. In cases like the Rohtak villages where we have a clan-expansion, the original founder is able to maintain a general hold over a large area, the greater part of which he does not cultivate till it is wanted; his claim is only manifested by the fact that if he has many cattle, he grazes them over it. Then, as each family grows up, there is land available which it takes up, perhaps by tacit consent; this goes on till the whole area is filled up. There is no kind of 'common holding' whatever, but only a sense of unity of origin, and the solidarity of clan interests which bind the various daughter-villages together.

family; and there could, of course, have been no anticipatory division of the area into 'villages.' When each village-group has in time developed, it will have sections within itself resulting from the fact that what was at first a 'close-kindred' has now expanded into a 'wider-kindred' composed of several close-kindreds all derived from the same head; and thus are formed *pānā* and *ṭhūlā* subdivisions, as they are here called. The individual holdings are *hal* or 'plough-lands'; and here, as so often observed, while the first or earlier degrees of descent from the founder naturally allowed the then few and simple share-portions to follow the ancestral gradation, as the numbers grew, the subsequent allotment within the main sections, was *per capita*—everyone was provided for, alike, according to his requirements. For this reason, as some families increased, and others diminished in number, the holdings of land were occasionally readjusted.[1] As usual, at the Revenue Settlement the individual shares were treated as so many *de facto* holdings, and were assessed at the proper acreage rate; but inside the villages, the primary divisions of *pānā* and *ṭhūlā* were demarcated as blocks, and the eldest member of the eldest house in each *pānā* was recognised as its official headman. The *pançayat* consists of the heads of *pānā* with the *thūlādārs*, or heads of the eldest households in the subdivisions. The *pançayat* still controls all matters of interest to the body—the cultivation of undivided common lands, the realisation of grazing-fees and house-rates,[2] the building of a village rest-house for guests, supervising the village watch, cleansing the common tank or pond, and settling any question of granting a rent-free plot to some pious person. I have not found any allusion in the Rohtak

[1] See *S. R.* p. 27. 'The local annals tell of half a dozen changes made at intervals in the shares on which each estate was held.' Mr. Fanshawe thinks this may point to the existence of a general redistribution; but this is not likely, for such a *general* periodic exchange is natural only where a clan already formed settles on land and each member is jealous of anyone getting a better lot than himself. There is no *raison d'être* for such a plan in the case of holdings added on, family by family, so to speak, to an original central village.

[2] The house-rates or hearth-fees (here called *kūdī-kamīnī*) are paid as usual by non-proprietors, artisans, &c., as an acknowledgment to the proprietors for their permission to reside.

Report to the feature, common in 'fraternities,' of making the holdings consist of specimen bits of each kind of soil. Here, perhaps, the land is too uniform to need such a device.

In the KARNĀL district, bordering on the Jamnā river, we frequently observe the same feature of a family expanding into a clan: the group of clan-villages begins, first, with the establishment of a central village (*thīkā*), and then by the gradual accretion of hamlets (*majrā*, or *garhī*, as they are hero called), which in time become independent. But Mr. Ibbetson has noted a number of interesting details. We are near the country where the earliest Aryans began to settle (in *Aryavarta*); and we find many Rājput owners; but the causes already mentioned prevent our tracing back the existing groups to any such primitive settlement. There is also a local curious caste or tribe of *Tagā* which I must pass over. The areas occupied by the clans are called *ṭappā*, or *thambā*, and the Imperial revenue officers made use of these divisions for official purposes.[1] The villages are all held by groups of real blood relations, being the areas added one by one, as each new little group of households grew up and started additional cultivation on an adjoining site. The village names often bear the addition *khurd*, or *kalān*, not meaning 'small' or 'great,' as the Persian words imply, but 'younger' and 'elder.' The clan connection between the villages in the *ṭappā* is kept up by the custom that 'when a headman dies all the villages in the *ṭappā* assemble to instal his heir, and the turban of the parent village is first tied on his head.' On ceremonial occasions—funerals, &c. (*meljor*)—the Brahmans of the parent village are fed first and receive double fees.[2] Though the *mājra*, or offshoot villages, are generally groups of the same descent, it should be added that sometimes relations of the wife's family (and therefore of another clan) are admitted to a share, and may

[1] *S. R.* § 185; the '*Āmils*, or Land Revenue Officers, made use of the heads of kindreds and families, whom they called *Çaudharī*, for collecting the revenue.

[2] § 181. Mr. Ibbetson mentions the case of a village which desired to change its *ṭappā*—*i.e.* not to belong to the group which was its natural sphere—because there were so many Brahmans in it whom the village had to feed! Of course it was held that a village might ignore or forget its origin, but could not change it.

possibly form one of the separate *mājra*; but the fiction of a common descent is maintained, and the person taking a share of another's land is said to be *bhūīṅ bhāi* (land-brother). The fact is, that the theory of family property is kept up because the whole is really (in spite of occasional gifts and admissions) one large family in its various groups of kindred; and, being all settled together, circumstances combine to maintain the memory of the fact. The interior divisions of the villages are here called *pannā* (the word meaning 'lot'—*pannā mārnā*=to cast lots). The subdivisions are *ṭhūlā*; and the features of these divisions and of the *pançayat*, are just like those described in Rohtak.[1] As usual, the first main divisions of the villages follow the ancestral grades—when the descent was in its first stages. Thus the *pannā* will probably mark the 'lots' of the original sons of the leader of the newly founded extension, and the *ṭhūlā*, the original grandsons; after that, as the numbers increase within the groups all are provided for *per capita*. We have here also the careful attention to soil varieties that marks the real *bhaiāchārā* tenure. 'The land,' writes Mr. Ibbetson, 'was carefully divided according to quality, so that each should have his fair share;' and 'the same rule was observed when a new cultivator was admitted to cultivate. The long dividing lines at right angles to the contours of the country which mark off the valuable rice land into minute plots,[2] and the inferior sandy soil into long

[1] Under the empire the heads of *pannā* and *ṭhūlā* acquired considerable authority, because the *'Āmil* worked through them entirely; the whole village was assessed at one sum, and these heads had to apportion the burden (*S. R.* § 233). It is worth while noticing that here the heads exempted themselves from duties of village watch and ward (*ṭhīk-kar*); and each has a menial (*çamār*) as a personal attendant, the *çamār* getting a free midday meal in return, but nothing else. The village *çamārs*, as a body, are made to give a day's free labour in each headman's field, but are fed in return.

[2] Special modes of division of valuable, but at the same time somewhat precarious, land on the banks of rivers and streams are sometimes observed; the plan being usually to divide into long and very narrow strips running at right angles to the stream: and these are usually reallotted every year. By this means everyone gets an equal share of the danger of diluvion and the advantage of the successive degrees of moisture further from the river. Two instances, with a diagram, will be found in *L. S. B. I.* ii. 142, 640. Captain Dunlop-Smith has recently called my

narrow strips including a portion of each degree of quality, and the scattered nature of each man's holding, still show how carefully this was done.'[1]

(2) *Illustrations from the North-West Provinces*

When we cross the river Jamnā from the Panjāb into the North-West Provinces we still find some of the districts supplying instances of 'clan-settlements.' In some cases, there are aggregates of estates mostly of one clan which are merely the remnants of long-destroyed chiefships or petty kingdoms exhibiting no clan union; but what our official reports call 'old cultivating fraternities' are real clan-groups of the kind we are considering at present: they have the true *bhaiāchārā* form of allotting the land. Sometimes they are Jat settlements; sometimes they are Rājputs of clans which took to cultivating or at least to land-owning, and had no Rājā and no pretensions to territorial rule. The North-West Provinces districts are much more thickly populated than the Panjāb, and they have been subject to such vicissitudes of war and changes of rule that it would not be surprising if such 'fraternities' had become broken up and intermixed, beyond recognition, with other cultivating village-communities. The usurpation or conquest of individual chiefs, the success of the revenue farmer and the auction purchaser, too, have altered the 'proprietary community' of so many villages that we rather wonder to find any examples of the clan *'ilāqa* and the *ṭappā*. Yet we do find them in parts; mostly, I believe, as examples of the expansion of a small group into a clan. The most typical instances occur in the MATHURA (Muttra) district, bordering on the South-eastern Panjāb and the Rājputāna

attention to the same custom in the Siālkot district north-east of Tahsīl Rāyā, where it is called *rassī būṭī*, or *bauṭī*—*i.e.* division by *ropes* (these being used in marking out the long strips), varying from 25 to 800 *kadam* (= 5½ feet) long and 1 to 10 *kadam* broad [*bauṭā* (H.), or in the feminine diminutive form *bauṭī*, means a slice, a piece]. This custom obtains among the Jat villages where they have a desire for good management and equal rights; while in other similar estates where it is not followed the owners are Rājpūts, 'whose local customs have always been in favour of the more powerful members of the different tribes.' (*S. R., Siālkot*, 1895, § 133.)

[1] *Karnal S. R.* § 240, p. 96.

States. In the famous cities of Mathurā and Bindraban we have the centres of the Krishnā cult; and although Jat settlers occupied much land, we are not surprised to find that throughout the district Brahman grantees figure largely among the proprietary communities holding village estates.[1]

The district is naturally divided, by the river, into a Cis-Jamnā and a Trans-Jamnā portion. In the former, the villages are of a distinct type. Though often large, they are essentially unit estates, the result of grant, purchase, or other acquisition by a single owner whose descendants are now the co-sharing proprietary bodies, and they are held on ancestral shares. In the Trans-Jamnā, on the other hand, we meet with 'villages' of the kind under our present consideration. As a matter of fact, in these clan-areas, the 'villages' are quite an afterthought, and are indeed the result of modern conditions or of accidental circumstances.

The *ṭappā* Rāyā and *ṭappā* Airā-Khera[2] offer as characteristic examples as could be desired. The Jat shareholders of the *Paçahrā* clan are all (really or by association) the descendants of *one family who originated the estate on its existing area.*[3] 'As the descendants increased and the cultivation round the old site grew, so new colonies of shareholders planted themselves in hamlets near their fields, separating off their cultivation, but still retaining their share in the ancestral *kheṛā*.' Airā-Kherā is a *ṭappā* covering nearly 18,000 acres, and it is now divided into 22 villages. Rāyā has 12,000 acres, now divided into 24 villages.

[1] Whiteway's *S. R.* 1879, p. 25 ff. This Report is specially deserving of the notice of students of village-forms, as is also the *Azimgarh S. R.* by Mr. J. R. Reid. Mr. Whiteway notices also that Brahmans constantly accompanied the bodies of Jat settlers as their priests, and that they got a share, or perhaps a whole village, given them (*S. R.* p. 31).

[2] We shall often meet with this term *kheṛā*; it means the parent village or original location when the clan was yet a family.

[3] And the same is true of the settlements of Nohwār and Narwār Jats (*S. R.* p. 33). The origin was with two brothers—A, settled in Noh; B in Narwār. A gave his Noh village to Brahmans, and founded two more for his own family. B founded Barauth in Narwār; and now there is a group of offshoots all round, belonging to the descendants. There are various groups of Jats, some of only three or four villages; but one, in Taluqa Soṅk, contains as many as twenty-one villages.

Airā-Kherā was started by one man with four sons about 200 years ago. In the lifetime of the ancestor the area was divided into four large compact blocks locally called *tarf*, one for each son; a fifth area was added for the Kasba of Sonāi, some kind of dependency, the exact history of which I do not know. The cultivation went on within each of the four *tarf* according to an understood division of the soil, so that each holding was made up of a number of strips and fields, some in each variety of soil. Gradually each *tarf* was subdivided into a number—four or five in all—of secondary groups, each having its own cluster of residences and called *thok*.[1] These have become the 'villages' of the official records; but the lands of the *thok* being taken, part in each different soil-area, are scattered over the whole *tarf*. Then again the 'village' groups (or *thok*) are internally subdivided into *naglā*. 'Within each *tarf*,' says the Report, 'the land of each of the four or five villages contained in it are intermingled in a singular fashion, and the *naglā* in these villages in a similar manner. The essential principle being that each *çak* [standard measure of holding] should contain the same relative quantity of good, bad, and indifferent soil, the properties are of necessity constantly intermingled. In some *tarfs* almost every alternate field belongs to a different one of the four or five *thok* contained in it.' In other *tarfs* long strips of land for the cultivating possession of the different *thok* were formed, and these areas were again subdivided, on the same principle, among the different *naglā*. 'And yet,' concludes Mr. Whiteway, 'with all this apparent intricacy I have hardly met with a disputed field, and not one case which was not easily and readily disposed of by the *pançayat*, which, like other *bhaiāchārā* institutions, exists here in great perfection.'[2]

As the *tarf* were compact blocks arranged to suit the wants and prospects of each main branch at the time when the numbers were few, it was not likely that each would contain exactly the same proportion of each class of soil, or that each

[1] It will be observed that not only do names of divisions vary locally, but sometimes in different places the same words imply a different grade of division—*e.g.* *thok*, which often means a smaller division of a *patti*, here means the first division within the *tarf*.

[2] *S. R.* pp. 39, 40.

would be equal in area; but it was possible to have a standard area of a certain value, so that each division might be valued to bear an equal proportion of revenue and other burdens or charges. And for this standard valuation they adopted a *çak*, which contained about 300 of the *kaççā* or locally used *bīghā*, or area measures of the different soils,[1] each such artificial lot as nearly equal in character and value as possible. The proportion of each *tarf* was as follows:—

	B.	b.	b.
1. *Tarf* Inchrāj	47	0	19
2. „ Rupāl	94	13	16
3. „ Bhareră	59	13	18
4. „ Sikam	72	15	6
5. *Kasba* Sonāi	39	7	19
Total . . .	313	11	18[2]

The main divisions, as usual, followed the natural ancestral grades as far as the four sons (*tarf*) and the *thok*, presumably shares of sons' sons, *i.e.* grandsons of the ancestor, and the *naglā* (great-grandsons); because at the time, the members being thus limited, it was quite natural to follow the divisions of the first or original close-kindred. But afterwards, as numbers increased, the holdings were allotted *per capita* according to the actual requirements of each household as it grew up;[3] but each could

[1] The normal *bīghā* is said to be *pakkā* = ripe or perfect; the local measure (usually smaller) is said to be *kaççā* = crude or imperfect. The *bīghā* is divided into twenty *biswa*, and that into twenty *biswāṅsī* (B. b. b. above).

[2] If we express the matter in fractions, it would come to this—that Inchrāj represents about one and a half tenths, Rupāl three tenths, Bhareră two tenths, Sikam two and a half tenths, and Sonāi one tenth. I do not know what the actual *kaççā* or local *bīghā* is; but suppose the entire area (arbitrarily) to be 45,000 *kaççā bīghā*, and the (imaginary) assessment to be Rs. 15,000; each *Çak* of 300 *kaççā bīghā* would represent Rs. 100 of revenue charge, and of this Sonāi would be responsible for about Rs. 10, Rupāl about Rs. 30, and so on; or, in total, Sonāi would pay Rs. 1,500, Rupāl Rs. 4,500, and so on.

[3] One of the reasons which in a clan-group of this sort tended to keep attention so much to the whole clan and so little to the actual family right, was the practice (*S. R.* pp. 32, 33) not only of *karāo*, or widow marriage, but also of allowing the children of any woman taken into the house (*dharaiçā*) to have an inheritance. This was extended in some cases to the children of a widow by a former husband (*lainrārā*).

bear its proportionate share of the burdens. 'On the same principle,' says Mr. Whiteway, 'a similar partition subsequently took place between—*i.e.* within—each *tarf* or quarter. The *pançayat* of each *tarf* adopted a *çak* of whatever number of actual *kaççā bīghās* was best adapted to their circumstances, always taking care that the relative value of each *çak* was the same, and subdivided the whole *tarf* into the four or five villages (or *thok*) in each, which again subdivided themselves as population increased into *naglā* or *patti*, on exactly the same principle.'[1]

We cannot expect to find such clan-settlements equally well represented in all the various districts; the Rohilkhand country, for example, suffered too much from the Rohilla rule to have preserved such traces; but we find them here and there.

Some of the best examples occur towards the eastern end of the province. Thus, in ALLĀHĀBAD, although most of the villages originated with single owners, there are one or two large clan-areas, *e.g.* in *pargana* Atharban, the *Bisen*, of whom we shall hear again, had a large community; and there are some Muhammadan clans in Karāri and Chāil.[2]

In the Bundelkhand districts there are several good instances of clan-settlements. In the HAMĪRPUR district there is a great tract called Kherailā-k͟hās, covering 28½ square miles, nearly all culturable and divided up into major group-areas and family lots. Here we have the *thok* also, which usually became the administrative village, and it is subdivided into *patti*.[3] Here also was the custom of the valuation by *çak*, or standard lots. Similar 'villages' are the Patāra area of 9,394 acres divided into twelve *behrī*, here the major-division or 'village'; and so in *pargana* Jalālpur-Kherailā is a group of eleven 'villages' with an *average* area of 8,294 acres, and one of thirty-four with an average of 5,111 acres. These were originally *behrī* of still larger clan-areas. In the BĀNDĀ district, where the *bhejbarār*, or custom of periodically adjusting the burdens to the actual relative value of the holdings, was once prevalent,[4]

[1] See Appendix to this section.

[2] *S. R.* Porter, 1878, § 22 ff.

[3] *North-West Provinces Gazetteer*, i. 179.

[4] The *bhejbarār* custom—which is not directly a question of tenure,

I find mention of a great clan area, at Khaptihā-Kalān (Pailānī *pargana*), of fifteen square miles held by some 3,700 co-sharers who still occupy one large central residence. And there are other instances of areas in which the more usual plan is observed of a parent-village with offshoot hamlets, which ultimately become separate villages, although their lands might be at first much scattered about.[1]

In the extreme East, the BALLIĀ district shows examples where 'each clan has its well-defined location . . . which the forefathers conquered from the aborigines or reclaimed from the waste.' The *Seṅghar* (Rājput) clan owned nearly the whole of the Lakhneswar *pargana*, and held it as a 'single estate' down to the time of the Permanent Settlement.[2] There are now 134 villages, but some groups hold lands scattered through every one of this number.

Of the GHĀZIPUR district I have already said something when describing the population. Mr. Oldham remarks that in Akbar's time the nineteen *mahāl*, or *parganas*, were all clan-estates of Brahmans, Rājputs, &c.[3] They were not all compact estates, for the country was jungle, and it appears that the clan-groups selected the most easily cleared portions first, and gradually, as their numbers expanded, the whole *pargana* would be filled up, and one 'estate' become conterminous with the next. But very often it would happen that before one clan had covered a large and continuous area, another clan would occupy a portion of the same area; in that case the different areas formed separate *ṭappā*, and a *pargana* might contain several such. The founders of these clan-settlements frequently came as adventurers in small numbers. Thus Mr. Oldham gives a tradition, for which there is some confirmatory evidence, that certain three *Çandel* brothers came as servants to a Bhaṛ Rājā,

though connected chiefly with the 'democratic' equal-holding or *bhaiāchārā* method—is described in *L. S. B. I.* ii. 143.

[1] See *S. R. Bāndā*, 1881, p. 30. Mr. Cadell has explained how the tenures of this district were upset by early maladministration.

[2] See Wilton Oldham, *Memoir of Ghāzipur District*, p. 52.

[3] See the list in Ayīn-i-Akbari (Jarrett), ii. 90, 162. Lakhnesar at that time had but 2,883 *bīghās* cultivated.

and that they conspired and slew him and founded an estate of their own.[1] In some of these cases there may have been the assumption of some kind of rulership, but not always, for Mr. Oldham expressly mentions that in many instances the 'land-holding fraternities' had no Rājā or territorial chief; and he speaks of *talūqas* containing 'scores of villages, and some of them paying 25,000 rupees of annual revenue, held by hundreds, and in some cases thousands, of co-sharers.'[2]

In the JAUNPUR district, clans have grown up often from small beginnings.[3] The Rājputs shew *Rāghubansi* (15,000), *Drigbansi* and *Bais* (of each 13,000) and *Çāndel* (7,000). The *Rāghubansi* was something like a territorial chiefship, as the report speaks of their holding a *beālisī* or territory of forty-two villages; but they began with a village at Tilochan-Mahādeo, 'and spread over the *pargana* from that place.' But as the clan recognised no primogeniture, the division of the territory went on as fast as the clan grew. The *Bais* colony came from Oudh and had been established for 700 years.

(3) *Illustrations from Oudh*

Among the twelve districts which form this province are to be found various instances of clan-areas with their groups of villages; and it is of no consequence, as far as this phenomenon is concerned, whether the villages have or have not since fallen under the power of a Taluqdār landlord. As might be expected, the clans are mostly Rājput, and some few are Muhammadans who came with the Mughal or earlier invasions.

Evidently, the earliest clan-settlements of all must have been of Bhaṛ, Ahīr, or other non-Aryans; but of such a state of things we have now no definite trace. Even the earlier Aryan kingdoms have all passed away; and such Rājput settlements as now appear are only in a few cases so old as even probably to

[1] *Memoir*, p. 48. The case is very curious, as 600 years after the alleged murder, a descendant of the Bhaṛ Rājā came forward to claim back part of the land which he understood was likely to be confiscated after the mutiny, owing to the proprietors (*Çāndels*) having harboured rebels.

[2] *Memoir*, p. 41.

[3] *North-West Provinces Gazetteer*, iv. 35.

go back to any very early location. We are here concerned with those villages which the writer of the *Gazetteer* calls 'democratic, where the superior clansmen, though they may have established themselves as lords of the soil, had no monarchical organisation, and did not establish anything resembling a kingdom. But it will be understood that in Oudh we have examples both of clans connected with monarchical States, and of 'democratic clans': and when the rulership of the former has long been broken up, and the descendants have settled as peasant proprietors in villages (either independent, or under Taluqdār landlords), it is not always possible to discriminate exactly as regards the origin. It appears, however, that the distribution of the non-monarchical clans with which we are directly concerned is, to some extent, traceable geographically. Thus I find the districts of Hardoi, Sītāpur, and Unāo, grouped together [1] as districts where some of the earliest settlements are found, and without any Rājās of their own. In Eastern Oudh, on the other hand, where war had to be waged against the Bhaṛ chiefs, as well as afterwards with the Moslem forces of the neighbouring kingdom of Jaunpur, the Rājput clans seem more readily to have adopted the monarchical system, as better capable of organising attack and defence.[2]

The first extensive clan-colony that claims attention was that of the *Raīkwār* Rājputs,[3] which once extended for sixty miles along both banks of the Ghāgrā river, in the districts of Bārabānkī, Sītāpur, Bahraich, and Kherī.[4] Some traces of this still remain. In the SULTĀNPUR district is a considerable *pargana* called Aldemau.[5] 'As far back as can be traced' it was divided into ten *ṭappā*. Eight different clansmen are traditionally said to have acquired a footing, under the Bhaṛ chiefs, in these territories; in one place, a long-established group of *Kurmi* cultivators was found by the adventurers. The *Gazetteer* traces

[1] And I may add the Partābgarh and Lucknow districts. See *Oudh Gazetteer*, iii. 532.

[2] *Ibid.* ii. 222.

[3] These are said to derive their name from a place in the Kashmīr Valley from which they are traditionally said to have emigrated.

[4] *Gazetteer*, i. 257.

[5] *Ibid.* i. 24. It was formerly included in Faizābād. The name of the place is derived from a Bhaṛ chief called Alde.

the history of the clans which grew up and filled these *ṭappās*. One, Sakarwār, I will mention, because of a feature frequently observed. One of the grandsons of the 'founder' became a convert to Islam, and two sections resulted, one for the Hindu sons born to him before conversion, the other for those of the Moslem wife. These were distinguished as *ṭarf*; one contains sixteen, the other nine villages. Another group seems to have been later occupied by some of the *Rājkumār* clan, claiming descent from Rājā Prithwī (A.D. 1193) of Delhi. One of the descendants (Barīyār Singh) had four sons, and these formed the heads of as many minor clans who established themselves in various places. One came to this *pargana* and ousted or absorbed a number of smaller family locations, 'partly by purchase, partly by force.'[1]

In the GONDĀ district (already alluded to as affording an instance of a Rājā unconnected with any clan monarchy) there is a good example of the clan settlement, the *Gorāha-Bisēn*, 'which alone exemplified the pure democratic form, each member of the family (*gens*) being equal in position, and receiving an equal portion in the inheritance of the clan.'[2] This is one of the older clans 'who have no recollection of a departure from some distant home in the West,' and 'they are unable to connect their countless houses by any intelligible pedigree.' They established a number of villages belonging to the different closer kindreds, and they obtained the full right over the area by grant of the local Rājā.[3]

In the neighbourhood, viz. in Kheri and Rāi-Bareli, we have instances of the spread of descendants of a local Rājā, and therefore these districts do not afford illustrations under the present head. But in the HARDOĪ district we have another case in point. To this day, the district is remarkable for its small independent proprietors and the absence of Rājās or chiefs.[4] 'It almost seems,' says the writer of the *Gazetteer* account, 'as if,

[1] *Oudh Gazetteer*, i. 30.

[2] *Ibid.* i. 510, and see *Gondā S. R.* § 33, p. 15 and § 88, p. 51.

[3] See p. 300, *post*.

[4] *Gazetteer*, ii. 40 ff. The remarks made on the causes of the absence of Rājās and of the aristocratic spirit in this district are interesting.

owing to the climate, a bolder, and more independent spirit animated the inhabitants of Unāo, Hardoī, Lucknow, and Southern Kheri, than in Eastern and Northern Oudh.' There were a number of separate clans settled, and owing to this and other causes powerful Rājās did not obtain dominions. 'But,' proceeds the writer, 'though these things account for large principalities never having flourished in Hardoī (South-western Oudh), they do not account for large clans like the *Nikambh*, *Çamārgaur*, *Sakarwār*, and *Puṅwār*, never having elected a Rājā. They show that even when a clan had mastered a compact estate the Rājā was regarded as an ornamental appendage, which might or might not be added.' It appears, indeed, that none of these clans have any tradition of their having come in force under any leader; and the writer adds: 'What took place was as follows: a single individual, or three brothers at most, settle in the country and prosper; they commence in all cases by dividing the property equally among all the sons, shewing that the idea of a *Rāj*, one and indivisible, had not entered their minds; they succeed by some process of natural selection or freak of fortune, other families give place to them, they multiply, and continue subdividing their property. If it happens that any call is made on the military prowess of the family (now become a clan), if they have constantly to fight for their property, it is not unlikely that their natural leader, the head of the elder branch, may be either nominated a *Rājā* by his clan, or be granted the title by superior authority.' The whole passage is interesting, but is too long to quote. It illustrates well how the monarchical organisation grows out of circumstances. But it will not be supposed that among the clans which have not adopted it there is no sense of the old patriarchal authority. 'There are clans in Hardoī who have their untitled chiefs, to whom in all times of turmoil their obedience is absolute.'

On the whole, both in Oudh, and the North-West Provinces, the instances of clan '*ilāqa* (or *taluqa*) and *ṭappā*, which have been formed by *the expansion of families from small beginnings*, are the most frequent; although we have a certain number of cases in which a clan has settled, *when already formed*. In the former case, it will be recollected that if the families have pretensions to nobility, it is quite likely that they will adopt a system of *ancestral shares,* as do the individual village estates when originating in one more or less 'aristocratic' founder. In the typical clan-settlements (whether of existing clans, or by subsequent expansion), the equal sharing (*bhaiāchārā*) method is the more characteristic.

APPENDIX

In connection with the *bhaiāchārā* method of dividing land, I cannot forbear alluding to a curious custom which is noted in the *Basti S. R.* (1891), §§ 93, 94 ; and Mr. Hooper informs me that it is found also in the Pīlībhīt district and perhaps elsewhere (near the *tarāi* country at the foot of the hills). It illustrates how this sort of division is applied in practice, and also how a *voluntary association* may have the appearance of a clan-group. I allude to the *halbandī* custom, where the whole village is let out by the small non-agricultural proprietary body to tenants who form among themselves a united subordinate village body, and I suppose have a *pançayat* to make the allotments. But the tenants are numerous, and even more ignorant and jealous of one another than the proprietors. They all cultivate separately and take separate receipts, and are often of different *status*, some being occupancy tenants, others tenants-at-will. In the old report of thirty years ago, Mr. Hooper tells me, these were considered as *partnerships* cultivating in common ; but if the scheme described was then also in force, I do not see where the feature of 'common holding' can come in, unless it is meant only to imply that the body have adopted this method of securing equal returns. Except that any man may have an extra plot (*ukhrā*) or cultivate some of the proprietor's home farm as *ukhrā*—*i.e.* outside the tenant partnership—the entire lands are treated as forming so many 'ploughs' (of from six to eight acres each). Thus, if the total rental is Rs. 800 and the ploughs are counted as 32, each plough will be answerable for Rs. 25. A man holds one plough or more or less, according to the cattle he possesses. But then the areas actually held must be made as equal in value as possible. For this purpose four ploughs will be grouped into a *thok* ; and with 32 ploughs there will be eight *thok* ; which practically means that there will be *eight series of fields arranged all as alike as possible.* Every separate quality of the village soil, the wheat land in the south, the more sandy lands in the north, the lands which are near a well or tank, the patch of potato or tobacco land near the village site, the flooded winter-crop land, the high and dry land beyond, and the best part between the two, &c., all are dealt with. 'I have seen,' adds Mr. Hooper, 'a little pond divided into *pātiā* because it sometimes dried up and grew winter crops (*jarhan*).' Each will be made into eight lots, and every *thok* will have its *pātiā*, or share, made up of one of each; and these have again to be divided between the four ploughs of the *thok*; and as the four may be held, say, A 1 plough, B ¼, C 1¼, D 1, E ½, it is no wonder that the individual fields are sometimes as small as one-fifth of an acre.

CHAPTER VII

JOINT-VILLAGES ARISING FROM FOUNDATION BY INDIVIDUALS

THE last chapter will, I hope, have made it plain that the clan or tribal stage of society has produced a very large proportion of the village-groups in India. But the tribal stage of society passes away, and yet the joint family and its customs of inheritance remain. Individual enterprises, the rise to local power of individual families, the establishment of Royal Courts, with the grants, assignments, and ultimately the revenue-farms, which they give rise to—these are the causes of the establishment of individual lordships over village, as well as larger, estates; and are equally the causes of the foundation of new villages in uninhabited country. We are not surprised, therefore, to find that so many joint-villages in the North-West Provinces and Oudh, and to some extent in the Panjāb also, are established, not on any tribal basis, but as the joint-estates of bodies descended from the one founder. Nor is the essential character lost by the fact that, in some cases, later additions have been made to the groups; or that, in other cases, two, three, or more separate families settled together, and are still remembered in the *sections* of the village which bear their name.

Under the head of 'individual' foundation I have also included some cases where the bond of union is not descent from one ancestor, but where the body originated in a voluntary association of independent colonists, or in the cohesion of groups for mutual defence; and the several groups have established major and minor divisions in the village to account for their several interests, accepting a joint liability for burdens imposed on the whole.

It is not, of course, possible to draw a hard and fast line

between the 'tribal' foundations and the 'individual,' merely on the ground of some special mode of sharing or form of constitution. It is quite possible that village bodies really of individual foundation may have adopted the *bhaiāchārā* method of equalised holdings usually observed in clan-settlements; and the latter may sometimes adopt the method of ancestral shares, which more commonly indicates descent from a single founder. A number of villages may appear locally in a large circuit, all of the same caste or clan, and yet there may be nothing 'tribal' about their settlement; the constitution of the villages is clearly based on individual founders' pedigrees and family joint ownership, not on tribal union. Still, in spite of difficulties of classification, I think the examples cited in the last chapter will have justified their separation.

In the class of cases now to be examined it will be observed that in a special sense the *village* is an essential and a distinct area; it is the limited group of lands in which the grant, or the conquest, or the usurpation, of the individual founder took effect. Or at least the 'village' is the result of a partition of a larger domain among the descendants of one founder or over-lord. Such villages, in the large majority of cases, are, or once were, held on the 'legal' or ancestral shares following from the place of each descendant in the 'genealogical tree.' The individual founder in general is remembered as having pretensions to some title or some position of superiority, and his descendants are proud of their 'inheritance' from him, and more or less jealous of each other: they desire to maintain their rank, even though they are but peasants. I do not mean to assert that all villages of the Rājput and other dominant races arising out of individual foundations are always held on this principle; but the majority are so; and the *pattidārī* rule will be found characteristic of land-holders of superior pretensions—Muhammadan grantee-families, Aryan Rājputs, and any other families of superior origin, whatever their real history. But there are cases where villages resulting from a purely individual foundation have adopted the plan of equalised holdings or some other special form of holding by 'ploughs' or other measures of land-allotment.

One other preliminary point deserves to be set down here. Villages of individual foundation are of all dates; some may be so recent that the single owner is alive; or the foundation dates back one or two generations, so that grandsons or great-grandsons of the acquiring owner may still be alive; in others a larger body of descendants and co-heirs may be holding the village still undivided, but sharing profits and burdens in the *ancestral* fractions proper to the several members of the agnatic group—*wārisān-yak-jadī*, as the phrase is. The older villages, again, will long have been divided, at least as far as the main sub-divisions which represent the grades of their first descent in the family group.[1] Hence it is conceivable that we may find instances of villages held by the *single owner*, by the *undivided body*, or by the *body partitioned*. This gives rise to the threefold division used in the official classification, which I will afterwards explain. It makes not the least difference, *from the tenure point of view*, which condition exists, or what degree of division or indivision subsists, as long as the *principle of sharing is the same*. While there is one owner he has of course the whole—he is sole 'sharer'; where there are many, it is *per se* immaterial whether the actual fields are divided for the 8 *āna*, 2 *āna*, or 1½ *āna* shares, or whatever they are, or whether the profits and burdens only are shared on the same rule, the lands being left undivided. Nor does it make any difference as to the tenure whether the partition has extended to the whole of the land or has left some part still undivided, as long as no new principle is introduced.

If we now proceed to set down, for convenience of further examination, the heads under which we can group some of the *known* origins of villages depending on INDIVIDUAL FOUNDATION, it will at once appear what a large number are connected with the existence, and also the decadence, of the Aryan monarchy, and with subsequent kingdoms and chiefships established on the same model. But this is not the only head. Let us at once adopt the following list:

(1) Villages arising in consequence of *grants* by the State; the descendants of the grantee forming the joint community. These are (*a*) sometimes ancient, and represent religious, family, or official grants and assignments by way of maintenance, pension, or reward under old Hindu States, or later of the Mughal

[1] See p. 238, *ante*.

Empire, and (*b*) of more recent times arising out of the Revenue farming of single villages.

(2) Villages which on the *disruption of an old State*, aided by family partitioning in some cases, remained in the hands of members and descendants of the once ruling houses; these, owing to their defeat or dispersion, descended to the grade of peasant-proprietors, and as such have clung to individual villages or portions of territory; they may from the first have had a closer connection with the land by residence and direct management, and have gradually become the actual soil-owners; they are now recognised in the persons of their co-sharing descendants, as *village proprietary bodies*.

(3) A number of villages scattered all over the country owe their foundation to *single adventurers*, scions of families who found no room at home and wandered away to seek new homes elsewhere; these not being connected with the establishment of any territorial Rājāship or other formal rule.

(4) Villages formed by voluntarily associated *groups of colonists* and others, mostly of no very ancient date.

It remains only to illustrate, by actual cases in the various districts, these several heads of origin.

Section I.—Villages connected with the Establishment of Local Kingdoms or Chiefships

(*a*) *Arising out of State Grants.*—We have already examined the origin of the Hindu State,[1] both when it is formed on the basis of clan-organisation—*i.e.* with a Rāja for the central territory and a *bhaiād* or series of kindred chiefs holding outlying territories and observing what we may call 'feudal' relations to the Rājā—and also when it is an individual rulership acquired by conquest or voluntary submission, and unconnected with any clan-organisation. The villages now to be spoken of may be said to be the more or less direct product of the Hindu Rāj (or any other State established on the same model) in the days of its prosperity, or in the course of its normal existence and administrative action.

[1] *Ante*, p. 192 ff.

Two points which have already been dwelt upon have to be borne in mind: (1) that the old Hindu Rājās made no claim to be actual owners of the soil of their dominions. (2) It is equally certain that in cases of local conquest, and in after times—especially when the great Deputies of the Mughal Empire set themselves up as independent sovereigns—the Rājās, Nawābs and other rulers ultimately claimed to be actual owners of every acre in their dominions.

It follows that all grants under the earlier *régime*, where they purported to convey villages already existing, were intended to transfer only the royal rights; it was not supposed that existing landholders would be ejected or otherwise made to suffer. At the same time, there was certainly no thought of legal principles or of defining the grantee's position; such a precaution would have been wholly impossible to the ideas of the time. The change of the grantee's descendants into proprietary communities was a matter of growth and gradual usurpation. Where, however, the grant was to colonise uninhabited land, the proprietory title was virtually conceded, as there was no antecedent private right to interfere. Succeeding generations would have the double customary title resulting from their inheritance of a *grant*, and of their representing the first establisher of cultivation.

Under the later *régime* all grants of *land*, as such, were proprietory grants. If such was not intended there would be express assignment of the land-revenue income only.[1] But even then, as such grants were often allowed to become hereditary, and as religious grants were never revocable, the

[1] In the palmy days of the Empire, a strict classification of grants was adopted: (1) where both the land and the revenue were conveyed (*milk*, *alṭamghā*, &c.), and (2) where the revenue only was assigned (*suyūrghal*, *jāgīr*, &c.) The earlier Hindu States had no such systematic terms, but a similar distinction was practically known. In cases of conquest, land-grants were made without the least thought of the existing possessors. *E.g.*, when the Rājās of Kumāon made grants, it was understood (probably thought a most humane concession!) that the grantee was not to take actual personal possession of more than one-third of the land. On that, he was at liberty apparently to eject the old cultivators or come to terms with them as he pleased. On the rest they must be left in possession, but became 'tenants.'

opportunities for the grantee, and especially of his later descendants, to become the virtual landowners were numerous and effective.

The causes or occasions of such grants are various; religion is perhaps the commonest. Every Hindu king distinguished himself by his liberality to Brahmans and by his gifts for the support of temples and shrines. Moslem kings rewarded Sayyads, Qāzis, Shekhs and holy persons, and endowed mosques and tombs. The number of these grants is so great, and their existence so notorious, that no special notice of them is needed. They mark every phase of government, of whatever period, whether Hindu or Muhammadan.

The secular grants, however, require more specific notice. When we look back to the early Hindu kingdoms such as the *Laws of Manu* picture to us, or such as are well known by tradition—*e.g.* in Northern Oudh—we must remember that the villages, largely if not wholly occupied by 'aborigines' or at least mixed races including the humbler classes of Aryan connection, were in the *raiyatwārī* form, each under its '*Pātel*,' or headman,[1] who had his dignity enhanced by the State allowance of some his plough-lands as free from land-revenue charges. The Rājā's grain share is peaceably collected,[2] as well as the dues of the artisans and other village servants. And there is no tendency for the village tenure to be altered. But the Rājā will certainly have cadets of his family who have a claim to maintenance, and courtiers and other persons whom he will desire to reward or to provide for. Some of them will be given grants in the virgin waste; but very often the grant is made of the king's *rights* in an existing village; and this would include the right to bring part of the ample waste in the vicinity

[1] *Pātel* is the Central India (Marāthā) title, but it is of *old* Hindi origin; copperplate grants, of the early centuries of our era at any rate, speak of the *Pātalika*.

[2] It may be remembered that not only do all early traditions and literary allusions represent the well-established early kingdoms as favourable to the agriculturist interest, but it must have been so, because the existence of the States were so dependent on agriculture and on the revenue. And all Rājās who were not mere marauders and desirous to 'make hay while the sun shone' would soon find it to their interest to protect their cultivating villages.

into cultivation for the grantee's benefit. Here is the beginning of the process by which a grantee becomes 'landlord' of the whole village and gradually turns the old 'soil-clearers' into his tenants. And when the days of wars and invasions begin, the chances of usurpers are multiplied; as the Rājā's needs increase, his grants also increase and he even makes them for a consideration; government becomes more and more lax, and the growth of local grantee landlordship progresses apace.[1] But even apart from the effects of actual bad government and an empty treasury (when it is so much easier to give a land grant than to make payment in money), the circumstances of an Oriental monarchy must have always tended to the multiplication of grants. To say nothing of relations and cadets of the family, all of whom expected support, there must at all times have been a great number of officials and attendants, every one of whom considered it his right to live by the Court in one way or another.[2] In the GONDĀ district of Oudh, Mr. Benett has clearly traced the history of the early local Rājās and their grants; this account is important, as all traditional and other evidence from literary sources proves that in its main features it represents what occurred in every Rājā's kingdom in the country. First it shows clearly that the original villages in the early states were *raiyatwārī*. They were simply aggregates 'of the people settled within the village boundaries and drawing their subsistence from agriculture.'[3] 'I believe,' continues

[1] It is interesting to compare the accounts of the growth of over-lord and manorial claims over once free villages in England, as stated in Pollock's *Land Laws* (The 'Citizen Series'), p. 32 ff.

[2] I have recently seen the account of a copperplate grant, believed to belong to the ninth century of our era, communicated to the Asiatic Society of Bengal by Mr. V. C. Batavyal (*Journal* for 1894, part i. vol. lxiii. No. 1). Here even at that early date we find what a vast number of officials there were; the Rājā's country was divided into *maṇḍala*, and again into *viçaya*; and the grant addresses 'all in authority assembled in the four villages' to which the grant relates, as *Rājās*, followers and relatives of Rājās, ministers (*Rājā-mātya*), commanders of troops, revenue officials, revenue collectors, purveyors, magistrates, police or executioners, officers of public works, of customs (*i.e.* transit duties), writers, and several others. It is not meant, of course, that all these would be found in the villages granted, but we see what a number of officials there were.

[3] *Gondā S. R.* pp. 44, 45.

Mr. Benett, 'that the similarity of sound between the words community and communism, the first meaning nothing more than a number of people living under similar conditions and capable of a joint representation, while the second describes a peculiar form of property, has led in the case of the Hindu villages to serious misconception. With regard to the cultivation of his fields and the disposition of the produce (after the customary shares were taken), each tenant holder was entirely independent of the rest.' But within these villages two forms of *grant* occasionally appeared—the right of the *birtiyā*, or receiver of a *birt*,[1] and that of the 'village *zamīndār*.' The former was originally a person who held a grant that merely assigned part of the royal grain-share for the subsistence or profit of the grantee. The *birtiyā* may have had opportunities for aggression, but his grant gave him nothing but the revenue share. But in the other case the Rājā granted his entire rights (which, as I have said, came afterwards to be collectively described as 'the *zamīndārī*'); the grantee could then appropriate the greater part of the waste for his own profit. He took all the tolls and dues, and the cultivators became responsible to him for the grain-share that formerly went to the State granary. Sometimes such rights were merely usurped, when the Rājā was weak; and in other cases the Rājā sold them *sub rosa*; but that was in bad times, and when he was out of possession or in an unstable position. These grants of the entire management are very old. Mr. Benett says that they may be found in the oldest cultivated tracts along the Ghāgrā river, and they are held by *Çhatrī* families, *Bisen*, *Bais*, &c., who were probably anterior to the *Kalhaṅs* Rājā. In what is now the Mahādeva *pargana*, a *Kalhaṅs* Rājā had granted *birt* rights, but one of the grantees, having done important service, asked for and obtained the full *zamīndārī* grant for his own and his family villages. *In each, accordingly, there grew up a proprietary community of the descendants; the village had become a joint or landlord village.* In after times all villages alike may have fallen under the power of Taluqdār chiefs, who are now

[1] *Birt* is the Hindi or Prakrit form of the Sanskrit *vṛttī* (= subsistence, maintenance). Pious gifts to Brahmans were often called *saṇkalp*.

recognised as superior landlords.[1] But that does not make any difference as regards the original position. Exactly the same thing might happen in the case of a grant of full right in a waste tract; the grantee would found a village with the aid of his own tenants and followers, and in a few generations we should have a joint body of co-sharers, forming a *pattīdārī* village.

It would not be interesting to collect a great number of cases of origin by grant, which must necessarily be very much alike. I will only recall a few instances which are specially noteworthy. In the ETĀ district, North-West Provinces,[2] mention is made of a number of villages owned by the descendants of five brothers, *Kaçhwāha Rājputs.* They had gained the favour of the Emperor Akbar, and one morning as they were riding with the Imperial party, each brother received a grant of a village. So again in the BALLIĀ district there are numerous estates derived from grants made to the revenue officers (*Qānūngo*) of the empire, and to *Qāzīs*, or Moslem judges, in towns.[3] So also there is an account of the estates derived from a grant to the two brothers Birshāh and Sūrshāh. To similar *grants* may be ascribed the wholesale growth of the Sayyad villages (*milk*) of MURĀDĀBĀD,[4] where indeed, in some cases, the grantees left the older possessors with some sort of status as owner, but also in others assumed the entire proprietory right themselves. I give these few instances merely to make my meaning definite; but in fact the royal grant has been incidentally illustrated or mentioned several times already; as it may equally be the origin of large clan-settlements as of individual families. And the essential point is that, whatever the precise nature of the grant, it leads to full proprietorship, and to the descendants forming a joint or co-sharing community of proprietors.

(*b*) *Revenue Farmers and Purchasers.*—More indirectly connected with State administration come the latter instances of village proprietary bodies grown up by descent from a person

[1] Village holders where the *zamīndārī* grant was held complete over the whole village would, at Settlement, become 'sub-proprietors' with a fixed payment, according to the provisions of a special law in Oudh.

[2] *North-West Provinces Gazetteer*, iv. 42.

[3] *Balliā S. R.* § 34. (Report on the Preparation of a Record of Rights.)

[4] *Murādābād S. R.* pp. 25, 26.

allowed to farm the revenues, or to stand security for the amount due by the existing village body.[1] The formation of village communities out of the descendants of such persons, or by the heirs of purchasers at sales for default in the village revenue payment, in the latter case indicating an origin not yet a hundred years old, would hardly need to be mentioned in the general history of Indian villages, except for the fact that such villages may exhibit all the features of a really ancient *pattīdārī* body; and in any case they form a very considerable addition, which goes to swell the total number of those 'joint-villages' which are held to be so widespread and important a class as to warrant a belief that they were the *universal* form of village once prevalent, and a form to be theoretically referred to archaic institutions and primeval ideas of communal-property. It is well to remind ourselves how easily the principle of *joint-inheritance* will produce a 'joint-village,' which may be held 'in common.' Every village which, as a whole, falls into the hands of a grantee, a farmer or a purchaser, will in time become a co-shared village estate.

The undoubtedly *raiyatwārī* villages of the Central Provinces for which the proprietary title was in 1860 conceded to *pātels*, *mālguzārs*, and the like, will have the same ending; the sons and grandsons of the 'proprietor' will (or may) hold 'in common' after the death of the first grantee, and as sharers multiply there will probably be a minute subdivision. If there is not, it will only be because the villages were granted to the 'proprietors' under such limitations as to the right of the existing landholders, that it may be impossible for the descendants of the *mālguzār* grantee of this nineteenth century to get possession, personally, of much land, and therefore they will have to divide the rents instead.

It is certainly the case that a respectable percentage of the entire group of the 'communal' villages of the N.-W. Provinces are villages held by the descendants of revenue-farmers under British rule. No grant of proprietory right was of course ever made to such persons; but having tendered for the Settlement year after year, having bought up lands, having ousted defaulting holders and taken their shares, having cultivated the waste,

[1] By this time a cash payment had been substituted for the old contribution in kind.

and done many other things to establish a virtually proprietary character, they have ended by having a sort of prescriptive title to the whole estate. Village bodies so originating are not found (or only locally) in the Panjāb, because by far the greater part of that province was not acquired, or at least bought under regular Revenue Settlement, till after the old vicious system of revenue-farms and immediate sale for default had been completely changed. The same remark applies to Oudh, except so far as estates may have originated in the farming arrangements of the Oudh Government before annexation; but, as far as I know, that Government did not employ farmers for single villages, nor sell villages individually for default.

As I have already given some statistics on this matter in my 'Land Systems of British India,'[1] I will only cite one or two prominent instances. In the BARELI district the writer in the *Gazetteer* goes rather to an extreme when he says that 'whatever proprietary tenures exist at all are *zamīndārī*' (*i.e.* have fallen into the hands of single proprietors and their heirs). We have seen evidences of other tenures here; but still, such have been the subsequent changes, that out of 3,326 village areas 2,611 became the property of single owners. Converting the numbers into percentages, we have 74·6 *zamīndārī*, and 25·4 co-shared villages of other kinds. The smaller percentage represents the older estates—*e.g.* of the Rājputs who would have ancestrally or otherwise divided villages; and we see also by the *caste*, that out of 23,122 proprietors recorded, 8,623 are still Rājput or Thākur, more than half of these being in the one *pargana* of Farīdpur, while the rest are Brahmans, Kayaths, Kurmis, and Muhammadans. The districts PĪLĪBHĪT, BUDĀON, and SHĀHJAHĀNPUR, having suffered from the Rohilla troubles, saw many of their village tenures destroyed, and the subsequent sole proprietory right was acquired by local headmen, by managers, and revenue-farmers. But in other places it was not the destruction of the old tenures by enemies that caused the change. It was

[1] Vol. ii. 116 ff, 122, &c., where also some account is given of the efforts made to reverse fraudulent sales in connection with defaults in revenue payment.

[2] *North-West Provinces Gazetteer*, v. 615. See *Bareli S. R.* (1874), p. 22.

the ignorance of the nature of the village-bodies that marked the first days of British rule; when, as Holt Mackenzie said, 'the interest of the persons made responsible for the revenue is so naturally conceived to be that of absolute and exclusive property.' The sole proprietory right thus passed into the hands of one of the older co-sharers, or of some person who became responsible for the revenue in the days when it was considered necessary that only one such person should be recognised.

In FATIHPUR the history would prepare us to expect a large majority of villages held on the *ancestral* share principle; but out of 2,145 village estates, we find that 1,555 have passed into the hands of 'sole proprietors' of the farmer or auction-purchaser class.[1]

I will only add that proprietors of this class were not by any means always chargeable with usurpation; for in many cases they took charge of villages and became responsible for them when there was really no one else to do so; former troubles had so depressed such cultivators as remained, that they were neither willing nor able to take responsibility as proprietors.

SECTION II.—VILLAGE ESTATES ARISING FROM THE DISRUPTION OR DECADENCE OF KINGDOMS AND CHIEFSHIPS

This head is perhaps the most largely illustrated of any, depending as it does on the existence at some former time of a local State, or chiefship, which has now disappeared, but has left its relics in the shape of villages and lands held by members of the once ruling families. In the Panjāb we do not find so many instances of the class, because Rājput or Aryan rulerships that have left any such mark were quite local, and are chiefly found in the more northern districts near the Salt Range. A few traces of *Çaurasī* groups[2] and similar marks of a local rule may, however, be found in some other districts. But, as might be expected, they are very numerous in the North-West Provinces and Oudh,[3] which were once covered by a network of

[1] *Fatihpur S. R.* (1878), pp. 9, 15.

[2] See p. 198, *ante*, where this term is explained.

[3] It may be truly said of the whole body of joint-villages in the North

such kingdoms and lordships. It may be advisable to add that when villages appear as the vestiges of some territorial rulership it is not necessary that there should ever have been a formally constituted 'Rāj,' or regular territorial kingdom; but there was always *either* such a kingdom *or* at least some kind of local chiefship, or usurped over-lordship, easily distinguishable from the mere establishment of a cultivating family expanding into a large fraternity.

And there is one other matter which perhaps had better be dealt with at once. The rule of *primogeniture* has a great effect in preventing the disruption of estates; and its absence, of course, directly facilitates it. It is somewhat remarkable that in the 'Laws of Manu' the right of the eldest is not connected with the royal title, or with succession to a chiefship. The eldest son is supposed to succeed to *any* family estate *if* he is particularly eminent, capable, or virtuous, and the rest are not so. The vagueness of such a rule is enough to have ensured its not being a practical one. The 'Laws' indicate a desire to place the eldest son (generally) in the position of the head of the family; and even when he does not succeed alone, he is given a larger share.[1] There is also mention of a special share for the youngest as well. But for our purposes it is enough to say that in general the rule of the eldest has practically been maintained only among the royal and noble houses, of whatever race, in India—in such higher families, in fact, as possessed some kind of title or dignity to succeed to, spoken of as the *gaddī* (=royal cushion or throne). But it is not possible to specify any particular degree in the social scale at which the custom ceases. I have known legal disputes in India as to whether property ought

West Provinces (putting aside those which are in reality artificial, as in Kumāon, Jhānsi, &c.) that they are derived—

(i.) From descendants of the revenue farmers and managers;

(ii.) From old 'cultivating fraternities' with a certain tribal connection;

(iii.) From relics of chiefships and local territorial over-lordships, and the grants connected with them.

[1] Sometimes spoken of as *jethānsī*. Mr. H. E. Seebohm has collected the quotations from Manu at p. 97 ff of his *Tribal Structure of Society in Greece*; see also Sir H. S. Maine, *Early Institutions*, p. 197. As to the honour shown to the eldest, cf. Manu, ii. 225 with iv. 180, 184, and ix. 104–119, &c.

or ought not to be deemed subject to a rule of primogeniture as a question of family custom. And in the case of some estates, *e.g.* those of Taluqdārs in Oudh and in Bombay, special rules have been adopted and legally enacted on the subject. In former times the custom was very various; and there are cases on record in which even families having the title of Rājā have divided the estate. In such cases, the tendency to split up the whole estate into a number of mere *villages* held by the co-sharing descendants of the divided branches is obvious. Even where an estate is theoretically preserved from dismemberment, it sometimes becomes so burdened with what are nominally maintenances and rent-charges, but practically are divided portions held by charitable grantees or by widows and cadets, that the estate as a whole is hardly able to pay its way. In the AHMADĀBĀD district of Bombay (Gujarāt), there are a number of relics of local chiefships, now called 'Taluqdāri' estates, which survived the formal resumptions and deductions of the Muhammadan conquest and the more open exactions of the Marāthās; the rule of primogeniture commonly prevails, but the chief is expected to share his rents, usually by whole villages or shares in villages, with every kind of relative [1] and family dependent.

And if voluntary, customary, partition causes a considerable estate to be dismembered into a number of joint-villages, still more does involuntary disruption, when the head of an old kingdom is defeated and slain, and members of the family manage to cling to a few villages here and there, relics of the territory they once ruled in independence. In such cases it is a question of circumstances, and of the degree to which dismemberment and decay have gone, whether the old territorial rulership still remains in the form of a considerable landlordship, or is marked by mere scattered villages or groups of villages. In many instances it is well known that the old territorial Rājā, or other titular chief, submitted to the Mughal commander, and accepted a *sanad* or patent, agreeing to pass on a considerable

[1] Similar troubles have affected the chief's estates in Ajmer as well as in North Bombay, and special legislative measures have had to be passed for their relief. See some good remarks in Mr. A. Rogers's paper on Bombay Tenures in *Transactions of the East Indian Association* for February 1882, xiv. 10.

share of his local revenue to the imperial treasury, or at least to hold his State as a tributary. Then he was favoured, or at least left alone, by the imperial Deputy, who knew only too well that he must keep the provinces quiet, and that defeated chiefs, if not conciliated, would be always ready, on the slightest opportunity, to give serious trouble. Thus we have, handed down to the days of British rule, all the varieties of Bengal *Zamīndār*, Oudh *Taluqdār*, and similar estates such as have arisen under other conquests in the Central Provinces, or in Northern Bombay; and we have also the *Janmī* of Malabār and *Mūlāvargdār* of Kānara on the west coast, and *Pālegār* in the south, as well as others whose existing landlord claims are derived in various ways from an earlier ruling or territorial position. With these 'landlord' estates this book is not concerned; but it is impossible to avoid mentioning the subject, because in the case of so many communities descended from a once noble family or a ruling chief, the difference between the *pattīdarī* village and the greater landlord estate is one of rank and degree rather than of kind; and the unity of the larger estate needs always to be supported by the primogeniture rule, or it tends to disintegrate. The immediate point, however, is that where the rulership was really broken up by misfortune and defeat, as it so often was, and the members of the family managed to cling to some separate fragments of the estate, they were brought close to the land, so to speak, in a manner that was never possible with a dignified chief living at his court or fortress at a distance. Thus driven to residence, and to taking part in the direct management, each family became virtual landlord of this or that village or group of villages —smaller or larger according to circumstances—and the multiplying heirs have formed the 'village community.' After a certain number of generations, such villages will be ripe for inclusion under some theory as representing 'archaic communal-ownership.'

It is curious to notice how completely, in the course of a few generations, the descendant of the former Rājā, or Rāo, is assimilated to the peasant grade, even if he is still able to keep his hands from the defilement of the plough. But though to alien eyes he is a mere peasant-proprietor, or village co-sharer, in his own eyes and also in those of his neighbours, his high caste and descent are still his own; and that makes all the difference. The popular saying of the BASTĪ district [1] shows how the idea of rank has come to be associated with the number of 'ploughs' (*i.e.* plough lands):—

Das hal kā Rāo, āth hal kā Rānā
Çār hal kā barā kisānā

'Ten ploughs are the holding for a Rāo [superior chief], eight for a Rānā; four are the holding of a considerable tenant-farmer, &c.' [2]

(1) *Illustrations from the Panjāb*

In the JIHLAM district I have already alluded to the (Rājput) Janjhūā villages. These are interesting because of the speculation—which, I fear, is quite baseless—that they represent some relics of primitive Aryan chiefships. However, there is every appearance that there was here a *local rulership* founded by conquest or adventure, and that the present co-sharing Janjhūā villages are the relics of it.[3] A particularly good instance occurs in the neighbouring district of GUJRĀT. Here the Chib Rājputs formed a local kingdom (still spoken of as the Chibhal), of which the main features can be traced, as it lasted down to the Sikh times, and indeed seems to have been overthrown by Mahārājā Ranjīt Singh.[4] Whether there was one

[1] *North-West Provinces Gazetteer*, 'Account of the *Bastī* District,' vi. 686.

[2] As a single instance of how pride of descent may cling to a purely peasant class, I may mention the clan of Manhāi in the Gujrāt district, Panjāb. They are really probably connected far off with some old Rājput stock by a mixed marriage—they say with Rām-Chandra of Ajudhiyā, which is much like being connected with 'Noah,' &c.! The Jamvāl Rājputs are their 'relatives,' and they came to the Panjāb at a remote date. They have long been completely agriculturist, but still they call all the *eldest sons* 'Rājā' and the younger '*Miāñ*,' and use the '*Jai*' or Rājput salutation (*Gujrāt Gazetteer*, p. 65).

[3] There is in the *S. R.* (Thomson's), § 61, &c., a very interesting account of Janjhūā rule and its gradual overthrow. It is too long to quote, and does not admit of being condensed.

[4] The older *S. R.* (Hector Mackenzie's), which gives full details, is no longer accessible, but it is quoted in the *Gujrāt Gazetteer* (2nd edition), p. 64. What is specially interesting is that this clan professes to be of great antiquity and superiority, and has a curious custom of recognising

Rājā or principal chief over the whole does not clearly appear; but it is probable, since there is still an existing 'head of the clan' named Rājā Sultān Khān, who has a considerable *jāgīr* (or revenue-free grant) from Government. The account given by Hector Mackenzie shows four major-territories, called *maṇḍī*, each containing twenty-two villages (*i.e.* a *çaubīsī*) and six minor divisions known as *dherī*, containing twelve villages each. The chief of the *maṇḍī* bore the title of *Rāi*; the heads of the *dherī* were *Thakkar* (= *Thākur*). 'The families in which the titles were formerly hereditary are known, but they retain none of their influence beyond their own villages.' As the clansmen would not cultivate the estate themselves, the best lands became occupied by others during the owners' absence in the petty wars of the period; 'and when the Chibs finally took to agriculture they were unable to dispossess these squatters.'

(2) *The North-West Provinces*

In these provinces, the instances of villages as relics of former kingdoms or chiefships are so numerous that I must make a limited selection taken from the characteristically different parts of the country. I have already remarked that the Rohilkhand districts have suffered much by various wars and invasions, and finally by the harsh rule of the Rohilla chiefs in the last century. When the districts came under the British Revenue-Settlement it was found that a large number of villages were virtually without owners, and the Revenue agreement was necessarily made with comparatively new men, who restored the cultivation and became owners. Nevertheless, the traces are abundant of former Rājput chiefships—sometimes constituting what may be called kingdoms, at other times being merely local over-lordships. It is worthy of notice that in these parts the Rājput clans are commonly called not Rājput but *Thākur*,

sons of the clan by cutting off a lock of their hair, left for the purpose, *at the ancestor's tomb*. (Compare H. E. Seebohm's *Tribal Greece*, p. 125.) They claim descent from the Katoch Rājās of Kāngra—a claim which is possibly confirmed by their calling their seven clan-divisions *mūi*, or *mūhī*. This term I cannot trace anywhere but in the Jālandhar Doāb, to which anciently the early Kāngrā Rājās' dominion extended. See p. 273, *ante*.

which word means 'Baron' or 'Chief,' and indicates that they were originally established as over-lords. It has been remarked that this over-lordship was freely accepted, and not infrequently invited, by local cultivating bodies; and it was doubtless a real protection in many instances.

It seems to have been a common procedure, that whenever a chiefship was established at a given centre, members of the family would go forth and take the direct control of smaller estates in the surrounding country. 'Among the Thākurs, successive branches continually left the family residence and settled in their allotments of country.'[1] This must have facilitated the ultimate dissolution of the territorial estate into small portions, often consisting of a single village.

In this country (SHĀHJAHĀNPUR District) the *Katheriyā* clan obtained such power that the name 'Kather' was formerly given to it. The clan long resisted the Moslem arms, and was only suppressed in the days of the Mughal Empire; but many villages held by *Katheriyā* still remain.[2] In one *pargana* (Golā) of the Pawain Tahsīl the clan had been so weakened by the departure of cadet members of their houses to other settlements, that when their chief was slain in battle, his widow, who was of course of another clan—in this case a *Gaur*, sent for her kinsmen to help. The *Gaur* leader came with his followers, but soon ousted all the remaining *Katheriyā*. A *Gaur* Rājā long retained his rule over the Pawain tract, but his family did not expand, so that we have a local landlord estate of some size, and not a number of separate villages. In another *pargana*, on the contrary, the Rājā of Khotar disappeared as far as territorial rule was concerned, but left a number of families of village proprietors, all of whom are 'Scotch cousins of the Rājā's.'[3] From the adjoining district of BARELI several examples might be given. One is that of the *Janghāra*, a branch of the *Tānwār* (or *Tumār*) clan, who seem to have been dispersed in the troubles which preceded the downfall of the Hindu monarchy of Delhi; some went to Budāon, others to Shāhjahānpur. I notice that this kindred was divided, owing to a very common cause, into two; the *Bhūr*, who are descendants of a regular marriage of

[1] *Shāhjahānpur S. R.* (1874), § 26, p. 60.
[2] *Ibid.* p. 107. [3] *S. R.* § 16, ch. v.

the ancestor, and the *Tarūi* group, descendants of a second (and perhaps inferior) marriage. When the *Çauhān*, with their famous Rājā Prithwī Chand, defeated the *Tumār*, five brothers of the dispersion led separate parties; the youngest crossed the Ganges to Bulandshahr; another, called Hemrāj, had three sons; one of these settled on the high land east of the Rāmganga river, and from him the *Bhūr-Janghārās* are descended. Since this settlement some fourteen generations are asserted to have passed, and the chiefships thus formed are now found to survive in some 3,150 co-sharing descendants in many villages.

It is, however, in the Doāb districts that we have some of the best examples of the results of a decadence of territorial rulership—how it leaves behind it proprietary village-estates. The country near Kanauj, as I have before remarked, was always a strong centre of successive Hindu rulers. The CAWNPORE district (in this vicinity) shows many traces of their rule, and Mr. Wright, in his Settlement Report, has given an account of the matter which is worth reading *in extenso*.[1] He was fortunately able to procure a *Vaṅsāvalī* or genealogical record of the *Çāndel* clan; and, making allowance for much exaggeration and for legendary additions, it has still an evident foundation of fact. It seems that the *Gaharwār* sovereign of Kanauj had been weakened, and ultimately driven out of his kingdom, by the early Moslem invasions; whereon a *Çāndel* chief, Sabhājīt, was advised to take possession of the vacant State. For eight generations a single son succeeded to the dominion. At length came a group of three sons, who formed three main branches of the family; the eldest took the title of *Rājā*, the second of *Rāwat*, the third of *Rāo*. The head of the first branch was removed to a new location in the Bithūr *pargana*, under circumstances which I need not detail; the second became extinct; the third, or Supāhi, branch before long again divided; the Rāwatpur section retained forty-eight villages, apparently a *bēālisī*,[2] and from this a *çaubīsī* was afterwards partitioned.[3] I

[1] *S. R.* (1878), ch. ii. p. 18.

[2] *Ante*, p. 198. The groups *çaurāsī*, *bēālisī*, &c., rarely keep to the exact number.

[3] One branch, having been leniently treated by the emperor (for their chiefship was no longer independent) in the matter of some arrears of

cannot follow the estate through its whole history, but partitions again and again occurred, till the entire territory was split up into quite a number of separate shares, and these, as usual, afterwards constituted a series of joint-village properties. In such cases some members of the leading houses may have a larger estate than the rest, holding together a certain number of villages as over-lords, and retaining a title of honour. In that case each will be the landlord or 'Zamīndār' of the group.[1] In the same way I might cite the case of one of the *Gaharwār* clan, who was expelled, as I have above noticed, from Kanauj, and obtained a new local chiefship in the south of *pargana* Bilhaur. In another case, a *Çamārgaur* chief named Pathardeo had seven sons. The father was murdered by a turbulent aboriginal tribe called *Meo*; in revenge, the sons attacked and defeated them, and thus obtained a number of local dominions. But here, again, partition split up the estates; and after various fortunes and many revenue sales at the beginning of the century, as well as subsequent losses during the mutiny, only a limited number of separate village-estates now remain.[2]

I can only allude to one more case, a *gens* of comparatively late origin, called *Gautam*, whose chief was first established at Argal, in the FATIHPUR district.[3] The family divided into groups with titles, *Rājā* for the eldest, *Rāo*, *Rānā*, and *Rāwat* for the others. So great were their territories, at one time, that they were in a position to make large grants of villages to chiefs of another clan—the *Çāndel*, to Brahmans, and to some *Āthya-Gautam*, who pleased the Argal Rājā by teaching him the game

land-revenue, paid him the compliment of ever after wearing their coats opening on the left side like Mussulmans.

[1] The policy of the early Settlements in the North-West Provinces was to encourage the village bodies, and to get rid of over-lord proprietors if possible—in some cases compromising their half-grown claim to landlordship by granting a 'Taluqdārī allowance,' which was a sort of rent charge on the estate, ultimately fixed at about 10 per cent. on the Government revenue. This policy formed the subject of considerable controversy at the time. (See *L. S. B. I.* ii. 157 ff.)

[2] The whole account is worth reading (*Cawnpore S. R.* ch. ii. §§ 25–35).

[3] See Beames' *Elliot's Glossary*, vol. i. (s.v. 'Gautam'). This clan is still numerous in Ghāzipur, and in some parts of Fatihpur and Cawnpore.

of chess.[1] In all these cases the history was as usual: soldiers of fortune acquire territories; their chiefs build forts and rule from those centres; in time they become possessors of many villages, both old and new; and ultimately, in later generations, appear sometimes with their principal member retaining a *landlord* estate over a number of villages, but the rest holding single villages, of which their descendants form the co-sharing communities. To complete the history of the *Gautam* of Argal, reference must be made to the Settlement Report.[2] The clan espoused the losing side of the Pathān Moslems, ultimately defeated by Humāyun and Akbar when the Mughal Empire was approaching its zenith. So they lost their possessions. The Argal Rājā, though much respected by all the Thākurs (Rājputs), is now only the petty 'Zamīndār' of two villages. But in Tappā Jas some of them continued to hold a *çaurāsi*; and many having become Muhammadans, they have still retained a considerable number of villages. I will only add that in the 'ĀZAMGARH district the *Gautam* chiefs were once so powerful as to rule nearly the whole, except the Mahūl portion. This was largely, however, due to the rise of the chief Abhimān-sen, who, in the seventeenth century, became a Muhammadan, entered the service of the Emperor Akbar, and grew rich; so he purchased extensive estates about Daulatābād. 'His descendants, and those of his brothers, systematically plundered their neighbours, wresting their estates from them one by one,' till, at the beginning of the eighteenth century, the whole district was held by them as above stated. It is interesting to trace from the Settlement Report of Mr. J. R. Reid,

[1] Another large grant was the origin of the Bais possessions across the Ganges in Oudh. Bhāo, a *Bais* chief, rescued the Argal Rājā's queen when, on a pilgrimage, she was attacked by the Mussulmans. Bhāo received a suitable bride as his reward, and was told he could have the lordship over as many villages as his bride could name in one breath. This remarkably well-winded lady, so it is said, pronounced the names of 1,440 villages!

[2] *Fatihpur S. R.* (1878), p. 9. I have already noted how in this district revenue-farmers afterwards gained possession of so many villages (*ante*, p. 304).

what has been the outcome of all this success.[1] First, let me mention the reporter's observation [2] that the population is now poor and dense, but the facilities for agriculture are considerable, and there has been a remarkable immunity from war and marauders. Many alien *grants* have been made, and many villages are held by descendants of the grantees. But in the greater part high caste proprietors are in possession; these are, in fact, remnants of the old ruling chiefs' houses; and therefore it is not surprising to find that the *pattidārī*, or 'aristocratic' system of village holding by ancestral shares, is in theory everywhere prevalent. The whole of the land has been excessively subdivided. The Government Review of the 'Report' notices that there are 5,532 villages (*mauza*), varying in size from little blocks of 1¼ to 5,500 acres in extent; the average being 248 acres. The groups of land held under one united title (*mahāl*) are 3,446. As to the nature of the *partition*, the principal feature to be noted is that the families are divided into *pattī*, which seem to represent a sort of minor clan or wide-kindred of the same house; each *pattī* is called by the name of the ancestral head. These *pattī* consequently represent the division only as far as the first or main branches of the original family;[3] for within the *pattī*, the component families and households often continue to hold undivided, the land being either rented to tenants (*parjas* land), or being held by individual co-sharers as tenants of the body. In the majority of cases division began long ago, probably in the time when the heads of branches (*pattī*), or their immediate successors, were alive; most of the cultivated lands and the profitable waste were then divided; but some still remained common to the whole major-group. Gradually the *pattīs* were divided into smaller family subdivisions, and then into minute holdings. Where there is complete division it has been carried to great lengths; on an average, there are nine fields to two acres.[4] The division is often made *khet-bat*

[1] *S. R.* (1877). The Report describes the fourteen *parganas* not permanently settled, which now alone form the district: this is the sixth settlement.

[2] *Ibid.* sec. ix. p. 87, § 307. [3] *Ibid. Government Review*, § 2.

[4] *S. R.* § 309. And there are sixty-five tables given in the appendix to the Report of different kinds of fractions (starting from the *rupee* as

(as the phrase is)—*i.e.* the number of geographical villages that belong to one large group of families and households are not allotted compactly one, or half a one, to each *pattī* (or whatever it is), but each *pattī* will have its lands scattered through a number of *mauzas*.[1] When the estate is divided into ancestral fractions it is said to be *khuntāitī* (= *pattidārī*), even though the shares held are not exactly correct to the scale. But it has often happened that the land proved so various in value that the fraction of the revenue and other burdens, which in theory ought to be identical with the land-fraction, became impossible, and the sharers converted their system into what is called *bīghādām*;[2] that means that each sharer was allowed to hold what he had, or to adjust his holding to what he could manage, but a really proportionate division of the land-revenue-charge was made to suit the holding. This *de facto* possession is sometimes recorded in acres, but sometimes it is noted in terms of the actual fraction of the whole that it represents. Doubtless, in time, it will be believed that this was the real 'ancestral' fraction. 'For,' says the reporter,[3] 'they never forget the descent from a common ancestor; and there is a sentiment against adoption' (*i.e.* the more or less artificial extension of the direct descent-table).[4] It seems, further, that although the incidence of the revenue has been adjusted by the *bīghādām* arrangement, the profits of waste and other like dues (*sāīr*), and possibly the share in the waste land, may still be regulated by the ancestral fractions; and so two scales come into use—*pattidārī māl* and *pattidārī sāīr*.

representing unity) used in the various divisions. (Cp. also *Cawnpore S. R.* § 107.) The following is No. lxiii. in abstract:

Rupee	*Āna*	*Gaṇḍā*	*Kauṛī*	*Dant*	*Kant*	*Reñ*	*Pheñ*	*Rāl*
1 =	16 =	320 =	1,280 =	19,200 =	288,000 =	(and so on	× by 15	each time)
	1 =	20						
		1 =	4					
			1 =	15				
				1 =	15			
					1 =	15		
						1 =	15	
							1 =	15

[1] This peculiarity is further described in the following chapter, p. 340.

[2] A full description is given of how this came about (see *S. R.* p. 92, §§ 326-8). The term means 'price or value *per* bīghā.'

[3] *S. R.* § 322 and note.

[4] Which would defeat the expectations of collaterals when the direct line otherwise failed.

All this is very different from the *bhaiāchārā* of the democratic family and the clan-settlement. It marks the sense of individual lordship, as jealously maintained by right of descent from the particular head of the family, which has branched off from the stem of the once royal or princely ancestor. We mark also the influence of the developed joint-family system ; in fact, the tribal and clan institutions of a wider character have begun to fade.[1] Where a certain number of families still hold undivided, it is always because they are closely related, and it is easier or more profitable to share the rents and other income than to squabble over the minute division of fields into patches, which will be unworkable when they are declared ; or perhaps it is because the land is held by tenants, and there is no object in dividing ; while if there is any waste reserved for grazing, the utility of it would be destroyed by partition.

It is not surprising to find, in this advanced stage of severalty, that the *pançayat* system 'exists only in theory,' and that the official headmen (*lambardār*) have practically nothing to do, and receive no *paçotra*, or official allowance.

I will conclude this series of illustrations of the North-West Provinces by only one more case in the Bundelkhand region, where we have not only the relics of the rulership, but also a definite memory of the loss of the princely title once enjoyed. In BĀNDĀ, Mr. Cadell has described in detail the rise and fall of the *Dikhit* Rājputs.[2] In the thirteenth century they had two capitals whence their chiefs ruled. 'But after the fall of the empire, even the inferior title of Rāo was lost to the clan, and whether owing to the discouragement of successive chiefs, or to the influence of the Hindu law of joint inheritance, there are now many *Dikhit* villages, but no *Dikhit* chief.'

[1] It will be remembered that in many cases in this chapter we have spoken of *clans*, because as a matter of fact the *clans* exist, and their number can be counted—if they are on compact areas of country. But nothing necessarily remains of any *clan feeling as to property* ; this is completely replaced by the ancestral individual right and by the co-sharing body as *representatives* of one original owner.

[2] *S. R.* (1881), § 72, p. 64.

(3) *Illustrations from Oudh*

The value of possessions in so fertile a country, and perhaps the influence of traditions of kingdoms believed to have been held by half-remembered ancestors or by legendary clan connections, must always have combined to tempt *Çhatrī* leaders to try and return to OUDH. They could reach it without difficulty either from their refuge in Rājputāna or when driven from settlements in Ujjain or Kanauj. Such possession was in fact acquired, sometimes by independent adventure, sometimes by joining the army of some Mughal or earlier emperor. The *Çhatrī* possessions and lordships thus acquired have given rise to proprietary-villages and to estates established on a footing clearly distinguishable from that of the apparently earlier land-holding communities, among whom no monarchical organisation or desire of territorial rulership was ever developed.[1] To give a complete account of the many conquering Rājās or local chiefs and of the estates held by their descendants, would be to transcribe a large portion of the account given of each district in the Gazetteers and Settlement Reports; the difficulty is to make a suitably small selection for the purposes of illustration.

In the SULTĀNPUR district I notice an 'estate' of 365 villages held by families of the *Bandalgotī* clan; the head still retaining, as landlord, the possession of 316 villages. This was due to the fact that up to the eleventh generation from the founder only one son was born; but at last there were more, and then the estate was divided and several village properties became separate.[2]

In BAHRAICH the great Ikhaunā estate might still be flourishing as an example of individual, territorial, foundation but for the events of the mutiny. It owed its origin to a single *Janwār* chief under Moslem patronage (for the chiefs long bore the military title of 'Risāldār'). Shāh Jahān made the estate revenue-free, and it became a landlord property. A number of villages (mentioned under the designation of *bhaiyāī*) were originally allotted to cadets of the family for their maintenance;

[1] *Ante*, p. 193, and cf. p. 288.

[2] *Oudh Gazetteer*, i. 47. As I have before remarked, it is perfectly immaterial, as regards origin, whether these villages did or did not in after times come under the power of Taluqdārs or landlords.

but after two or three generations they were found as independent estates having no connection with the chief, and were afterwards reduced to paying rent, separately, to a Taluqdār.[1] For the KHERI district (northern part) the writer of the Gazetteer notice makes some good remarks on the manner in which Rājput chieftains came to be able to establish their local rule. 'The *Çhatrī* ascendency,' he says, 'might be simply described as the re-establishment of local Hindu government under the native chief. There was no elaborate design or settled plan. A conqueror appeared and was often welcomed as giving some security against the oppression of neighbouring chiefs or of the suzerain government. The Rājā once established could . . . dispossess any of his subjects who showed signs of treachery or disloyalty. . . . He had many wives and many sons, bastard and legitimate; all the waste lands were his; all lapsed and forfeited villages also became his; with such lands he provided for the scions of his house.'[2] In this way much of the actual ownership of the land passed into the hands of his family. Four-fifths of the district, it is said. belonged to *Çhatrīs*, and three-fifths were under their ruling chiefs. Indeed, in Akbar's time, of the 223 *mahāl* (or *parganas*) of Oudh, eighty-seven were held by Çhatrī lords. Other tribesmen, as *Kayaths* and *Kurmīs*, might obtain village estates, but they never became rulers. But an able and adventurous *Çhatri* of noble descent could always get a local territory; and villages, as already remarked, would often gladly place themselves under him.[3] The Moslem Emperor was content to take a general revenue or tribute from such a chief, leaving to him the administration of justice; and the whole estate ceased to be borne on the imperial registers as *khālṣa* or directly subject to the imperial administration. It was merely a natural progression of things that 'the subjection of the land to the Rājā became first confused, and then identical, with his proprietorship.' In Oudh it often

[1] *Gazetteer*, i. 117, 122, 177 ff. [2] *Ibid.* ii. 140, 215 ff.

[3] *Ibid.* 207. Several instances are noted where the village landholders voluntarily placed themselves under the protection of the Rājā. This *hāth-rakhāi*, or *commendation*, is frequently found. The villages always ended by passing under the complete ownership of descendants of the chief's family.

happened that the Rājā became Taluqdār, and utimately was created *landlord* of the whole or a portion of his demesne; but, if the estate happened to be partitioned or the Rājā disappeared, being put to flight, or slain in battle after some unsuccessful revolt, the villages would continue to be held by some members of the family, and would become so many separate village-estates.

A most remarkable instance remains to be cited, and it illustrates the direct process of the division of a Rāj into both village-estates and larger landlord-properties. I refer to the case of the *Tilok Çandī Bais* estates in RAI-BARELI.[1]

The whole history is too long to be even summarised here, but the main facts are these: the district contains 1,735 villages, of which 1,719 are owned by descendants of Tilok Chand, who died shortly before Bābar ascended the throne of Delhi (A.D. 1526). The dominion, indeed, began before the chief's time, but he consolidated the position. He acknowledged the Mughal suzerainty and never assumed the title of Rājā personally; it was only taken by his eldest descendant at a later date.[2] At the present time there are about forty landlord estates containing several villages each and ranking as 'Taluqdāri' estates, and a great number of village-estates.[3] This resulted from the family at first admitting of partition and then agreeing to stop it. The elder branch represents the estate of Murārmau, in which the title of Rājā was afterwards taken; it was the several grandsons who, separating, originated the larger estates; and these again became variously subdivided in the course of time.

'The accounts,' writes Mr. Benett,[4] 'of the half century which elapsed between the death of Tilok Chand and the accession of Akbar are very meagre. . . . It may be surmised that the Rājā of Murārmau, the Rānā of Khiroñ, and some other chiefs of a different stock, each exercised on a smaller scale the sovereign powers of the first great Rājā (*i.e.* Tilok Chand).

[1] The whole history will be found in the *Gazetteer*, iii. 208 and 225 ff, and in Mr. Benett's *Chief Clans of Rai-Bareli* (Lucknow, 1870).

[2] *Gazetteer*, iii. 230–1.

[3] I cannot separate the single villages held by Tilok Chandī Bais from some held by Moslems and Kānhpurias; but out of the whole 1,735 villages 537 are independent of any Taluqdār over-lord.

[4] *Clans of Rai Bareli*, p. 53 ff.

Under the vigorous administration of Akbar and his successors, the Hindu clans were naturally much depressed, and driven, so to speak, nearer to the soil. Their connection with the villages in their domain became much closer; new villages were founded, and the increasing numbers of each family led to the establishment of the non-cultivating village-proprietors who are now known in our courts as the "*old zamīndārs.*" The intervention of a foreign ruler, and the diminished danger of invasion from without deprived the Rājās of half their attributes: the principle of unity was lost sight of, and each member of a leading house was able, when he separated, to assume, in his new home, almost all the privileges retained by the head of the family. The ties of kinsmanship were, however, still vividly recognised, and at the end of this period, instead of a few unconnected Rājās, we find hierarchies of powerful *landowners, each the immediate proprietor and landlord of a few villages from which he drew his subsistence* . . .' (the italics are mine). In this case it will be observed, although a clan unity so far prevails that kinship is acknowledged and kept up by the survival of the military spirit (always a strong incentive to its preservation), and by the fact that the Emperor would call on the chiefs to furnish levies for the imperial army, there is nothing of clan-custom observable in the mode of land-holding. The tenure is 'aristocratic' either in the form of larger landlordships or of jointly-owned, single, villages.

SECTION III.—VILLAGES FOUNDED BY INDIVIDUAL ADVENTURERS AND SETTLERS UNCONNECTED WITH THE STATE OR WITH TERRITORIAL CHIEFSHIP.

While a large number of villages have had their origin in some individual chief or dignified founder connected with a State or chiefship, it is also true that other founders have been private adventurers, settlers, or purchasers, without any territorial connection. It is convenient to separate the cases, because it facilitates discussion to classify our known origins of villages as far as possible. There is often, however, room for doubt whether in any given case the foundation more properly belongs to one specific kind or another; we may set down a case as apparently one of private adventure, though really there had been a royal grant, or the founder represents a remnant of a forgotten local rulership. This degree of doubt necessarily arises where the foundation is remote in time and the evidence chiefly traditional. The possibility of such error is, however, of slight importance so long as we can preserve the main distinction between the village arising out of the *clan or tribe*, and that arising out of *individual* foundation—in one form or another. For wherever we have the *clan*-group, and the clan sentiment of equal right, we have a different basis of constitution from what is observed in the case where an individual ancestor is remembered as the direct originator of the estate.

A typical case in point occurs in the GUJRĀNWĀLĀ district of the Panjāb, where we have a group of eighty-one communities (*pattidārī* in their original state) descended from a single founder. I do not know any evidence or traditional opinion that there was any local rule or chiefship; but the founder was himself of good family: the *Cātta* houses [1] claim descent from a *Çauhān* Rājput stock—indeed, from Rājā Prithwī Chand himself. But a single adventurer of the family, named Dhīru, in the tenth or eleventh generation, left his home and settled in a village called Sidhkot: he married two wives and had eighteen sons, from whom all the village-bodies are descended. Both in this district and in Siālkot, although the general prevalence of the *pattidārī* form of village indicates that a great number are held by bodies descended from adventurers or founders of some pretension to good birth, there is no definite trace of local rulerships out of which they sprang. Nor, on the other hand, does there appear to be anything of the *tribal* character in the villages in question. In SIĀLKOT as many as 2,155 villages are shown as shared on the 'ancestral' principle, of which 106 are held by the families undivided; [2] only 633 are put down as *bhaiāchārā*,

[1] The family finds a place in Sir Lepel Griffin's *Panjāb Chiefs*, where their history is given in detail.

[2] Unless I am misled by the term *zamīndārī* without any qualifying addition, which is much misused; it may mean villages owned by a single purchaser, &c., or by a group remaining undivided. Probably the latter (*shāmilāt* or *sānjī* villages) are meant. (*Siālkot Gazetteer*, 1883-4, p. 48.)

which, as the term is used in the Panjāb, includes villages that probably were originally 'ancestral,' but in which the ravages of time and circumstance have caused the regular shares to be modified or forgotten altogether. It is worth noting that in the earlier Settlement, Mr. E. Prinsep, illustrating the varieties of village as regards sharing, takes, as the standard natural to the district, the case of '*the founder* of a village who secures a property by purchase, grant, appropriation, or conquest;' and he goes on to show how the sons will hold undivided, how they ultimately separate, and how the *ancestral* shares of the separated houses are changed into *de facto* holdings or some other shares which have become 'customary.' This series of changes would be wholly inapplicable to cases where the estate did not begin with *one* founder, but where a whole clan had divided the conquered land, or where a clan grew up under its own customs of holding.

I have already alluded to a specific case from the GUJRĀNWĀLĀ district; but the totals of the different kinds of village in the whole district are also worthy of notice; though here a considerable number of villages are held on shares of a special kind which may indicate a different origin. But even allowing for these cases, the number of villages derived from *individual* founders is considerable. An analysis of the tables[1] shows a total of 1,199 villages, classifiable thus:—

Ancestral shares	138	held by single owners (40) and undivided families;
	211	wholly or partly divided,
	118	*partly* on ancestral shares,
	459	by a system of shares in *wells*,
	188	by a system of 'customary' shares,
	85	held 'on possession' only.
	1,199	

Even of the eighty-five, in the last line, it is quite possible that some really belong to the other classes, only that from one cause or another the shares have been completely lost. It is noteworthy that among the villages which acknowledged *shares*, no less than

[1] *S. R.* (Nisbet), printed in 1874. The figures are gathered from the tables at the end.

395 agreed to return to the correct list, some by voluntary surrender of excess lands, others by making up to those who had less than their proper share by additions out of the undivided culturable waste.[1]

These examples have been selected from the Panjāb Reports without difficulty, owing to the circumstances of the country. I have not been able to do the same for the North-West Provinces and Oudh, because, with a denser population, with a much greater number of local kingdoms and chiefships, and the wider prevalence of revenue-farming, in former days, it becomes almost impossible to separate the cases of private enterprise from those connected with territorial rulerships. It is not, however, to be doubted that villages due to private, individual, foundation, are just as common in the Ganges plain as they are in the Panjāb.

SECTION IV.—COLONIST ASSOCIATIONS

I do not at present include those ancient traces of villages in the Madras Tamil country, regarding which our most reasonable conclusion is that they were due to colonist families of an energetic agriculturist caste settled under patronage of a local prince, and who adopted an interesting method of co-operative village cultivation. It is only traces and traditions of these southern villages that now survive; and before I could bring them forward as instances of the formation of joint-villages by voluntary association, I should have, as I hope to do in a future chapter, to argue out the case for their existence, nature, and origin.

Here I am concerned with villages of a type actually existing and known. Such cases must necessarily be confined to sparsely populated districts, where large areas were, even in late historic times, awaiting cultivators energetic and patient enough to cope with the initial difficulties of establishing cultivation. The South-eastern Panjāb exhibits a natural field for such founda-

[1] It may also be noted that if we deduct 138 single owner or undivided villages, the remaining 1,061 (shared or held in severalty) show, as a whole, 636 in which the original system has undergone no change, and 425 in which under stress of time and circumstance it has been altered.

tions; and we are not surprised to find them quite characteristic of certain districts or parts of districts in that locality. In such villages there is no question of 'holding in common' except in so far as the unappropriated waste and grazing ground is so held. The villages have accepted the joint-responsibility under the modern revenue system, because their association would expressly contemplate cohesion for such purposes, not to speak of other countervailing advantages, such as acquiring defined rights in the adjacent waste area, which they may not have possessed before.

Villages founded by associated colonists are treated as cases of *individual* foundation, since the associates are neither a gradually expanding clan nor a tribal-group already formed. If some of the members happen to be connected by blood, which is quite likely, it is an accidental circumstance, and may have produced some sharing (as a family) of particular holdings, but not of the whole village. Complete extracts from the District Reports describing the mode of foundation, the planting of the stake (*moṛi*) to mark the central village-site, and the drawing lots for the 'plough-lands,' have been printed in my *Land Systems of British India* and need not be repeated here.[1] We find villages of this kind in the districts of FIROZPUR and what was formerly SIRSĀ.[2]

There is no doubt also that a similar origin may be ascribed to villages in other parts. It will be enough to call attention to the main features—viz. that the headman is the leader and spokesman of the party, who has perhaps conciliated some neighbouring chief or governor, and obtained his countenance to the projected settlement. Major and minor divisions of the culturable area were, or might be, arranged in the first instance to suit the requirements of different groups—probably different castes or different family aggregates; within these, the several 'plough-lands'—such is the general unit—were arranged and assigned to each settler according to his means, *i.e.* with reference to the plough cattle he possessed, and the number of hands he could bring to the work of cultivation; the plough-lands

[1] Vol. ii. p. 678 ff, and p. 689.

[2] The Sirsā district has been abolished, part of the territory being added to Firozpur, part to Hisār.

were taken by drawing lots for each, so that there might be no unfair distribution. As to the adjacent waste area, it was so little considered that no definite boundaries at first existed; and long afterwards, anyone of the settlers who chose could break up a new portion, outside his former allotment. Indeed, this was the cause of some trouble after the Land-Revenue Settlement was introduced, and a tenant law was provided. For then the waste was definitely surveyed and included in the village boundaries, and became *formally* the joint or 'common' property of the whole body, who were, under the system in question, regarded as the co-proprietors of the whole village. Consequently, after the survey and record of rights, no one could make a new field in the waste without proceedings for partition, or without asking permission of the whole body. Moreover, additional cultivators had been formerly allowed in as tenants, on the understanding, perhaps rather tacit than expressed, that the land they cleared and subdued to the plough would be left in their possession for ever. Under the first of the tenant laws (1868) such persons might find themselves treated as tenants *at will*, and be offered the option of a rise in rent or of notice to quit—a proceeding which, however legal, they regarded with indignation.

It is extremely difficult to apply the term 'collective ownership' to the rights in a village so constituted, at least before the days of Revenue records and surveys. The body was united for its own interest, and it accepted the joint liability for the Government Revenue, as one of the most natural objects of its association.[1] It is also curious to note that in some cases the headman and his sons managed to push themselves forward into a sort of proprietary position over the whole village, and exact some kind of rent from the other cultivators; in that case the village was distinguished as *boledārī* (*bolā*=agreement). In revenue parlance, the others were called *bhaiāchārā*, though not in the correct sense in which I have always used the term. I do

[1] As I have had occasion to observe before, in the days of bad or oppressive revenue management, it was a great matter for a combined body to be able to bargain for a lump sum which the collector would agree to, because it saved trouble; the village was thus secured from the inquisitorial visits and vexatious interference of the revenue-farmers' underlings.

not know of any specific instance where existing village bodies known to have originated as colonies and associations have adopted any other method of allotting the land than that of assigning separate numbers of 'plough-lands' taken by lot. But there are still many villages the origin of which is uncertain; and I suspect that not a few villages holding by shares in wells and in other modes (to be mentioned in the next chapter) are voluntary colonist associations. In any case, the form of sharing adopted will depend on the local conditions of agriculture. If such a colony, instead of being planted in open dry plains and prairies like those of Firozpur and Sirsā, had been formed in a dense jungle country like that of Southern India (*Tondai-maṇḍalam*) they might have adopted a different method; they might have all combined to clear an area gradually, and to work the land without any final allotment, determining year by year what portion each co-sharer should take in hand. We shall see, later on, reason to believe that this was really the mode of working in the villages in Southern India, which were once held 'jointly' under a noteworthy colonising enterprise.

Having now passed in review the various known origins of actually existing joint-villages, and seen how—apart from any general *a priori* theory—these villages, really grew up, it is evident that we have two great causes for union—(1) the existence of a tribal or clan stage of society with all that this stage implies, especially in the way of a right to share equally in the tribal acquisition; (2) the influence of the 'joint-family' and its law of joint-inheritance. And to these we might perhaps add a third—voluntary association and combination. Villages, or areas larger than villages, constituted under either influence are found to be divided into certain general—major and minor, primary and secondary—divisions of the land, and finally into individual shares. Thus, there are certain liens which tend to make each village, in some sense, a unit-estate. They are, therefore, brought under a system of Land-Revenue Management which, devised to suit the *prevailing* form of tenure, subjects all the village estates in the province to a similar system of demarcation, survey, and record. The system also applies a common nomenclature to them all; and thus, as it were, varnishes over the whole group with an appearance of uniformity which goes beyond any degree of similarity they naturally possess.[1]

It now remains to examine some details of the internal structure of joint-villages, and to note both the minor variations which occur and the modifications that the form of constitution may undergo. We have finally to notice the special cases of joint-village which are believed once to have existed in certain other parts of India, but which have become a subject of dispute because only traces of them now exist. These are very interesting to the historian as showing the growth, or at least the probable growth, of over-lord claims over what would otherwise be independent villages of the *raiyatwārī* type, and also the formation of villages under special circumstances in a joint or co-sharing form as exceptions to the prevailing tenure. If our inferences regarding these mostly long decayed landlord-villages are at all just, we shall have the phenomenon of the *raiyatwārī* village and the joint-village occurring in juxtaposition. But such a juxtaposition is not confined to these doubtful cases, nor is it dependent on inferences regarding the past; we shall also take occasion to describe certain cases where it can be seen in existence at the present day.

[1] By such a remark I do not intend to imply any disparagement of the system. As a matter of fact, in practical working, the North-West Provinces Revenue-system initiated by Regulation VII. of 1822 (and applied, with local modifications, to Orissa, to the Panjāb, to Oudh, to Ajmer, and to the Central Provinces) has proved remarkably elastic. In Orissa, for instance, the working is as nearly *raiyatwārī* as possible; and so in Ajmer, where the principle of the joint-responsibility has been reduced to a mere shadow. Indeed, the system is able practically to admit both the landlord right over large estates (as in Oudh and parts of the North-West Provinces) and what are really separate holdings in villages nominally joint.

CHAPTER VIII

THE VARIETIES AND MODIFICATIONS OF VILLAGE FORMS

We have seen hitherto that the existence of a group of agricultural holdings forming a village does not necessarily imply a single or uniform plan of internal constitution. The village may be a group of independent holdings; or it may be in one sense a unit, a share in which is held by every one of the resident owners who form the 'village community.' Or again it may be a group of lands which has been almost accidentally formed, the real area of 'collective ownership' (as far as the term is applicable) being something much larger than a village. In any case, the constitution may differ. The main forms or principles have now been discussed—the tribal, the joint-family or *pattidārī*, and the 'equalised-share' methods, &c. But each such method may exhibit in its application certain minor variations, just as in plants we may have 'species,' and under each a number of 'varieties.' Apart from this, modification arises subsequently owing to what I may call 'wear and tear.' Original shares are lost, sometimes partially, sometimes altogether, without any constitutional difference of principle.

There is one form of village which in the nature of things does not vary: the *raiyatwārī* form, being merely an aggregate of independent holdings, has no original varieties; nor can any change be introduced short of its conversion into a joint-village either by reason of some artificial process of Revenue management, or, so to speak, naturally, by the reduction of the cultivators to the rank of 'tenant,' under the influence of a co-sharing family, which establishes over-lord rights over the whole as the proprietory community. This is, however, not a variation of form, it is the supersession of one form by another. The superimposition of landlord rights has, no doubt, constantly occurred wherever conquering clans have settled, and wherever adventurers have acquired a dominion, or Rājās and Emperors have made grants, or the revenues have been farmed to some village-manager. But until such an over-lord arises, the independent group of land-holders, with its hereditary headman and its staff of artisans and menials, must necessarily remain unchanged.[1]

But when we come to the joint-villages—those held on some system of co-sharing—there is ample room for variety, both original and induced by accident.

In the first place, I may mention a general cause of modification which may affect any kind of really joint-village. There may be a portion of the village area not yet divided; and this circumstance, though of no particular interest in itself from the tenure point of view, may be of practical importance to the administration. We shall see presently that the official classification provides a distinct head for the *wholly* divided, and another for the *partly* divided villages. In the former there is neither arable nor waste land, except the site of the village temple or mosque, the graveyards, roads, and other such naturally indivisible areas, left unpartitioned;[2] in the latter, which is by far the larger class, an area of waste either wanted for grazing and wood-cutting, or not yet wanted for ploughing up, is still held in common. Sometimes, also, a portion of the arable is left undivided, because it is all in the hands of tenants—perhaps 'occupancy' or irremovable tenants—and the proprietors have no object in dividing it. This question of partial or total division may affect management in various ways;[3] but there is one

[1] I have already discussed the possibility of rights being destroyed and originally homogeneous bodies dispersed under the effects of harsh revenue administration; but nothing of the kind tends to alter the *raiyatwārī* form.

[2] Land which is unfit for cultivation and is otherwise impartible is spoken of as *ghair mumkin*; while the waste for grazing, &c., that may one day be utilised, is *mumkin—i.e.* 'possible' to cultivate. The village-site is often partitioned, because it gives the different co-sharers not only their due allotment for their own houses, but enables each to charge rents and derive other benefits from the house-sites which fall to his share.

[3] It may also be conveniently borne in mind that when a village is divided into *major* and *secondary* groups (called *pattī*, *thok*, &c.), the whole of the land may be divided between the groups, so that nothing remains

point where it also touches custom and the tenure form. It is sometimes observed that, while the divided arable land is held on one existing scheme of shares or on the basis of mere *de facto* possession, the common land and the profits from grazing, wild fruits, thatch-grass or similar produce, as well as other common profits or dues—house rates and the like—may be enjoyed or divided on a quite different set of shares. This usually indicates that the *original shares* of the foundation have been disturbed or forgotten, as regards the cultivated holdings, and yet the co-sharers do not like altogether to ignore their proper principle; they cannot help abandoning it as regards the lands that have long been held in severalty, but they still adhere to it as regards profits or lands which have not been yet divided.

We may now proceed to the more specific varieties. It may be a convenience shortly to recapitulate the list of *primary* joint forms before specifying these *variations*. We have: (1) villages held on a tribal basis. As a rule, the several allotments are made as equal as possible: of this class the frontier and some other Panjāb villages form our best examples. Here the 'joint-holding' depends on the sense of unity as a clan, and on the feeling that all are equal and may have to submit to exchange holdings with a view to giving effect to that equality. There is no particular bond constituting *village*-groups as such. (2) Villages held by 'cultivating fraternities,' where there has been no territorial rule and no aristocratic title in the family, but where, beginning with a small household-group settled on a wide area, there has gradually grown up a large clan. In some cases a group of villages has been formed like a number of buds shooting out from one parent stem, and then separating into so many full-blown new 'villages.' In other cases certain

common to the whole village (*shāmilāt dih*); but each *pattī* may have internally divided only part of its land, leaving some still common to the section (*shāmilāt pattī*). It very frequently happens that smaller family (or close kindred) groups hold their shares jointly because it would be so inconvenient to divide them. The co-sharers may recognise a fractional interest in a *pattī* which is represented by $\frac{1}{1000}$th part of a 'rupee' or less (see p. 315, *ante*); but such an interest cannot always be divided out on the ground, and must be enjoyed jointly with others or it would be useless.

primary, secondary, and tertiary divisions of the whole estate-area have been established in the days when there were but a few family members; but after that, all the multiplying descendants have obtained land *per capita* according to the actual requirements of each household as it came to maturity. There was no thought of any particular aliquot parts of the whole; only care was taken that *an equal division* of good and bad lands should be observed, and more especially that a valuation should be made so that the share of the burdens (land-revenue or any other charges) borne by each might be in just proportion to the value and extent of the land held.

In contrast with this cultivating-fraternity form, where some traces of *clan* feeling are still in evidence, stands the very large class of villages (3) where one individual, or one or two together, obtained or founded the village-estate; and here it is solely the 'joint-family' fully developed, and its consequent law of joint-inheritance, that has produced the joint-community. Here, too, the 'village' is essential; it is the limit of the grant or acquisition. The heirs will divide strictly on the *ancestral shares* indicated by the 'genealogical tree.' It is in this form that we have the stages, first, of the sole owner, then of his heirs holding undivided, and finally of complete or partial severance of the holdings. But in many such estates the division was made at a remote period. And there are some few cases where a kindred already numerous enough to form a village-group or something larger have, on acquiring a new domain, formed it and continue to subdivide it into so many *ancestral shares*, rather than into the *equal lots* of Nos. 1 and 2. The ancestral-share system is peculiarly open to give dissatisfaction as time goes on; it is also peculiarly liable to become modified by external agency.

(4) There is a class of village still having certain features of 'joint' holding—*e.g.* the common responsibility for the revenue, which is best described negatively; it is not 'tribal,' it is not *pattidārī*, nor is it held on the 'artificial *çak*,' or equalised-holding method. There is locally some peculiarity, derived from some unknown source: perhaps the village is a small surviving remnant from some once larger body which has gradually disappeared; often it is a voluntary association of cultivators, who

have combined for protection into a 'joint-body.' In these cases the 'shares' are of various kinds.

(5) Lastly, there is a large list of villages which is only separable because we are in the dark as to their real original mode of constitution. The 'co-sharers' hold each a certain separate area, and the fact of possession is the only known measure of right. The official classification has a special head for these '*de-facto*-holding' villages.[1]

Let us notice each head separately, and see what minor varieties are possible.

(1) It is difficult to say that there is any typical or normal form of the purely tribal village of the Panjāb. Regarding the co-sharers as persons, the village depends on the family connection which associates a number of kindred in one separate group, and on the conditions of life and locality which compel many small hamlets, or one large *ābādī*, as the case may be, to be formed. All we can ask is what is the type of tribal-*share*? The examples I have given show some variety in this respect which is evidently original and not induced. Generally, both in Bilūchī and Pathān tribes, the *larger* divisions follow the branches of the first ancestral family up to a certain point; [2] but within the *khel*, or other ultimate larger group, the single shares are *per capita* and equal. More rarely ancestral shares seem to be followed throughout, and up to the existing families. The principal changes that occur in such a distribution of holdings are more a matter of anticipation than anything else. The clan-connection, not being exercised in war, or by other occasions, will fall away and be forgotten; the general sense of the area as 'the clan possession' in which each member has his personal share or right will also fade away, especially with the abandonment of the old custom of periodic exchange of holdings which kept it alive, but which becomes impossible when time and labour expended for years past have produced well-cultivated fields and farms, and when records of title and maps of permanent holdings

[1] See Appendix to the chapter on the official classification of villages for statistical purposes.

[2] Even then the *ṭappā*, &c., are not made of equal size and value; they are larger or smaller according to the number of houses and families in each.

have been prepared. Under the system of dividing the land into lots composed of several pieces of different soils, there will be, I suppose, a gradual tendency for original differences to disappear under long cultivation, manuring, and watering; fields will then be voluntarily exchanged, and by these means holdings will in time become consolidated lots in one place.

(2) But in the communities which I have called the '*true bhaiāchārā*,' and of which the Airā-kherā estate in the MATHURĀ district[1] is a perfect example, there are several natural varieties if not subsequent modifications. It will be remembered that in all these cases of clan-holdings and fraternities growing up on the spot there is never anything in the nature of holding 'in common.' Certain large divisions may be established at an early stage of the growth of the body, and within these the household lots or shares for the later descendants in each group are added on, one by one, as the families increase. In these cases very large areas are usually occupied; and the first modification they undergo is that some of the family groups within each main division, having each built separate groups of houses, but regarding themselves as offshoots from the parent village and not at first disconnected from it, gradually blossom out into completely separate villages. Thus a large estate in the HAMĪRPUR district called Kheraila-khās, and containing 28½ square miles, was divided into six main *thok* or sections, and these have now become separate village estates. So in the same district, Patāra, an estate of over 9,000 acres, was divided into twelve sections (there called *behrī*), which have become as many 'villages.' The building of the separate residence, the increase of the houses, and the consequent completion of the village establishment, is what makes the separate 'village:' the lands belonging to it may still be scattered, and only brought into an aggregate in the official registers. But sometimes a large portion of the land happens to lie in one block, and then in the course of time outlying fields will be exchanged, and so the village and its land will be brought into a ring fence. Lastly, special customs of distributing the revenue charges according to standard valuation lots (*çak*, &c.) will be given up in favour of paying according to

[1] Described at p. 282 ff., *ante*.

the differential acreage-rates for soils established for assessment purposes by the Revenue-Settlement Officer.

But the *method of sharing* also shows some variation. Thus, in the BĀNDĀ district, if the village was composed of no more than the three chief varieties of soil—*mār*, *parwā*, and *rākār*—it was not necessary to make any complicated artificial lots, and for valuation of the holdings; it was sufficient to treat the members of the community as holding each a certain number of *bīghā* measures of land; but the *bīghā* of the worst soil was in fact two or three times as large as the *bīghā* of the best soil.[1] In MAINPURĪ, examples occur of villages in which advantage was taken of the natural belts into which the cultivation in the North-West Provinces generally is observed to fall: there is the *gauhān*, or land nearest the village site (central group of homesteads), which is always well irrigated and easy to manure, and is thus the most valuable and most successfully cultivated; next there is the *mānjhā*, or 'middle land,' not quite so good, because not so easily supplied with manure, and irrigation is perhaps less certain; lastly, there is the *bārhā*, or outlying zone of the poorest soil, probably rarely manured and largely dependent on the rainfall. Each holding will be represented on the basis of an artificial *tor* (or *tauzī-bīghā*) made up of a certain area in each zone of the best, middle, and outer land.[2] The holdings here are scattered, but very much less so than under the elaborate system of soil classification sometimes followed—such, for instance, as that noted from the Bastī district.[3]

I have not met with other specific forms of originally various (or afterwards modified) *bhaiāchārā* custom. The '*bhaiāchārā*, lot or share' must naturally vary with the simplicity or complexity of the actual soil distribution in the village. In a very uniform

[1] *Bāndā S. R.* p. 40. So that when the revenues are distributed at a uniform sum 'per *bīghā*,' the payment is in fact fairly equal.

[2] *North-West Provinces Gazetteer*, iv. 600. Thus, in one village the standard lot was large, viz. 90 *bīghās* (actual measure), composed of 25 of the best + 30 of the middle + 35 of the poorest. In another village, where the lots were numerous and consequently smaller, I find 819 lots each of 24 actual *bīghās* (6 of the best + 8 of the middle + 10 of the outer soil-zone).

[3] See p. 291, *ante*.

locality the shares may be of the simplest description;[1] where the soil varies much each share or lot will be a very composite one. In the latter case serious practical difficulty is to be looked for in the future. The tendency in such estates (as noted, *e.g.*, in the ETĀWĀ S. R., which is worth consulting on the subject), is for the shares to become excessively subdivided; and then the fact that the holding is already perhaps in three or five or more portions tells awkwardly; for each portion has to undergo the same process of subdivision. The result is that unless the cultivators are of superior energy, or are able to devise some remedy and to send off their surplus hands to some other occupation, they will surely fall into poverty and lose the ownership altogether. In this district, the prospects of the much divided *bhaiāchārā* estates are not very promising: the Settlement Officer notices that the *paṭwārī* (village accountant) is the only person who knows how to keep the accounts of the numerous little separate holdings, and how to apportion the revenue payment; he rules them all accordingly; the *pançayat* has ceased to exist, and 'self-government' is a delusion.

(3) The ancestral-share, or *pattidārī*, villages are the most likely to change of any. Here it will be remembered that, theoretically, if a man owns (owing to his place in the genealogical table) say $\frac{1}{8}$ of $\frac{1}{3}$ of $\frac{1}{4}$ ($= \frac{1}{96}$) of the *pattī* or main branch to which he belongs, he ought to be holding $\frac{1}{96}$ of the cultivated area, to be entitled (on partition) to the same fraction of the waste, and to be paying $\frac{1}{96}$ of the assessed land revenue and common expenses of the *pattī*. But long before the village has got to this number of small shares it will probably be found that the correct fractions[2] have been partially, at any rate, lost sight of. The causes are several; they are sometimes natural,

[1] It is to be regretted that the method of sharing in the large Jihlam clan-estates or villages (*ante*, p. 270) is not on record. I believe, however, that it is by simple plough-lands allotted in each group according to the requirements of the households at the time, there being great similarity of soil throughout.

[2] It will always be remembered that the arithmetic of vulgar fractions was not known in former days to the village population, any more than it was to the devisers of the extraordinarily clumsy provisions (as they appear to us) for dividing the estate under the Muhammadan law of inheritance.

but still more often they are the result of external pressure on the village resources. In the first place, after the co-sharers had gone through a certain term of practical experience of working their separate shares, it must often have proved that two portions designed to represent perfectly equal fractional-shares are by no means equal in working value; at least, they are not equally productive in the hands of the actual holders. When this inequality is general, the co-sharers will probably not alter the holdings, but will give up the attempt to distribute the charges according to the proper (corresponding) fractions, and will agree to a *bāçh* (as it is called), which will re-distribute the burdens in a more equitable manner. And then the holdings themselves rarely remain unaltered in extent: one man finds himself able to cultivate more waste land and increases his holding; another sells a part of his share to his neighbour, or becomes poor and leaves the village, in which case his holding is distributed perhaps between not more than two who are willing to undertake to pay the revenue; or it is absorbed by the headman, &c. This goes on till a great many sharers have more or less than their true fraction. But a still more fruitful cause of change is the heavy lump-assessment laid on the village by some former rapacious native governor; all the holders had then to pay what they could and to cultivate what they could to make up the total and avoid being ruined or ejected from their ancestral home. Possibly, too, they would have to call in outsiders to help; and these may have needed to be coaxed by promises of admission as co-sharers or as tenants with special privileges—such as paying nothing beyond the Government assessment on their land. Case after case occurs in our records where this has actually happened. In the Panjāb it was indeed the normal state of things under successive Sikh governments; with them it was the regular plan to take everything that could be got, from everyone—no matter whether he was owner or tenant—who held land. Shares then ceased to have much practical value; and it is not surprising that the correct scale was often forgotten or voluntarily abandoned or altered, while the village body were unwilling to give up their ancestral lands

Hence division by fractions was always a roughly and clumsily performed operation. Cf. p. 263, *ante*.

en bloc if they possibly could help it. After some years, or perhaps a generation or two, it is too late to rectify the shares, when better times come round; the larger holders will stand out for their *de facto* holding on the ground of their larger payments; the weaker ones will have to submit; and the only relief is that the existing revenue assessment can, by law, be distributed in accordance with the actual holdings, or at rates per acre, of the different kinds of soil.

I expect also that irregularity must frequently have arisen from the mode in which the land was held before formal partition.[1] Each co-sharer gets possession of a certain home-farm, or *sīr* land; and this he continues to hold on the understanding that when a regular partition is demanded he will have to submit to give or take as the case may be; for the land held by each in this way may be more or may be less than the proper fractional share of the whole village, or of any section of it. When at last a partition is made, there is a struggle, in which each sharer hopes to keep what he has previously been enjoying; and it is quite possible that some irregularity is submitted to by the weaker members, and that the stronger come off the gainers. But, whatever the cause of the inequality, it is first made tolerable by dropping the fractions, as far as revenue payment is concerned, and making the charges correspond to the area actually held. In the end the villages frequently consent to remain 'as they are.' Sometimes they will allow the *de facto* holdings to be recorded, and then, of course, the change is stereotyped. Sometimes they will desire to have the proper list of shares recorded, but the possession does not, in fact, correspond; this means that there is some lingering idea that one day or other the correct shares will be restored. But it must be remembered that there is in most communities considerable pride taken in the *pattidārī* form, as being intimately connected with the maintenance of the family dignity; and I have given an instance of at least one district where the co-sharers agreed to correct the existing holdings either by surrender of excess lands, or by making up to those whose holding was deficient, by means of a special allotment out of the culturable common waste.[2]

[1] See *post*, p. 347.

[2] *Ante*, p. 323.

It is also frequently observed that, while *de facto* holding has been acquiesced in as regards the old cultivated land, the 'manorial' profits of the waste lands, or from fruits, grass, grazing fees, house-dues, and other miscellaneous sources, are still divided on ancestral shares, and that the culturable waste will be partitioned on the ancestral shares also. In such cases we have estates partly held on shares and partly on *de facto* possession. This is one of the reasons why the official classification provides a separate heading for 'imperfect *pattidārī* villages,' which means that part of the land is undivided, and possibly *also* that the divided and undivided portions are shared on different principles. It may be added that for the same reason an 'imperfect *bhaiāchārā*' may exist; part of the land may be retained in common; and there may be cases where a different principle has been introduced in the two portions. (I do not, however, know of any such, at least in the real 'customary share' class of village.)

If we tabulate the variations of the *ancestrally-shared villages*, we have:

1. Held on fairly correct shares; at least the principle is acknowledged throughout.[1]	
2. Held partly *de facto* (home farms out of proportion to the correct share); and the rest (common land, profits of a miscellaneous kind, &c.) divided on the correct ancestral shares.	*a.* Separate (existing) possession has become unalterable by record in the Papers of Settlement. *b.* Separate possession has not been recorded.
3. Ancestral shares have become completely lost or upset and disused.	*a.* Existing possession fixed by record. *b.* Only a list of shareholders recorded, and cultivation arranged for each year.[2]

[1] These occur where the land is partitioned, and also where the whole land is held by tenants, and managed by one man on behalf of an undivided body, who share the profits ancestrally.

[2] Mr. Whiteway, author of the *Mathura S.R.*, informs me that such cases do exist, but are very rare.

The effect of heavy revenue-assessments in producing tenure modifications is not confined to *pattidārī* villages; it may be observed in any class; it may break down whatever system of shares existed. It was doubtless this oppression that led to the *bhejbarār* custom, which prevailed at one time, especially in the districts of Bāndā, Allāhābād, &c.[1] Here, quite irrespective of any original or theoretical distribution of burdens, the revenue charge was in former days periodically redistributed so as to suit the actual cultivation of each member; and the liability of an insolvent member was distributed rateably among the others. This was done, not because they held the land in common, which they never did, but because they were still one clan or one 'wide-kindred,' as the case might be, and this was the most feasible mode of preserving their united existence as land-holders. Over-assessment, too, must have led to various arrangements for admitting new cultivators; and especially to the absconding or withdrawal of some of the co-sharers, who some years later would seek to be readmitted, but most probably would be allowed a smaller holding than they had once enjoyed, and perhaps an inferior position.

In the GUJRĀT district of the Panjāb, Mr. Tupper[2] notices how oppression under Ahmad Shāh Durāni led various sections of different tribes or families to club together and effect 'a much greater concentration of the village communities' than had existed before. We have seen how, in distant Kāchār,[3] the settlers formed joint-stock communities, doubtless to enable them unitedly to meet the revenue charge, and to ward off internal interference with their affairs. And so they did under the *vīsābadi* system in North Madras. In some of these cases we observe the effect of a sense of strength given by voluntary combination; but in others, as in the GUJRĀT district, the elements combining were already tribal, or at least kindred groups, and the natural sense of tribal-union maintained the combination; but each group kept to itself, and formed a distinct

[1] This custom is fully described in *L. S. B. I.* ii. 143. It was certainly, while it lasted, an expression of the solidarity of the village; as all consented to a periodical readjustment of their proportionate payments, and in some cases to a correction of holdings.

[2] *Cust. Law*, ii. 31.

[3] *Ante*, p. 140.

turf, or section of the village. In most cases, too, the result of heavy exactions was to confuse the co-sharers with their tenants and cultivators: 'responsibilities were imposed on the founder's kin, or immigrant outsiders indifferently.' Naturally, in after times, the outsiders, who had borne the burden equally with the nominal 'owners,' claimed their just privilege, and the modern Revenue Law cut the knot by creating for them a special status of *mālik maqbūza*, or 'proprietors of the holding,' without any interest in the general management of the village or share in the common lands or miscellaneous profits of the whole.[1]

There is also a curious feature connected with the *pattidārī* principle of sharing which is observed in Oudh and the North-West Provinces and possibly elsewhere. It will be found in cases where the existing proprietors are groups of families which had established their over-lordship over a number of village-areas already existing; and they have declined to accept the existing villages as the 'shell' into which the growing communities will fit. As the landlord family multiplied, it partitioned, and then the sections partitioned again. Such a partition might have given, say, a single village to each branch of the kindred, and that would be subdivided into *pattī*, &c., for the lesser branches; then we should have a number of separate and compact village-estates, each owned by the descendants of the particular head to whom the village was allotted. But very often, actuated by a desire to secure a more equitable division of the property, the heads of groups who were to receive the separate major-shares got part of their allotment in one geographical village, and part in another, or in several others; so that here the

[1] This is only one way in which such cases of limited or secondary proprietary-right to plots of land within the village estate come to exist. In other cases such persons have been recognised in view of the fact that originally they were full proprietors, but their rights had been overborne by the growth of a new general proprietary body over their heads as, *e.g.*, in the case of the *mālik maqbūza* in Central Provinces villages, or with the *'arāzidār* and *mushakhsidār* in parts of the North West-Provinces.

It must be remembered that in the old days the village 'solidarity' was much more felt than it is now, and that there were many cases (even in the North-West Provinces) where tenants were welcomed to help cultivate, and *no one thought of taking rent from them.* The burdens were distributed rateably over the whole, and all paid alike.

estate, or *mahāl* (group of lands held under one title), has to be gathered together on paper, and cannot be a compact area on the ground. In the 'ĀZAMGARH district, for example, to which I have so often referred for illustrations from its curiously subdivided villages, 'one *pattī* may hold its land in one or two *mauzas* (geographical or survey village), another *pattī* in another *mauza* or two, and a third *pattī* in a third, while all the *pattīs* hold in the remaining *mauzas*; but generally all the *pattīs* have shares in all the *mauzas*.'[1] As the families are much attached to certain places of residence, which are also divided, it happens that many groups of land belonging to one section of a family, have *no village site*: the owners continue to reside at some other centre. Such areas are technically said to be *be-çirāghī*, or 'without a lamp.'[2] It is often only the larger and important villages that are finally subdivided down to the household shares; in others the lands for the whole *pattī* have long ago been defined, but the families within the *pattī* manage their holding jointly—very probably collecting and dividing the rents obtained from the tenants. This peculiarity, it will be observed, affects the land; it does not alter the ancestral shares or the constitution of the groups of families. Such groups may be subject to the loss of their correct share-system and so forth, just as if they were enjoying a compact area of land.

(4) I have made this head—for the remaining villages, sometimes colonist groups and sometimes of other origins, in which neither the tribal nor the *pattidārī* methods of division are followed. Colonist villages—known to have had that origin—have been described as a well-known feature of the South-eastern Panjāb. But when we have taken note of those *known* origins which we can classify, there are still a large number of villages found here and there with local, special, or apparently exceptional methods of sharing, of which the origin is not always known. Any small tribal or family group may locally adopt some method of sharing which is peculiar. Thus, among the Ghakar clans of the Northern Panjāb, in an *'ilāqa* or tribal territory called Sohān, the allotment of lands was made with reference to military

[1] *Azimgarh S. R.* 'Government Review,' § 2.

[2] *Ibid.* §§ 326-8, pp. 92, 93.

rank, as horseman. or foot-soldier, or *asāmī* (ordinary person). The share for the former was one-third as much again as the latter. For family purposes the 'horseman' share was divided into four *sum* (=hoof). And so in a village in the Hazārā district I have noticed shares (called *dogī*) each subdivided into four *pair* (=feet), and each *pair* into four *kharsandi* (or toes).[1] These are some of the exceptional and local cases.

A much more widely spread mode of sharing is found in the Panjāb, and occasionally in the North-West Provinces; we are led to suppose that the villages adopting it are frequently groups of voluntary associates. It is observed when cultivation is carried on by means of irrigation-wells. The settlers have combined to sink the number necessary, and shares in the village are reckoned by shares in the wells which water, or at least partially protect, the whole arable portion. One well, with the area nominally attached to it, will be divided among three sharers, another among six, and so on. The actual watering is managed by each sharer taking possession of the well apparatus, attaching his own bullocks, and working it (letting the water run into his own channels) for so many hours in the working day, or on so many days in the week. In the JHĀNSI district, North-West Provinces, there are whole villages (called *kūābādī* villages) worked in this way; but there is a peculiarity in the management, as all the fields are not always irrigable, nor the same fields under crop; so the revenue is assessed in a lump sum *per* 'well,' covering both the land regularly watered and the outlying fields, which can only occasionally in favourable seasons get irrigated.[2]

In villages of uniform soil, another common mode of sharing is to divide the land into lots (of varying number of acres), called 'ploughs,' the unit being the quantity of land which it is supposed one pair of oxen can plough. If necessary, the 'plough' is subdivided into 'bullocks,' and each 'bullock' into 'legs.'[3] Sometimes the division is effected by counting the cattle and allotting the area into so many portions representing each 'one bullock'—one family will hold two, another ten, and so on. Here the only 'joint' element in the village is the 'common

[1] *L. S. B. I.* ii. 639. [2] *North-West Provinces Gazetteer*, ii. 281.
[3] See *L. S. B. I.* ii. 143.

waste' allotted to the village, and recorded as their joint-property, and the common responsibility for the land revenue; the actual holdings are, and always have been, separate.

It is hardly necessary to specify separately, as cases of modification, the change of a joint-village of one form into a village of another form, by sale, or grant, or by some voluntary adoption of a new plan of holding. Yet such cases do occur. I have elsewhere given an account of a village in the Tirohān *pargana* (BĀNDA district) where a *bhaiāchārā* village became granted to three Brahman proprietors, and so technically became a *pattidārī* village. A village called Tūrā was another case in which part became held under one principle and part under another.[1] The largest class of transformation cases is where the old constitution has been lost completely, without any apparent or traceable grant, purchase, or usurpation of over-lord rights—where, indeed, no definite explanation can be given.

(5) And this will serve to remind us that after enumerating the varieties and *known* modifications of the several forms of village, it is necessary to take account of the many villages which, having made no objection to the joint liability under the North-west Land-revenue system, and having accepted the common area of waste attached to their group, are reckoned as 'joint-villages,' and yet there is no trace of any particular foundation, or of any share-system; the cultivated land is held simply on the basis of *de-facto possession*—*i.e.* every member of the community has come to hold a certain area of land—how, he does not know.

Each holding is enjoyed in complete severalty, but the whole village admits its joint responsibility for the revenue. Should it happen that there is a waste area to be divided, the division will take place *ḥasb-rasad-khewat*—according to the proportion of land held in the arable, or to the amount of revenue paid. Even if this 'possession' is believed to represent a modification of *an earlier system of regular ancestral or other shares*, still it is now irrevocable. But very often nothing *is* remembered; and the holders say that their holding was always

[1] Both the cases are given in detail in *L. S. B. I.* ii. 147, 148, and need not be further described here.

merely according to what they wanted or could manage (*kāsht ḥasb maqdūr*), or that their holding was what 'Providence gave them' (*dād illāhi*).

In some such cases, possession is now the sole measure of right in the arable land; but the existence of ancestral or other shares is acknowledged as regards the waste and the manorial profits. These cases have been already alluded to.

There is, however, one class of cases in which '*de-facto* possession' is the sole measure of right throughout, in which it is highly probable that original shares are unknown because there never were any; the villages were originally *raiyatwārī*, and no landlord family happened to have acquired them. Such villages merely became 'joint' by the example of the neighbouring estates and the application of the prevalent Land-revenue system.

In some districts such a change has been artificially effected. For example, in the little province of AJMER (the only British possession in Rājputāna), the villages were *raiyatwārī*, but were brought under the North-West Provinces Settlement, and made 'joint' by the grant in common of the adjacent waste; but the joint responsibility was so little adapted to the circumstances of the communities that at the later Settlements it has been virtually abrogated.

In the CENTRAL PROVINCES the same thing happened, only in a peculiar form; for there the whole village was not treated as the joint proprietary body, but the headman, or more frequently the Marāthā Revenue manager, or *māl-guzār* (as he was afterwards called), was made sole proprietor, only with large reservations of the rights of the original cultivators; so that there we have the peculiar feature of landlord-villages, only that the landlords have no power of interference with the rent-payments, or with the management of a considerable portion of their tenants.[1]

Then, again, there are the districts, like Kāngrā and Kumāon, where, as we have seen, there were no villages, but the hamlets have been aggregated into circles, and certain areas of common waste and forest given to each, and so the circles have been

[1] The Ajmer and the Central Provinces systems are fully described in *L. S. B. I.* vol. ii.

formed into villages. The same thing happened with the isolated 'wells' in the South-western Panjāb. Here the *land* has practically come to be a bond of union, as the separate farms formed into groups have accepted the joint constitution; they have even adopted the custom of pre-emption, basing it, as might be expected, on the principle of mere contiguity or vicinage. 'Individuals,' writes Mr. Roe,[1] 'have sunk wells in the waste, receiving a grant from Government of from sixteen to fifty acres of land; and where such grants lie near together they have been formed into a village and the intervening waste thrown in as common land. I myself as Settlement Officer, have created several such villages in the Montgomery and Multān "Bār" dry tract. More were so erected under native rule, and very probably in some cases the families have come together of their own accord.' In these isolated and afterwards artificially aggregated holdings, some curious customs of right have sprung up. In the first place, in many cases, families of some pretension have gained the over-lordship over such villages, or, may be, over a considerable tract of country, and have been able to exact a kind of over-lord fee.[2] Sometimes the landlord also settled a cultivator under what is known as the *ādhlāpī* custom, by which the cultivator who sinks the well (without which tillage would be impossible) becomes customary owner of *half* the land, and the landlord of the other half; very frequently the well-sinker would also permanently occupy the landlord's half, paying him rent for it. Under this state of things also appears another custom, the *kasūr khwār* (=eater of fractions), where the owner of the land employs someone with capital to sink the well, and the latter receives certain dues (*kasūr-sil-çāh*) or portion of the produce 'for the bricks of the well.' In Sikh days, the local governors often ignored the over-lord, and assumed their own right to locate settlers on *çak*, or allotments of waste. These settlers were then able to sink wells and hold on what is called a *çakdārī* tenure. It might be that the grantee (*çakdār*) was unable himself to sink the well, and put in a tenant who

[1] *Tribal Law in the Panjāb*, p. 8, and *note*.

[2] See *L. S. B. I.* ii. 661, and iii., chapter on Sindh. It was in this way that the 'zamindārī' rights in Sindh grew up over aggregates of scattered settlements which answered to villages.

did so; in such a case the tenant became irremovable, and is now recorded as 'inferior proprietor;' he is entitled to take the produce after paying the revenue, the over-lord's *ḥaq*, or fee. if there is one, and certain dues (in kind and called *kasūr*) to the *çakdār*.

While time and circumstances have thus produced many varieties in the holding of village lands, there has been one thing that has perhaps tended to preserve the constitution to some extent, and that is the facility with which the revenue and other burdens can be specially distributed over the holdings by a *bāçh*, or scheme in which (without altering the extent and character of the holdings themselves) earlier methods of fractional or artifical-lot valuation are given up and the revenue is distributed over the actual holding, either by an all-round acreage-rate sufficient to cover the total sum, or by different acreage rates, which vary with the value of the soil, or by some other method. Mr. D. G. Barkley enumerates eight such methods, used in the Panjāb;[1] but this includes the methods which are normal, viz. where the payment is according to the proper or theoretical shares. Omitting these, the other methods adopted are—(1) to pay by a rate on each whole *well* (*kūhgārī*), (2) by a rate on the actual *ploughs* possessed by each co-sharer (*halsārī*), (3) by an *all-round acreage* rate, (4) by *rates* varying with reference to the land being irrigated or unirrigated—*i.e.* dependent on rain-fall, (5) by rates on the *several descriptions of soil*, (6) by a rate on the *houses* or families (*garh sārī*) proportionate to the number and ability of each, (7) by a rate according to the *cattle* possessed (*dum sārī* —*i.e.* counting 'tails.') Whatever general method is in force, there may be different ways of applying it. It may be, for instance, that rents of the tenant lands, and rents, usually light, applied to the lands in the possession of the several co-sharers, are all levied and collected, or, at any rate, brought to account, at contract or customary rates. This sum, together with all miscellaneous and 'manorial' income added, is first applied to pay the revenue and rates and the common expenses of the village—entertainment of guests, repairs of village public buildings, and, I fear, we must add, bribes to officials, and cost

[1] See his Panjāb edition of Thomason's *Directions to Revenue Officers*, p. 44.

of supplying free rations to man and beast, as shown in the shop-books of the grocer, the grain dealer, the money-lender, or the headman, who disbursed them in the first instance, and then the surplus is distributed according to shares. Otherwise the proceeds of tenant-rents on the undivided land, and other items of general income, go to pay the revenue and expenses, and, if they do not suffice, a rate is levied on the co-sharers' holdings, according to one or other of the above methods, just sufficient to make up the total charges. There are no profits, of course, under this latter system.

It follows almost naturally, from this, to pass on to explain what is usually meant by holding a village 'in common.' I do not here speak of the mere leaving to the common use and enjoyment a certain area of waste and grazing ground. Such land is often left undivided, not because of any inherent idea of community of goods of which this is a relic, but for reasons already stated. I refer to the areas where the *whole village* is held 'in common' by the proprietors themselves. This usually happens in villages where the community are the coheirs of one founder; they are jealous of each other, and regard partition as likely to give an undue start to some one or more members, which will give him or them an advantage over the rest. More rarely it happens, when there is some peculiarity in the soil, or some other circumstances which make it desirable for the body either to cultivate the land, and, after paying the revenue and expenses, to divide the surplus on *known shares*, or else to manage the cultivation by an arrangement effected year by year; each co-sharer takes up, for the year, such a plot as is assigned to him, without calling it his own; in that case each takes the produce of what he has actually cultivated; this is the most usual plan.

In the Panjāb, for example, I may quote Mr. Roe's description; and I believe that it correctly represents what happens in other places where there are undivided villages cultivated by the proprietors. Each co-sharer actually takes as his 'home-farm'—*i.e.* some area which he holds in possession, though as yet there has been no partition—and he enjoys the whole produce of that, either paying a light rent for it to the common fund or otherwise. After observing that there is no such thing as a common house or common table, and that each family has its own 'house with its surroundings, the privacy of which is strictly guarded,' Mr. Roe continues:

'Nor do we find . . . even in joint (*i.e.* undivided) villages, or even in joint holdings, that the produce of the cultivated lands is ever really brought to a common stock, and then distributed. What happens in practice is that each cultivating proprietor takes the whole of the produce of whatever portion of the joint land he actually cultivates, and pays the land revenue assessed on it, and perhaps a light rent in addition. This rent, and all rents paid by tenants, and all income derived from the waste, go to the common fund or *malba* [1] . . . If there is any surplus, it is not distributed in cash, but the headmen with whom the administration of the common fund rests, if they do not embezzle it themselves, apply it to payment of the land revenue, thus reducing the amount to be paid by each shareholder.' [2]

From these considerations we shall now be able to summarise the actual *varieties* of the different kinds of village, as we have already summarised the various *origins* from which the bodies of owners sprang. A reference to the *Appendix* will then show how the official vernacular terms come into use, and how the classification adopted in all general returns is valueless *as far as the real tenure distinction is concerned.*

(i.) The *raiyatwārī* village, which has remained as such in all those provinces where no attempt has been made to establish middle-men, or to aggregate the separate holdings artificially, *i.e.* to make a general estate by including a portion of waste, which may be partitioned, and imposing a joint responsibility for a lump sum of revenue assessed on the estate as a unit.

(ii.) The *zamindārī khālis*, or 'sole landlord' village, where one single person concentrates in himself the right to all the land and all the rents, &c., in the village.

(iii.) The *zamindārī mushtarka*, or jointly held, undivided village, where the body of nearly related agnates, descendants of one original landlord, own the village, and have not

[1] This term has been explained above.

[2] *Tribal Law in the Panjāb*, p. 9.

divided it at all—*i.e.* by any formal partition. In rare cases, a joint-holding, as I have remarked, may result from other causes.

(iv.) The village partitioned and held on *ancestral* shares—the legal, or fractional shares of the law or custom of inheritance pure and simple. Rarely these shares are correct or perfect; but if the principle is acknowledged over the whole of the land, the village is rightly put in this class. We have in this case either the result of a formal partition made recently, or at all events subsequently to a known period of previous undivided holding; but very often a state of division has immemorially existed. In most cases, however, it does result from the antecedent holding of some founder, or a small number of such founders whose names still adhere to the *pattī*, or main sections. In certain cases it may be that a sufficiently numerous family has conquered or gained an estate, and has divided it out, on settling down, in *ancestral* fractional shares throughout.

(v.) The purely *tribal* village, usually held in shares on some plan of equal holding, such as we see in the definitely tribal cases of Bilūchi and Pathān frontier villages, and in some large tribal villages in the North Panjāb and elsewhere.

(vi.) But we also include the 'cultivating fraternities' of 'democratic' or non-monarchical clans, exhibiting many of the same features of connected groups of hamlets, occupying a large and continuous area. The shares are usually equalised lots made up of different soils, and subject to a peculiar mode of calculating value. These villages ought to be called (and only these) *bhaiāchārā*.

(vii.) All villages held on 'ploughs,' 'well-shares,' and other 'fancy' methods of allotment, always divided, which may be colonist-associations voluntarily formed out of more or less miscellaneous elements; or they may be tribal or family groups, which have adopted this particular method for reasons which are not now discoverable.

(viii.) We have also to add villages now retaining something of the corporate feeling, the relics of a family or a tribal union, but who have lost or never possessed any *calculated share* of the unit-estate, and have separate holdings, of which all that can be said is that possession is now the sole measure of interest.

(ix.) Lastly, we may make a class, or rather two sub-classes, for what are officially termed the 'imperfect' forms of partitioned village estates. If a portion of the estate is left undivided, this fact alone puts the village, for official purposes, into the 'imperfect' class, whether of *pattidārī* or other. From a tenure point of view, this partial indivision is only interesting when it involves the fact that one method of sharing is applied to the divided cultivated land, and another, *very probably the old or original scheme* of the estate, to sharing the waste, or dividing the common profits. So that really this class gives us the 'transition' village, where the loss of the ancestral or some other kind of share is not quite complete—the village is not yet wholly relegated to the eighth head, where *de-facto* possession is alone recognised. This head, then, includes the 'imperfect' *pattidārī* and the imperfect *bhaiāchārā*, or any other kind of *shared* estate.

With these nine heads of real difference and variety, it will now be easy to compare the heads of classification which were indicated in Mr. Thomason's *Directions to Revenue Officers* in the forties; these have, with singular infelicity, been adopted ever since for official purposes, the terms getting slightly, or sometimes completely, misused in different places.

The headings of the statistical tables are:[1]—

(i.) '*Zamindārī*' generally employed to mean *either* a sole landlord *or* an undivided body. I suppose because it was troublesome to write the distinguishing vernacular additions—*khālis* (sole), *mushtarka* (joint), which alone give any sense to the term.

(ii.) *Pattīdārī*, divided on legal or *ancestral* shares, often, however, allowed to include other settled schemes of shares besides.

(iii.) Imperfect *pattīdārī*, partly so divided, *and* including the large class where the two portions are shared in different ways.

(iv.) *Bhaiāchārā*, which in the Panjāb has been strangely appropriated[2] to mean villages held *on possession only*, but which

[1] The *raiyatwārī* village is acknowledged, but it does not appear in Mr. Thomason's list, as such villages are not recognised under the North-West system.

[2] See Barkley's edition of the *Directions*, p. 44.

is, in practice, used to include also any kind of 'equal-lot,' 'plough,' 'well,' or other kind of shares which are not 'legal' or 'ancestral.' [1]

(v.) There is the 'imperfect' form of No. 4, either where there is merely part of the land undivided, or where part is undivided, and also enjoyed on a different principle.

If the 'imperfect' class is held to refer mainly to the fact that *two parts of a village estate are held on different principles*, then, of course, 'imperfect' *pattidārī* and imperfect *bhaiāchārā* can be, and very often are, lumped together in official returns.

In the light of our present knowledge of custom and our general interest in tenure-forms, such a classification is worse than none at all. When it was first invented, it served as a rough and ready means of distinguishing villages for office and administrative purposes. It had, and was intended to have, no other use or value.

In conclusion, it may be well to remark that there is considerable practical difference betwern joint-villages held by owners of a completely non-agricultural caste and those held by Jats and other agricultural communities. The distinction is not, however, formal, nor does it give rise to actual variations of tenure.

In the Panjāb, it will be remembered that by far the larger number of villages are cultivated by the co-sharing families themselves; even the women take a large share in the work. When there are tenants, it is because the co-sharers have more land than they can manage, and are able to call in 'tenants at will;' or because in the old days a tenant class was associated to help in 'the founding,' or were called in to help cultivate more land to make up the heavy demands of the State Officers. Sometimes such tenants (or, may be, 'inferior-proprietors') are reduced members of earlier, once proprietary, families, or of grantees or other families who have gained a footing in other ways. In such cases it is quite common to find 'tenants' paying no rent—they are, in fact, only cultivators, just like the proprietors, with the exception that they have no concern in the profits of the estate and no voice in its management. But the revenue and

[1] *E.g.*, the artificial villages of Ajmer and Kāngrā are so classed, and most of the Panjāb tribal villages, which are really a class apart.

cesses are distributed rateably over the whole of the cultivated land—sharers and tenants alike.[1]

In the North-West Provinces, again, it is much more common to find the village co-sharers non-agricultural; and then either the whole land is managed by tenants who may or may not have been located by the owners, or, which is very common indeed, a large portion of the land is held by tenants who represent the original cultivating body over whom the 'community' of proprietors grew up. In such a case the whole estate may be simply managed by one man, who collects the rents and divides them, after paying revenue and expenses. Or, more commonly, each co-sharer will have taken a certain holding, called his *sīr*, or home-farm. This farm he cultivates by his own personal tenants and farm-labourers, while all the rest of the 'tenant'-land is held by cultivators regarded as the tenants of the whole body. Frequently this area is not divided, for why should it be? It is much easier to divide the rents collected by the head-man or other manager; or perhaps these rents go *en bloc* to pay the revenue, and the surplus only is divided. In the Panjāb we rarely hear anyone speak of *sīr* lands, because the co-sharers generally work the whole of their share themselves, and such tenants as there are naturally appear as holding land under this or that co-sharer.

In the Panjāb the co-proprietors generally look for cultivating profits only. In the North-West Provinces they expect an income from rents, besides the yield of the home-farm. At least, that is the case with the largest class of villages. I believe the true *bhaiāchārā* or cultivating fraternities are oftener cultivating bodies of agricultural caste, or of one that has taken to cultivation. Contract-rents based on competition are much commoner in the North-West Provinces than they are in the Panjāb. In the former, they are so common as to form the normal standard of the value of land for assessment purposes; in the latter, they are neither sufficiently common nor really based on competition to furnish such a standard; they can only be referred to as a supplementary means of checking rates calculated in other ways.

[1] Mr. Whiteway tells me that a few such cases may be found in parts of the North-West Provinces; and were formerly common.

APPENDIX

THE DEFECTS OF THE OFFICIAL SYSTEM OF CLASSIFYING VILLAGES IN THE AGRICULTURAL RETURNS

It will readily be understood that the remarks made in this note are not intended to criticise the published Agricultural Tenure Returns as they are in themselves, and for the *purely official* or *administrative purposes* for which they were alone designed.[1] What I have to point out is (i.) that these returns are not only quite useless, but distinctly misleading, *for any purposes connected with the history of institutions*, and as regards the interesting question of the survival of the *different tribal and family origins* of the villages.

The British Government has done much to preserve the Archæological treasures of British India. Old buildings and inscribed monuments have been protected, repaired, and strengthened; elaborate drawings have been made, photographs taken, and measurements and sections placed on record in the invaluable *Technical Art Series* of the Imperial Survey Department. My plea is that something of the same interest should be shown by an attempt to preserve the archæology of Indian institutions which do not exist in stone or in material monuments, but in customs and forms of tenure. I do not think it would be an impossible task, gradually, and after such modification of detail as must necessarily be made in any plan submitted, to take a kind of *census* of the 'joint'-villages of the Panjāb, North-West Provinces, and Oudh, and to improve the general returns as regards the *raiyatwārī* provinces.

(1) As to these last-named provinces: in Madras we wish to know the number, and if possible the population, whether miscellaneous or of chiefly one or two castes or tribes, of the purely *raiyatwārī* villages; the number of villages included under Zamindārīs or other great landlord estates; and it might be possible to give for each district the number of villages in which *mirāsi* rights are in any degree of survival, carefully noting that *mirāsi* is used only to mean relics of *old shares* in the village land, and is *not* to include the hereditary *ex-officio* remuneration of village headmen, officers, artisans or servants, and the like, which have never decayed, and are part of the natural constitution of *raiyatwārī*

[1] Though it must be admitted that the obscurity or diversity of meaning which has been allowed to attach to the vernacular terms used must have a tendency to produce error even for the purposes mentioned.

villages. The usual official record of villages held in *In'ām*—*i.e.* free of revenue, or liable to a fixed reduced payment consolidated by 'enfranchisement,' would conveniently be added, though they are of less interest from the tenure point of view.[1]

In BOMBAY it would surely be possible[2] to show the *narwā* and *bhāgdārī* villages, which represent local survivals of the co-shared village, and the number of villages in the *kasbātī* estates.

(ii.) But it is in the provinces of UPPER INDIA that the returns fail to preserve any information regarding the real nature of the joint-villages which are there the prevailing form.

It is necessary to explain that in the official classification used in the *local* returns[3] for the North-West Provinces and in the *Imperial* returns for Oudh and the Panjāb (where the classification is added) the heads are derived from §§ 85 ff. of Thomason's *Directions to Revenue Officers*. It must be admitted that these paragraphs, affording an explanation of the system, are very obscure. In the Panjāb edition of the work (1875) the attempt was made to elucidate them by adding explanatory matter in square brackets, but the result is not satisfactory. The whole classification was only intended to be provisional, and to suggest a few 'obvious distinctions' which would assist the Settlement Officer in his attempts to understand the constitution of the villages. The degree of separation between the several properties, a matter of no interest to the *tenure* student except as already explained, is taken as a matter of distinction, which no doubt from the Collector's point of view is really important.

The heads adopted are :—

(i.) Communal—*zamindārī*, i.e. *zamindārī-mushtarka* (where there is but *one* landlord it is *z.* *khālis* (§ 87 of the *Directions*).

(ii.) *Pattīdārī*—held in complete severalty (§ 88).

(iii.) *Bhaiāchārā*—which the *Directions* does not define : the term is only mentioned afterwards in §§ 89, 93. The term is explained in the *Panjāb* edition, in an added par. (§ 104) ; but in this case the word is given a sense which is only partially adopted in the North-West Provinces and in direct contradiction to what is sometimes there meant. *Bhaiāchārā* thus appears to

---

[1] In Form I. (E 3), Madras is fairly complete ; but it might be possible to add the number of villages in which *mirāsī* right is still recognised.

[2] In the same Form I. (E. 3).

[3] In the Imperial form for the North-West Provinces, *all* details of villages-forms are omitted ; and the vicious mode of recording the villages twice over under different heads increases the difficulty.

include everything that is not *pattīdārī*, but especially to signify villages held 'on possession' as the only measure of right.

(iv.) Imperfect *pattīdārī*—where part of the village estate is held undivided, *and* where very frequently the two parts are shared on different principles—only one retaining the original shares.

(v.) Imperfect *bhaiāchārā*—ditto, ditto in bhaiāchārā villages.

Now, considering that most of these terms are obscure, and that probably in no two District Reports are they used in exactly the same sense, it is quite intolerable that they should continue to serve as headings.

A few remarks on each term will make the difficulty more evident.

'*Zamindārī*.' This term implies simply that the land is held by a landlord or a proprietor. The owner or co-sharing owners of the village are in fact peasant proprietors of the whole, arable and waste together. The term in itself has nothing whatever to do with 'joint' or 'several,' 'communal' or 'individual.' It only acquires these meanings when another word is added. *Zamindārī khālis* means that there is one landlord, a sole surviving sharer, or a sole owner, whose family has not yet branched out into a number of co-sharers. *Zamindārī mushtarka*, again, means the 'communal,' or joint holding of a number of co-sharing proprietors whose interest is not separated by the several allotment of shares on the ground.[1] There are villages of this kind almost always held by a body of co-heirs succeeding to a previous single owner; and in this case they have their *defined shares*, though the holdings are not partitioned. Hence from a *tenure* point of view they are not distinguishable from *pattīdārī* in the true sense of the word. Rarely there *may* be village estates held by a voluntary association 'in common.'

Pattīdārī was *originally* employed (and so Mr. Thomason seems sometimes, but not uniformly, to have employed it) to mean any kind

[1] Whether the whole phrase in the vernacular was too long or what I do not know, but quite early they began to use *zamindārī* as if it meant 'communal.' Thus in an old law (Reg. xix. of 1814, *sec.* 30) *zumeendary* was used to mean 'joint-estates held in common tenancy, where all the sharers have a common right and interest in the whole estate without any separate title to distinct lands forming part of the estate.' Strictly speaking, this definition is somewhat defective, as it omits the important qualification that every 'tenant' has a *defined share*, most commonly a legal fractional share, on which the profits and burdens, though not the land itself, are in theory divided. Property is only held *in common* when there are *no* fixed *shares* and each takes what he needs.

of village, so long as it was divided out on the ground into distinct shares or lots.[1] But it soon came to mean, and now ought always to be restricted to, pure *pattīdārī—i.e.* where *only the ancestral* or *fractional shares of the law of inheritance* are recognised. In this sense I have uniformly employed the term in this book; nor is it necessary that the shares should be strictly accurate, as long as the *principle is accepted throughout* the village estate.

In the Panjāb, some District Reports use the word as including *either* ancestral *or* customary shares, which is fatal.[2]

'*Bhaiāchārā.*' This term is the most unfortunate of all, since it has now lost all definite meaning; and a column so headed in the returns is a veritable statistical melting-pot in which all sorts of interesting origins and varieties are confused together. Properly, in its original sense (as used in Duncan's early Report of 1796 on the Benares co-shared villages), it means held on the custom of the brotherhood—*i.e.* by the association of families, usually a clan grown up out of one single family on a large available area which fortune preserved for them till they had filled it all. It implies that peculiar method of equal allotment of which the type is best illustrated by the oft-quoted Mathurā Jāt villages,[3] and Mr. Whiteway correctly uses the term accordingly. Holdings *made up of specimens of each kind of soil* are the characteristic. This is the true (1) sense.

But the term has also got to be used (2) for all kinds of share systems, viz. by 'wells,' 'ploughs,' &c., other than the legal or ancestral (*pattīdārī*) shares, and (3) to include also all villages in which shares have become wholly extinct or never existed, and where *de-facto possession* is now the sole measure of right. In the PANJĀB the term is officially provided to be used for the cases where the shares 'have become quite extinct, and each man's holding is or has become the sole measure of his right' (Barkley's edition of the *Directions*, § 104). But even in the Panjāb this use is not uniformly kept to; *e.g.* the artificial Kāngrā villages are shown as '*bhaiāchārā*,' and so are many of the tribal-frontier villages, where the shares are not

---

[1] It is so used, *e.g.*, in an old Act (I. of 1841). It is evident that in § 88 Mr. Thomason so uses it, while in § 93 he clearly uses it in the restricted sense.

[2] In practice, the Panjāb returns have the effect of *ignoring all tenure distinctions except*—

1. Undivided or sole.
2. Divided { i. on *any kind* of shares. / ii. on no shares, but possession only. }

[3] *Ante*, p 282 ff.

in the least extinct, but perfectly definite, only that they are not ancestral—*e.g.* are *per-capita* shares. In the NORTH-WEST PROVINCES the term is variously used in different districts, sometimes to mean the *de-facto* possession and extinct-share class, sometimes to mean the real old custom of the 'democratic' cultivating fraternity.

The resulting confusion is easily understood ; the *Imperial* compiler of *Provincial* tables cannot know in exactly what sense the term has been used ; nor can the *Provincial* compiler know exactly in what sense each *District* officer has used the word.

Under any general head of this kind, in the tables, we therefore find *thrown together indiscriminately* the following varieties :—

(i.) Real *bhaiāchārā* villages of the 'cultivating-fraternity' type (Mathurā Jāts, &c.).

(ii.) Panjāb tribal-villages where the *ancestral* scale is not followed throughout.

(iii.) *Pattidārī* villages which have acquiesced in the complete, or virtually complete, loss of the share-scale, and are held 'on possession.'

(iv.) Villages held on shares in 'wells,' on 'ploughs,' shares of 'bullocks,' &c., &c.

(v.) All kinds of villages held on *de-facto* possession of holdings.

(vi.) Artificial aggregates of individual holdings, i.e. villages converted under the revenue-system (Kāngrā, Kumāon, Jhānsī, Ajmer, &c.).

The student of village-tenures who calls to mind the distinctions I have endeavoured to explain and illustrate in this book by examples taken from 'real life' will regret the confusion of so many interesting varieties in one undistinguished heap. The 'imperfect' classes (of *pattīdārī* and *bhaiāchārā*) are, as I have remarked, sometimes lumped together ; in which case, since a majority of shared-villages have *some* land still in common, the result is that a large proportion of the whole number escape any distinctive classification whatever.

I think that any final list of new heads to be adopted will naturally require local consideration ; and a writer at a distance cannot satisfactorily produce one offhand. But I venture to think that some principles may be suggested which may usefully be borne in mind. Vernacular terms will perhaps have to be retained because of the local compilers who do not use English. It might be possible to distinguish :—

(I.) (*zamindārī khālis*) Villages where there is *one* landlord—

whether paying revenue or holding revenue free—will naturally be distinguished. It is for consideration whether it would be advisable to confine the term to villages of native origin, and not apply it to mere plots of granted land, or to leases under the waste-land rules. The head of 'undivided villages' (z. *mushtarka*) also calls for no alteration ; except that surely we might distinguish between cases of co-heirship, and the rarer cases of a joint-holding for some local convenience or by some voluntary association.

(II.) *Pattīdārī* should be uniformly and solely used for the village *divided* on the *legal or ancestral shares throughout*, and as long as the *principle* is acted on, even though the shares of land are not quite correct, and though the revenue-assessment is not paid in corresponding fractions.

(III.) 'Villages on a mixed system' should, for a tenure study, be separately recorded, meaning those in which there is a different mode of sharing recognised in different portions of the whole village—*e.g.* where in the divided lands the ancestral shares have been lost and *de-facto* possession is recognised, but where in the common or undivided land, and for miscellaneous profits, the ancestral shares are still followed.

The term *bhaiāchārā* as a heading should be abolished, or confined strictly to the old 'equal lot' or artificial (*bhaiwādi-bīghā*, *tauzī-bīghā*, &c. &c.) system. The Panjāb use should be altogether abandoned, as there is really no excuse for it, since villages held *on possession only* can much better be called *Qabzewār*. Whatever is done, however, with regard to terms, it would surely be possible to distinguish—

(IV.) Frontier tribal-villages, noting the number that are held on the *ancestral* shares throughout, and not merely as regards the principal divisions, while the interior shares are *khulāvesh*.

(V.) Villages held by clans grown up on the spot, or old 'cultivating fraternities,' having some form of *equal allotment* or artificial measures made up of specimens of each kind of soil. Some means may be adopted to indicate clusters of villages that are simply offshoots or divisions of a single parent estate as in Rohtak, Karnāl, &c.

(VI.) Villages held on *special shares*, such as 'wells,' 'ploughs,' 'bullocks,' &c., not being either *ancestral shares* nor those under V.

(VII.) Villages now held on *de-facto* possession, which are *known to have had shares* of any kind *and lost them completely*.[1]

---

[1] The rare cases where *de-facto* possession is not recorded, under the vague idea that one day the real shares will be restored, can easily be noted.

(VIII.) Villages held on *de-facto* possession as the measure of right, where either *no recollection* of any shares can be traced; or where they *never existed*, as in artificial villages, or those converted, as in Ajmer; and possibly some colonist villages, where each man took what land he pleased without any idea of share or allotment.

There will be no occasion (for a *tenure return*) to notice any 'imperfect' class in the sense that merely a part of the estate is held undivided: the only case where notice is called for, is when each portion is governed by a different plan (see under head III.) It would be quite possible to note under the general heads that so many villages had *waste* undivided (for the whole estate), and so many had part of the *arable* undivided.

It will be observed that heads I. and II. are really sub-heads of the same principle; so long as the *ancestral* rule has been observed by the family, or will be so, it is immaterial whether one owner is holding, or a number of co-heirs, or whether they have actually made a partition.

So with reference to heads V. and VI., it would be of less importance if they were conjoined, provided we could know, in a column of remarks, &c., how many of the old true *bhaiāchārā*, 'democratic,' and usually clan-forming villages (always, I believe, in local groups) exist; and in the Panjāb, how many of the purely 'colonist-associations' in the south-eastern districts.

So also it would be no great loss if it were held more convenient to club the cases VII. and VIII. together.

This is necessarily only a suggestion of a preliminary nature; but I think it is quite clear that if all knowledge of the approximate numbers, and relative importance locally, of the different kinds of joint-village are not to be rapidly lost beyond recovery,[1] *something*

[1] It will be no doubt a question how far the *village* can be separated as a defined group. In the tribal-areas of the Panjāb, for instance, the *k͟hel* is rather a considerable area of land with scattered hamlets over the whole; in Malabār there are no 'villages,' &c. But as in the compilation of *district* statistics (and it is these separately that will most interest the student) the compiler will add his notes and remarks, such difficulties will be got over. In some cases the Revenue Administration has already made and recorded separate villages, and these will be accepted; in others, the artificial circle, *amisham*, *māgane*, and what not, will serve, with explanatory notes. This difficulty will not be found insuperable, and the very effort to meet it will result in the most interesting statistical facts.

that will obviate the confusion of the official *pattidāri* and *bhaiāchārā* is urgently called for.

Let me only add a reminder that our students at home rejoice in the existence of a 'Domesday Book,' or the 'Extenta' of Wales, which have furnished us with the basis for the most valuable historical research. May we not hope, before it is too late, for a table of village statistics for India that will be an historical and economic record worthy to be placed beside the other splendid records that the Government of India has produced in the more tangible and material, but not necessarily more instructive, departments of archæological and historic art and architecture?

There is only one more point to be added. Would it not be possible to collect information as to the *origins* of villages of the joint-form wherever it is known or fairly inferred? Even a very loose classification would be useful. Villages originating directly in *tribal* occupation would probably be confined to the Panjāb frontier; but village groups formed by expansion on clan principles could be noted, colonist villages in South-eastern Panjāb and others similar; so, too, villages which are the vestiges of an earlier Rājāship or territorial rule; villages founded by individual ancestors, royal grantees, &c., and later by revenue-farmers and auction-purchasers. Even some such general classification, and if it were followed by an unfortunately large group ('origin not discoverable'), would be of great interest.

CHAPTER IX

THE TWO TYPES OF VILLAGE IN JUXTA POSITION LOCALLY

WE have been latterly so much occupied in discussing the joint- or landlord- village, its origins, and the variety which may be found to mark its internal constitution, that the first chapter may have been forgotten, as well as the contrast in which it was attempted to delineate both the *raiyatwārī* type of village and the common features of the *joint type*. It will now serve to emphasise the distinction if we proceed to consider the cases in which we can trace these two types or forms growing up, or existing, side by side in the same locality.

I will dispose first of two cases of the early appearance of joint-villages, in Madras and in the Bombay Dakhan, for they are of historic importance, and must be kept separate from the later and *still existing* instances to be found also in parts of Bombay and in Rājputāna.

In one of the cases now alluded to—that of the Dakhan—the tenure of villages by co-sharing families can hardly be said to have had any actual existence at the time when the inquiry was first made about them; but there were certain local traces of claims to village rights, certain surviving terms in use, and a few written records preserved; and it was a matter of historic probability and of just inference to determine what these traces meant. In the other case, that of Southern India, there certainly were *some* distinctly shared villages still in existence in 1790–1814; but their *status* had been much impaired, even in the districts where they were most clearly in evidence; while in other districts it was only traces of this form of tenure that could be found.

SECTION I.—JOINT-VILLAGES IN MADRAS

I will deal first with the most important question of the ancient joint-village in Madras. This must be examined in detail, for some writers have built on the existence of these villages a theory that anciently 'a tenure in common' prevailed over the whole Presidency. Yet no complete examination of the facts has been placed on record, as far as I am aware, in any one book or report. Briefly stated, the facts were these: Among the earliest territories to be acquired in the Madras Presidency was a district near the city of Madras now known as Chingleput, but in 1765 called 'the Jaghire.'[1] It had passed under the rule of the Nawābs of Arcot; and, besides being cruelly misgoverned by them, it was ravaged by an incursion of the Mysore Sultāns. Even after its acquisition by the British Government, pursuant to an Imperial grant, it was much mismanaged owing to lack of experience in the earlier British authorities. But at the close of the last century, Mr. Lionel Place was made Collector; and he found that throughout the district, and indeed in a considerable area round it, there was in most, if not in all the villages, a class of persons who claimed to be owners of the *entire area of village-lands in shares.* As we have so often found to be the case elsewhere, they claimed this right as their *kāniādsī*, which in Tamil means 'inheritance,' and which the Muhammadan officials had rendered by the usually employed Persian term *mīrāṣī*, having the same meaning. By making his Revenue Settlements with these co-sharers as a body, Mr. Place obtained considerable success, although time and misgovernment had already done much to limit and to confuse the rights actually enjoyed. When, some years later, the Madras Government were anxiously considering what would be the best Revenue system to adopt, a general inquiry into village tenures was made; and then it appeared that the existence of co-sharing bodies claiming right over the villages was not confined to Chingleput.[2] In the course

[1] Properly Chengalpat. For the history of it, see *L. S. B. I.* iii. 6, 14.

[2] The cause of this general inquiry should, perhaps, be briefly stated. The Indian Government at Calcutta, fresh from the completion of the

of this inquiry, Mr. Ellis, of Madras, produced a valuable Memoir full of information about the villages in the Tamil country; some, more or less, distinct evidence was also obtained from other districts; but a number of other reports left the matter very uncertain, owing to a cause I will presently notice; while others again either distinctly negatived the existence of such villages or returned no answer, an omission only partially supplied from other sources.[1]

The importance of the question to the historian is considerable, for the reason above stated.

It may be as well to say at once that the universal prevalence of these *mirāsi* villages[2] is certainly not proved. On the other hand, their existence, in certain specified localities, is proved as well as anything of such early date can be. And it is remarkable that they existed just in those districts where they would most naturally grow up, supposing them to be, as I believe they were, privileged tenures by the grants of early Princes, apparently by that time 'Hindu,' or else the result, in their most important centre, of a privileged colonising enterprise undertaken, and after several failures successfully accomplished, under the patronage of one of the Çoḷā princes.

Permanent Settlement of Bengal, and guided doubtless by the fact that in the northern part of Madras there were native chiefs in the position of 'Zamīndārs,' conceived that the Bengal system might be applied to the whole of Madras, and peremptorily insisted on such a Settlement being made. The attempt, of course, proved (except in the northern *Zamindārīs* and a few similar estates in other parts) a complete failure. The Madras Revenue authorities then directed their attention to the village-tenures. If it was true that a class of co-sharing hereditary proprietors could be found over the several villages in each district, such a fact, if only partly or locally true, might be an important factor in facilitating the working of a plan which the Board of Revenue then regarded with favour—namely, that of dealing with each village-group as a unit, and thus avoiding what was in those days thought the difficult task of dealing direct with each separate land-holder or *raiyat*.

[1] A selection from the evidence thus collected has been republished in the form of a reprint of the more important papers in a volume called *Papers on Mirasi Rights*, printed at Madras by Messrs. Pharaoh in 1862.

[2] For the sake of brevity I will continue to speak of *mirāsi* villages, always meaning those which were at one time possessed by co-sharing bodies, exactly, in fact, like some varieties of the joint-village of Upper India.

One preliminary point must be mentioned as concerning the *general* prevalence of such a right, and as regards several of the reports which deal with the subject in an extremely vague manner. The idea of the joint-village, so readily seized by the resident of Upper India, was not at all easy of comprehension to the Madras officials of eighty years ago, accustomed as they were to the *raiyatwārī* tenure, and to the then firmly established custom that the sovereign was sole land-owner. The village owned *as a whole*, in shares, by a body of *mirāsi* or hereditary proprietors, was quite a strange idea. When, therefore, various *other* hereditary rights and privileges appeared which were commonly described by the same name—*i.e.* as *mirāsi* rights—there was a not unnatural confusion. Very often it will be noticed that, when the reporters asserted *mirāsi* right to exist in the villages of this or that district, they did not really mean the right to a share in the village as a whole, but some special privilege, which has nothing to do with the question at issue, such as the hereditary *māniyam*, or free-holding of village headman (which is essentially a mark of the ancient *raiyatwārī* village), or the hereditary grain fee (*swatantram*, or *merāi*)[1] of the village artisans and servants (which equally exists in *raiyatwārī* villages.[2]

In order, then, to do justice to the question of the former

[1] It ought hardly to be necessary to point out that the Tamil *merāi* has no connection whatever with the Perso-Arabic *mirāsi*; but I have seen the mistake made. Moreover, the term *mirāsi* became current, just as other Persian or Arabic words did, from the Moslem Revenue Administration—the only one that was in any degree systematic or had regular official terms. It was not intended by the use of the word to imply any depreciation of the right. On the contrary, *mirāsi* was always used in the Dakhan kingdoms, where it originated, to indicate the highest type of direct right in the soil.

[2] This confusion is often made in the early Government Minutes, *e.g.* Board of Revenue, 1796, § 23 (*Mirāsi Papers*, p. 35); in the report on *Dindigal* (p. 111), where the *headman's* privilege is spoken of, and in many other places. Cf. the North Arcot letter at p. 394 (and especially p. 396), where the confusion is very evident. And so at p. 408, where there is a hopeless mixture of the two things. The *distinction* is noticed by Mr. Ellis (pp. 180, 181), and clearly by the Board of Revenue Minute, §§ 67, 68, p. 373.

existence of co-sharing villages, it is necessary that we should completely exclude all evidence referring only to such ordinary hereditary holdings and privileges. We must confine our attention to the *traces of co-sharing bodies claiming the whole village as their mirāsi.* It is obvious that the claim originally included, and necessarily so, the right to the entire area of the grant, or of the land on which a village was established—*i.e.* the waste and arable together.[1] Naturally the co-sharers would claim a rent or 'landlord's share' (called *tundu-vāram*, or in Brahman villages *swāmi-bhogam*=landlord's or owner's share) from such lands as were held by tenants of whatever class, not being co-sharers. In short, there cannot be the smallest doubt that if the *mirāsi* village claims were anything at all, they were claims which, originally at any rate, constituted the holders jointly, according to their shares, the proprietors of the villages exactly as such co-sharers were in other parts of India. Lists of the shares (called *pangu-malai*) very often existed. Each village had its own *pançayat*, or managing body, and consequently, as always in such a form of village, there was only an official headman, or *manegār*, with no power nor hereditary land-holding (as headman), nor privilege (as there would have been in *raiyat-*

[1] There was some little doubt caused on the subject of the claim to the waste which was admitted by Mr. Ellis. But this is easily understood. It was very probable that in the days of encroachment and exaction the Revenue Agents of the local Governor would begin to assert a right to put in tenants on culturable waste where the *mirāsdār* did not or could not provide for it himself (this was the case, *e.g.*, in some places under the Sikh Governors in the Panjāb), and in this way it would come to appear doubtful whether the *mirāsdār* had a right to the waste. But even if this is not so, it is quite possible that there may have been some internal village custom affecting the waste. For example, the waste (*tārisu*) was classified into *shekāl karambu* (culturable waste) and *anādi karambu* (permanent 'immemorial' waste). The latter included roadways, land occupied by trees wanted for the general convenience, and so forth. It is easily conceivable that village custom may have early imposed on the co-sharers themselves a prohibition against cutting down such trees, stopping such roads by making them into fields, and the like. Such acts would be resented in the co-shared villages of the Upper provinces, but no one would think that such a restriction militated against the general proprietary right over the whole village.

wārī villages).[1] It is necessary to emphasise this character of the *mirāsi* as a claim of general village-tenure, because some of the documents relating to these cases speak as if they thought the *mirāsi* right to be merely some kind of superior status as regards a particular field or holding.

Naturally enough, in the early years of the nineteenth century, the *mirāsi* claims having been continually overborne in the past, the right was not, in most cases, complete or intact. As time went on and rapacious local officers under the Nawāb began to oppress the people, these privileges would be gradually broken down; heavy assessments might cause some co-sharers to give up the attempt to hold the lands, and their co-partners might be unable to relieve them. Then holdings would begin to lie waste and the revenue to be in arrears. The Governor would accordingly assume the right to locate new cultivators and to take revenue from them direct. Such persons would naturally resent any attempt of the *mirāsdār* class to demand landlord's fees from them; and thus the co-sharing proprietors' superior right to the whole estate, and especially to those parts of it not in their direct possession, would come to look more and more doubtful, especially to observers whose previous experience had not taught them to look for anything of the kind, and to whose ideas of expediency it was opposed.

It is impossible, however, not to perceive that the institution was really unknown in some parts, and that in others it had existed but was fallen into decay. It was in a limited area that there was clear evidence of its survival, though whether, even there, it could have been restored in its integrity, as a working tenure, is problematical.

When, in the light of modern experience, we sum up the evidence, the conclusion, I venture to think, is irresistible that these villages, owned by co-sharing families or groups of families, were the growth of special circumstances, and certainly did not represent any universal custom of land-holding. Still

[1] For a clear exposition of this, see *Chingleput D. M.* p. 204. It is necessary carefully to distinguish the old headman's hereditary (and sometimes revenue-free) holding in virtue of his office, and the partial revenue-free grant allowed in the Tondai country to encourage the colonist villages generally.

less is there any evidence, or even tradition of origin, that lends any countenance to the idea that they represent survivals of a primeval communal land-tenure, which indeed nothing that we know of old Dravidian customs would lead us to expect.

Such villages in fact consisted :—

(i.) Largely of *agrahāram*, or villages held on hereditary grants (in this case free of revenue payment)[1] to Brahmans. They are especially numerous in districts which had been the demesne of the ancient kingdoms of *Çoḷā* and *Pāṇḍyā*. These Brahman communities held villages sometimes *samudayam* (or undivided), sometimes (and more usually) divided (*pattidārī* as would be said in the North, or *arudi-karai* in Tamil).[2]

(ii.) A certain number of other villages, held by secular castemen, appear in the districts of Tanjore, Trichinopoly, and Tinnevelly, and probably Madura.

(iii.) The largest and most important group is found in part of the country formerly known as *Tondai-maṇḍalam*, which, roughly speaking, embraced the country between the north and south rivers, both known by the name of Pennai.[3] It does not follow that villages of this kind covered the entire country, but they were found surviving chiefly in Chingleput and the adjoining districts of Arcot.[4]

Ad (i.). The existence of the Brahman villages and their origin in a religious grant will not be disputed by anyone. As they were also revenue-free, they did not excite that administrative interest which others did, and therefore it is not so readily and at first sight apparent that they were *mirāsi* villages, with just

[1] As we shall presently see, Brahman *mirāsi* villages (*agrahāram*) were revenue-free. Others held by secular castemen (*Çūdra*) were not. In the Tondai country (Chingleput, &c.), the *mirāsi* villages were observed uniformly to claim the exemption of a *part* of their land from the revenue share, the reason of which is traditionally explained.

[2] *Samudayam* is Sanskrit, and so may properly be applied to *Brahman* villages. I doubt the correctness of its use in the Tondai country among the Vellālar. Mr. Ellis says the Brahman villages were generally divided. (*Mirāsi Papers*, p. 295.)

[3] On maps shown as Penar, Pennaur, and Penner. The Southern river runs into the sea between Pondicherry and Cuddalore.

[4] See *D. M. North Arcot*, chapter iii. p. 89.

the same sort of proprietary right as that claimed in others—and just as much held in *family shares*.

Ad (ii.). When we have once ascertained that Madura was the capital of Pāṇḍyā, and that Tanjore and the adjacent districts were the demesne of the *Çoḷā* king, it will not surprise us that many privileged tenures or grants should have existed.[1] In TANJORE, Colonel Blackburne's evidence is definite; he saw that such villages arose out of *grants*, though too long ago, he thought, for him to trace their beginning. But it will be recollected that no attempt appears to have been made to ask the people themselves for their traditions, or for their genealogy, or for lists of co-sharers preserved in villages, such as in the North of India can readily be obtained, and actually were obtained in Chingleput. The State spoken of had then for some time been under the foreign domination of a Marāthā prince, whose position was due to a recent and unqualified act of seizure and marauding. The State officials were not likely to trouble themselves about existing titles and tenures, which it was their object to tax to the utmost, at least in those cases which were not due to their own grants. But the Tanjore figures show quite sufficiently what the general type of village was. The total number of villages is reported[2] to be 5,783. But this must be at once reduced to 3,976, as the difference represents 1,807 so called *ekabhogam* villages—mere hamlets or parts of villages of which the *single owners* with pretensions to rank, and who had given their names to the places, got permission to have recorded as separate possessions; this has obviously nothing to do with primitive or even ancient custom. But out of the balance, as many as 2,202 are *arudi-karai* (or

[1] It is, nevertheless, remarkable that the *D. M. Trichinopoly* contains no notice whatever of the existence of *mirāsi* villages, and the allusions in the *Mirāsi Papers* are vague and general. Before 1805, Trichinopoly and Tanjore were united in one collectorate, after the lapse of Tanjore to the British Government.

[2] *Mirāsi Papers*, p. 95. *D. M. Tanjore*, p. 400, mentions 62,000 persons as having *mirāsi* claims; of these, 16,000 were Brahman grantees and 43,000 (I give round numbers), Çudra. But these numbers appear evidently to include holders of *all sorts of 'inām' and hereditary rights and privileges*.

phālā-bhogam [1]) held in severalty; and there is nothing to show that many of these were not ordinary *raiyatwārī* villages, in which the cultivators had combined to share the revenue. That possibility, however, is not very material, as I do not think it can be doubted that, besides the Brahmans, Vellālar settlers, being energetic agricultural castemen, had been encouraged to hold villages on the superior tenure. It is worth while noticing that while in the Tondai country, as we shall see, it was necessary further to encourage such grantees by allowing a part of the villages they created to be held free of revenue, such a concession was not necessary in the rich delta land of Tanjore, where there was hardly any waste, and a *mirāsi* tenure was quite sufficient inducement of itself.[2] Of the remaining villages, 1,774 were *samudayam* (or in Tamil *pasaṉ-karai*—*i.e.* held in some form of undivided holding); a considerable part of these would certainly be Brahman villages, where the Sanskrit term would be most naturally used. And, as the Brahmans would be non-agriculturists, it is quite likely that some families would hold jointly—*i.e.* dividing the income, while family quarrels and jealousies would lead others to divide the land itself.

In all these village lands we may notice first the same plan of division of the produce and payment of revenue in kind which we know to have been originally universal all over India. The lands yielding produce, as distinguished from the waste and the revenue-free lands, are generically called *vārampat*. The produce, if there is no *mirāsi* class, is simply divided into the *mel-vāram*, the State share, and the *kudi-varam*, or occupant's share: that is to say, after the fees (*merāi*) of the village servants, watchmen, &c., &c., have been satisfied out of the grain-heaps. When there is a body of *mirāsi* proprietors, then there are *three* instead of *two* to share: *mel-vāram*, as before, is the royal share;

[1] Tanjore being ruled by Marāthās, the prevalence of Marāthā terms is explained. Such are *ekabhogam* (single owner); *phālābhogam* (in separate lots); and so *kunbhāvā* is the equivalent for *kāniādsī*, or *mirāsi*. (*D. M. Tanjore*, pp. 403, 409.) *Phālā bhogam* is sometimes said to be a half Sanskrit compound with the Tamil *pala* = 'many.' I think it much more likely that it is the Marāthī *phālā*, a share.

[2] This is clearly put in the *D. M. Tanjore*, § 10, p. 403.

tundu-vāram is the landlord's (*mirāsdār's*) share; and *kudi-vāram*, the cultivating occupant's, as before.

Turning to the other royal demesne of MADURA and TINNEVELLI, the evidence is much less satisfactory; but we can hardly help believing that the kings' and chiefs' courtiers and relations, and others, would gradually acquire the *mirāsi* right in certain villages; and hence we find it reported that, at any rate in the Tinnevelli 'pollams' or chief's territories, *mirāsi* villages were found. In the early report,[1] the existence of Brahman *mirāsi* villages (*agrahāram vādagai*) is noticed in the TINNEVELLI district, and it is stated that other villages held by Çūdras were also *mirāsi* and held on shares, and that these latter are called *panḍūra-vādagai.* It is noteworthy, however, that these words merely mean that the villages are on the list of those paying revenue to the treasury (which the *agrahāram* are not); or, in other words, that they are what elsewhere would be called *k͟hālsa*, or revenue-paying, villages. Nothing appears about the origin or the nature of the tenure; the details given refer solely to the Brahman grantee villages;[2] still, it is certainly intended that both Brahman and Çūdra villages were held on the same sort of superior title, and were divided into *pangu* and *karai* = major and individual shares. But further, it is added (and this is important), that, *beside* the shared villages, there were others held by non-proprietary (*payakāri*) holders, who had no system of shares.[3]

As to MADURA, the author of the District Manual expressly states that certain villages in which *karai-kāran*, or 'persons holding shares,' were stated to exist, there was no privileged or superior tenure, but the term merely indicated a method by which the cultivators formed a voluntary association for the

[1] *Mirāsi Papers*, pp. 77, 105, 283. The two latter Reports are long-winded disquisitions on property in general, giving no facts of any kind, and showing that the writer was confusing in his mind all sorts of rights, including the special holding of the headman, which is certainly not existent in *mirāsi* villages under any circumstances whatever.

[2] *Mirāsi Papers*, p. 79 (Mr. Lushington). When the writer comes to the Çūdra villages, he only makes some unimportant remarks about the caste, and gives a deed of sale with nothing to show to what class of village it refers. He says nothing as to how the Çūdra tenures originated.

[3] See this clearly stated by Mr. Ellis (*Mirāsi Papers*) p. 386.

purpose of meeting the revenue demand. Mr. Ellis, on the other hand, evidently thought that joint-villages once existed in Madura; and it must be admitted that in the demesne territory of an ancient kingdom it is likely enough. No great importance, however, attaches to the question; but it is evident that throughout these districts there is no single incident or feature in the evidence which does not coincide with the supposition, in itself so very probable when judged by the experience of other 'Hindu' kingdoms—viz. that the co-sharing or proprietary villages were the superior or privileged tenures resulting from royal grants to Brahmans, or to other (secular) grantees for various purposes, including, very possibly, the direct revenue management or the extension of cultivation to new lands. As such they may date back several hundred years; and they may have been held by the descendants of the original grantees acting on the usual custom of joint-succession.

Ad (iii.). When we come to the CHINGLEPUT district, which is the centre of the larger group of Tamil *mirāsi* villages, we find the evidence much more complete, and the whole subject studied with great care and with an amount of detail that is quite remarkable for the period. The evidence mainly consists of surviving share-lists in many cases, and other evidences of proprietary possession, while the origin of the villages is explained by a detailed and ancient tradition, the substantial truth of which was accepted by every one of the officers who had local experience, from Mr. Place in 1796 to Mr. Ellis (1816) and Mr. Smalley (1822), Mr. Graeme in North Arcot, and a learned native gentleman (B. Sankarayâ) in Madras.[1] We are not bound to accept the entire details of the tradition; but there can hardly be a reasonable doubt that its main idea was a true one, and that the villages were established in a fertile but originally almost wholly forest-clad country, at the time held, and partly at least inhabited, by *Kurumbar*—a pastoral tribe who were then ruled by *Pallava* chiefs, who had established twenty-

[1] The principal reports are in *Mirāsi Papers*, Place (1796), p. 36, ff. For his final Report in 1799, of some 750 paragraphs, and full of long-winded disquisitions of no interest, but containing also many valuable facts, see pp. 38–70. Ellis (1816), pp. 172-217; B. Sankarayâ, p. 218; Graeme, p. 393; Smalley (1822), p. 424.

four *kuṭṭam*, or territorial divisions, each protected or commanded by a fort. The days came when a *Çoḷā* prince advanced into the country and conceived the idea of colonising part of it.[1] The settlement of the first families of Vellālan castemen was not a success, but ultimately Vellālar from the north-west country of Tuluva were induced to settle; and then the colony was established. Some remains of the earlier families of the Vellālar are stated by Mr. Ellis to have still held lands, but the principal proprietors were the Tuluva Vellālar.[2]

The general evidence as to the past history of the villages is given by Mr. Ellis in some detail. He quotes the verses that have become tradional or are found in early Tamil literature bearing on the subject, as well as lists locally preserved showing how the Vellālar divided the territory into *nādu* under chiefs (called *Nāttān*), and how these new divisions were related to the twenty-four *kuṭṭam* which their predecessors had organised. The records include some lists of the nādūs, and some calculations of the number of villages which each contained.[3]

It appears to me that attempts to identify the *entire country* included in the traditional and literary limits of *Tondai-maṇḍalam* are very doubtful. Equally so the attempts to calculate, from certain temple records, the number of families of Vellālar. The fact seems quite clear that so large an area could never have

[1] The name generally accepted by Mr. Ellis and others is that of a (Hinduised) prince, *Athondē*, or *Adaṇḍā-Chakravarti* (the last member being a Sanskrit title meaning 'suzerain'). The full detail is given in the *Chingleput D. M.*; but as Wilks's description of a purely *raiyatwārī* village is quoted, and this is mixed up with the account of the village held in shares, some mistakes are the natural result. The dates seem also somewhat confused. The author suggests that the Vellālar colonisation began before the time of Manu (p. 207): on what this rests I have no idea. Afterwards it is suggested that the Vellālar *from the Tuluva country* came during the first centuries of the Christian era. (See p. 208, and compare p. 25.) The supposition that jointly-held villages existed before Manu, and before Sanskrit was known in the South, is entirely unsupported by any kind of evidence. The traditions all point to their having been privileged under Adaṇḍā, who reigned at a time when the Hindu religion had long been introduced. He may have extended the privilege to the remains of earlier settlers of superior race, as indeed would be natural under the circumstances.

[2] *Mirāsi Papers*, p. 230.

[3] *Ibid.* pp. 236–240, 242.

been occupied from end to end by colonists, even if it was really conquered and annexed by the *Çoḷā* dynasty; and that the special location and grant of privileges to the Tuluva Vellālar villages must more reasonably be confined to that part of the country where they are proved to have been established by the fact that a considerable group of them was in some degree of preservation at the time when British rule began. It is quite a gratuitous supposition that such villages at one time existed *all over* the whole area vaguely included in 'Tondai-maṇḍalam,' but that over the greater part they had been rooted out—the villages entirely, the people almost—by subsequent Moslem and Marāthā conquests.[1] It is true that we have more reason to believe the villages were held on a *mirāsi* tenure in some other districts (Tanjore, &c.), and it may be that these are included in the general limits of Tondai-maṇḍalan described by Mr. Ellis.[2] But the districts of Chingleput and Arcot were also equally harassed by wars, and afterwards by the harsh rule of the Nawābs of the Carnatic, as Mr. Ellis's own papers show; and yet *there* the *mirāsi* villages were, though much injured, not at all destroyed, nor was the Vellālan population rooted out. It is surely sufficient to establish—and of this there is no doubt—that in Chingleput, in the Madras Collectorate, and in the neighbourhood, there were unquestionably *mirāsi* villages, and that in many of them the *pangu-malai* or records of shares were preserved, a fact which demonstrates that the institution in question was certainly 'the joint or co-shared village.'

It is not at all easy to fix a date for these Chingleput colonies. Mr. Ellis thinks that the country was early brought into a fairly flourishing state, since there are names of places which can plausibly be identified with those mentioned in Ptolemy's geographical account (about the middle of the second century). Hence Mr. Ellis thinks the colonisation must have begun before the Christian era.[3] But such recognition of

[1] See *Mirāsi Papers*, p. 246. Races speaking Telugu and Canarese cover the whole of the so-called Upper Tondai west of the 'Coromandel' ghat.

[2] He proposed to prepare a map, which was never completed; and the coloured portions were to show whence the Vellālar possessions had now disappeared, and the uncoloured the parts where they survived.

[3] *Mirāsi Papers*, p. 230. See *D. M. Chingleput*, p. 25.

names, if it is a fact, does not show that Adaṇḍa's colonising enterprise was so early; for (as the *Chingleput D. M.* points out), up to the eighth century, the Pallava, Pandu, and Kurumbar tribes were in possession,[1] and furnished the origin of the still existing 'Pallar,' a low caste of farm labourers. It was only about the eighth or ninth century that the *Çoḷa* dynasty extended its influence northward to the jungle-clad Tondai country, and overthrew the Pallava chiefs. After this it began to lose ground, and finally fell about the eleventh or twelfth century. I think that, on the whole, we may more probably attribute the special foundation of privileged villages to some period not far removed from the eighth or ninth century. This does not conflict with the possibility of some still earlier and partial Vellālar settlements.

Coming, however, to the actual survivals at the time of the British rule, Mr. Place in 1799 enumerated 2,241 *mirāsi* villages in Chingleput.[2] Of these, a considerable number had passed into the hands of Brahmans, but the bulk were still Vellālar. In his time as many as 15,994 *mirāsi* shares were held by 8,387 sharers, but a number had been abandoned owing to the heavy revenue demands which, here as elsewhere, deprived landed property of its value.[3] Mr. Place, indeed, adopted the extreme measure of granting the *mirāsi* right in vacant lands. Mr. Place explains that the 8,387 sharers represent only the heads of kindred; and that there were many more minor shares—apparently subdivisions of $\frac{1}{4}$, $\frac{1}{8}$, $\frac{1}{16}$, $\frac{1}{24}$, &c.—the fractions known to the Tamil arithmetic.[4]

It has been remarked that the Vellālan village-owners were not of common descent; but this, I think, is very natural. For colonists would be volunteers gathered from a number of different families and centres. From the accounts we possess, it is probable that the colonists kept together in village groups, and that the head of each separate family-group would represent a major share in the village; there is no reason why these major

[1] The *D. M., North Arcot*, p. 20, states that it was a Pallava chief who formed the twenty-four *kuṭṭam* above alluded to.

[2] *Mirāsi Papers*, p. 251.

[3] See *ibid.* pp. 382, 383.

[4] Mr. Place's long report of 1799 is also printed in the *Fifth Report*, ii. 299-314.

shares should not have often been held by separate families, who, associated as clearers of the forest, had no lien of blood beyond the common ties of caste or tribe. But within these major shares (*patti* or *tarf* as they would be in North India), the minor holders would all at first be 'kindred'—*i.e.* descendants of the same ancestor. This, I think, is the only reasonable inference to be drawn from the facts as stated by Mr. Place.

The villages of the Vellālan special colonisation were, as I have said, privileged by being allowed a portion of the land free of revenue, and by certain other dues; privileges which it is noticed particularly do not occur in any other *mirāsi* villages elsewhere.[1] The larger shares alluded to seem to have been called *pangu*, and the minor shares were *karai* (whence the generic term *karāi-karan*, or 'co-sharers').

As to the *form of joint tenure* prevalent, the villages were chiefly what are called *pasaṇ-karai*, a term which has led to some rather extravagant notions about ancient community of property. But, as a matter of fact, all the evidence points to this having been a voluntary and perfectly natural arrangement of association made when new cultivation was to be established, and when a well-cemented union of effort, both in clearing forest and in creating the means of irrigation by digging tanks, was necessary. Under this system, moreover, two varieties were observed. The absolute *pasaṇ-karai* meant that the village body worked without any separate or permanent allotment of lands; the 'council' determined each year what portion of land each group should undertake. Whether each took the produce of what they actually cultivated, or whether all was collected and divided according to the known fractional shares, does not clearly appear.[2] But for this mode another was sometimes substituted, viz. the *karaiyīdu*, which meant that

[1] See *Mirāsi Papers*, p. 375, § 85. I make no apology for repeating this, for it is important as showing that there must have been something special about their villages, and so far confirming the tradition of their origin.

[2] Mr. Place speaks of such joint bodies working together so that 'the labours of all yield the rent = the Government revenue (?), and they enjoy the profit proportionate to their original interest' (*Fifth Report*, ii. 314). This may refer only to the general idea of the association.

the holdings were separately allotted for a time and then exchanged.

Mr. Place gives several examples of the shares in these villages.[1] The major-shares, as I have said, were those of the heads of each branch or group, taking part in the establishment of the cultivation; and there were sub-shares. Mr. Place instances a village in which there were actually thirty sharers, but they remembered the four major-shares of the foundation, and adhered to that division. Another village had 160 *original* shares; this probably includes both the major and minor shares. 'It was deemed essential,' says Mr. Place, 'that the shares should be equal.' As might be expected, there were many slaves and serfs, doubtless the original inhabitants who were reduced to this condition; and many followers who held lands on an inferior tenure.[2] In one of the *Mirāsi Papers* mention is made of the formal grant by the *mirāsdārs* of a cultivating, but not co-sharing, right in perpetuity. And it was this, and possibly the occasional existence of previously established cultivators, that led to the distinction between the *ūlkudi*, or hereditary tenant, and the *parakudi*, or tenant-at-will, especially in Brahman or other villages in which the co-sharers were non-agriculturist and would rely on tenants for farming their lands.

When, in the course of time, the shares, for any reason, were allotted and *permanently* divided, the village was said to be *arudi-karai*. This division was foreign to the original plan of co-operative colonisation, and was, as Mr. Place notes, against the caste feeling. It appears either as a later change in the Vellālar villages, or as a more frequent family division in the Brahman villages, and perhaps in those of other (*Çūdra*) grantees.

[1] *Fifth Report*, ii. pp. 299, 300, &c. This exchange, Mr. Place says (p. 385), was 'to obviate, I imagine, the inequality to which a fixed distribution would be liable.'

[2] In the *D. M. Chingleput*, there is a curious account of the *serfs* and their being rather proud of being *adscripti glebæ*, because they had a certainty of land to cultivate and a fixed livelihood; and they had a kind of annual ceremonial strike—for such it was, for the details of which the original must be consulted (pp. 211–214).

I think that a variety of circumstances taken together are strongly in favour of the view that the joint-holding, or *pasaṇ-karai*, in the Tondai country was essentially a device for holding together and equalising the *colonist associates*, each in his own group or major-share division. It will be recollected that we start with the uniform tradition that the *Vellālar* were established with the grant of a superior right, which was to attach them to the land and encourage them to persevere in their difficult task.[1] Then we find that this permanent right was still so much valued in 1799, that Mr. Place declared[2] that 'it was indispensable to assign *mirāsdārs* to the unappropriated lands; without it,' he says, 'I found that they could not be rented—*i.e.* the revenue-settlement accepted; but the idea of permanent property was such an inducement that I was not only able to fill up the vacant shares, but to convert the most stubborn soil and the thickest jungle into fertile villages. "Give us the *mirāsi*, and we will both rent the lands, and employ all our labour to make them productive" was the common observation . . .'

Then, again, it is noted that the *mirāsdārs* would 'assemble and execute a joint-deed divesting the defaulter of his share in the "*mirāsi*," transferring it to the others, which looks very much like a strong association, the basis of which was that all must pull together to meet the assessment.[3] For in village bodies dependent on common descent from a single ancestor nothing of the kind is ever recorded. And, again, it is noted in Madura, as I have already observed, that the *pasaṇ-karai* was actually adopted in existing villages as a means of meeting the

[1] 'There is a distinct tradition of some of these (Vellālar) having deserted the undertaking. The manner in which the difficulty was at last overcome, and the son of the Cholā king able to report to his father the completion of the enterprise, is set forth in the following story, which has always been current in the country. Kullatanga (Rājā) asked his son how he had been able to settle the country so well? The latter replied that he had forged a chain for the inhabitants of such strength that they would never be able to free themselves. By this he meant that the affections of the people were so riveted to the land of their new country by *kānīādsī*, or property in the soil, that they would not desert it. This story is no doubt very ancient. . . .' *D.M. Chingleput*, p. 217.

[2] See *Fifth Report*, ii. 303.

[3] See *Mirāsi Papers*, p. 223, and cf. p. 389, *post*.

revenue charge by combined action. And so in North Arcot it is expressly said that when it became 'necessary to add . . . new cultivators to the original proprietors to assist in repairs of tanks, in the distribution and settlement of the different lands, and to regulate the irrigation,' *pasaṇ-karai* was adopted by voluntary association, and the new-comers were 'partners in the profit and loss of the cultivation of all the lands,' though they had no share in the original privilege by which the co-sharers had a certain portion of the land free of revenue, and received certain special grain-fees (*kuppatam*), &c.[1]

I also note with regard to the method involving *exchange* of lands (*karaiyīdu*) that it is stated in the Report on South Arcot that newly cleared 'wet' lands under new water are to this day frequently exchanged in order that each might get the good as well as the bad lands in his turn.[2]

I do not think, then, on the whole, that there can be any reasonable doubt that the relics of *mirāsi* right indicated the establishment of a superior co-sharing village tenure, which existed locally, and contemporaneously with the *raiyatwārī* tenure; such superior tenure being connected either with *grants* to Brahmans or to other (secular) castemen—very likely cadets of families and other persons gaining privilege from connection with the ruler, or with a direct privilege granted to encourage and confirm a colonising settlement.

That such should be the real history is exactly in analogy with the evidence we have everywhere that, given a 'Hindu' State and Rājās, we are sure to find joint-villages growing up, either by grants of land or by colonising enterprises under the patronage of the Rājā.

I would only add that, in another connection,[3] I have shown how in the old Oudh kingdoms the villages were naturally *raiyatwārī*, and how by the king's grant leading families obtained the lordship of the village, and how waste land grants would result in the establishment of villages on the superior tenure (co-shared village). I believe that the Madras history is

[1] See *Mirāsi Papers*, p. 395, § 106. [2] *Ibid.* p. 412.
[3] See p. 300, *ante*.

just the same thing in another form. That it affords any example of a general primeval tenure of 'land in common,' quite contrary to all we know of Dravidian custom, I see not the remotest reason to believe.[1]

[1] In concluding the whole subject I take occasion to observe that no attempt has been made to account for the unquestioned survival of the joint-villages, with their *pangu-malai*, or share lists, and, in the Tondai territory, their special privileges, on any other basis. The chief if not only dissentient voice is that of Sir T. Munro in his Minute of December 1824 (*Mirāsi Papers*, p. 430). But this illustrates what I have elsewhere had occasion to observe, that the Minutes of our great Administrators are not always to be appealed to for points of history and details of tenure. Sir T. Munro's main object was to argue for the practical adoption of a *raiyatwārī* Settlement and for a great reduction of revenue; *that* would make the country flourish and save it from middlemen. This important principle, to the adoption of which Madras owes all its subsequent prosperity, seems obvious enough now; but in those days it needed all the advocacy of a powerful personality to obtain consideration for it. But with this one object in view, Sir T. Munro had no concern with tenure details. He frankly says he does not care to inquire about the alleged *mirāsi* villages. Had he stopped there, and pointed out that in their then existing condition the surviving right, such as it was, could easily be provided for under his system, and that its past history had no practical bearing on his proposals, it would have been well. Unfortunately, the distinguished writer endeavoured to add a brief criticism, which, it must be admitted, was without sufficient foundation. He says that the existence of the joint-village is 'without the least proof' and is only Mr. Ellis's opinion. This certainly is not the case. He then briefly adds that if such colonists settled (to the number of fifty or sixty thousand) it would have depopulated the country whence they came; and that they would have perished before the task of clearing the jungle was accomplished. But Mr. Ellis expressly shows that the Tuluvā country was well able to support sending out a colony (see *Mirāsi Papers*, p. 249), of which of course the numbers may have been exaggerated. And, as to the likelihood of their perishing in the attempt, since the country certainly *was* somehow colonised, and that, unquestionably, at no recent period, the objection has no weight: colonisation was just as possible in, say, the eighth century as it was at any subsequent but still ancient date. In fact, the whole argument—as far as it appears in the Minute—would not need to be seriously noticed at all if it were not for the great name it bears.

SECTION II.—TRACES OF OVER-LORD RIGHT IN THE DAKHAN VILLAGES

When we turn to the Dakhan districts of the Bombay Presidency, the traces of co-sharing right, also called *mirāsi*,[1] are more doubtful; or rather, I should say, it is more doubtful what interpretation we should put on the evidence. That a distinct class of superior holders once locally existed there can be little doubt; that share-lists, showing how the families allotted the lands, were actually obtained by Colonel Sykes is also clear; but to what extent this superior tenure of whole villages prevailed, or whether in some cases the traditional evidence does not rather relate to shares in the headman's privileged special landholding (or *waṭan*), there is some room for question.[2] On the whole I think it is more probable that these villages were subject to a local but really widespread over-lordship, which is by no means impossible to account for. It will be observed that in no case is there any suggestion of any common-holding of village lands. The families whose shares (*thal*) are spoken of may, or may not, be descended from common ancestors. Colonel Sykes notes particularly that the major shares were called by the names of the founders—men of 'ancient Marāthā families.' We have no sufficient evidence as to who they were. Very probably they may be traced to the earlier Aryan or semi-Aryan clans, long before the name 'Marāthā' was in use—though at a date when

[1] It will be remarked that the term *mīrāṣī* was derived from the early Moslem revenue systems which originated in the Muhammadan kingdoms of the Dakhan and thence become generally current. Malik 'Ambar, the famous minister who made the Revenue Settlement of these parts, was always anxious to resuscitate, if he could, the *mirāsi* families and make village Settlements with them. See *Berar Gazetteer*, p. 90, and G. W. Forrest's Minutes of M. Elphinstone (Captain Brigg's Report), p. 385.

[2] There is in the Reports something of the same confusion already noted in Madras; for the terms *watan*, *watandār*, which apply to the headman's and village-*officers'* privileged holdings, are sometimes applied to the *proprietary* shares in the village; at any rate, it is not certain which is meant. Hereditary holdings of headmen and officers are common in, and even characteristic of, *raiyatwārī* villages; so that their existence is no proof at all of any joint-tenure of the whole village as a unit estate.

the Hindu co-sharing family institutions were already developed. Buddhism, we know, from architectural remains, had obtained a hold in the country, but was afterwards supplanted by the later Brahmanic institutions. The early 'Marāthās' disappear from history and only emerge with the revival under Sivājī in the seventeenth century.[1]

Whenever the process of destruction of these early village over-lordships began, and whether it was chiefly due to Moslem victories or was before that period, these ruling families were defeated and deprived of their estates, except in so far as some of the descendants may have clung to villages here and there or to shares in such villages. Under the rule of a new conqueror, a change naturally begins: the lands still belonging to certain branches of the landlord families cannot bear up against the heavy assessment that is imposed; the families, already weakened and dispersed by defeats, having lost prestige and also had many members slain in battle, gradually disappear. The local governor, without much care for anything but immediate profit, puts in some *upari*—*i.e.* non-proprietary cultivators—to till the vacant lands, and they in time become permanent holders with prescriptive rights. In any case, as time goes on, the few remaining *mirāsdār*, or co-sharers, and the cultivating *uparis*, become reduced to the same level, and both appear as mere *raiyats* occupying lands the superior ownership of which has become claimed by the ruler.

I think this view will be generally confirmed by the evidence which is derived partly from the inquiries directed by the Hon. Mountstuart Elphinstone previous to his well-known Report of

[1] The Dakhan districts, covered with hills, afford the greatest facility for building forts and strongholds from which the early chieftains and noble families would dominate the villages in the 'tal,' or level country below. The old over-lord families were sure to have been non-agriculturist, and when their forts fell before their enemies they would lose their hold on the village lands to a great extent. In this respect they would be unlike the village bodies of Upper India, who, holding strong posts in the centre of their village lands, and being in close managing connection with the land and themselves agriculturists, were able to defend them and to secure their possession. I may refer to p. 111, *ante*, where some account is given of early Aryan contact with the west of India.

1819 on the 'Territories acquired from the Peshwā.'[1] These inquiries were made at a time when real historical investigations into tenures were not understood, and they naturally leave much to be desired. A further inquiry was made by Colonel Sykes; and his papers on 'Dakhan Tenures' are to be found in vols. ii. and iii. of the *Journal* of the Royal Asiatic Society. The then well-remembered distinction between *mirāsi* holders and *upari* holders, which is held to mark the existence of co-sharing families over the villages, did not extend to Khāndesh, nor to the South Marāthā country; but it was found in the Dakhan Collectorates of Ahmadnagar, Pūnā, and Dhārvār. Here, too, it was noticed that many lands not in possession of *mirāsdārs* were popularly known as *gat-kul*, which implied that the landlord family (*kulā*) was 'gone' or destroyed (*gatā*). Colonel Sykes found that in many villages lists of shares still existed. And there is some reason to suppose that the larger share was called *thal*, while the minor or individual share was *tīkā*.[2] Colonel Sykes's papers are well worth reading, but it has to be remembered that the author was not familiar with the joint-village, as found elsewhere; there is nothing strange, for example, in the lands of one family branch or *thal* lying scattered about, as the result of some family partition. And our author sometimes confuses the *haq* and the *watan* holdings of headmen and village officers with the shares in the hereditary

[1] This is printed in Mr. G. W. Forrest's *Official Writings of Mountstuart Elphinstone* (London: R. Bentley, 1884). Unfortunately, the *whole* of the Reports of Chaplin, Robertson, Thackeray, and others are not reproduced, but only those portions which Elphinstone attached to his official Minute.

[2] These words are, nevertheless, rather puzzling, perhaps, owing to faulty record of the real word. *Thal* means the 'ground, 'soil,' and 'place' in general; *tal* means 'level.' The correct word I cannot ascertain. *Talkari* may mean a person holding land in the level plain as opposed to *gaḍhkari*, a person employed in the forts, or *gaḍh*, which crowned the hills in the high land of the Dakhan and were doubtless the head-quarters of the chiefs of the clans which dominated the villages. *Tīkā* (or *thīkā*?) again suggests either a spot, a blotch, or patch, or, if the second form is correct, a lease or farm; but the latter is less likely, for farming the revenue of villages could not have been in use in early days. Captain Robertson thought *thal* was used in the sense of a 'field.' (Forrest's *Elphinstone's Minutes*, p. 379.)

estate of village proprietors. Lastly, he is much too ready to infer the general existence in the Dakhan districts of the *thal* system, where no trace of it was actually found. It can justly be inferred to have existed only where it *also* appears that there is at least the memory of *mirāsi* holdings in the village.

Each *thal*, it is interesting to observe, just like the *patti* of Northern India of which it is the counterpart, bears, as I have said, the name of the head of the branch to which it belonged. As the early volumes of the Royal Asiatic Society's *Journal* are not readily accessible, I will make one or two characteristic quotations :—

At Nimbi, in the Nagar (Ahmadnagar) Collectorate (writes Colonel Sykes), there were twenty-three *thal*, of which eighteen were *gatkul*; at Kothal, nine *thal* and five *gatkul*. In the first case eighteen families out of twenty-three are extinct, and in the second, five out of nine. . . . At the village of Belwandi (*pargana* Kardē, Ahmadnagar district), there was not a single representative of an ancient family remaining in A.D. 1827, the whole of the lands were *gatkul*. There were nevertheless some half dozen *mirāsdārs* who had purchased their lands from the Pātel six or seven and twenty years back.[1] The Kulkarnī even denied the existence of *thals* ; but, one of the *mirāsdārs* having told me that he had his land on the *thal* of an extinct family, I urged their existence so strenuously that a *thaljārā*, or list of the estates into which the village lands are divided, was at last reluctantly produced, an old worn paper dated Saka 1698=A.D. 1777. In this list I find the *thals* minutely detailed, together with their possessors, the number of names of *mirāsdārs* who had purchased *mirās* rights from the village authorities on the *thals* that had become *gatkul*, and, finally, the names of the different *uparis* (tenants-at-will) renting land on the *thals*. In 1827 there was not a single person alive a descendant from the possessors of *thals* or *mirās* rights in 1777 ; it would appear that in Holkār's inroad into the Dakhan in 1802, war, famine, pestilence, or flight had depopulated the village ; that the few people that returned died subse-

[1] *Journal R. A. S.* ii. (1835), 209 ff. It will be remembered that in later Marāthā times the Pātels were made responsible for the revenue of their village ; and it was their duty to provide for the cultivation of abandoned holdings ; and they would assume to sell the *mirāsi* right occasionally, either for their own profit or as an inducement to cultivators to take lands and to remain permanently.

quently, and that in consequence there was not an ancient 'heritor' remaining. The lands of Bāghroza (one of the constituent villages of Ahmadnagar) are divided into *thals*, each having a family name with descendants of the original proprietors in possession of many of them. It might have been supposed that the Mussulmāns would have dispossessed the Hindus ;[1] but with the exception of one *thal* which from time immemorial[2] had been in the possession of the descendants of Husain Khān, whose name it bears, there is not a Mussulmān name to any of the *thals*.

An instance is afterwards given of a 'town' Wamori (or Wambori, in the Ahmadnagar district) in which *thals* do not exist by that name, but there is a list found called *Jamīn-jārā-jathāwār* = list of lands according to families (*jathā* means 'company,' hence family), and there were thirty-four families. The individual holders were members of these families, holding the land divided into *tīkā ;* the family lots were apparently not contiguous. In this instance, however, we have a case of the superior ownership being recently assumed by a family of some pretensions; for it was known that Wamori had been devastated by Bhīls, and that the inhabitants fled and the lands lay waste till some of the hereditary village officers returned and took possession of what lands they pleased. The Patārā family holding the *pātelship* (there were then five *pātels*) had annexed no less than thirty thousand acres between them; and the family of the *kulkarnī* (accountant) had also taken possession of a large number of *tīkā*.

Colonel Sykes thinks that the *thal* system could be traced in three-fourths of the villages in the Ahmadnagar and Pūnā

[1] This, however, would not be likely; the Nīzām Shāhi kings (in this part) took the rule only and could not have furnished foreigners sufficient to dispossess any considerable number of land-holders. Moreover, it appears to have been their policy to preserve the old land-holders and superior families, regarding them as the best guarantee for a permanent revenue.

[2] This is an exaggeration, for the dates of the conquest, and of any possible Mussulmān proprietor, are perfectly well known. Probably the share was acquired between the fourteenth and sixteenth centuries; but here we have the original process repeated; a Musssulmān locally replaces *as over-lord* an earlier Hindu whose ancestor may have been lord of the whole village or more, and who probably gained his position by similar conquest in the first instance.

districts. It is curious that, though the superior tenures were, as so often observed, originally free or at least privileged holdings, they afterwards (in Moslem and Marāthā times) were made to pay at a rate which was higher than that of ordinary occupants, and was distinguished by the term *swastīdhārā*.[1] And, characteristically, the Marāthās, not liking to openly surcharge this, levied once in three years an *extra cess*, which they called *mirās-patti*, a special tax on the privilege of superior tenure! Under such circumstances it is no wonder that in the course of time the distinction between *swasti* land and other, or between the representative *mirāsi* occupant and the *upari* or tenant, soon became a matter of memories and names only. It owed such partial preservation as it actually had to the feeling of attachment to hereditary lands and to pride of superior origin. The *mirāsdār* as such would be able to marry his daughters, and secure social advantages that would be denied to the *upari*, however wealthy. Nor is it surprising that the Moslem and Marāthā Governments respected at least the title to *mirāsi* lands; this was partly because they had a natural fellow-feeling with the higher families, partly that they themselves felt that customary respect for hereditary land which was never altogether extinct,[2] partly also because such lands could be made to pay more than the others. Ordinary tenants not attached by hereditary sentiment to any particular village will not be induced to cultivate unless tempted by terms that on the whole are advantageous.[3]

[1] Corruptly, *sosthi* or *susthi*; the word means 'well-being'—*i.e.* a rate (*dhārā*) proper for land held on privileged or superior tenure.

[2] The *private* lands of the governing classes themselves would necessarily be held on an analogous if not identical tenure; this also might make them have some respect for the *mirāsi* holding in general.

[3] This opportunity may be taken to mention that, besides these traces of the tenure of co-sharing landlord families over villages, there were, in a few villages, locally surviving divisions of an older nature, as indicated by the purely Dravidian terms used. The lands were divided into larger areas called *muṇḍ*, and smaller ones called *kās*. The writer of the *Ahmadnagar Gazetteer* (*Bombay Gazetteer*, xvii. referring to xiii. p. 550), justly points out that the division had nothing to do with co-sharing families in superior possession; for where these existed they were of Aryan origin and had the Sanskritic names of *thal*, *tīkā*, &c. Nor do

SECTION III.—MODERN (OR EXISTING) CASES OF THE JUXTAPOSITION OF THE TWO TYPES OF VILLAGE

(1) *The Gujarāt Districts of Bombay*

We have just seen that in the Dakhan districts, whatever groups of landlord families holding villages in shares once existed, they have died out. In one or two of the GUJARĀT districts we find a number of 'shared' (*i.e.* jointly held) villages still surviving, but having a different and much later origin; and they are found side by side with the ordinary *raiyatwāri* village. We shall find them, in fact, held by families of Bohrā (or Voharā), and by families of the enterprising agricultural caste called Kunbī. In both cases the co-sharing tenure is due to the families having originally taken the management, as revenue-farmers, or in some analogous capacity; and now their descendants have sub-divided the villages into many shares, and have long held the whole as virtual owners. That many more villages had formerly come under the same kind of 'ownership' there can be no doubt, but they did not survive the Marāthā rule. In fact, it is largely due to the fact that the Nawābs of Bharoch encouraged such villages that they survive as much as they do.

Before describing these tenures it will be well very rapidly to review the position of the GUJARĀT country as a whole; for it

they indicate any Marāthā method of revenue-management; though doubtless the revenue officers, finding these old divisions of fields still remembered, made use of them to impose lump sums of revenue on the whole, making the cultivators distribute the amount among themselves. Thus the idea arose—which is quite without any foundation—that those few villages where the *muṇḍ* areas were known had some resemblance to the North Indian *zamīndāri* or *pattīdāri* villages. The terms *muṇḍ* (cf. *muḍā*, *muṛka*, &c.), and *kās* indicate larger or smaller areas or lots as measured by the quantity of seed required to sow them. This was a very ancient mode of estimating area, still traceable in Kānara and other Dravidian districts. The word is also found in Berār (*Berār Gazetteer*, p. 93), where it is used (*muṇḍkarī*) to mean an old original cultivator of a holding. It is quite possible that these terms may connect the present with the old form of Dravidian village, and indicate the establishment of different lots or holdings for the headman, the *māhato*, the priest, &c. (Cf. p. 179, *ante*.)

illustrates well how these joint or shared ownerships of villages (where we have nothing to do with clan movements and the foundation of villages in a new territory) always originate in some dismembered territorial over-lordship, or in some position of vantage gained by a revenue-farm, or grant of the revenue-management of a village.

In the Dakhan districts, the early and probably only half-Aryan chiefs who once dominated the country disappeared, as I have stated. In the richer GUJARĀT districts, a much larger and longer continued series of local chiefships attract our attention. For the earlier centuries we have no detailed knowledge; but there is every reason to believe that besides early Aryans coming from the Indus Valley, and probably other Northern leaders also, Greek Princes (connected with the name of Menander) had the rule; and at one time Asokā, the Buddist Emperor of Magadhā, extended at least his suzerainty thus far. But at some date long subsequent to the establishment of the Aryan clans in the Ganges plain, and when the Rājput chiefs had spread into Rājputāna and Mālwā, we begin to have historic glimpses of powerful Rājput dynasties, still strictly localised. They were of the later Aryan type, either Buddhist, Jain, or Brahmanic, being of the *Agnikulā*, or 'Fire-born' houses, the *Chāwarā* (locally *Chāvaḍa*) of Anhilwārā, the *Solankhai*, and later *Bāghelā* princes. In the fourteenth century the 'Hindu' rule came to an end, and there succeeded a series of Moslem Sultāns, the results of the early conquests subsequent to Mahmūd of Ghazni. Their rule lasted some 165 years, till Akbar conquered the country in A.D. 1572. A number of local 'estates' or lordships, the remnants of the old chiefs' dominions, were the natural result.[1] With these we are not now concerned. But it is hardly wonderful that under such a varied series of rulers, all desirous of making the best revenue possible, and rewarding their followers, there should be occasional examples of petty lordships over *villages*: such were the tenures enjoyed by persons called *nāik*, *gāmeti*, *mālik*, *kasbāti*, &c.

The class of village under Bohrā or Kunbi families, which is

[1] There is a particularly good account of Gujarāt in the *Asiatic Quarterly Review* by the late Mr. W. G. Pedder. I think it was in 1889. I have a copy of the article, but, unfortunately, not the reference.

what we have immediately under our consideration, arose out of revenue-farming arrangements. When the time came at which the old fashion of collecting the revenue in grain proved too troublesome, the natural resource was to fix a lump sum in demand from the whole village, whether at a full estimate or at some moderated sum (*udhaḍ-jama*). This was especially the Marāthā system; and the local officials looked about for some village manager to be responsible for the total sum; he in his turn being entitled to take grain or cash (or both) from the villagers, as he best could, to recoup himself. When there was any local chief or *gamēti*, or *kasbāti*, of course he was the person who managed the village. When it was an ordinary *raiyatwāri* village, either the *pātel* (indigenous) headman might be employed, or some outsider put in. It was merely a question of opportunity and circumstances whether such a revenue-manager grew into being virtual owner of the village, in which case the family would divide the property into shares. In the cases before us—chiefly in the districts of Broach (Bharoch) and Kairā (Kheḍā)—the revenue-managers had contrived to retain their villages, and had handed them on to their descendants as their own property.

In principle, these estates are joint-villages like those of Upper India. As late as 1827 such villages were more numerous than they are now.[1] Two kinds are now in survival: one is called *bhāgdāri*, or 'held on shares;' and the shares are (in origin at any rate) the ancestral fractions of the law of inheritance, and, in fact, correspond to the *pattidārī* tenure of Upper India. In the Kairā district the prevalent form is the *narwādārī*, which has a somewhat different constitution, and in Upper India would be called a form of *bhaiāchārā* tenure—*i.e.* fractional shares resulting from the law of inheritance were not observed, but a scheme distri-

[1] The example of a *raiyatwāri* Settlement all round, and the fact that the revenue officers assessed (in general, for there was some difference in detail) every field and holding, would give a great impulse to the co-sharers already holding in severalty to adopt the survey-rate on their holding, instead of their own fractional shares or other customary modes of levy; and if they consented to give up any waste numbers not in cultivation, they would become practically *raiyatwāri*. The only drawback was a certain loss of dignity by giving up the 'shared' tenure.

buting the charges for revenue and expenses was made out according to the value and advantages of the several holdings. The word *narwā* itself means a schedule or scheme of rateable or proportionate payments assigned to each sharer. And the shares or holdings were valued by reference to the *urd-bhāgwāri*, which I understand to be certain artificial land-measures adopted for the valuation of the different shares relatively, like the *bhaiāchārā-bīghā* of Northern India.

In Bharoch the co-sharing holders (*bhāgdār*) have, I understand, become much mixed as to family and caste. But the prevailing caste of proprietors seems still to be the peasant or agricultural section of the Muhammadan Bohrā or Voharā.[1] These families appear to have acquired a hold over a number of villages at a date which is uncertain, but cannot be many generations ago. They got their footing as revenue farmers, or by the familiar process of lending money, or becoming sureties for village revenue payments; this naturally ends by transferring the land to the surety. In 1818 as many as eighty-four villages were found to be held by Bohrā families, who had undertaken the joint responsibility for the revenue, and accordingly had divided both the land and the responsibility into family shares.

The Kairā villages, again, are mostly held by Kunbi communities; the precise origin has not, as far as I know, been traced; but it seems likely that these enterprising agricultural castemen undertook, on the acknowledgment of a permanent lease or other superior tenure, to be responsible for the revenue, possibly restoring the villages after some calamity had for a time thrown them out of cultivation. They have kept together better than the Bohrā communities, probably because the *narwā* system tended better to prevent the disruption of the community, and secured mutual co-operation and support in meeting the revenue demand.[2]

[1] I cannot find proof of the correct spelling. In the local dialect the *w* is usually pronounced as *v*: hence *narvā*, *vāntā*, &c. (*narwā*, *wāntā*, &c.), and so with *b* and *v*.

[2] It is to be wished that we had a more definite detail about the *classes* or castes actually holding shares, and about the people's own traditions of origin and history. There is a valuable Report on these tenures, by the late Mr. W. Pedder, C.S.I., in the *Bombay Revenue*

The difference between the *narwā* and *bhāgdāri* villages is usually treated, by the Bombay writers, as a question of the *form* of *assessment*; in the *narwā* village, it is said, the revenue was, at first at any rate, assessed in the lump for the whole village, according to former custom, and the people prepared the distribution list according to which the co-sharers arranged to pay the total amount.[1] In the *Bhāg* villages, on the other hand, every share-land or family holding, being separate, was separately assessed; and the fields held by tenants were valued at the usual survey-rates. The revenue on the tenant lands was paid accordingly; but the rest was added up together, and the total distributed among the co-sharers, according to their own fractional shares. I cannot believe that this is the real *tenure* distinction; the different mode of assessing must surely have been the consequence, not the cause, of a difference which already existed, and which I have attempted to describe. It will be well to examine a little more in detail the features of each class of village, as it may show that here, in fact, we have the same varieties as naturally occur in joint villages elsewhere. In both cases the origin was, as I have stated, in an arrangement made by individuals of sufficient influence who undertook the responsibility for the revenue-assessment of the whole

Selections, one of those monographs which ought to be reprinted, with notes and explanations added, by some intelligent inquirer of the present time. Some good remarks are to be found in Mr. A. Rogers's Paper on Bombay Tenures in the *Journal of the East India Association*, and in the *Bombay Gazetteer*, iii. 88 (Kairā); for the Broach (Bharoch) district, ii. 377, 483; and for some remains (in Daskroī) of Ahmadābād shared villages, see iv. 156.

[1] None of the reports give any detail as to how a *narwādāri* holding is actually made up; I have no doubt it is of various proportions of each kind of soil; and that the customary valuation is effected by some artificial standard-lot (which is the system called *bhaiāchārā* in North India), and it was worked also with the annual or periodic readjustment of burdens known in the North as *bhejbarār*; both features are certainly implied by Mr. Pedder's Report. It seems to me probable that our first Settlement officers, finding this apparently complicated method, thought it better not to try and assess the *holdings* separately, and so assessed the whole of the *narwā* lands *en bloc*. I can only offer that as my suggestion. It is a fact that the *narwā* lands were assessed in the lump, and the *bhāgdāri* field by field.

village. Thus, as regards the Kairā villages, we are told:[1] 'Under this, the *narwā* system, the headman's responsibility was divided among the members of his family. In such cases, the different branches of the family were traced back to their common ancestor, and the village divided into as many *bhāg*, or primary divisions, as that ancestor had sons. Each share was made over to the representatives of one son, and they divided it into as many lots as there were men (heads of households) in their branch. The head of each branch was called *bhāgdār*, or *pātel*. He acted for the other shareholders, but interfered in no way with the management of their shares.' The families—and sometimes there was only one to a whole branch, would either till their own lands or let out the fields to tenants. Shares were sometimes sold,[2] and outsiders thus brought in. The peculiar *narwā* feature was this: 'Every year the Government demand (*ānkdo*) was divided equally among all the branches, and in every branch each shareholder had a lot, called *phālā*, assigned to him. If he failed to pay, he forfeited his right to the land, and the other sharers might force him to give it up.'[3] But this was not always insisted on, for the others also might fail to pay, or the *parela*, or lapsed shares, might have to be managed direct by the State officer.

The shares were expressed in *ānas* (fractions of a rupee) on an artificial scale. Thus, in a village called Sandesar, in Pitlād, there were seven branches, and the revenue demand was Rs. 7,854. The whole village was treated as = 84 *ānas*, of which 12 were assigned to each of the seven *bhāg*. There were 403½ *bīghās* held undivided, and the income of this, Rs. 294, was first devoted to the revenue payment, leaving Rs. 7,560 to be met by the remaining lots held in severalty and covering

[1] *Bombay Gazetteer* (Kairā), p. 88 ff.

[2] The complicated and readjustable *narwā* share would be less easy to sell than the fixed, demarcated, fractional share of the *bhāgdāri* village; perhaps this was the reason why the latter villages have become more miscellaneously held (p. 389, *ante*).

[3] This is noteworthy, as confirming what I said about the Madras Vellālar (p. 377, *ante*). Such a power does not exist in the *pattidāri* communities descended from an 'aristocratic' ancestor in Upper India. It shows a voluntary association for colonising or revenue managing.

1,505 *bīghās*. Each *āna* thus corresponded to a holding of 17 *bīghās* and a fraction (17·9 × 84 = 1,504 nearly).[1] As there remained Rs. 7,560 to be paid on 1,505 *bīghās*, that gave Rs. 90 for each *āna* share (90 × 84 = 7,560). The *majmūn*, or common land, was managed for the community by the headmen. On the whole, the *narwā* village evidently much resembles the democratic *bhaiāchārā* community of Northern India.

In the *bhāgdāri* village the method is somewhat different, and approximates to the ancestral fractional-share system, or *pattidārī*, of the North-West Provinces. In the example selected by the writer of the notice in the *Bombay Gazetteer*, the village has a total area of 2,500 acres, of which 1,800 are held divided and 700 held jointly. Now in Bharoch there might be three 'ancestors,' or representatives of three major shares of four *ānas* each, leaving the undivided land as a kind of fourth *share* to represent the remaining four ānas of the unit rupee. This, it is true, would not be the case with an '*imperfect pattidārī*' village of Upper India, held on fractional shares in descent from an original founder. In such a village, if there were only three *pattī*, each could represent one-third of the whole ($5\frac{1}{3}$ *āna*), and each would be liable for the same fraction of the revenue, and would take the same fraction of the undivided land when it came to be partitioned, and meanwhile each would have one-third of the rents and profits.[2]

But in the Bharoch example, each of the three sharers holds 600 acres as a four-āna share, and 700 acres are in common (3 × 600 + 700 = 2,500). The total revenue is assumed to be Rs. 10,000, of which Rs. 4,000 come from the manorial dues and income of the common land, leaving Rs. 6,000 to be met by the three sharers. Each of the three *bhāgs* would thus have to find Rs. 2,000, which would again be distributed in regular fractions among the sub-sharers; thus, two '*pātīdārs*' (secondary sharers) of the first *bhāg*, would pay Rs. 1,000 each; or, if they were further subdivided, say into eight minor shares, each of

[1] See p. 389, as to the different soils in each holding; and the note at p. 335, *ante*.

[2] In practice, the rents and profits of the common would probably be first taken to meet the revenue demand, and it would be the balance that would be met (one-third by each) by the main shares.

these would find Rs. 125 and so on.[1] In prosperous times the common land would be held by tenants, and so managed as perhaps to cover the whole or a large part of the revenue demand; but under the Marāthās an assessment would be laid on every separate portion, and the village total would be raised accordingly; and I expect that the arrangement noted above, of treating the tenant land or 'common' as a sort of separate share, arose out of this necessity.

The villages all keep their list of the shares and sub-shares, which is called *phalāvni*. The major share is here locally called *motābhāg*, and the minor share *petābhāg*. Each family share is *pāti*, and the holder of it *pātidār*. This is the usual division of the estate according to the degrees of *the original* family—sons, grandsons, and great-grandsons of the founder.

The people, Mr. Pedder notices, are unwilling to give up the status of co-sharer, because they would lose '*abru*,' or dignity; they can marry their daughters much better with this claim to superiority. On the other hand, the convenience of the *raiyatwāri* method, surrendering the ownership of unused waste to Government, and having to pay just the fixed assessment on the particular field, must in time tempt them to abandon the original form.[2] It is curious how few villages, comparatively, became definitely constituted like the *narwādari* and *bhāgdāri*. In North India, under similar revenue-farming arrangements, and under the forced sales and similar transfers which they occasion, revenue farmers and purchasers at auction have become the proprietors of a respectable percentage of the total number of village-communities in the North-West Provinces. But the Marāthā administration was never favourable to these growths. Though there were farmers in abundance, they were too strictly looked after, and not allowed to continue long enough, to become

[1] It would often happen that one of the *bhāg* would have part of its land undivided among its own members (*majmūn-bhāg*), then they would meet their 2,000 rupee share just in the same way, as above stated for the whole village; they would first apply the proceeds of the common land to the payment, and then provide the balance according to their shares.

[2] The people call the *raiyatwāri* villages *sanjā* (in Gujarāt *sejā*), which means 'joint,' or not shared; not because there is or ever has been any joint-holding, but because there are no *bhāg*, *pāti*, &c., but all are on the same footing of equality.

proprietors; and the same is true of the village officers, who in later times presumed greatly on their powers, and in some cases acquired very large holdings,[1] by forced sales and mortgages in their village.

(2) *The Bīkaner State.*

We have another instance yet to notice, in conclusion, of a Native State in which both kinds of village exist side by side. I do not doubt that many other cases could be found; but it is only under favourable conditions that they come to notice and get recorded. If the general land system of a province happens to be based on the prevalence of one form or the other, the tendency must be for any other forms that may exist naturally, to assimilate to the one contemplated by the system. In the provinces of Northern India where *raiyatwāri* villages existed of old, as no doubt they did, before the landlord villages grew up and Jat and other invaders established themselves, it is quite likely that some at least would remain without falling under any landlord class; and yet in the present day no distinction would possibly survive after our surveys and records, which are prepared to suit the joint form.[2] So in Madras, the general system being *raiyatwāri*, the tendency for the local, and already decaying, *mirāsi* or joint-villages to become merged in the prevalent form proved irresistible.

The circumstances of the State of Bīkaner have made it possible for both kinds of village to survive together. Bīkaner is situate in the northern corner of Rājputāna, in a sandy plain which stretches north and north-west of the Arāvālī mountains. It is possessed of a generally poor soil and is thinly populated,

[1] For example, in the case of the Wamori Pātel above alluded to. See also a curious account in *Bombay Gazetteer*, iv. 485 (referring to Forbes's *Oriental Memoirs*, ii. 419). The District Accountant (*majmūdār*, or *despāndyā* of other parts), named Lallubhāi, attained to such pretensions in the Bharoch district as to go about 'with mace-bearers running before him proclaiming idle titles.' This was in 1776. Had this happened under more favourable circumstances, or in Bengal, he would have ended by becoming a great 'Zamindār.' Unfortunately, under the Marāthās, an end was put to his career by a revenue-farm which he was tempted to bid up for against a rival. He got it, but on terms that proved his ruin.

[2] *Ante*, p. 344.

so that the villages are more easy to observe and to classify. About the latter half of the fifteenth century, a clan of Rājputs (of the *Rāhtor* stock) established a dominion and divided the territory into a *k̲h̲ālsa* demesne for the Rājā and into chiefships held (on the usual *pattā* or quasi-feudal tenure) by the Thākur or 'barons.'[1] In the *k̲h̲ālsa* area we find two kinds of village—those established in independence, before the Rāhtor dominion, by Jāts,[2] and villages established since the dominion and mostly within the last century or so. It is probable, says Mr. Fagan, that originally neither the Rāhtor Rājā nor his fief-holders claimed any definite ownership in the soil; but they held the over-lordship as rulers, each realising the grain-share in his own territory. Mr. Fagan goes on to remark that, though primogeniture has to some extent secured the chief's 'estates' from partition, still the issue of grants of villages and maintenance provision for members of the family (which assign the chief's grain-share and the right of cultivating the waste), have virtually created a number of petty estates, in which there is a distinct tendency for the grantee to draw closer to the land and to become the direct owner or village landlord.

In the Rājā's demesne, the chief's connection with the land could not, in the nature of things, be as close as that of a resident landlord; and, consequently, the Rājā collects his revenue and exercises his right of disposing of the waste, without directly influencing the tenure of the land in general.

The Jāt villages, in the absence of any other dominion at the time, established an independent position, and are held in joint ownership by co-sharing bodies—representatives of the original 'founders.' In the Thākur's estates above mentioned, this position has now been overborne by the Thākur's assertion of the superior landlordship; but the original right is still so far recognised as to give a claim to hold permanently and on an hereditary title. It is chiefly in the Rājā's demesne that the joint-village is more distinctly in evidence; but side by side with

[1] *Report on the Settlement of the Khalsa Villages of the Bīkaner State*, 1893, by P. J. Fagan, C.S. (Panjāb Government).

[2] *S. R.* iii. § 19. Here the name is Jāt. It will be observed that the Rājputs furnished only the ruling house and its army. Had they been more numerous, they might have formed co-sharing villages, as elsewhere.

the Jāt villages, all the other villages are groups of independent cultivating holders who have settled together under a headman (or *çaudhrī*), who was their spokesman in applying for leave to establish cultivation. Here, as in the South-eastern Panjāb, the people commenced the village by driving in a stake or pole on the site of the *ābādī*.[1] Sometimes permission was not formally asked, but as soon as the new village became known the Rajā's officer would go to the spot and settle terms. In the village itself (land being in this case abundant and irrigation from the *johar* or tank being well-nigh indispensable) there was no formal allotment of holdings; each settler took what he could manage. 'There was no partition,' says Mr. Fagan, 'of the whole or part of a definite area by virtue of a joint-landlord claim over it.' Where population is scanty and the area wide, no objection is made to anyone extending his fields into the adjacent waste, or even to new-comers doing the like. But in the more thickly populated parts of the Eastern Tahsīls, only the original settlers can so extend their holdings; new-comers (called here, as often elsewhere, *sukhbāsī*) must get the headman's permission to cultivate. The *çaudhrī* acts in this respect, not as landlord, but as representative of the State. Mr. Fagan particularly notes that the *çaudhrī* has no superior position as claiming general ownership over the village. Nor were the oldest settlers or 'first clearers' owners of the whole area jointly; their position is only marked by exemption from certain local fees, or taxes on marriages, or on weighment of grain, and by their having greater freedom in taking up additional waste to extend their holdings. The actual boundaries of each village, and the jurisdiction of the *çaudhrī*, became settled in time by practice, and by the definition which results from contact with the areas of neighbouring villages.

It does not appear whether the Jāt joint-villages are in the *pattidārī* form, or whether (as is more likely) they are in the form of the clan-villages settled on some form of *bhaiāchārā* tenure. It is true that the *raiyatwārī* villages are not of ancient origin; but many joint communities in other parts are

[1] In the Panjāb, it will be observed, owing to the system, such villages are classed as 'joint-villages' and are so treated; in Bīkaner they appear in their natural *raiyatwārī* form.

no older, and there must surely be a real difference in the custom and constitution of the Jāt clans who preceded them. The co-sharing among the latter was due to their sense of superior position, either as descendants from individual founders, or as members of a clan obtaining a new home as a matter of conquest or adventure, and bringing with them this characteristic of clan feeling. The other settlers have no such pretensions; they assert merely a right to their own holdings in virtue of the first clearing and establishment of tillage which they have accomplished. This is not a decay of the former feeling, but one characteristically different.

CHAPTER X

GENERAL SUMMARY AND CONCLUSION

Section I.—Ideas of Property, Collective and Individual

The numerous instances of village formation which have been collected from the Settlement Reports and similar authorities can hardly have failed to suggest the impossibility of disposing of 'the Indian Village Community' by referring the whole of the phenomena to some one theory or generalised view of the subject. But such a conviction does not preclude us from drawing certain general conclusions which appear to arise naturally from a comparative view of the various forms and kinds of village presented to our observation.

One of the first questions which the facts naturally suggest, is: seeing that the village is a group of *persons* as well as an aggregate of *land*-holdings, what kind of right or title was really acknowledged? or, in other words, what kind of connection is there between the *persons* and the *land* of a village? And this question involves the two subordinate inquiries—(1) how has any idea of ownership or right in land in India grown up? and (2) how have these rights been recognised—as residing in the individual, or father of the household, or in a body of wider kindred, or in a still larger body, such as a whole clan?

(1) *Early Ideas of Right in Land*

The sense of ownership in land, if we judge solely on the basis of what has occurred in India, seems to have arisen and progressed in a manner which is purely natural, and which does not, at any rate, *need* for its explanation an *a priori* assumption of 'collective ownership,' or holding 'in common.' If any evidence exists of actual collective ownership, at any stage of the development of tenures, that is another matter; but, in so far as it may be regarded in the light of a necessary postulate, it may be not out of place to remark that 'collective ownership,' as a very early phenomenon, is a hazardous thing to assume the existence of; the very name or term is one which it is difficult to employ without bringing in a number of ideas of a kind which, instinctively as they arise in our own minds, can hardly have existed in the minds of primitive or early tribal settlers. We have become so accustomed to a mental analysis of 'ownership,' and to say, at least in general terms, what it involves or in what it consists, that it is not easy to think of any right in land apart from such conceptions. When, for example, we think of the periodical exchange of holdings which is found among certain clan-settlers, and assert that this indicates 'common ownership' because (to use M. de Laveleye's words[1]) 'le fonds continue à rester la propriété collective du clan, à qui il fait retour de temps en temps, afin qu'on puisse procéder à un nouveau partage,' this seems to imply that a precedent conception of what 'collective property' *is* existed in the minds of the clan, and that in consequence of such a conception the surrender of the holdings became required by custom. But it is impossible to suppose that any distinction of the kind was even vaguely understood: exchange was the custom because it gave every one an equal chance; not because the tribe realised the idea of a joint-property, which, in the juristic nature of things, was capable of being recalled and redistributed. Every tribesman knew that he had joined in conquering or seizing a territory, and that he would fight to keep his hold on it. He acknowledged that his chief's word was his law, and that the share allotted to him and his fellows must be observed. His sense of right to his own allotment would make him equally ready to fight for it; and if asked why? he would in all probability reply, because his clan had conquered it, his chief had allotted him 'his inheritance,' and he had cleared and ploughed up the land.

Putting aside the temptation to read modern juristic notions between the lines, it would seem that the right to land grows

[1] *Propriété Primitive*, &c. p. 5.

out of two ideas; one being that a special claim arises, to any object, or to a plot of land, by virtue of the labour and skill expended on making it useful or profitable; the other, that a claim arises from conquest or superior might. In a very early stage, a body of primitive settlers comes to a 'boundless' area of wooded or jungle-clad but fertile plain. As each household group laboriously clears and renders fit for cultivation a certain area, the father, or the united family, as the case may be, regards the plot as now connected with himself or themselves specially, in virtue of the labour expended on it. This claim is recognised by all, because every other member of the clan has the same feeling as regards the field he has cleared. The feeling of right is further developed when each holding is the result not merely of a random choice, but of some regular procedure of allotment by the clan chief.[1]

If there are no other human beings to contest the ownership, although the clan occupies a more or less compact general territory, the sense of any wider or more general clan-right is not as keen as it afterwards becomes when other, very likely unfriendly, clans lie all round, and each has to maintain its own limits against aggression. The idea of clan-right to the territory as a whole—both the cleared holdings and the waste which is grazed over and from which wood is cut, must soon, in the natural course of events, become definite. Not only is there sure to be some clan collected together at the time of first settling,[2] but the families, naturally and by choice grouped together, must help each other a great deal in clearing the jungle, building the cottages, digging the tanks or wells, and in many similar works. Hence, even if there were no general sense of kindred, which long residence together has fostered, there would still be a certain sense of union. The right to the holding selected and cleared by the family is, however, naturally superior to the clan-territorial claim, being more definite: it is, in fact, dependent on the sentiment which originates the notion of

[1] The sentence of the Patriarch and the result of casting lots, are both of them in early times, vested with a semi-divine cogency or significance.

[2] I refer to the first general (Dravidian) movement, probably unopposed, to a permanent agricultural settlement.

'property' in general—that which a man has 'made' or rendered useful and profitable he has a special title to enjoy.

Professor Kovalevsky, in his interesting lectures on the development of the family,[1] has quoted the curious reflection of Rousseau: 'Le premier qui ayant enclos un terrain, s'avisa à dire "Ceci est à moi," et trouva des gens assez simples pour le croire, fut le vrai fondateur de la société civile. Que de crimes . . . . n'eût point épargné au genre humain celui qui arrachant les pieux ou comblant le fossé eût crié à ses semblables: "Gardez-vous d'écouter cet imposteur; vous êtes perdus si vous oubliez que les fruits sont à tous, et que la terre n'est à personne."' The natural sense of the community unfortunately was that the person who did tear up the stakes of the fence or did fill up the ditch would be an enemy and a wrongdoer; everyone consented that the clearer of the waste had a real claim to the field he had made. The sentiment is observed among all tribes when they have made a permanent agricultural settlement; it was, in fact, Nature herself who prevented the early existence of the philosopher who should cry 'Beware of such a supposition,' though it arises instinctively.

The naturalness of such a feeling of appropriation is the more obvious because in early times there is nothing to prevent its action; there is no prior claim nor obstacle to the customary allotment by the clan chiefs: the wide expanse of virgin jungle is as free as the air or water. The modern Socialist asks as against the present possessor of a farm or a park, 'Although you have spent money in draining, planting, and, in fact, in creating the utility and value of the plot, what right had you to deal at all—for any permanent purpose—with that particular section of the surface of the national land?' He considers it an economic wrong that the growth of custom and law should have allowed a permanent individual appropriation. But, in truth, it is only the operation of an instinctive feeling of human nature. The early tribesman, under sanction of custom, appropriated his field, or his share of the tribal land, as he would appropriate a tree to make a canoe or a plough.

But very soon another factor comes into the question: when

[1] *Tableau des Origines et de l'Evolution de la Famille*, &c. (Stockholm, 1890), pp. 50, 51.

tribes multiply, and, moving east or west, come into conflict, and one is superior in energy and in power of combination to another; the possession of land no longer remains a matter of first appropriation in the absence of all other claims. Might becomes right; and conquest gives a new title. The title by 'first clearing' is overborne by the title by conquest, notwithstanding that the claim by first clearing will probably be acknowledged by the conquerors as among themselves. This claim by conquest and superiority the next generation will euphemise as the claim by 'inheritance.' It is curious to observe that a people so advanced as the Romans, and so apt to make that legal analysis of things which has influenced all subsequent views regarding ownership, not only conceived the idea of *res nullius*—*i.e.* crude material or potential property as yet unappropriated—but they boldly held that when war broke out the lands and property of an enemy reverted to a state of nature and once more became *res nullius*. The conquerors began over again the process of customary appropriation.

Out of this new growth—the right by conquest or 'inheritance'—some further factors in the making of land-tenures are sure to spring. In India, among early tribes like the Mongoloid and Kolarian (as far as we can trace their habits), the cohesion was extremely loose, and the idea of centralised rule quite wanting. This appears to have been gradually improved upon by the Dravidian races; but it is later conquering tribes like the Aryan, the Indo-Scythian, the Jat and the north-west frontier tribes, that had the best developed powers of combination and organisation. Hence we find ideas of the right of a whole clan to a certain territory, in which every member has his share or his equal interest; and we find families expanding into clans, and still keeping up something of this same notion.[1]

But it is also a further phase of clan development, under the necessity for military discipline, and organised movement, that the patriarchal rule of chiefs gives way to a system of king

[1] In such a case the sense of individual appropriation exists side by side with the sense of the collective appropriation; and while each gets his separate share, the custom of periodical exchange of holdings is the expression of the *equal right* which results from the unity of the whole body.

and barons, or subordinate chiefs. And no sooner are these dignities acknowledged than there arise various kinds of territorial lordship, which may take the form of a kingdom, or local chiefship, or a sort of manorial holding of smaller portions of land. This right of lordship over an estate has nothing to do with the question of labour or expense incurred in clearing and cultivating the soil, but is an over-lordship, based on caste or family superiority, attained by conquest or otherwise; and it expresses itself by taking a share in the produce raised by tenants, dependents, or a pre-existing body of agricultural settlers. It is made tolerable to the now subordinated original settlers by the degree of protection which the over-lord, even in his own interest, affords to the villages from which he derives his revenue or income.

So far, then, we have the two natural and often concurrently active factors, the sense of right by 'occupation' and 'first clearing,' and the right by 'inheritance'—a term which we shall now understand without further comment, and which has already met us in so many forms as *mirāṣī*, *wirāṣat*, *wāriṣī*, &c.

It is hardly possible to avoid the suggestion that the main distinction between the *raiyatwāri* and the joint or landlord village (these terms being only provisional, and adopted for want of better) is in some way the outcome of these two principles. The former originated with early unopposed tribes, who, like the Dravidian had strong agricultural instincts and had passed out of the nomadic and pastoral stage: their struggle was more with the forces of Nature than with any human enemies, and their idea of right was that they were *bhūīṅhār*, the original soil-clearers and settlers. The latter originated with 'inheritors,' who acquired the lordship of existing villages, or founded new ones in the same sense of superiority. If, as in the case of the Jats, the clans were not only superior in conquest and adventure, but also addicted to agriculture, they would combine both feelings of right to their settlements.

Granted, however, such a natural foundation for 'ideas of ownership' in the abstract, it is a further question whether either kind of right is understood to attach itself to the individual, or to the family, or to the whole clan settled in one compact territory.

We can attempt to judge of this by the aid of the actual cases of clan-settlement, family-village, and separate-holding village which we have had before us.

(2) *Collective and Individual Ownership of Village Lands*

This last remark reminds us that some preliminary explanation is necessary to connect the question of the form of ownership with the existence of land-holdings *in village groups*. We remember, in the first place, that the village group does not in any case represent a fixed circle of kindred extending to any particular degree. We talk freely of a 'village community' as owning the land 'in common,' but it will at once strike us on reflection, that the formation of village groups of families is not necessarily connected with any idea of soil-ownership at all. In the case of some clan-settlements, we have seen that there may be a degree of unity maintained over the whole area, or at least over its major divisions, and that villages are quite a secondary, almost accidental, result of the fission of the area. In India, south of the Vindhyas, again, we see an almost universal *village* formation, but there is no claim, either joint or individual, to the ownership of the whole village;[1] there the village is a group formed of several families who settled, or are now resident, together, but whose contiguous holdings within the village boundary are independent, and always have been so, as far as any evidence goes. And where, in Northern India, the *village* as an area of land is also the essential feature, not a casual result of the fission of a clan-area), and where such a village is jointly owned, it is really that the 'village' is the limit of the original acquisition by a single person, and continues as the sphere of ownership of a possibly numerous but still singly descended close-kindred which has succeeded by joint inheritance to the right of the founder or originator.

In the first instance, no doubt, the aggregation of holdings in a 'village' of limited dimensions, and the establishment of a central (perhaps rudely fortified) place of residence, is, under the circumstances of most Indian provinces, a purely natural

[1] The cases in which such an ownership had probably at one time existed or still exists are so far exceptional as not to invalidate the statement in the text for present purposes.

condition under which permanent cultivation can best be established and maintained. There are districts where the nature of the ground or other conditions render any considerable aggregation either of fields or of residences impossible; but in the plains, let us say, in a moist and densely-wooded region, the erection of a group of dwellings on a fairly elevated spot, the united clearing of an area to give breathing room, and the united defence of the cleared fields against the depredations of wild animals—all these things imply the aggregation of families in a village; and the aggregate must be limited in size, or the machinery for its self-government and the supply of its needs would fail to act. Or again, in a dry climate, a similar combination would very likely be necessary with reference to providing or utilising the means of irrigation. But in the second place, the fact that kindred, especially in a tribal stage of society, naturally keep together, and that as the groups expand they must necessarily separate and form a new series of similar aggregates, these facts, and others like them, also furnish the conditions of village formation.

But there is nothing in the causes of such formation to suggest any new form of ownership as resulting from their operation; and as a matter of fact, and looking to the largest number of instances we can recall, we shall find that the sort of ownership which is actually found in villages corresponds to one or other of the following three heads:—

(1) The family or individual holdings are all separate within the village.

(2) The village is an accidental aggregate of kindred families; and the joint ownership or collectivity, such as it is, is in the whole clan; where any further (real) joint ownership appears, it is between members of the 'family' or close kindred.

(3) The village is really the limit of the acquisition, by whatever means, of one founder or originator;[1] and the joint-

[1] It may happen that one geographical village may contain two originally separate groups, but in that case all the phenomena of joint-ownership will exist only within the groups. Where a village has come to be miscellaneously owned, by the intrusion of various strangers there is no joint-ownership at all. Should outsiders have been formally admitted to shares, then there is the fiction of family membership.

ownership now appearing is due to the main branches representing, according to universal custom, the three primary grades of descent, and to such families, descendants of these, as remain joint among themselves being subject to the operation of the 'joint-family' custom and the law of joint-inheritance.

We sometimes find it insisted that the order of these *three* modes ought to be reversed. I do not, however, desire, by placing them as I have done, to imply *any* theory of sequence of development.

It will be well, however, as such a theory has been propounded, to consider the modes of ownership in connection with it. We may readily admit some plausibility about the general idea that (1) the *joint-ownership of land by a whole clan* is natural as a first stage; that (2) this dissolves into the ownership of isolated joint-families; and, finally (3), that family shares are lost sight of and there remains nothing but the modern individuality of title to the several holdings. But I do not think that the evidence in India will really bear out such a succession. For whatever clan-ownership can be asserted, it is not of a kind to change into or produce the real joint-ownership by a family. I should rather say that the process was just the reverse: that the earliest idea was appropriation by the individual—*i.e.* the father of the family, whose power was a sole and unrestricted power; that this gradually develops into an idea of equality between all the sons in succession to the father's property, which again leads to the restraint of the father's power to deal with ancestral land, and so to the idea of a joint-ownership by a close-kindred of which the father is the head. When a number of such families of common descent, kept together by circumstances, continually fighting side by side and conquering together, have acquired and settled on a new land, they constitute a *clan*, and there is, further, a kind of collective sense of right to the whole, which is over and above the family right to the several lots that fall to each, and is largely dependent on the sense of unity which clan life naturally produces, and on the sense of the right of every member to share in the common acquisition.

But let us briefly recall and analyse the kinds of tenure which we have found to result from the settlement *where a clan-union is still to some extent maintained.* The details have already appeared in Chapter VI.

We may pass by those early Kolarian and Dravidian clan settlements which resulted in the *raiyatwāri* village, because we have no evidence on which to found any assertion of collective ownership among them.[1] Whatever indications they afford of growth of ideas of ownership relate to the family and to the father of the household and not to the clan as a whole.

The clan settlements of Upper India, which introduce us more directly to the question of clan-ownership, are some of them of comparatively late date, but they show tribal ideas in full force, and, at any rate, are the only examples of clan-settlements which afford us any details as to the principles on which the territories occupied were held. It will be remembered that we have two forms of such settlement—(1) of already formed clans; in this case clans with a strong sense of union under patriarchal authority; (2) of clans grown up on the spot out of a single family of settlers on a wide area; so that in this latter case we had the family estate, only expanded in a manner and to an extent that was impossible in the limited area of an ordinary village, and, because of the blood connection of the cultivators throughout the whole area occupied, it preserved some of the features of a clan-settlement.

It is not known, in either case, whether the settlers had had any experience of permanent cultivating ownership of land in any previous home. It cannot be said with certainty that, for example, the frontier tribes, on settling in our north-western districts, emerged for the first time from a nomadic stage and took to agricultural life; probably not. Nor do we know how far the Jats had any experience of settled agricultural life before they came to India. But all tribes possessed herds and flocks, and they necessarily possessed the idea of individual or family property as far as moveables were concerned.

Our north-west frontier tribes certainly exhibit a strong sense of territorial right, which is necessarily a collective one,

[1] If, too, we may take such surviving cases as the Kāndh and a few others as representing very ancient custom—and they very probably do so—they do not show any collective ownership in the clan; and even the 'family' is not regarded as collective owner.

and exhibits itself in the acknowledgment of an '*ilāqa* for the whole body and of certain sub-territories for clans and minor clans, each of which certainly constitutes a unit area. These territorial areas correspond to the main branches of the family of the founder with whom the clan originates. Consequently, the names of the primary divisions follow those of the sons, grandsons, and great-grandsons of the founder respectively. All later and now existing families belong to one or other of the thus established groups and sub-groups, and take shares within the territory belonging to each: there are no new designations given to subsequent divisions. Only, should a certain group move off to another locality, then the whole process would begin anew.[1]

Two sentiments appear to have taken hold of the tribal mind: the territorial right to the main divisions as so many units or wholes; and the right to a specific—usually equal, but sometimes ancestral—share within the proper unit-territory. The action of the tribal heads at the time of the settlement seemed to go no further than allotting the primary or major divisions or territories: inside each, the further allotment of actual holdings was made by the minor or sectional chiefs. The space relatively required by each recognised group was roughly estimated by counting the number of single shares which represented the total population of the group. The whole process seems designed to provide for the separate enjoyment of the individual family share.[2] The shares being intended to be as equal as possible, equality was further ensured by the custom of periodical exchange, which, however, did not apply where the holdings were specially prepared for irrigation, or, in any case, there were circumstances of expenditure which tended to evoke

[1] It is true that sometimes a new series is begun within the lowest original division, called *khel*. We may have the *khel* divided into *kandi*, and that into *thal*—a new series of three grades. This, however, only emphasises the principle. Evidently, here the tribe is old and has much expanded, so that it is convenient to begin again; the lowest of the original divisions has become so big as to be itself a clan.

[2] In dividing a large surface into a great number of small equal portions, the process is obviously facilitated by first making a few large divisions to start with.

more particularly the natural sense of individual right to the plot.

The shares were assigned on one of two principles: either (1) there is a *per capita* distribution—*i.e.* every man, woman, and child was counted, and each household thus received the number of shares which the count of heads indicated; or (2) the ancestral shares were calculated according to the pedigree table, in descent from the heads of each recognised group. The lots might consist of various bits of different kinds of soil scattered through the whole major-divisions (a *ṭappā*, or a *khel*) dealt with. Diagram I. (on the next page) explains this.

It is quite possible that groups of close kindred will cultivate their shares jointly; it being more profitable to do so than to split up the land into small severalty holdings.

As regards the tenure of the whole major division, nothing in the nature of 'holding in common' ever appears; for in any real sense, 'common holding' implies that all should join in cultivating as large an area as necessary, and that each should then receive a portion of the harvest suitable to his wants, without thought of any particular share calculated on any principle whatever, and without thought of the proportions between the amount of sustenance required and the actual amount of labour and capital, or the number of cattle, contributed to the common task.

Nor is there any evidence of 'joint-holding,' save for special reasons, in special plots of land. I am now speaking, it will be remembered, of the joint-holding by a whole clan or clan-section. Whatever the rule of distribution, partition, or allotment on the ground of the several holdings, appears to take place as soon as may be after the settlement of the clan. Some portion of the area may be left undivided, either because it is not yet wanted for cultivation and is reserved for future extension of the family holdings, or because it is grazing ground, or jungle for wood-cutting, which would be rendered useless by division. If there is any area of cultivated land left undivided, it is for special reasons, and the shares are defined though not partitioned. On the other hand, some kind of 'collective right' may very reasonably be asserted, which is something more than that mere territorial claim which every nation, even under modern conditions of life, feels with regard to its own country. The clan has not only its

DIAGRAM I

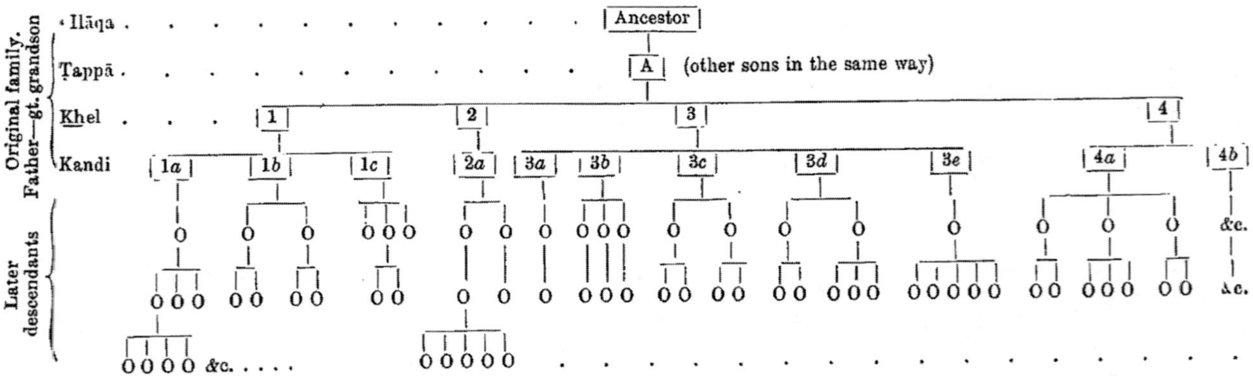

I. Tribal sharing (*khulāvesh* or *per-capita* method). There will be as many *tappa* arranged as there are sons of the founder, A, B, &c. [Only one of these is followed out in the above table.] *Ṭappā* A will be divided into four *khel*, which will contain 3, 1, 5, and 2 *kandi* respectively. Here the descent of the first rank, counting from the ancestor, ends. All the existing heads of households at time of settlement (represented by the last complete line of little circles) will be counted, and each will get such a number of unit shares as represents the number of *heads* in each.

II. Sharing by the 'ancestral' method. Here the division up to the *khel* areas will be as before; but *khel* 1 will be divided into three equal portions for *kandi* 1*a*, 1*b*, 1*c*. The whole of *khel* 2 will descend to the *kandi*, as there is only one. *Khel* 3 will be equally subdivided among five *kandi*—3*a*, 3*b*, 3*c*, 3*d*, 3*e*, and so on.

And coming to the lowest line in the scale, the whole *kandi* 1*a* will go equally to the three sons; that of 1*c* will go between two surviving descendants, two being deceased without heirs. So with *kandi* 3*a*, the one son will take the whole, while 3*c* will have to be divided among four equal descendants, so that the shares or lots actually held will be very various; the families with fewer members will have larger holdings.

Supposing the *ṭappā* to be 40,000 acres, the four *khel* in A would have 10,000 acres each, and *kandi* 1*a*—1*c* would have each 3,333⅓ acres, *kandi* 2*a* would take the whole 10,000, *kandi* 3*a*—3*e* would each get 2,000, and so on.

Under the first method (which is common) the *khels* would probably have unequal areas, roughly proportioned to the number of houses in each: *khel* 3 having many descendants might be much larger than *khel* 2, for instance. Supposing 15,000 acres to be the area, as the *khel* 3 has eighteen existing houses, each containing (say) five souls or a total of ninety, then taking ninety shares of 166⅔ acres each, *kandi* 3*a* could take five (for its one house); 3*b* would take fifteen, and so on.

general boundary, which it would be prepared to defend resolutely as a whole, but every clansman has an indefeasible right to a share in that territory.[1] They will also combine as regards the responsibility for land-revenue and similar charges. All this, however, seems to me to point much more to the sense of kinship and personal obligation to mutual help than to any idea as to the soil being owned jointly. Union is the life of a clan; each section of it must be prepared to send its quota of fighting men to the field, to pay its portion of the contribution necessary for defence, and so forth. Moreover, there is the patriarchal feeling of the obedience due to the chiefs. In a family, as distinct from a clan, there is a recognised bond, which is that of felt blood-relationship, and may be accompanied by a system of joint inheritance and co-ownership. This kind of connection ceases to apply to purely collateral branches, who are only connected at a point a long way back in the pedigree table, and in the person of an ancestor whose very name is probably unknown to a number of the families; but if circumstances have maintained a large circle of ancestral connections through a whole clan, the connection of one family with another is kept up by other feelings: clan-union and all that it implies has survived. I can see no evidence that this ever amounts to a real joint-ownership of the territory by the entire body, such as is observed when a number of co-heirs have each (in theory at least) a definite fractional share of an estate inherited from one original owner and possibly held without actual partition.

This question of joint-ownership by a whole clan is further illustrated by that other case of clan-settlement illustrated in Chapter VI., which is in fact the converse of the one just described: the clan does not arrive ready made, but a family obtains a wide area, and expands, upon it, into a clan. The districts that presented the requisite conditions favourable to such a development are only occasionally to be met with. There must have been a wide extent of suitable land (sometimes twenty to fifty square miles or even more), and circumstances of position such that the entire area has been preserved to the group without disturbance all through the long period during which only

[1] See p. 49, *ante*, as to the effects which physical conditions of agricultural life have on the form which the tribal union takes.

a limited portion could have been actually occupied, and up to the time when the multiplied families had become numerous enough to fill the whole. But here again, judging from the instances which have already been given, though the first family were evidently in a stage of society in which they regarded themselves—father and sons together—as joint-owners, it can hardly be said that this sense of joint-ownership continued as between the more and more distantly related families that grew up and branched off, but still lived on part of the same great area. We observe some cases in which no definite sections of the area corresponding with main branches of the family are demarcated. The *whole area is held directly in separate household-holdings*, usually consisting of so many 'ploughs;' and they appear to have been added on to the first centre of cultivation, one by one, as the different male descendants came to an age at which they needed their own separate home with its farmland. Nevertheless, a certain union is maintained all over the estate; but the union appears to consist essentially in a clan-feeling of readiness to defend the common interest in this settlement, and to resist any intrusion of strangers. In India such a union necessarily involves the acceptance of a joint responsibility for the revenue demanded by the sovereign. Sometimes we have the case of a number of smaller compact circles of new cultivation, established round, and in extension of, the original location; and as the original village-site becomes too small to accommodate the new families, fresh hamlets spring up in the centre of the blocks of new cultivation. These in time become completely separate villages; and the only remaining bond of union is some social and ceremonial connection with the parent village on occasions of rejoicing or mourning, of appointing a new headman, and the like.

In other cases of this kind we find that the whole area was, at an early stage, *divided into certain large primary blocks* which represented the sons, and perhaps, further, the grandsons, of the original family; here anything that can be called union is maintained chiefly within the several major divisions. And it depends on the nature of the soil and the conditions of agriculture which have suggested a certain form of holding what sort of union is maintained. Sometimes the plan of cultivation, within the primary divisions of the area, may have been one according to which each connected group holds its land in several portions—as many portions, in fact, as there are recognised kinds of soil. In that case, groups which under other circumstances might have formed distinct villages must remain intermingled, by reason of the scattering of their lands; and they arrange to distribute the burden of the revenue and expenses by treating the holdings as representing certain artificial measures each containing a certain number of actual measures of each quality of soil, first, second and third—good, bad, or indifferent. Here, again, the household-holdings are very probably minutely subdivided, and are held in complete severalty; but these groups and sub-groups cannot appear on a map as compact local blocks. The groups are only separated in the official records; and the closely connected families retain a joint responsibility as among themselves and for the joint estate they represent. This arrangement will be easier to remember by reference to Diagram II on the next page.

It is chiefly in cases of this kind that we look for those peculiar *bhaiāchārā* arrangements of equally valuated holdings which are characteristic of the clan-expansion.

Thus, in the case of a 'clan-expansion area' the nature of the soil and other circumstances may produce either one of the three varieties we have successively noticed in this class of settlements. We may have (1) the whole of a large area (*e.g.* cases in the Jihlam district, p. 270) held directly in a great number of separate individual or household shares; (2) the area represents the original location of a parent village, with numerous subsequent hamlets, as offshoots from it, developing into separate villages (*e.g.* South-eastern Panjāb, p. 276); and (3) the more complicated *bhaiāchārā*, where the holdings are, within certain main subdivisions, all intermingled (*e.g.* the Mathurā district villages, p. 282). How joint-ownership, beyond the ultimate groups of closely connected relations, can be said to exist in these large areas, I am at a loss to understand. What really exists, or formerly existed, is a personal sense of clan-connection which facilitated distribution of holdings, local government, and the like, while it induced a general willingness to accept a joint liability for the revenue.

DIAGRAM II

Partition among descendants of four sons (of the Founder) whose areas (*tarf* I–IV) were separated in the lifetime of the Ancestor. The *thok* are the groups by sons of the *tarf* holder; the *ṭūlā* are the sons of those again: all existing houses are aggregated under one or other *ṭūlā*.

Tarf (I) alone is shown entire. We suppose it to include holdings for five *thok* (grandsons of founder) A, B, C, D, E. We assume also that the managing committee recognise three qualities (having different practical

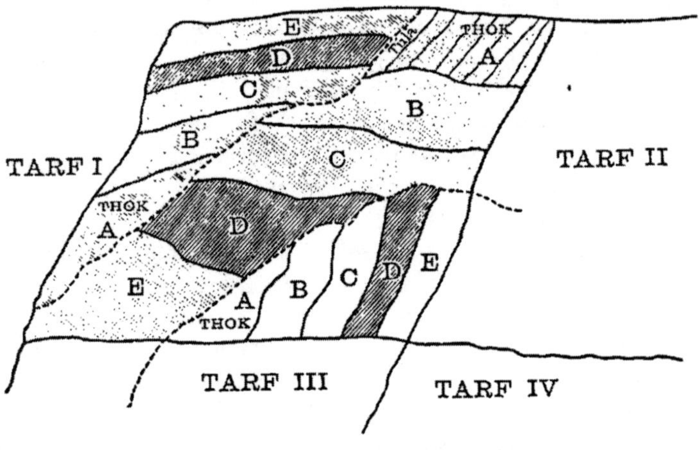

values) of soil (white, and shaded in two degrees), but in many cases there will be more. Each *thok* for equality's sake must take part of its allotment in each kind of soil. Each such part has again to be subdivided among as many *ṭūlā* as the *thok* contains. The allotment of one *thok* (D) has been made darker so as to show more readily how the *thok* lands lie about, and hence how the *thok* cannot form separate compact 'villages,' at least not until in course of time exchanges of land, sales, and other accidents have brought their holdings more within a ring fence.

I venture to doubt whether, on the basis of the Indian phenomena alone, we should ever have heard anything about a common or joint-ownership of a whole clan, had it not been for the fact that, in one way or another, these large areas do tend to split up into smaller groups; and, as the bond of clan-union is forgotten under modern conditions, the several local sections are assimilated in many respects with that larger class of real 'villages' which began as the estate of one founder, or one or two conjoined. These latter villages, though never held *in common*, may really be long held *jointly*; as long, that is, as the existing households are sufficiently closely related. Beyond a certain limit of blood-relationship the joint-holding never goes; and when the primary divisions (*pattī*, *thok*, &c.) have become established by partition in the earlier stages of the family history, the subsequent families in each group may again continue to hold their land jointly within them. Our North-West Provinces Revenue system was mainly adapted to this latter class of village; and, naturally, the revenue terms and the forms of land-records were also adapted to it. But the same terms and the same forms were applied also to all varieties of village, and to the larger (clan) areas, where there were shares of one kind or another, and where the joint responsibility for the land-revenue of a given area, whether large or small, was not objected to. Hence a much greater appearance of uniformity resulted than is actually in the nature or constitution of the estates.

Constitution of the 'Family'

This leads us directly to consider the constitution of the *family*; for it is on this that the existence of joint and co-sharing forms of village-estate really depend. Whatever the source of the idea of ownership, it is obvious that the right to any kind of property may be felt to reside in an individual—*i.e.* in the head of the family or household; or, again, that it may reside in what we call a 'joint-family'—*i.e.* in the head conjointly with his sons, grandsons, and great-grandsons, if he lives to see them.[1] When-

[1] It is hardly necessary to remark that with the superior agricultural tribes leading a simple, healthy, outdoor life, where polygamy is rare and

ever we see an actually joint and undivided family holding, whether extending over a whole village or a smaller area, it will always be found to consist of members of the close-kindred.

Every reader of Indian books is familiar at least with the term 'Hindu joint-family.' But it is perhaps hardly realised that, though this is in itself an ancient institution, it need not be primeval, nor, in all probability, was it the form of family-union recognised by the earliest tribes. As we know it in the text-books of Hindu law, it bears the marks, I may say, of legal elaboration. If, for instance, we compare the customary rules of succession and those on the connected subject of adoption (*i.e.* artificial succession) and the right of the father to alienate ancestral land, as acknowledged by the various Jat, Gujar, and other agricultural tribes of the Panjāb, we observe that they differ in many respects from the rules of the law-books; and also, quite essentially and in principle, from the inheritance rules of the Muhammadan Law. Still, the idea of the joint family exists; and that is why there can be so much general similarity between the Aryan-Hindu, the Jat, and other superior tribes, in their village institutions.

But if we go back to the still earlier customs, of which vestiges remain among Kolarian and Dravidian tribes, it would seem that the head of the family is much more like the sole owner and representative of the share in the tribal possessions —whether divided, as in our Indian examples, or not. In the Welsh tribes it has been observed that as each son came to a certain age he had a claim to an additional maintenance-area of land, which he had, not as a share of his father's possession, but as a member of the clan. The father's authority, at a certain stage of tribal development, is in fact regarded as almost of divine right, and is doubtless the origin of the great influence

confined to the few wealthier owners, and early marriage the rule, it is no impossible thing to find, say, a great-grandfather of eighty-eight years, a grandfather of sixty-five, a father of forty, and a son of nineteen—himself just married, all living on ancestral land. In the earlier ages what reduced families so much was the continual loss of male members in wars, feuds, and forays. Local famines and epidemics must have been rarer because population was smaller and so localised; but when they occurred, as there was no means of combating or relieving either, their effects must have been very severe.

of the tribal and sectional chiefs and patriarchs which lasts long after the power of the head of the individual family has become much restricted. In other words, the *patria potestas* is much more complete at one stage of tribal life than it is at another. In the developed Hindu joint-family, it has almost disappeared except in certain ceremonial and religious aspects. The head of the close-kindred or family is now little more than the manager and elder member of a coparcenary body. Every son, as soon as he is born, has an inchoate interest at least in all the ancestral property. But in earlier (and non-Aryan) custom it was different. Among the Kāndh tribes, who evidently represent a very early (and probably little changed) tribal system quite unconnected with the Hindu law, we find the father regarded as the sole owner during his life; and this would imply in many cases a long continuing ownership in the presence of adult sons and grandsons. But here we observe that the rule has already been established that, on the father's death, the sons will all share equally. There is no primogeniture, which indeed appears to be a custom connected with some dignity or chiefship, and not to prevail in ordinary (not joint) families under their customary law.[1] In some tribes, indeed, it is the youngest who succeeds to the paternal house and homestead, the elder sons having established separate houses elsewhere, possibly on a certain holding that they were entitled to claim as clansmen, irrespective of what their father had.[2] Where, however, we find tribes of an historically later date, and therefore (presumably) in a later stage of progress, like the Jat or the Panjāb frontier tribes, there it is not surprising to find that the family-holding is already completely regarded as joint-property: a custom has been established that the house-father should not make an alienation of the 'inheritance' to the prejudice of his descendants and that a sonless co-sharer should not adopt an heir except from among the near agnates, and even then with consent of

[1] Primogeniture seems to be connected with the growth of the joint-family, because of the desire to keep someone as the head and representative where the divided members do not themselves become so many separate heads. This sentiment is also counterbalanced by the affection of a father for his 'youngest'—'the son of his old age.' Manu, it will be remembered, suggests a special share to *both* (p. 305, *ante*).

[2] p. 132, *ante*.

the rest. From this it is not difficult to pass to the stage at which a body of coheirs remain joint for a long time. The causes of this are various. If the family is of any pretensions, all the descendants are jealous of their equal representation of the dignified founder (equal, *i.e.*, in their proper grade of descent and kinship). And they avoid division for fear lest one or the other should gain an advantage over the rest. Sometimes it is that the land can better be held jointly because the greater part is in the hands of tenants, and the rents are as easily divided as the tenancies themselves. And in a joint-holding among cultivating proprietors, what usually happens is that various members have *de-facto* holdings, which are theoretically liable to be readjusted (partly or entirely) on a formal partition; some of them do not wish for change, and resist a partition as long as possible. Such a joint-holding, as I have before remarked, never continues outside the circle of the close-kindred. At least I have found no case on record; and if instances exist it would be extremely interesting to have them detailed and the circumstances of the holding stated. We are constantly, however, meeting cases in which the larger groups of shares have been separated to a certain degree, and there are groups of close-kindred still holding jointly within the first divided areas.

Just as I have suggested that one of the main types of village (the *raiyatwāri*) is connected with the idea of ownership by 'first clearing' and conversion of the jungle, and that the second type exemplifies the principle of right by superiority or conquest, so, on the further question of the right as residing in the joint-family or in the single head, it may be suggested that the *raiyatwāri* village seems to depend originally on the idea that the house-father is the separate and sole owner, whilst the *joint-village* represents the more developed idea of the joint-family and the limitation (not to say extinction) of the *patria potestas*. In the former case, the father may have remained very long in possession of the holding after the sons and grandsons had grown up to an age to cultivate land for themselves; and both on this account and on account of the growing inability of the elders to take an active part in the cultivation, there must have been a temporary partition if the holding was large, or the acquisition of fresh lands by the increasing junior families till (on the limit of the direct descent being reached) a final partition was made (among second cousins). Thus there would be a continuous tendency to separate off the holdings; and as every village was composed of a group of such separate holders, and there was no one person who was regarded as the owner of the whole village, there was no possibility of a body of heirs having joint rights over the whole. At the present day, when Hindu law has introduced the Hindu family ideas to a great extent, the change has not affected the *raiyatwārī* village; it is still the individual holding that has to be partitioned among as many of the co-sharers as can get a sustenance out of it; if they are too numerous, some of them must take a compensation for their small shares, and go elsewhere. But in the case of the joint-village (*i.e.* in one numerous class of cases) the ownership of the whole village has originated with (or passed into the hands of) one man, and it is probable that a partition will have been made as soon as the first series of descents from the ancestor was accomplished. The *patti*, *thok*, and *ṭūlā*, or whatever other names are used locally, will have been demarcated on the ground, and it is only the subordinate families within each that remain joint. This is at least the case with the typical *pattīdārī* form of village; and it evidently marks a stage where the joint-family has developed fully, and where there is often some aristocratic feeling, and pride of family and caste. The curious 'Āzamgarh joint-villages cannot be explained on any other principle; we have here a number of families descendants from Rājput over-lords who acquired a right over a series of villages already to some extent marked out and existing.[1] But the joint-families and bodies of coheirs of the last lords declined to fit into these shells: they did not accept the village-areas as they stood, and assign them, one by one, to certain groups of connected families. They made a number of shares, parts of which were found in two, three, or more of the villages. The family groups can only bring their estates together into one whole on paper; and the lands of each such major-group are now divided into many varying fractions, because

[1] The over-lord families may have added many new villages in the course of their growth, but there evidently were a number of originally established villages to start with.

of the sense of *family* property existing: there is no democratic equality of a whole clan.

In that other class of joint-villages which have something of a clan-connection, and a more 'democratic' constitution, we may also trace the joint-holding to a family ownership, although in this case it is modified, by a larger sense of equality of all later descendants, which savours rather of the clan-feeling than of the strict joint-family. Still, in the Jat settlements and in those of non-monarchical and non-aristocratic tribes whose villages must for convenience be placed in the joint class, the people certainly show a sense of family-property; their custom, as I have said, always objects to alienation by the head of the family; and adoption, as defeating the expectation of other agnatic heirs, is more or less restricted. Such customs cannot be explained, except on the basis that ancestral land is regarded as belonging to the whole family. At the same time, there is a desire for equality, and a consequent tendency to disregard the exact fraction which depends on the grade of descent, as well as on the number of sons, &c., in each house.[1] When the whole land has become fully occupied, this desire cannot any further be given effect to, because there must necessarily come a point at which, of two existing holdings which we will suppose are equal in extent and value, one is inherited by a single son and the other is inherited by seven sons jointly, and no more land is available in the village or estate. It is only in the earlier stages of the growth of such a community, when waste land is still abundant, that the seven sons could add on enough out of the waste to make each of their holdings, if not quite equal to that of the more fortunate sole-heir, at least sufficient for their wants. So in some communities (usually holding large areas) we find the ancestral descent only followed in making the *primary divisions*, when it was the natural and indeed the only possible basis of allotment; after that, the later families have all acquired holdings, added on one by one, as the numbers and general requirement, of each indicated.

[1] In fact, in some of the old *bhaiāchārā* areas, or 'cultivating fraternities,' we find exactly the same idea of equal holdings for all existing households that we found in the Panjāb frontier tribes under the *per capita* or *khulāvesh* custom. (Cf. Diagram I. at p. 410.)

To resume the general conclusion shortly, I believe that individual ownership of the personally cleared and prepared holding in the tribal territory is quite consistent with the customs of tribal society at an early stage. Actual joint-property does not exist among the whole clan: at best, there is an appearance of collectivity caused by the common origin and close defensive and offensive alliance of the whole clan; by the equal right of everyone to share in the land obtained by the united exertion of the clan; and by the obligation to obey the patriarchal authorities, and to submit to that equalisation of holding in the tribal territory to secure which custom decreed that all holdings should be periodically exchanged.[1] Actual joint-ownership is exhibited in the records of the Indian villages, as far as I can discover, only (*a*) among the *families* forming separated groups on a clan territory, (*b*) where there has been one owner of the whole village and his direct heirs continue to hold it without partition, (*c*) when the cultivation of an entire village has been undertaken by a group of colonists who prefer to arrange for each year, or cultivating season, what area or what fields each member shall take up, according to the number

[1] I have seen it argued that joint-ownership by a family necessarily implies an antecedent joint-ownership by a whole clan; but that is on the supposition not only that the idea of the joint-ownership as between a father and his sons existed when the clan began its growth and continued unchanged till it had reached its full dimensions, but also that the same joint idea was maintained through wider and wider circles of relatives so long as the whole body as a 'clan' were able to keep together, there being no limit to the degree to which joint-ownership can extend. Now, certainly it is not possible to assert that the notion of the family as a body of co-owners has never varied; and equally certainly it is possible to assert that we have no evidence in any tribe in the world of any jointness or common estate kept up to an unlimited degree of relationship. There is always a customary limit—usually of three descents, as I have explained in the text. It is possible theoretically that a whole clan may acknowledge a joint-ownership of an entire area conquered and settled by it on the ground of equal right to the acquisition by the united effort, but not because the original family was joint or because the jointness has been continued throughout the widening circle; of that no kind of proof exists. It is equally possible also that the idea of the joint-family may develop at any stage, and under varying circumstances. It has certainly not been uniformly found among any large number of tribes.

of hands, number of cattle, &c., he can bring to the work. The most extensive instance of this kind is that which has been fully explained in Chapter VIII., in connection with the traditional *Vellālan* colonies in the Tamil country. (*d*) It is also possible that particular plots of land may be always held in a sense jointly by a number of sharers, who may represent even an entire group of village owners, when there is some peculiarity, as for instance when a portion of the village lands are along a river, and so are both liable to be washed away at one time and added to at another, and also to be exceptionally valuable, a little further inland, owing to the unfailing percolation of moisture; here, besides devices of making narrow strips which run at right angles to the river course,[1] we often find that permanent shares are not allotted, but a series of holdings for the year only are arranged, and these are held in rotation by the different co-sharers. In all these cases the shares are perfectly well known.

If there are other forms or cases, of joint-holding, it will be very interesting to hear of them; but it is necessary that they should be reported in their actual form, and not merely called 'joint' or '*zamindāri*' or by some such indefinite name. I have not met with any such.

The theory, then, that all joint villages *begin* with a 'common ownership'—that this, by a process of natural evolution, goes on to strict shares; that, next, the shares become irregular; and, finally, that mere individual *de-facto* holdings emerge; is distinctly contrary to the facts. It is based on a false generalisation from 'joint villages' of different kinds and origins; and it ignores the fact, that when, in any given village, there has actually been a joint holding, followed by a partition into ancestral fractional shares, and these have been transformed into simple *de-facto* holdings, the joint condition was not original, but consequent on a prior *single* title of the founder, grantee, &c., of the village;

[1] This simple device secures each strip having a portion of all the advantages and disadvantages of the situation. If, for instance, the divisions were drawn *parallel* to the river, those nearest the water would be all liable to destruction or injury by flood; the few next would be of exceptional value, being moist and yet safe from erosion; and the furthest series would be all equally deprived of the benefit of moisture altogether.

the joint holding was the result of the joint-succession (on ancestral shares) to that one founder. There is no progress of ideas, or evolution, in the matter.

SECTION II.—SOME PRACTICAL CONSIDERATIONS REGARDING THE VILLAGE FORMS

It has been the argument throughout these pages, that the *raiyatwāri* village is of distinct origin from, and of quite equal importance with, the joint-village of Upper India; and that there is a fundamental objection to theories which, albeit unconsciously, ignore the one as an independent form, and, further, are based on a view which really takes in only one kind or class even of the joint-village. It may be interesting now to take note of some practical results which arise from the difference in question, and also those which arise from differences in the internal constitution of the joint-village. These points of difference have a direct bearing on the value of the 'village' as a form of aggregation in agricultural society with reference to economic and administrative considerations. In the first place, something should be said about the difference in the *modern title* to the land in each form of village, which is the outcome of their past history.

The origin of the claim of the ruler to be owner of the land in India, has been explained, and no further mention of the subject in this place is called for.[1] But the effect produced in former days on the two kinds of village, by the assertion of this claim, deserves to be noted. In the *raiyatwāri* countries[2] the several cultivating land-holders were in general regarded as, and called, 'raiyat' (*ra'īyat*=dependent, subject, &c.), a sort of indefinite name which well expressed the actual relations where the land-holder had theoretically no ownership-rights at all, and practically (under every settled and well-conducted Native Government) had all the assurance he needed of tolerably certain hereditary tenure, from which ejection was unheard of. The

[1] See p. 207 ff. *ante*.

[2] It will be perhaps useful to remind the reader that the term includes Bengal Proper (as far as its villages are concerned), the Central, Western, and Southern districts of India, and it practically includes Assam and Rājputāna.

State demands left him enough to live on, but no more; but he was not pressed in a bad season; and, on the whole, his position, if one of constant labour, and little prospect of accumulating wealth, was by no means intolerable.[1] In the Dakhan and in the South, the raiyat was not allowed to sell his land; indeed, it may be questioned whether as a rule it had any market value, as there was no surplus profit or value when the revenue was paid and the subsistence of the family taken into account. Ownership was only acknowledged in land granted revenue-free by the State, and apparently in lands held on the privileged tenure of *waṭan* (land held in virtue of office in a village or district). In the Dakhan also we remember that there were vestiges of the *mirāsi* right, that of superior families who once held the lordship of villages. We are told that even the Marāthā rulers would pay for land held on a *mirāsi* title when it was wanted for any State purpose. It is curious to remark that the privileged tenure was not unattended with corresponding drawbacks; for the rulers appear invariably to have taken advantage of the attachment which these older families, with pride of origin, had to their ancestral lands, to assess them at a much higher revenue-rate than could be taken from the raiyat, whose resource was flight when a rate was imposed which he could not pay.

It might be thought that, as the joint-villages of Upper India were held on a superior tenure and by more energetic and self-asserting agricultural and fighting tribes, and largely by

[1] I may once for all explain that in speaking of the old administrations, I refer to the normal earlier governments under well-established sovereigns, and not to exceptional (and generally later) times of war and turmoil, or to the precarious possession and temporary rule of Rohilla chiefs and the like, or the local tyranny of bad governors—which things, terrible as they were, can only be regarded as occasional at least in comparison with the entire period of history and the entire extent of Indian kingdoms. There have been periods at which, and countries throughout which, the raiyats have been cruelly robbed and oppressed, and land-holding made a burden rather than a profit; but these are abnormal, and it would not be fair to cite them as specimens of Native rule in general. And when I speak of the condition of the raiyat as 'not intolerable,' I mean with reference to the ideas and state of Eastern society at the time. Such a condition of life is obviously inconsistent with modern notions of political freedom or intellectual advance.

bodies having pretensions to dignified descent and general superiority of rank or caste, the State governors would have treated them differently. But in theory it was not so; the village co-sharers were just as much tenants on sufferance of the ruler, as the 'raiyat' of Central and Southern India; only that the joint constitution enabled the villages, on the whole, to make better terms, and at least to escape much internal interference, by their power of combining to meet the demands made on them. It certainly was the practice of former rulers to care nothing for forms of tenure, and to take every revenue from actual occupier, irrespective of his proper position as owner or tenant. Indeed, it may fairly be said that most Native revenue systems, before the universal adoption of revenue farming, were as nearly *raiyatwāri* as possible. No doubt, where there was some local 'Zamīndār,' who could be held responsible for the revenue of a given area, he was dealt with, because it saved trouble, or, in the case of an hereditary chief, was politically necessary. And so the local 'Āmils or revenue officers found it profitable to deal with districts made up of joint-villages all of one clan, and also with the stronger joint-villages generally, by making the local *Çaudhari*, or the village headman, responsible to bring in the required revenue total. In the Panjāb, to take another example, the Sikh governors took the revenue (here very generally collected in kind) from co-sharer and tenant alike; they made no distinction; the land belonged to the *Sirkār* (the governing power), and whoever held it must pay.

When we find Marāthās according a certain measure of respect to the higher family tenures, it was perhaps because these belonged to (virtually) the same rank or caste as the rulers themselves; and the Muhammadan kings of the Dakhan respected similarly privileged holders, because it was their policy to deal with the cultivators through them; but in the North the Moslem rulers would feel no particular sympathy with higher caste Hindu communities or with Jat co-sharers. When any special village-tenure was respected, it was because of some State grant, or religious obligation, as in the case of Sayyad communities or others which it was politic to preserve or countenance.

While the State theory did not distinguish, the people themselves cherished very different feelings. The *raiyatwāri* villagers may perhaps have acquiesced in the position they had as 'Crown tenants.' It has been observed that in some cases they were more anxious to secure the power of relinquishing the land when they could not make it pay than to have a fixed title. The Northern joint-villages would never have admitted any such change in their position, at least not to themselves. When a heavy revenue was demanded, they combined to meet it and called in other settlers to help; they always acted as far as possible as owners of the land. The State claim to the land was not one of defined principle, nor of declaration by Imperial decree, but of tacit assumption; it did not alter the position of the villages ostensibly. When proprietary communities lost their right and fell into the grade of tenants under a new proprietor or a new family of over-lords, it was that the latter had individually gained the upper place by reason of some revenue-free grant, some opportunity of farming the village revenue, or standing security for it to the State Collector; and not infrequently by reason of the village body voluntarily putting themselves under the protecting lordship of some neighbouring magnate. The State ownership of itself, produced no such ostensible degradation. It is probable, on the whole, that, owing to the power of combined effort and an internal sense of abiding right, the joint-village holders were more rarely interfered with or driven from their homes than the villagers in the *raiyatwāri* provinces.[1]

The practical distinction became manifest when British rule began. In Upper India, the joint body of village co-sharers was recognised as the proprietor of the entire village, arable and waste together, the limit being ascertained by inquiry and equitable adjustment, and fixed by formal demarcation and survey. It is true that no proclamation was put forth acknowledging or conferring this right in set terms, as was done with the landlords of Bengal under the Permanent Settlement; nor did the first Settlement Law (Regulation VII. of 1822) of the

[1] Not that the *raiyatwāri* villages were always helpless. I think it is in the *Chāndā S. R.* (Central Provinces) that there is an account of how the *pātels* (headmen) defended their villages and fortified their *garhī*, or central residence, for the purpose.

North-West Provinces declare the right in so many words; but the fact of ownership is implied throughout the Regulation, as it is in the subsequent Land Revenue Laws; and it is evident from the terms of the land-records. The joint-village tenure is *zamīndāri*—*i.e.* a proprietary or landlord tenure, with no greater limitations than those which accompany the tenure of the Zamīndār or Taluqdār of Bengal or Oudh.[1] In both cases alike, the right is subject to certain limitations owing to the existence of subordinate rights and to the lien of Government on the land for its land-revenue; and the mere fact that the amount of the revenue is or is not liable to periodical revision makes no difference whatever in the tenure. The village co-sharer can sell and mortgage his land,[2] and lease it to whom he pleases, subject of course to any special rights of tenants; and so long as the Government Revenue is paid the owner is at liberty to cultivate or not, or to build on the land if he pleases.[3]

On the other hand, in the *raiyatwāri* countries, where the Settlement deals direct with the several landholders in the villages, as in Bombay, or Berār, or Madras, there were various reasons why the British Government did not, as a matter of policy, completely or formally renounce its own proprietary right in the soil and confer it on the raiyats. Only in the Central Provinces was a proprietary title to most of the villages, under many limitations, exceptionally conferred on certain persons;[4] and so the villages ceased to be *raiyatwāri* and became *zamīndāri*. Speaking generally, the difficulty was this: the raiyat holdings had been so crushed by excessive revenue charges under the

[1] It is for this reason that I have called the joint-village also the 'landlord village.' It is always held on a superior sort of tenure, at all events throughout Upper India and the Central Provinces.

[2] Subject to any restrictions of his own tribal or caste law or custom, such as pre-emption, &c., but to none directly imposed by the State.

[3] There is some difference about the subsoil right to minerals, which in the Panjāb and other provinces are expressly reserved by law to the State. In the North-West Provinces those rights, in all the plain districts, belong to the village owner, as the Secretary of State expressly allowed in a despatch of 1880.

[4] It would be unnecessary here to go into any detail on the subject. The history of the conferment of right in the Central Provinces villages is given in some detail in my *L. S. B. I.* ii. 455 ff.

later Marāthā and Moslem rulers, and especially during the period when Central India became the focus of the wars of contending chiefs and armies, that the first relief required was to lower the charges, especially as the British system was at first much stricter and less elastic than the Native rule.[1] But such reduction was especially unpalatable to the authorities under the constant pressure which the times produced on the State Treasury, and it was but tardily acquiesced in. So much, however, was gradually conceded, that the raiyat might relinquish his holding, at a suitable season, if he felt unable to pay the revenue; and this rule came to be a fixed principle of the *raiyatwāri* revenue system. It operated as an efficient test, in many cases, as to whether the revenue really was excessive or not. I am not, however, writing a history of the revenue management, and can only so far allude to the subject as helping to show why a formally 'proprietary' title was not recognised. A holder who can give notice that he will not be responsible for land after a certain date can hardly be called 'owner,' even under the ordinary limitations of Indian law. Accordingly, in Madras the question of the raiyat's title has been left undefined by law, though judicial decision has left no doubt that he has the practically proprietary enjoyment of his holding. But in Bombay, the holder of land is, by express legislative enactment, called 'occupant;' and in Burma and Assam, which are *raiyatwāri* provinces in principle, though not formally so designated, he is called 'land-holder.' The right is legally

[1] The Native rulers in general put down the revenue demand at a high figure; but their officers were extremely good judges of the power to pay in each particular season, and were adepts in alternately squeezing and letting go by rule of thumb and without any system whatever. The British power was irresistible, and worked with mechanical regularity. Our early authorities sometimes forgot this, and were disposed to think that rates must be equitable when they were no more than former rulers had entered in their assessment-rolls, and when peace and security were now assured to the cultivator in a manner previously unknown. Hence it was that rates not nominally enhanced, but collected with strict regularity, proved intolerable in the first years of our rule. Those who wish to see specific examples will find plenty in Mr. A. Rogers's *Land Revenue in Bombay* (2 vols., Allen, 1892) and in the Madras *District Manuals*, *passim*.

defined as a permanent hereditary and alienable right of occupancy.[1] In prosperous times, under our modern well-adjusted assessments, nobody ever does 'relinquish' permanently cultivated land under any ordinary circumstances, but the power is there.

It may be noted that this theoretical distinction between the 'proprietary' tenure of the Upper Indian joint-village and the 'occupancy' tenure of the several holdings in a *raiyatwārī* village, as well as the fact that in one case the right applies to the village as a whole, and in the other to the holding only, is the immediate cause of the difference between the Provincial Land Revenue systems. These distinctions are now well understood; but they would have been unintelligible to an Imperial Revenue officer of the seventeenth century, or, at all events, to one after the reign of Aurangzeb, in the early eighteenth century. For the old systems cared nothing for tenures as such, and in fact acknowledged none but the tenure of 'Government' land, and that of land held by some hereditary chief, or held in free grant [*milk*] which was an exceptional favour. In general, the country was classified into two large divisions—one that was *k͟hālsa*, or paying revenue to the State; the other that was held in *jāgīr*—*i.e.* the revenue of the land was assigned to and collected by the grantee, the great State official, or the military tenant, who had the assignment. The assignee was bound to apply the revenue, to the amount fixed, to the support of the local administration, to the maintenance of a certain military force, and to the support of his own state and dignity. The grants (charitable, religious and special) of lands or villages revenue-free, and therefore free of all State claims, might be found in either division, but more commonly in the *k͟hālsa* lands. The only considerable change in the system was brought about by the general introduction of revenue-farming on a large scale. It was a change, because then the details of villages and lands included in one 'farm' all disappeared from the Treasury Books; nothing was entered but the total due; and the farmer had the entire management. This

[1] See *L. S. B. I.* iii. 269, 403, 498. The difference is technical or legal rather than practical—*i.e.* affecting the actual enjoyment of the holding. The Madras theory is discussed, *ibid.* iii. 128 ff.

system of farming very often resulted in the farmer becoming so far owner of the land, whether a village or a larger estate, that in after years it was hardly possible to deny the title to his descendants.

The British Government went on an entirely different principle: it started with the avowed policy of defining, and confirming on an equitable basis, the right of private persons in the soil. At first, this right, from the experience of Bengal, seemed to reside in some one landlord; but, as further provinces came to be settled, it was found that other kinds or forms of right had to be acknowledged. It followed that whoever was entitled to the chief interest, whether called 'ownership' or 'occupancy,' that person was the one to be primarily and directly responsible for the land-revenue. Consequently, each provincial revenue-system differed according to the character of the legal tenure which was most generally prevalent.

In Bengal, land was held for the most part by great landlords; and hence the system was designed to suit the case of owners whose revenue assessment the Government thought it politic to fix in perpetuity, and whose title it was thought right explicitly to declare. In Northern India, again, in spite of the fact that in Oudh there were great landlords called Taluqdārs, and that similar landlords appeared in some parts of the North-West Provinces, the prevailing feature was the tenure of joint-villages; accordingly, the system provided primarily for dealing with these as units, fixing a sum of revenue on each, which was engaged for by the representatives of the village body, and distributed among the co-sharers according to their own custom and constitution. The minor variations of the system necessitated by the peculiar conditions of the Central Provinces, Ajmer, and the Panjāb, caused subordinate varieties of the North-Western Provinces system to be formulated; but they are the same in general plan and principle.

There remained the Central, Western, and Southern districts, where, in general, the country was not held either by landlords or by joint-villages, but by separate holders in *raiyatwāri* villages; and here the two varieties of *raiyatwāri* management, the Madras system, and the Bombay system, were perfected in the course of time. Each holding is here dealt with on its own independent merits, and assessed by a special method of valuation purely based on the consideration of the quality and value of the soil. Here, of course, the right of each holder extends only to the assessed holding; no area of waste is included in a village to be partitioned or held in common. Thus it will be evident that the difference between the great revenue-systems essentially depends on the difference of prevalent tenure, whether of a great landlord, a joint-village body, or the separate village land-holder.[1]

It may be advisable here to note that a suspicion may arise in some minds that the *raiyatwāri* village, as it is under existing systems of adminstration, is something very different to what it was in old times; and that the system of revenue administration is quite different from that in use in former days. No doubt our modern surveys have defined, demarcated, and recorded the separate holdings in a manner that was never attempted in old days, but it certainly has not altered the characteristic custom by which the holdings are essentially separate, and the boundaries of each known. And so the modern mode of collecting the cash revenue is different from the old plan—first, of taking a share in the grain from each holding, and afterwards of calling on the entire village to arrange among its members for the payment of a total estimated cash sum. But the old method, equally with our own, recognised the individuality of the holdings; it never supposed that the raiyats were co-sharers, and that one was, under all circumstances, liable for the default of another. When injustice was done, or rights ignored, it was not by reason of any theory of land-tenures, it was simply from the oppressive methods of the farmer or the tax-gatherer.

It is curious to notice how the two ideas, now so easy to us, of the joint-village as a unit-estate, embracing arable and waste together in one general co-shared right, and the *raiyatwāri*

[1] Hence the absurdity of the attempts which were made in former days to compare and discuss the relative merits of this system or that. No comparison is possible, for each is only good for the particular sort of tenure it is designed to fit. Any one may be, and has proved to be, capable of great improvement in itself, and all of them may have certain features in common; but it is impossible to look upon one as intrinsically better than another, because each is based on a different groundwork.

village as a collection of individual families, each having its own holding without any joint responsibility to Government, struck the minds of the early revenue officers at the end of the last and the begining of the present century. When the co-shared villages of Benares and the Upper Provinces first came to the notice of officers accustomed to the Bengal system of individual landlords over considerable areas,[1] they were at first quite puzzled : there must be, so they thought, some one person who is landlord, and with whom the Settlement of the village-estate ought to be made. The idea of the village as an 'estate' within a certain boundary, consisting of arable and waste together, was intelligible enough; and it was understood that the Government claim to ownership, [except as to some residuary and super-eminent right] was given up; what they could not understand was that the title should reside, not in some one village-head, or other individual, but in a joint body under a more or less complicated constitution. It needed all the arguments of Holt Mackenzie's gigantic Minute of 1819 to make it understood. In the South, on the other hand, it was the idea of a village-estate, as an area of arable and waste in a ring fence and owned by the 'raiyats' as a whole, that was so difficult to realise. Here they felt that the Government was the absolute owner of the soil, except indeed where there was some special 'inām' (revenue-free) grant or some greater 'Polygar' or 'Zamīndār' landlord, on whom had been conferred a patent 'of perpetual ownership.' The raiyat in a village was secure enough, no doubt, in the enjoyment of his individual holding; but he could not have a right to anything beyond the fields for which he held the Collector's *pattā* or lease; and the Collector would also insist on his duly cultivating the land, or else the revenue could not be paid. Hence, when the inquiry was made (as detailed in Chapter IX.) as to the former existence of a number of village-estates held by co-sharing bodies (*mirāsdārs*), the officials could not well take in the idea.

[1] And these landlord tenures, as confirmed in 1793 by Lord Cornwallis's legislation, seemed to them to be in accord with the natural order of things. In early 'Minutes,' papers, and books, we often find expressions which indicate that in the mind of the writers, the tenure of land by a landlord with tenants under him was the natural and necessary order of things—the only conceivable kind of permanent tenure, in fact.

And so they confused the alleged village-estate rights with other hereditary claims to special privileges, which had nothing whatever to do with the question. This difficulty of conception is reflected in the laboured judgments of some of the courts on the claims of alleged co-sharers to such village rights, and in the language of most of the district Reports; and not least in the lengthy but very ill-designed series of questions which the Board of Revenue of those days circulated to District Officers with a view of elucidating the existence and history of *mirāsi* claims. Mr. Ellis, and, before him, Mr. Place, seemed to grasp the idea of the joint-village, but hardly anyone else; and it was little wonder that the joint-villages, which were no doubt in an advanced stage of decay, perished altogether.[1]

But there is yet another practical result of the difference between the *raiyatwāri* and the joint-village. In the former, as a simple aggregate of individual cultivating holdings, held together by local ties and under the authority of the hereditary headman and village officers, there were no superimposed rights, at least not as a general rule. The holder was the separate occupant, and held by hereditary descent[2] possibly from the first clearer of the soil. If he employed a tenant, as he often did, the tenant would, in most cases, have been located by him; there would, in short, seldom be anything but a simple contract tenancy. Here and there, no doubt, it would be otherwise. In the northern parts of the Bombay territory we have various local instances of over-lord tenures, where the occupants themselves have to pay rent to some *taluqdār*, *kasbāti*, *gāmetī*, or other superior intermediate between them and the State. And even in ordinary villages it has happened that particular persons have been able to acquire lands and be recorded as the occupant, although cultivators were on the soil before them, and are now 'inferior occupants' or tenants

[1] The practical treatment of the remains of such rights is described in *L. S. B. I.* iii. 126.

[2] It will be remembered that the 'inheritance,' which is referred to by such terms as *mirāsi*, *warisī*, &c., is always the landlord or superior title; it has nothing to do with ordinary holdings, which, notwithstanding that they pass from father to son by inheritance, are not held in virtue of any conquest or superiority, and so are not *mirāsi* in the technical sense.

whose position did not originate in any contract. In such cases there may be some express local customs about rent-payment, which, on proof, the Courts will give effect to. But, speaking generally, the practical effect of the *raiyatwāri* tenure has been to avoid tenant-right difficulties.[1]

But in provinces in which joint-villages are prevalent it is otherwise. We have seen how often this tenure has arisen (especially in the North-West Provinces and Oudh) by grant, conquest, or usurpation (in the more or less distant past) over the heads of earlier cultivating bodies probably in the *raiyatwāri* form. Very often, too, the present body of co-sharers are the descendants of one or more 'farmers' or other intruders who have borne down the rights of an earlier joint-community who once had the village lordship, and are now reduced, in their turn, to being tenants. Then, there are sure to be distinctions of grade and privilege among the tenants: some will have claims as 'ex-proprietor,' or as descendants of a family that once held the village in grant and perhaps did much to improve it; and on other grounds also.

Even where, as in the Panjāb, the joint-villages are more commonly original foundations by superior agricultural clans and families, it is often found that tenants have claims by custom, as having taken part in the work of founding and having held their lands ever since; or they may be absentee co-sharers who have returned after many years, and have been admitted to cultivate, but have not been allowed their old place in the co-sharing body. Or they may be persons who were called in, in the days of Sikh or Durāni rapacity, to help cultivate enough land to make up the heavy revenue demanded, and have never paid anything beyond their quota of the total amount. It would be unjust not to recognise those who had borne the heat and burden of the day as entitled to consideration. To put it shortly; the joint-village tenure, being of the superior or over-lord character, is constantly associated with subordinate or inferior interests in particular plots or fields, and sometimes with interests extending over the whole of the older cultivation, if not over the whole village area. There

[1] In fact, they only appear in such special cases of superior tenure as the Khot's estates of the Konkān districts, and certain others, in which case there is a special provision made by the Legislature.

are, then, besides the ordinary class of contract-tenants located by the proprietors, others whose position is due to no contract whatever, and is on the basis of *status*. Fortunately, each province has been able, on the ground of an historical and practical view of the actual kinds of claim, to formulate its own tenant-law, which defines what circumstances have to be established, and what degree of privilege, as to fixity of tenure and non-liability to enhancement, or limited liability to enhancement, attaches to each kind of tenancy. It should, however, be added that a difficult question of tenant-right of a more general character arose, as it did under the Bengal landlords, chiefly in connection with the village estates of the North-West Provinces, where a number of the villages were owned by communities of non-agriculturist castes. In such cases, the lands were naturally entirely in the hands of tenants; and it became difficult, and sometimes historically impossible, to distinguish between tenants that had been located by the landlords, and who might be presumed to be tenants on some basis of contract, and those who were the old cultivating holders of the land, and over whom the co-sharing community of proprietors had grown up. Hence a general (arbitrary but equitable) rule was laid down of a presumption in favour of every tenant who had held, under certain conditions, for twelve years.

In the Panjāb the villages were so much more generally the result of original location, and were so frequently cultivated by the co-sharers themselves, that there this difficulty was not seriously felt; and the tenants who are protected by law are the purely natural classes, the circumstances of whose position it is not difficult to prove.

It is not within my present scope to justify these rules or to give a detailed account of the different kinds of tenant which are to be found in joint-villages, and in larger landlord estates,[1] but what has been said will have been sufficient to show the difference between *raiyatwāri* and joint-villages as regards the existence of tenant-right.

[1] If a succinct account of the chief features of the Tenancy Laws in Bengal, Oudh, North-West Provinces, Central Provinces, and the Panjāb is desired, it will be found in ch. vii. sec. 5 of my *Short Account of the Land Revenue Administration in India* (Clarendon Press, 1894).

As regards the social and economic advantages of the village grouping of agricultural society, I find it impossible to make any choice between the two forms. That the 'village' formation (of either kind) facilitates revenue management, and is favourable to arrangements for police, sanitation, irrigation, and other matters of public administration, will not be doubted. But the advantages which can be claimed do not appear to me to depend much, if at all, on the internal constitution, whether joint or several.[1]

No doubt, in past days the joint-village was especially well adapted to confront the class of difficulties and dangers peculiar to the times; though I suspect that the successful maintenance of so many villages intact was more dependent on the character and spirit of the castes and clans which furnished the proprietary families, than on the special features of their joint-holding. However that may be, the strong sense of union which exists, or once existed, in the North-Indian joint-villages, especially those that had a clan-origin, or that were proud of a connection with a common ancestor, was no doubt valuable in times of continuous war and local feuds and raids, and when defence was also needed against extortionate Revenue officers. But in modern times these evils have no longer to be guarded against; and the joint constitution does little for the village except that it keeps strangers out, to some extent, through the exercise of the power of pre-emption; and to some extent it promotes mutual help. But there is an undoubted tendency for the joint-villages, in some cases, to fall too much under the power of the official

[1] I do not propose to discuss the advantages of the village-aggregation with regard to the revenue administration. I will only mention that in former days it was supposed that the task of dealing with a multitude of individual holdings or 'survey-numbers' was beyond the power of any Collector, and that either a landlord-middleman or at least a dealing with whole villages as units, was the only practicable method. Such ideas have long since been exploded. The Collector of Bombay or Madras makes his annual demand accounts (*jamabandi*), and deals direct with every holding in every village in his district, with perfect facility; and the *raiyatwāri* revenue management is just as easy and as efficient as that of the joint-village. Indeed, though in the latter only the village-total is (in theory) looked to, as a matter of fact, the local revenue officers have almost as much concern with the individual holdings in the villages as they have under the other system.

lambardārs or headmen, who presume on their position, so that they, with a few of the larger and wealthier shareholders, exploit the rest to their own advantage; while in others bitter party spirit arises and strong factions. This party spirit (*dhardāri*) is marked in the northern districts of the Panjāb, and is often the cause of affrays and even of more serious crime.

The actual condition of the joint-villages and the degree of good feeling which exists among the 'brotherhood' varies, of course, in different places. Officers whose experience is in one place will regard my remarks as needlessly depreciatory; others with less favourable experience will probably think I am too laudatory; over the wide extent of Upper India, it is not possible that any one estimate can be true throughout. I can only note specific points which are certainly true locally.

Excessive subdivision of holdings is certainly found in many villages, and it is a serious evil. This subdivision, to be sure, is not confined to holdings in joint-villages; for now that in the *raiyatwāri* countries Hindu caste and inheritance-customs have been established for many generations, it is quite possible that the *raiyat* holding may be much subdivided among the heirs of the 'occupant.' As a matter of fact, however, in *raiyatwāri* districts subdivision is only carried to any length in the richer soils; and the Revenue rules about demarcation and record of shares, though liberal enough, act as a salutary check on the process. In the joint-village there is no limit; and where the holdings still consist of little strips in different parts of the village, representing so many varieties of soil, minute subdivision of each of these again, becomes a source of great confusion, and throws the people into the power of the *paṭwāri* (or village surveyor-accountant, who alone can know how the little plots are distributed. Hence the local saying, '*G͟harīb kā ustād paṭwārī*'—'The accountant is the teacher (or master) of the poor landholder.'

The tendency undoubtedly is towards partition, and to a separate possession which shall be unalterable. And the strict fractional shares of the *pattīdāri* system (as well as some others) tend to be lost, and to be converted into *de-facto* holdings, sometimes to the advantage of a few of the stronger, and the loss of the weaker, shareholders.

As the distribution of the revenue-charge over the holdings is always recorded, and each holder knows, or can know, exactly what revenue his particular plot has to pay, the practical difference, as regards value or profit to the holder, between the *raiyatwāri* holding and the joint-village share, becomes less marked, especially when all the common land has been divided up. In the North-West Provinces, if the several holders have any difficulty in getting credit for their share-payments, they can easily get permission to pay, and obtain receipts, direct from the local and subdivisional (*Tahsīl*) treasury. In these Provinces, too, 'perfect' partition—that form which not only separates the holdings but dissolves the joint-liability to Government, and so constitutes a number of separate 'estates' (*mahāl*)—is not objected to, when all concerned agree to apply for it. In the Panjāb, the law restricts the power of such partition much more; but the joint responsibility, though useful as indirectly keeping up the 'brotherhood' ideal, and acting as an incentive to exertion and to combined action within the community, now but rarely needs to be enforced. The fact is that with our moderate Revenue demands there is not often any reason why in a tolerable year (or even under a short succession of bad seasons), a thrifty peasant owner should ever be in serious difficulty to meet his revenue instalments.[1]

The power of relinquishment which exists in a *raiyatwāri* village, and is a feature of the tenure, was once (as I have explained) of consequence, but now has practically ceased to be so. The joint-village is owner of the whole estate; the co-sharers cannot therefore get rid of the responsibility which is the condition of ownership: but this again is not in any way a burdensome necessity, as no one wishes to give up land; and if

[1] I cannot of course say the same of the unthrifty or the lazier classes of agriculturists. Of late years great attention has been paid to a most important subject; the proper arrangement of several—but not too many—instalments in which the revenue is payable, so that the demand shall come when the rents are got in and crops profitably disposed of, and the means of payment are at hand. And the power of the Collector *at once* to suspend the demand in case of serious general or local calamity has been enlarged. Such suspension may or not be followed by total or partial remission, as the case requires. These, however, are matters of revenue administration. and are beyond my scope.

he does, he can easily find a buyer or a lessee. If in any case it were not so, that would argue something wrong with the assessment, or some other defect, in which case the revenue would probably fall into arrear, and the Collector's action would be sure to result in discovering the error and effecting the necessary remedy.

Another feature is that the *raiyatwāri* village-holdings can only consist of the 'numbers' actually held and occupied; all surplus land belongs to Government; but, as long as any such lands exists, there is no obstacle to the increase of holdings for growing families. A person desiring land has only to apply for the vacant number and agree to become responsible for the revenue. And, as to the waste, as long as there is any, Government always allots to the village an area for its *use*, and this is secured as permanent grazing-ground (or for wood-cutting as the case may be). The Government ownership of such land is a positive advantage in some ways. In the joint-village, the estate being one, it naturally includes whatever land, arable or waste, lies within the boundaries. And in any case, even if the boundaries as regards the uncultivated area were uncertain, some provision was always made, at the first Settlements, for the natural expansion of the village; and a suitable area of the adjoining waste was always allowed to be included in it. This land is useful as grazing-ground, and also makes it possible that, as the several co-sharers' families expand, a partition can take place, and additional holdings be so provided. When there is no more land to partition, new families must necessarily go elsewhere. In this respect there is no greater, and no less, difficulty than occurs in the *raiyatwāri* village, when a similar limit is reached and there are no more unoccupied numbers to apply for. But as the waste in a joint-village is thus at the absolute disposal of the co-sharers, no one can interfere, so long as the co-parceners agree to partition it,[1] even if it should be economically unadvisable to break up the land, and more profitable to keep it as grazing and wood-cutting ground.

[1] I have known cases where a contractor for railway fuel has persuaded a village to cut down the whole of a wooded tract, under the temptation of the several hundred rupees which he would offer and which would be divided at the moment. Yet the future inconvenience, which

A few words may be added as to the effects of the modern legal title to the land recognised in either kind of village respectively. I have explained in another connection the theoretical difference between the title to the land in a *raiyatwāri* holding and that in a joint-village; and here it may be added that this difference does not seem to have any practical effect as to the value of the land for sale or mortgage. It is a question on both sides of which much may be said, whether in adjusting and conferring private rights in land, Government was well advised in conceding the power of free alienation to the peasantry in the joint-villages, and the power of selling their interest in *raiyatwāri* lands. The practical result of the claim of Native Governments to be owners of the land was to deprive the peasant-owners of the right to sell the land; and even the sale of the occupancy was restricted, partly because only the best holdings would be saleable at all (under the conditions of the time), or, if they were bought up by a person desirous of forming a great estate or holding, he would be wealthy, and the Governor could exact a handsome fine or fee for sanctioning the transfer. It is not surprising that, following Western notions of jurisprudence, our administrators should have thought the power of alienation to be an essential feature of free ownership, and have thought it wiser to leave the matter to a natural economic solution than to

was never thought of, might often be serious, since a village is not likely to adopt the measures necessary to reproduce the wood on the cleared area. As to the disappearance of village wastes generally, however, it may be reasonably questioned whether permanent cultivation is not better than the maintenance of the wretched natural grazing which is found on the waste lands in all the 'drier' districts. This aspect of the question is one that is often forgotten, but it would be going beyond my subject to discuss it. It is sometimes asserted in argument that the people *must* have this wretched natural grazing ground; but it may well be doubted whether it would not be a positive advantage that they should be compelled by circumstances to grow grass and to cultivate grass-lands, as is done in Europe. The idea that grass cannot possibly be grown profitably in India is quite a delusion. It is not so long ago that our cavalry regiments used to be given the control of enormous areas of waste land—ten times greater than they really needed—on this supposition. But of late years, with irrigation and proper cultivation, they have found it easy to produce much better and more abundant grass on a much smaller area, giving up the rest to the plough.

attempt to impose any artificial limitation. It would be impossible *now* to return to a policy of prohibiting the sale of land in villages; but whether it would not have been a wise measure originally is another question. The general result of the power has been, among the less energetic castes, to facilitate the transfer of village-lands to a money-lending or trading and non-agricultural class. The loss of lands usually commences with a mortgage; and as payments on account are made in kind at practically the creditor's own valuation, and as the peasant keeps no accounts, and rarely knows how to preserve evidence of his payments, even by endorsements on the bond, it is very likely that the debt with interest will eventually reach such an amount that payment becomes hopeless and a sale completes the transaction. It will be observed that such a sale does not always, or even frequently, involve the removal of the landholder; he still lives on and cultivates as before, only that he is now tenant to his vendee, and has to give a cash rent, or a share of the produce by way of rent. Should he, however, fail to pay, or let the land fall out of cultivation, there will be the ordinary legal remedy against a defaulting tenant available, and then he must go to the wall altogether.

As regards the facilities, which either form of village affords for local government and rural administration, I have expressed my belief that it is the 'village' as such which offers them; and that in this respect there is little if any choice between the forms. The *pançayat* was once the special feature of the constitution of the joint-village. A council of the heads of houses took the place of a single hereditary head, as the agency for managing village affairs. But, regarded as a means of deciding disputes in general, the agency of a *pançayat* was just as commonly resorted to in *raiyatwāri* villages. In tribal-communities, the permanent village *pançayat* (and the tribal *jirgā* on the frontier) are still active institutions, and are made much use of. In the *raiyatwāri* village, the strong position of the hereditary headman or *pātel*, has also been utilised; and he is armed with small civil and criminal judicial powers, with or without the aid of assessors. The *lambardār* of a joint-village not being originally connected with the institution, his position is apt to vary exceedingly with circumstances: I know of few if any cases where he could be allowed to act magisterially as the *pātel* is. Sometimes he has too little influence, sometimes too much. One source of weakness is that there are sometimes too many of them, one for each *patti* or section. In the Panjāb this is to some extent remedied by appointing a 'chief-headman.' And to aid in the repression of crime, and in rural administration generally, the Panjāb villages are often formed into circles (*ẕail*), over each of which an honorary officer, being a local landowner of respectability and influence, is appointed, with the title of *Ẕaildār*. There is no doubt, however, that more use might be made of village *pançayats* in disposing of petty judicial cases, both civil and criminal; and the legislation of the Madras Presidency is worthy of study on this subject.

Village organisation is admirably adapted for facilitating measures of sanitation, drainage, local communications, and education; provided such measures are not overdone and are kept to very simple and intelligible lines. In another important matter—the regulation of minor questions connected with canal or tank irrigation, the equitable distribution of the water, and so forth, the villages have of old been accustomed to manage for themselves; nor would it be difficult to form a union of several villages for such purposes when necessary. Generally, where there are a number of small hamlets, it is easy to aggregate them in circles;[1] and if the hamlets have a clan connection (such as has been described), the union will be still more easily maintained and managed.

It may be added that it is very probably owing to the village-system that Indian provinces dispense with a Poor Law and feed their own indigent and helpless (rural) residents.

It must be remembered, in schemes for local government by village agency, that while there is a natural tendency on the part of modern administrators to resort to the idea of a democratic and elective council, popular election in India (at any rate in rural districts) is still a very tender plant; and it is rare to find an election which means anything but the most unblushing

[1] As an instance, I may mention that the *patwāri*, being now a much better paid and educated and responsible officer, is usually (in Northern India) appointed not to a single village but to a 'circle' (*halqa*) of villages.

sale of votes or the exercise of personal influence. The fact is that in India, in spite of all modern and more superficial aspirations, there is a strong underlying current of aristocratic feeling; and to ensure the success of village councils, and the like, it is essential that well-chosen and educated chiefs or presidents, of really respected family as well as of local influence, should be induced to become associated with them.

Those who have hoped to see in the joint-village anything of a communistic or socialistic type will, I fear, be disappointed by a study of the real facts. By far the larger portion of the joint-villages were in origin the result not of communism but of conquest; of tribal and caste superiority, and of family pride in the common descent from a house that once held sway in the country round. Not a few are the descendants of successful 'farmers,' auction-purchasers, and land-speculators, who in common with others acknowledge the joint-family law and the consequent joint-inheritance. Even among the 'democratic' tribal settlements of Jats and the old free 'cultivating fraternities,' the sentiment of equality is all within the brotherhood and not in the least for the outside; their tenure is as much a 'landlord' tenure as any other form of joint-village community.

Village councils left uncontrolled would be a failure; there must be a chiefship and an efficient supervision, which, however, must be exercised with such wisdom as not to deprive the *pançayat* element of real influence or of its self-respect. This may be difficult of attainment, but it is not impossible. The danger always is that, when it is found necessary to define by law the powers which such local and rural boards are to exercise, the provisions may be too refined and complicated, and, with the best intentions of preventing mistakes and obviating sinister influences, the provisos and restrictions may defeat their own object.

One remaining point deserves notice, and that is, that the village-system enables a complete series of working and practically sufficient land-titles to exist throughout India.[1] The land-records prepared under the Settlement proceedings are now *kept correct* by annual and periodical revisions, and the

[1] Except in the landlord estates of Bengal. All other revenue systems include the survey and record of rights.

maps are also kept continually in accord with the facts, and this by the agency of the *paṭwāris*. It is comparatively of little importance whether deeds of transfer are drawn up or not; the village records make all titles as clear as possible. No extensive search or examination of documents is needed. There is a simple procedure for notifying and recording the fact of every permanent transfer by sale, gift, or inheritance. The system is only possible where the holdings are first aggregated into villages, each with its own staff; for these villages are then naturally grouped into 'Talūkas' or 'Tahsīls' or other convenient revenue-subdivisions; and thus a number of local centres, as well for the receipt of revenue and taxes as for the compilation of statistics, are distributed over the country. From the head offices of these subdivisions the various inspectors of revenue, and of land records and statistics, continually move about through their respective circles. Every one of these local centres is in charge of one or more intelligent native officials. And these are under obligation to submit various returns and reports and diaries, which enable the Collector—the District Officer—to keep himself informed of everything that goes on. Moreover, the 'District' being so distributed and subdivided, it is possible at once to localise any complaint, or to trace the progress of any cattle disease, or agricultural calamity, or any economic change that affects the welfare of the people.

It would be easy to enlarge on the facilities which the village organisation gives for the discovery and repression of crime; and I might describe the customs by which (in the Panjāb, *e.g.*) cattle stolen and traced into one village must be traced beyond it again, or else the village becomes liable for the loss: these and other matters are connected with the 'village' as an institution; but I cannot go beyond the more directly 'tenure' aspects of the question.

I should like only to notice one interesting modern development, which is taking place in the dry plains of the Panjāb,[1]

[1] In the Panjāb, in spite of the fact that each village had an area of waste adjoining it, and which became part of its property, there were enormous areas of waste in the centres of the tracts between the rivers which had never belonged to any existing village, and which, on the usual rule, are the property of Government.

where extensive areas of Government waste land have been made culturable by carrying out great works of canal irrigation. The Government might, of course, at once auction these lands to capitalists; but a wiser plan has prevailed. The lands are mostly level, at any rate are so situated that the canal branches and distributories can be arranged at pleasure to suit special schemes of locating colonies of peasant land-holders who are encouraged to emigrate from the over-populated districts. The result has been to form what will be artificial villages of peasant lessees. All the holdings will be in squares or half-squares of a fixed size, so that boundary disputes and difficulty in identification of grants, will be impossible. The canal distributories have already been arranged exactly to suit the wants of these aggregates of holdings; and a certain proportion of each group is to be kept as grazing ground. The peasant-holdings will be 'Crown-tenancies' without rights of transfer. Thus we shall have '*raiyatwāri* villages' in the course of time. It is not intended to make the whole of the reclaimed areas into such peasant tenancies: a certain number of large holdings (not exceeding 550 acres) will be offered for sale to capitalists, and a certain number will be made available (140 acres is the limit, in one instance, of such grants) for cultivators of the yeoman class. So that every type of land-holder will have a fair representation; but the peasant-lessee will be the principal figure. Provision is also made for reserving certain areas, which are to be stocked with wood for fuel and other purposes.

These details have been taken from one particular locality—the Chināb Canal Area: other smaller colonies also exist; and similar schemes will, as years go on, be doubtless extended, on the great scale, to the other tracts of open country between the Panjāb rivers, and will in future play a not inconsiderable part in the rural economy of the province.[1]

[1] I may commend to the reader's notice a paper by Sir J. B. Lyall, giving many interesting details about these colonies and other matters connected with the Panjāb and its canal system. See *Journal of the Society of Arts*, xliv. 285 (February 21, 1896).

INDEX

(*Rai.* is used to abbreviate *Raiyatwārī*)